# THE YEAR BOOK

## OF

# WORLD  AFFAIRS

## 1978

*Published under the auspices of*
*THE LONDON INSTITUTE OF WORLD AFFAIRS*

WESTVIEW PRESS, INC.
Boulder, Colorado

All editorial communications should be addressed
to the Director, London Institute of World Affairs,
Thorne House, 4–8 Endsleigh Gardens, London
WC1H 0EH


Published in 1978 by
Stevens & Sons Limited of
11 New Fetter Lane, London
and printed in Great Britain
by The Eastern Press Limited
of London and Reading

Published in the United States
of America in 1978 by Westview
Press, Inc., 5500 Central Avenue,
Boulder, Colorado 80301

Frederick A. Praeger, President and Editorial Director


Library of Congress Catalog Card Number: 47–29156


ISBN   0   89158   824–8

Printed in Great Britain

# CONTENTS

# TRENDS AND EVENTS

THIS annual survey is intended to serve three purposes:

(1) With every additional volume of the *Year Book*, it becomes increasingly difficult for new readers to derive the fullest benefit from the material available in earlier volumes. This survey brings together references to themes examined in the past which have particular current relevance.

(2) The specific object of an annual publication is to make possible analyses in a wider perspective and on the basis of more mature reflection than may be possible in a quarterly or monthly journal. Thus, it is not the object of this *Year Book* to provide instant information on current issues of world affairs. Yet, international affairs have a stereotyped and, largely, repetitive character, so that, frequently, a "new" happening, or "modern" development has been anticipated in one or more of the earlier volumes of the *Year Book*. *Trends and Events* provides evidence of some such continuity as may be traced over a span of years.

(3) References to earlier contributions also offer readers an opportunity to judge for themselves the adequacy of the conceptual and systematic frameworks chosen or taken for granted in the papers selected:

## (A) THE WORLD ECONOMY

Alexandrowicz, C.: *The Study of International Economics* (4 Y.B.W.A., 1950)

Cohen, P. M.: *The Future of Gold* (31 *ibid.* 1977)

Desai, R. R.: *World Monetary Reform* (20 *ibid.* 1966)

Fisher, A. G. B.: *The Future of International Economic Institutions* (1 *ibid.* 1947)

Goldsmith, P. and Sonderkotter, F.: *Equality and Discrimination in International Economic Law* (*IV*): *The European Communities* (28 *ibid.* 1974)

——: *Equality and Discrimination in International Economic Law* (*V*): *The European Communities and the Wider World* (29 *ibid.* 1975)

Goodwin, G. L.: *GATT and the Organisation for Trade Co-operation* (10 *ibid.* 1956)

——: *United Nations Conference on Trade and Development* (19 *ibid.* 1965)

Harrod, J.: *Non-Governmental Organisations and the Third World* (24 *ibid.* 1970)

James, A. M.: *The UN Economic Commission for Asia and the Far East* (13 *ibid.* 1959)

1

Kaplan, G. G.: *Equality and Discrimination in International Economic Law (II): The UNCTAD Scheme for Generalised Preferences* (26 *ibid.* 1972)

Kojanec, G.: *Recent Developments in the Law of State Contracts* (24 *ibid.* 1970)

Mahajani, U.: *Foreign Aid at the Operational Level in South-East Asia* (19 *ibid.* 1965)

Modelski, G.: *The Corporation in World Society* (22 *ibid.* 1968)

Paenson, I.: *The Problem of East-West Trade* (10 *ibid.* 1956)

Penrose, E.: *Monopoly and Competition in the International Petroleum Industry* (18 *ibid.* 1964)

Ramcharan, B. G.: *Equality and Discrimination in International Economic Law (III): The Commonwealth Preferential System* (26 *ibid.* 1972)

Robertson, D.: *Proposals for a North Atlantic Free Trade Area* (23 *ibid.* 1969)

Ross, L. W.: *The Washington Monetary Agreement* (26 *ibid.* 1972)
——: *Flexible Exchange Rates* (30 *ibid.* 1976)

Scamell, W. M.: *International Economic Co-operation and the Problem of Full Employment* (6 *ibid.* 1952)

Schwarzenberger, G.: *An International Investment Insurance Agency* (23 *ibid.* 1969)
——: *Equality and Discrimination in International Economic Law* (25 *ibid.* 1971)

Seidl-Hohenveldern, I.: *Multinational Enterprises and the International Law of the Future* (29 *ibid.* 1975)

Shaw, C. A.: *Dilemmas of Super-Growth* (30 *ibid.* 1976)

Stoiber, C.: *Equality and Discrimination in International Economic Law (VIII): The Multinational Enterprise* (31 *ibid.* 1977)

Strange, S.: *The Economic Work of the United Nations* (8 *ibid.* 1954)
——: *The Commonwealth and the Sterling Area* (13 *ibid.* 1959)
——: *Changing Trends in World Trade* (16 *ibid.* 1962)

Sutton, A.: *Equality and Discrimination in International Economic Law (VI): Trends in Regulation of International Trade in Textiles* (31 *ibid.* 1977)

Vaizey, J.: *International Inflation* (30 *ibid.* 1976)

Verdross, A.: *Quasi-International Agreements and International Economic Transactions* (18 *ibid.* 1964)

Wells, S. J.: *The Kennedy Round* (20 *ibid.* 1966)

#### (B) INTERNATIONAL VIOLENCE AND ITS CONTROL

Bellany, I.: *The Acquisition of Arms by Poor States* (30 Y.B.W.A., 1976)

Boyle, Sir Dermot: *Thoughts on the Nuclear Deterrent* (16 *ibid.* 1962)

Bull, H.: *Two Kinds of Arms Control* (17 *ibid.* 1963)

Burns, A. L.: *Military Technology and International Politics* (15 *ibid.* 1961)

Burton, J. W.: *The Declining Relevance of Coercion in World Society* (22 *ibid.* 1968)

Coffey, J. I.: *The Limitation of Strategic Armaments* (26 *ibid.* 1972)

Cowley, Sir John: *Future Trends in Warfare* (14 *ibid.* 1960)

Curle, A.: *Peace Studies* (30 *ibid.* 1976)

Dinstein, Y.: *Another Step in Codifying the Laws of War* (28 *ibid.* 1974)

Douglas-Home, C.: *The Arms Sales Race* (23 *ibid.* 1969)

Erickson, J.: *The World Strategic Balance* (23 *ibid.* 1969)

Foot, M. R. D.: *Resistance, War and Revolution* (31 *ibid.* 1977)

Garnett, J. C.: *The Concept of War* (30 *ibid.* 1976)

James, A.: *Recent Developments in United Nations Peace-keeping* (31 *ibid.* 1977)

Johnson, J. T.: *Just War, the Nixon Doctrine and the Future Shape of American Military Policy* (29 *ibid.* 1975)

Joynt, C. B.: *Arms Races and the Problem of Equilibrium* (18 *ibid.* 1964)

Lee, R.: *Safeguards Against Nuclear Proliferation* (23 *ibid.* 1969)

Martin, L. W.: *Ballistic Missile Defence and the Strategic Balance* (21 *ibid.* 1967)

Millar, T. B.: *On Nuclear Proliferation* (21 *ibid.* 1967)

Mitchell, C. R.: *External Involvement in Civil Strife: The Case of Chad* (26 *ibid.* 1972)

———: *Peace-keeping: The Police Function* (30 *ibid.* 1976)

Radojković, M.: *Les Armes Nucléaires et le Droit International* (16 *ibid.* 1962)

Ranger, R.: *Arms Control in Theory and in Practice* (31 *ibid.* 1977)

Roberts, A.: *Civil Resistance as a Technique in International Relations* (24 *ibid.* 1970)

Schwarzenberger, G.: *Hegemonial Intervention* (13 *ibid.* 1959)

———: *The Law of Armed Conflict: A Civilised Interlude?* (28 *ibid.* 1974)

Smart, I.: *Alliance, Deterrence and Defence* (26 *ibid.* 1972)

Smith, H. A.: *Modern Weapons and Modern War* (9 *ibid.* 1955)

Smith, W. H.: *International Terrorism: A Political Analysis* (31 *ibid.* 1977)

Williams, G.: *The Strategic Nuclear Balance and the Defence of Europe* (27 *ibid.* 1973)

## (C) EAST-WEST DÉTENTE

Boardman, R.: *China's Rise as a Nuclear Power* (25 Y.B.W.A. 1971)

Burmeister, W.: *Brandt's Opening to the East* (27 *ibid.* 1973)

Burnham, C. G.: *Czechoslovakia: 30 Years After Munich* (23 *ibid.* 1969)

Erickson, J.: *The World Strategic Balance* (23 *ibid.* 1969)

Ginsburgs, G.: *Socialist Internationalism and State Sovereignty* (25 *ibid.* 1971)

——: *The Constitutional Foundations of the "Socialist Commonwealth"* (27 *ibid.* 1973)

Martin, L. W.: *Ballistic Missile Defence and the Strategic Balance* (21 *ibid.* 1967)

Millar, T. B.: *On Nuclear Proliferation* (21 *ibid.* 1967)

Radojković, M.: *Les Armes Nucléaires et le Droit International* (16 *ibid.* 1962)

Ranger, R.: *Arms Control in Theory and in Practice* (31 *ibid.* 1977)

Schwarzenberger, G.: *An Inter-Camp Agenda* (18 *ibid.* 1964)

Smart, I.: *Alliance, Deterrence and Defence: The Changing Context of Security* (26 *ibid.* 1972)

Yahuda, M. B.: *China's Nuclear Policy* (23 *ibid.* 1969)

### (D) China's Emergence as a Super-Power

Adie, W. A. C.: *China and the Developed Countries* (20 Y.B.W.A. 1966)

Bell, C.: *The Containment of China* (22 *ibid.* 1968)

Boardman, R.: *China's Rise as a Nuclear Power* (25 *ibid.* 1971)

Buchan, A.: *An Expedition to the Poles* (29 *ibid.* 1975)

Erickson, J.: *The World Strategic Balance* (23 *ibid.* 1969)

Fitzmaurice, G. B.: *Chinese Representation in the United Nations* (6 *ibid.* 1952)

Frankel, J.: *The Balance of Power in the Far East* (7 *ibid.* 1953)

Keeton, G. W.: *Nationalism in Eastern Asia* (1 *ibid.* 1947)

Lewisohn, W.: *Basic Problems in Modern China* (3 *ibid.* 1949)

Lindsay, Lord: *Chinese Foreign Policy* (15 *ibid.* 1961)

Mahajani, U.: *Sino-American Rapprochement and the New Configurations in Southeast Asia* (29 *ibid.* 1975)

Meissner, B.: *The Political Treaties of China and the Soviet Union in East Asia* (27 *ibid.* 1973)

Schwarzenberger, G.: *Beyond Power Politics?* (19 *ibid.* 1965)

——: *From Bipolarity to Multipolarity?* (21 *ibid.* 1967)

Wittfogel, K. A.: *The Russian and Chinese Revolutions: A Socio-Historical Comparison* (15 *ibid.* 1961)

Yahuda, M. B.: *China's Nuclear Policy* (23 *ibid.* 1969)

Yalem, R. J.: *Tripolarity and World Politics* (28 *ibid.* 1974)

Yu, G. T.: *China in Africa* (24 *ibid.* 1970)

## (E) LATIN AMERICA

Ball, M. M.: *Recent Developments in Inter-American Relations* (3 Y.B.W.A., 1949)

Blakemore, H.: *Chile: Continuity and Change* (27 *ibid.* 1973)

Crossley, J. C.: *Agrarian Reform in Latin America* (17 *ibid.* 1963)

Ferns, H. S.: *Argentina in Travail* (29 *ibid.* 1975)

Gorinsky, C.: *Cultures in Conflict: Amerindians in New Societies* (24 *ibid.* 1970)

Graber, D. A.: *United States Intervention in Latin America* (16 *ibid.* 1962)

Hilton, R.: *Castrophobia in the United States* (18 *ibid.* 1964)

Hutchinson, G. W.: *The Coup in Chile* (29 *ibid.* 1975)

O'Shaughnessy, H.: *Christian Democratic Upsurge in Latin America* (21 *ibid.* 1967)

Parkinson, F.: *The Alliance for Progress* (18 *ibid.* 1964)

——: *Santo Domingo and After* (20 *ibid.* 1966)

——: *International Economic Integration in Latin America and the Caribbean* (31 *ibid.* 1977)

Salera, V.: *Economic Relations between the United States and Latin America* (14 *ibid.* 1960)

Strange, S.: *Cuba and After* (17 *ibid.* 1963)

Tannenbaum, F.: *The Continuing Ferment in Latin America* (10 *ibid.* 1956)

Whitaker, A. P.: *The Organisation of American States* (13 *ibid.* 1959)


## (F) MIDDLE EAST

Frankel, J.: *The Middle East in Turmoil* (10 Y.B.W.A., 1956)

James, A.: *Recent Developments in United Nations Peace-keeping* (31 *ibid.* 1977)

Kirk, G.: *The Middle Eastern Scene* (14 *ibid.* 1960)

Mitchell, C. R.: *Peace-keeping: The Police Function* (30 *ibid.* 1976)

Neumann, R. G.: *The Near East After the Syrian Coup* (16 *ibid.* 1962)

Parkinson, F.: *Bandung and the Underdeveloped Countries* (10 *ibid.* 1956)

Rodinson, M.: *Israel: The Arab Options* (22 *ibid.* 1968)

Roth, S. J.: *World Jewry and Israel* (28 *ibid.* 1974)

Strange, S.: *Palestine and the United Nations* (3 *ibid.* 1949)

——: *Suez and After* (11 *ibid.* 1957)

Troutbeck, Sir John: *Stresses Within the Arab World* (12 *ibid.* 1958)


## (G) AFRICA

Butterworth, R.: *The Future of South Africa* (31 Y.B.W.A., 1977)

Doxey, G. V. & M.: *The Prospects for Change in South Africa* (19 *ibid.* 1965)

Doxey, M.: *The Rhodesian Sanctions Experiment* (25 *ibid.* 1971)

Hudson, D.: *The World Council of Churches and Racism* (29 *ibid.* 1975)

Legum, C.: *South Africa: The Politics of Détente* (30 *ibid.* 1976)

—: *The Future of Ethiopia* (28 *ibid.* 1974)

Longmore, L.: *The South African Dilemma* (8 *ibid.* 1954)

Spence, J.: *The Strategic Significance of South Africa* (27 *ibid.* 1973)

Stent, G. D.: *Colour Problems of South Africa* (2 *ibid.* 1948)

Taylor, T.: *President Nixon's Arms Supply Policy* (26 *ibid.* 1972)

## (H) INTERNATIONAL LAW AND ORDER

Aaronson, M.: *Political Aspects of International Drug Control* (9 Y.B.W.A., 1955)

Beloff, M.: *Problems of International Government* (8 *ibid.* 1954)

Butter, W. E.: *Eastern European Approaches to International Law* (26 *ibid.* 1972)

Cheng, B.: *The First Twenty Years of the International Court of Justice* (20 *ibid.* 1966)

Corbett, P. E.: *Law and Society in the Relations of States* (4 *ibid.* 1950)

Engel, S.: *The Changing Charter of the United Nations* (7 *ibid.* 1953)

Falk, R. A.: *The Logic of State Sovereignty Versus the Requirements of World Order* (27 *ibid.* 1973)

Hambro, E.: *The International Court of Justice* (3 *ibid.* 1949)

Kojanec, G.: *Recent Developments in the Law of State Contracts* (24 *ibid.* 1970)

Ramcharan, B. G.: *The International Law Commission* (29 *ibid.* 1975)

Rosenne, S.: *Relations Between Governments and the International Law Commission* (19 *ibid.* 1965)

Schapiro, L. B.: *The Soviet Concept of International Law* (2 *ibid.* 1948)

Schwarzenberger, G.: *Civitas Maxima?* (29 *ibid.* 1975)

—: *Neo-Barbarism and International Law* (22 *ibid.* 1968)

Vallat, Sir Francis: *International Law—A Forward Look* (18 *ibid.* 1964)

Vincent, R. J.: *The Idea of Concert and International Order* (29 *ibid.* 1975)

Yalem, R. J.: *The Concept of World Order* (29 *ibid.* 1975)

Yuen-Li Liang: *Methods for the Encouragement of Progressive Development of International Law and its Codification* (2 *ibid.* 1948)

Zemanek, K.: *The United Nations and the Law of Outer Space* (19 *ibid.* 1965)

## (I) World Portraits

Bonn, M. J.: *American Statesmen* (5 Y.B.W.A., 1951)
—: *The Demise of the Adenauer Era* (18 *ibid.* 1964)
Burmeister, W.: *Brandt's Opening to the East* (27 *ibid.* 1973)
Hilton, R.: *Castrophobia in the United States* (18 *ibid.* 1964)
James, A.: *U Thant and His Critics* (26 *ibid.* 1972)
Nicholas, H. G.: *The Nixon Line* (25 *ibid.* 1971)
Pickles, D.: *France Under General de Gaulle* (16 *ibid.* 1962)
Sceats, R.: *The Continuity of French Policy* (26 *ibid.* 1972)
Vincent, R. J.: *Kissinger's System of Foreign Policy* (31 *ibid.* 1977)

# DÉTENTE AFTER HELSINKI
## *ATTITUDES AND PERSPECTIVES*

### By

### FRANS A. M. ALTING VON GEUSAU

THE Conference on Security and Co-operation in Europe (CSCE) which had opened on July 3, 1973, and was concluded on August 1, 1975, owes its historical significance in East-West relations to what did not happen.

It did not end in failure, although no basic agreement was reached on any of the outstanding differences between East and West.

It did not conclude with a belated peace treaty or a new charter for European co-operation, although every effort had been made—endless negotiations on the precise wording of paragraphs and a final summit festival—to give it the appearance of such an exercise. It did not make any meaningful contribution to overcoming the political and ideological division in Europe, although all participating States are on record for "recognising the indivisibility of security in Europe." It did not lessen the military confrontation nor influence the course of parallel negotiations on force reductions, although "the complementary nature of the political and military aspects of security" was considered an essential consideration from which to proceed.

The States participating in the Conference entered negotiations with divergent, if not conflicting, objectives. Their policies and statements ever since the conclusion of the Final Act indicate that each side has maintained its own objectives, despite the compromises achieved in the texts of the Final Act.

CSCE therefore cannot be seen as the beginning of a new era in relations between States in Europe. The exercise and its outcome, however, may assist in better understanding the process of East-West relations, as the Act at least is offering a new common framework for analysing divergent policies and objectives.[1] This new common framework consists of the fact that all States have accepted the promotion of détente as their common objective. It may be useful, therefore, to devote this survey of détente after Helsinki, to the attitudes of participating States towards this objective.

---

[1] For an in depth analysis of the Final Act, see in particular: V. Y. Ghébali, " L'Acte Final de la Conférence sur la Sécurité et la Coopération en Europe et les Nations Unies," in XXI *Annuaire Français de Droit International* (1975), pp. 73–127; and H. S. Russell, "The Helsinki Declaration: Brobdingnag or Lilliput?" 70 *American Journal of International Law*, No. 2, pp. 242–272.

## I—DÉTENTE: THE SOVIET VIEW

It is common knowledge that the convening of CSCE had been made possible by the reluctant agreement of NATO countries to such a conference, proposed by the Soviet Union since the early fifties. Although the use of the term "détente" is fairly recent in Soviet statements, it is now being forwarded as the most appropriate one for identifying the present state of relations between "socialist" and "capitalist" States. Détente as a consequence is the name for the current stage in an "irreversible" process of relations between the "socialist" States and those of the "opposite camp."

The following quotations may assist in giving the Soviet view on détente its proper post-war perspective: "This war does not resemble previous ones. Whoever occupies a territory, imposes his own social system. Everybody imposes his social system as far as his army can advance. It could not be otherwise." (Stalin to Tito, March 1945.) ... "After the war two camps were formed—the imperialist and anti-democratic camp having as its basic aim the establishment of world domination of American imperialism and the smashing of democracy, and the anti-imperialist and democratic camp having as its basic aim the undermining of imperialism, the consolidation of democracy, and the eradication of the remnants of fascism." (*Founding Declaration of the Cominform*, September 1947.) ... "Peaceful co-existence of the socialist and capitalist countries is an objective necessity for the development of human society ... (it) implies renunciation of war as a means of settling international disputes . . . (it) affords more favourable opportunities for the struggle of the working class in the capitalist countries and facilitates the struggle of the peoples of the colonial and dependent countries for their liberation . . ." (*Program of the Communist Party of the Soviet Union* (CPSU), adopted at the 22nd Party Congress, October 1961.) ... "Détente and peaceful co-existence have to do with inter-State relations . . . Détente does not in the slightest abolish, nor can it alter, the laws of the class struggle... We make no secret of the fact that we see détente as the way to create more favourable conditions for peaceful socialist and Communist construction." (L. Brezhnev at the 25th Congress of the CPSU, February, 1976.)

The stages of post-war relations between the Soviet Union and the outside world—as seen by the Kremlin—can be clearly discerned from these quotations.

The imposition of the Soviet system in Eastern Europe after the Second World War by force of arms was proclaimed as the end of the period of Stalin's socialism in one country and the beginning of a new era. The founding declaration of Cominform defines the Soviet view of the new era: the world, henceforward, is divided in two hostile camps.[2]

During the late 1950s, the development of nuclear weapons induced the Kremlin to revise its doctrine on the inevitability of war. Khrushchev, as a consequence, adapted Lenin's doctrine on "peaceful co-existence" in such a way that it could also be used as a "new" principle guiding relations between States belonging to the two hostile camps. The use of this new term has proven to be most rewarding. Many non-Marxist commentators have come to believe, erroneously so in my opinion, that the *addition*—the avoidance of nuclear war— and not its *origin*—the international class struggle—are now the essence of the principle.

The extent to which this belief is misinterpreting Soviet thinking becomes clearer, since détente has been added to the ideological jargon.

Détente, we are told, indicates a new stage in relations between the two camps, in which the changes in the "correlation of forces" have compelled the "capitalist" States to give a wider recognition to the principle of peaceful co-existence. Détente, therefore, represents a shift in power relations between East and West in favour of the Soviet Union. The reasons given for this shift are: the crisis of the capitalist system (the oil-crisis); the increasingly anti-western attitudes of many developing countries; and the continued strengthening of Soviet and Warsaw Pact military forces.

As the military balance of forces between the Warsaw Pact and the North Atlantic Treaty Organisation (NATO) is apparently shifting in favour of the former, one should not be surprised to observe that the objective of avoiding nuclear war is receding to the background in Soviet strategy and military planning. As Paul H. Nitze wrote recently: "unfortunately, I believe the record shows that neither negotiations, nor unilateral restraint have operated to dissuade Soviet leaders from seeking a nuclear-war-winning capability—or from the view that with such a capability they could effectively use pressure tactics to get their way in crisis situations." [3]

Even more indicative are the conclusions of a recent study made by Joseph D. Douglass and based on Soviet open-source military literature. "(1) To the Soviets, theater nuclear weapons are a fundamental part of their warfighting capability rather than a deterrent adjunct to conventional forces . . . (2) The Soviets view nuclear weapons as powerful and effective means of tactical combat. The

---

[2] Which indicates progress in ideological terms, as the new era was preceded by the era of capitalist encirclement of one country.

[3] P. H. Nitze, "Assuring Strategic Stability in an Era of Détente," 54 *Foreign Affairs*, Nr. 2, January 1976, p. 232.

Central Committee of the Communist Party of the Soviet-Union has adopted and promulgated a strong, offensive, nuclear-oriented, warfighting doctrine. The Soviet military strategy is clearly offensive, with nuclear weapons playing the leading role. . . . (3) An in-depth, massive, surprise nuclear strike, in conjunction with an immediate, high-speed air and ground exploitation, is still the dominant Soviet concept for war against NATO." [4]

The Soviet view of détente—as shown through their public statements—can no longer be seen as the ideological expression of a communist dream (world revolution), disguising the political reality of Soviet fear for western aggression, and revealing a willingness to accommodate with the West. The addition of détente to the official, ideological jargon is the expression of a new " arrogance of power " in Moscow. This new arrogance of power appears to have replaced the balance between an ideological interest in world revolution and a historically rooted national, Soviet interest in improving its security against the West. Previously this balance of interests appeared to leave room for East-West agreements. In the present phase of détente, ideology and "national" power politics have become mutually reinforcing incentives, by which the room for agreements is being further narrowed.

## II—Détente: The United States View

Détente as a policy, rather than a doctrine or a principle, originated in the West. Like the American policies of confrontation and containment during the era of the Cold War, it is meant to deal with an adversary relationship. Détente as a policy can be traced back to former President Kennedy's handling of the Cuba Missile Crisis in October 1962. It was intended to improve the political climate—to reduce tensions—and thereby create better conditions for negotiating agreements, particularly in the field of nuclear arms-control. Its scope gradually broadened, especially during the Kissinger era, to include most aspects of the Soviet-American relationship. According to Henry Kissinger, the concept of détente "was designed to prevent competition from sliding into military hostilities and to create the conditions for the relationship to be gradually and prudently improved." [5]

In 1967 the pursuance of a policy of détente was explicitly stated to be the second function of the Atlantic Alliance, alongside the

---

[4] J. D. Douglass, Jr., "The Soviet Theater Nuclear Offensive," I *Studies in Communist Affairs* (1976). (Published under the auspices of the United States Air Force.)

[5] H. A. Kissinger, "The 1976 Alastair Buchan Memorial Lecture," *Survival*, September/October 1976, p. 198.

function to maintain adequate military strength and political solidarity to deter aggression.

As Kissinger said: "Alliance policy toward the East has had two necessary dimensions. We seek to prevent the Soviet Union from transforming its military power into political expansion. At the same time we seek to resolve conflicts and disputes through negotiation, and to strengthen the incentives for moderation by expanding the area of constructive relations. . . . We must conduct a diplomacy . . . that resolves issues, nurtures restraints and builds co-operation based on mutual interest." [6]

American détente policy does not imply a renunciation of basic post-war foreign-policy aims. Said Kissinger in the same lecture: "We are determined to deal with Eastern Europe on the basis of sovereignty and independence of each of its countries. We accept no spheres of influence and no pretensions to hegemony. . . . And we will continue to pursue measures to improve the lives of the people in Eastern Europe in basic human terms—such as freer emigration, the unification of families, greater flow of information, increased economic interchange, and more opportunities for travel."

Despite some very superficial similarities in the Soviet and American concepts of détente, their aims and policies are essentially different. The basic difference resides in the completely different relationship between the United States and Western Europe on the one hand, and the Soviet Union and Eastern Europe, on the other. [7] Furthermore, as the Soviet Union sees détente as an opportunity to exploit perceived western weaknesses, the United States sees (saw) détente as an opportunity to promote mutual restraints and further agreements.

### III—Détente and the "Allied" States on Both Sides

During the 1960s, détente primarily indicated a change in the Soviet-United States relationship. It served, however, the interests of some of the smaller European States gradually to improve their bilateral relations in a number of non-military fields. Charles de Gaulle's policies against the United States appeared for some time to encourage the growth of national identity in some East European States. Smaller States in Europe began to favour multilateral talks on European security and co-operation. [8]

The 1968 invasion of Czechoslovakia quickly terminated those efforts towards truly multilateralising the improvement of intra-

---

[6] *Ibid.*
[7] See *e.g.* Brzezinski, "America and Europe," *Foreign Affairs* (1971).
[8] See *e.g.* F. A. M. Alting von Geusau (ed.), *NATO and Security in the Seventies* (1971).

European relations. Within the Soviet system, the year 1968 saw the beginning of Brezhnev's efforts to employ both bilateral ties and multilateral instruments—the Warsaw Pact and Council for Mutual Economic Assistance (CMEA)—to strengthen Soviet control of Eastern Europe. It opened a new drive for a European Security Conference aimed primarily at obtaining Western recognition of the post-war *status quo, i.e.* Soviet hegemony in Eastern Europe. CSCE, as a consequence, showed a high degree of socialist unity amongst the States of Eastern Europe, with the exception of Romania. This unity is further reflected in the comments and statements of those socialist countries which in the late 1960s had manifested a tendency to play down the ideological component of East-West relations. Janos Nagy, for instance, writes: "The Socialist countries lay stress on the long-range factors. Determinant among them is the shift in power relations in favour of socialism. This is the firm foundation which ensures that the process of détente becomes irreversible." [9] A similar thought has been expressed by Marian Dobrosielski, when discussing the reluctance of NATO countries to hold a Conference: "It was, however, difficult for the opponents to East-West détente and accord to give up the idea of their policy 'from the position of strength' despite the fact that such developments as the strengthening of the unity and cohesion of the Socialist countries, the growth of the military power of the U.S.S.R. and the whole of the Warsaw Treaty, the increasing importance and political authority throughout the world of the Socialist alliance—demonstrated how unrealistic and dangerous this policy was." [10]

It should be anybody's guess, how "firm a foundation" détente may find in a "shift" in power relations. The attitudes reflected by such statements, however, are bound to undermine rather than strengthen the political foundations of détente.

The outcome of CSCE appears to have further strengthened Soviet control in Eastern Europe as is indicated by the recent treaty between the Soviet Union and the Democratic Republic of Germany, the new Polish Constitution, and the *rapprochement* with Romania.

Despite these clear indications, French officials are still reported to see détente primarily as "a process by which medium and small Powers could assert their autonomy and independence." [11] This

[9] J. Nagy, "The Spirit of Helsinki," XVII *The New Hungarian Quarterly*, Nr. 64, Winter 1976, p. 7.

[10] M. Dobrosielski, " Conference on Security and Co-operation in Europe: A Polish View," *The Conference on Security and Co-operation in Europe*, Polish Institute of International Affairs, Warszawa (1976), pp. 25–26.

[11] P. de Vries (*Rapporteur*, International Secretariat), *Report on the Activities of the Subcommittee on Détente*, Political Committee, North Atlantic Assembly, November 1976. (Doc. TI70 PC/D(76) 12.)

concept of détente, however, lost most of its relevance in 1968. More important, so it appears is the West-German concept of détente. It was the "Ostpolitik" of Chancellor Brandt since 1969 which created the necessary conditions for convening CSCE. For the Federal Republic of Germany détente was reported to be "a very fundamental process of normalising relations with her neighbours" . . . "It is in our interest to restrict areas of conflict, to calm down existing conflicts, to define areas of technical co-operation, after asking the question as to whether the independently defined interests of the two sides can be brought over a common denominator. And finally, an aspect that is doubtlessly more important from the West's point of view than from that of the other side: how can we help human beings at the same time? Individual groups, minorities, the oppressed, but in the full knowledge of where the limit lies as to what can be negotiated and positively influenced."

The geographic position of the Federal Republic of Germany has also induced her to comment more cautiously on some post-Helsinki developments: "Even considering events in Angola there was no alternative to a realistic long-term strong détente policy since no-one could wish for a return to confrontation." [12] Other western governments basically hold the same concept of détente as a process which ought to produce progress especially on arms-control, troop reductions and less restricted human and humanitarian contacts.[13]

## IV—DÉTENTE AND THE NON-ALIGNED EUROPEAN STATES

Détente as we have seen in the previous sections is identified as a specific stage in a relationship between adversaries: the two super-Powers, two opposing systems or two military alliances. By definition, the term is unsuitable to characterise relations between the non-aligned States and those States belonging to one of the two alliances. A reduction of tension between the two blocs can be seen, however, as a primary interest for non-aligned European States, as it is likely to promote an evolution more conducive to their own independence and security. For this reason, one can expect the non-aligned States to be more interested in tangible results rather than ideological definitions of détente. The non-aligned States, furthermore, tend to look at the role they can play in bringing the adversaries to agreements by which relations in Europe can move *beyond* détente, *i.e.* beyond a Europe divided into blocs. Finland, Austria, Sweden and Switzerland served as an *ex-officio* mediation group during

---

[12] Statements from Brandt and Wischnewski as reported in *North Atlantic Assembly*, *loc. cit.* in note 11 above.

[13] See *e.g.* M. van der Stoel (Netherlands Minister for Foreign Affairs), "East–West Relations: Limits and Possibilities," *NATO Review*, Nr. 6, December 1976.

CSCE negotiations. Finland and Yugoslavia, especially, stressed how détente should contribute to different (*i.e.* from inter-bloc), relations between States in Europe.

President Tito affirmed at Helsinki: "The present positive trends in the policy of reducing tension would doubtless soon face a crisis if détente were reduced to an understanding between the blocs instead of increasingly becoming a method of understanding between all peoples on the principle of respect for independence, sovereignty and equality." [14] The non-aligned countries therefore underline the principle of the Final Act that relations will be developed "irrespective of differences between political, economic and social systems." [15] For them also, CSCE marked another important change: "The stage of détente previous to the convening of the CSCE was characterised by the bilateral character of agreements made. In this respect the CSCE marked a new stage, for it moved partly into an era of multilateral security and co-operation systems." [16] In other words: CSCE "has been rightly described as having marked itself a multilateralisation of détente by having expanded the number of those involved and interested in it so that the actual process has begun evolving from bloc frameworks to the broader international level. This expansion of the process of détente has led to a certain amount of democratisation of the foundations on which it should unfold, as was manifested in both the organisation and method of work of the Conference itself. . . ." [17] In all, ". . . the CSCE, while recognising present realities, adopted a new platform for democratic relations and co-operation in Europe, as contained in the Final Act." [18]

In a number of important matters, the non-aligned countries clearly took their distance from the Socialist countries. They did not follow the ideological approach to détente as a manifestation of peaceful co-existence applicable only to relations between States. Like most western countries, they see détente as a process to be made more viable through concrete steps and measures, primarily in the first (military), and the third (human contacts), "basket."

## V—ATTITUDES TOWARDS DÉTENTE: THE CRUCIAL PROBLEM

It should be clear from the foregoing survey that the common objective of promoting détente disguises widely divergent attitudes.

[14] President Tito in his address to the Third Stage of CSCE at Helsinki.

[15] O. Apunen, " The principles of relations between the States of Europe," *Yearbook of Finnish Foreign Policy* (1975), p. 36. [16] *Ibid.*

[17] D. Ninčic, " The Spirit and Letter of Helsinki," XXVII *Review of International Affairs*, Nr. 626, May 5, 1976, p. 6.

[18] M. Pešic, " The Conference on Security and Co-operation and Current Developments in Europe," XXVII *Review of International Affairs*, Nr. 629, June 20, 1976, p. 2.

Each of the three main attitudes towards détente—the NATO, non-aligned and Warsaw Pact ones—moreover suffer from intrinsic contradictions.

United States and, more generally, western policies of détente are based on the assumption that a balance of forces between the Soviet Union and the United States is a factor of stability and an opportunity for negotiation. As it involves a "balance of terror" at the same time, the dangers of nuclear war are assumed to be additional incentives for negotiating arms-control and arms-reduction agreements. Technology and ideology, however, are bound to make the East-West "balance" an inherently unstable one. While the Soviet Union—during the last decade—has embarked on a massive programme of strengthening its military power, NATO countries' defence policies have manifested a striking ambivalence: technologically the arms race continued, while some member-States began to reduce their defence capabilities in advance of East-West agreements.

The détente policies of the non-aligned States are—and rightly so—pursuing the overcoming of bloc divisions in Europe. Détente to them signifies improvement in an adversary relationship. It should be replaced by a different kind of relationship, if it is to be more than a temporary interlude. At the same time they tend to ignore that strict adherence to national sovereignty—while being necessary today—is a shaky basis for organising European interdependence in the future.

It should be clear that the Soviet and Warsaw Pact approach to détente suffers from the most fundamental, intrinsic contradictions. It is simply inconceivable to any reasonable mind to advocate reconciliation, accommodation and agreements in an adversary relationship, while at the same time presenting détente as a manifestation of a policy to shift power relations in favour of Socialism. The roots of this contradiction, no doubt, are in Stalin's post-war European policies.

During and after the war, United States planners embarked on a policy of reforming international structures in an effort to create new frameworks for co-operation and security in which States would be better able to deal with threats to peace. Stalin embarked on a basically backward policy to ensure Soviet security, by, amongst other things, subjecting the peoples of Eastern Europe to Soviet external and ideological domination, and resisting any effort to reform international structures in Europe. His backward policy, however, was presented to the outside world as *the* example of progress towards a new system of (Socialist) inter-State relations. American efforts to reform international relations, as a consequence, had to be presented as examples of backward imperialism.

Marxist-Leninist ideology served as a useful instrument to distort and confuse the meaning of any understandable notion, and of political reality itself. The proclamation (at the founding of Cominform) of a world divided in two hostile camps was the ideological expression of the Soviet policy of creating its sphere of security. Western opposition to this artificial division of Europe, was then twisted into a presumed policy of artificially dividing the continent into two groupings. After having put the blame for Europe's division to those who opposed it, the Socialist camp was henceforth presented as the grouping which—while insisting on the acceptance of the political *status quo*—tireless strove to overcome division.

"An entirely different approach to the problem of security in Europe and in the world was, and continues to be, presented—in theory and practice—by the Soviet Union and other Socialist countries. It stems from the idea of peaceful co-existence among countries with different socio-political systems; it adopts as the starting point for all-European solutions the acceptance of the realities resulting from the Second World War; it aims at overcoming the artificial divisions of Europe into conflicting military groupings, at disarmament, at replacing the balance of fear with co-operation and military conflicts with peaceful competition." [19]

A statement so packed with contradictions can be understood only in terms of an entirely different approach aiming at the *victory* of Socialism. Détente—contrary to anything a reasonable mind may assume it to mean—is the phase, then, by which the victory of Socialism is being transformed from an ideological article of faith into a realistic political expectation.

Unless the West is appeased or defeated, détente, like peaceful co-existence and confrontation, expresses the continuation of a policy to keep Europe divided into hostile camps, adversaries or military blocs. Unless the West accepts that one-party, repressive rule is an example to admire, rather than a humanly unacceptable system to criticise and change, albeit peacefully, tensions and conflicts are bound to re-occur inside the Socialist system, between the Soviet Union and Yugoslavia and in East-West relations. Ideology, repression and division are the fundamental problems Europe has to cope with after Helsinki, just as much as it had to before. Of the three, ideology is the most serious threat to world peace. Ideology gives repression its justification. It divides the world into two species, reducing "them," the others, to abstract categories of evil like capitalists, imperialists or aggressors. It is this organised lie, this reduction of "the other to a category for vilification," which in our days prepares the human mind to accept and eventually wage war.[20]

[19] Dobrosielski, *op. cit.* in note 10 above, p. 15.
[20] See G. Marcel, *Les Hommes Contre l'Humain* (1951), p. 114 *et seq.*

Or as Solzhenitsyn wrote: " Ideology—that is what gives evildoing its long-sought justification and gives the evildoer the necessary stead-fastness and determination. That is the social theory which helps to make his acts seem good instead of bad in his own and others' eyes, so that he won't hear reproaches and curses but will receive praise and honours ... Thanks to *ideology*, the twentieth century was fated to experience evildoing on a scale calculated in the millions. This cannot be denied, nor passed over, nor suppressed. How then, do we dare insist that evildoers do not exist? And who was it that destroyed these millions? Without evildoers there would have been no Archipelago." [21]

In the final analysis it is the ideological attitude to détente which constitutes the most formidable barrier to overcoming the artificial division of Europe and building a structure for European peace and reconciliation. It is not those who propose a free exchange of people who undermine détente, but those who state: " peaceful co-existence fixes the principles of relations between States with different social systems and the forms of co-operation, and does not apply to the ideological sphere. Ideological confrontation is an objective necessity which follows from the difference of social systems." [22]

Ideological confrontation is an objective evil standing in the way of creative efforts to build a structure of peace in Europe.

## VI—A " Code of Conduct "
### for Détente?

The extent to which the ideological attitude to détente is hampering the improvement of East-West relations has manifested itself all too clearly during the " Follow Up " meetings of the CSCE in Belgrade.

At least two separate but related new developments in 1977 have again emphasised, how far policies and objectives of the participating States continue to diverge, despite their joint signatures under the Final Act of Helsinki. I am referring here to: (1) the human rights movements inside the Soviet system; and (2) some important changes in American foreign policy towards the Soviet Union and Eastern Europe.

The ever present opposition against totalitarian repression in the Soviet system took a new form with the publication in January 1977, of the Czechoslovak Charter 77 Manifesto.[23]

---

[21] A. Solzhenitsyn, *The Gulag Archipelago 1918–1956* (An Experiment in Literary Investigation: I–II; translated from the Russian by T. P. Whitney, 1974), p. 174.

[22] Nagy, *op. cit.* in note 9 above, p. 10. This is said to be the Hungarian position.

[23] A translation of this impressive document appeared in the *New York Herald Tribune*, February 1, 1977.

The strength of this new movement resided in the fact that it did not ask for political change, but for the application to all citizens of those fundamental human rights to which their own governments had subscribed. This clearly reasonable, if not pressing demand, to respect at home, what had been used as a tool of ideological struggle abroad, was especially disturbing for the communist rulers. It was bound to focus attention in the CSCE review conference on Soviet-bloc violations of the seventh principle of the Final Act. The ruling élites predictably reacted with measures of repression, villification, unlawful imprisonment, harassments, etc., . . . only to make things worse for them.

Repression of these human rights movements also was an important cause for the emerging dispute between the CPSU and some West European communist parties.

The human rights movements in Eastern Europe coincided with the coming to power of a new democratic Administration in Washington. Among the changes President Carter initiated in American foreign policy, the following ones are especially relevant: a renewed determination to promote respect for fundamental human rights; the elaboration of a more radical approach to arms control and disarmament; a renewed commitment to " open " government; and an insistence on strict reciprocity in Soviet-American relations in all fields.[24]

Related to the two other developments, already mentioned, President Carter's emphasis on human rights is a most unwelcome change for the Kremlin, especially in the year of the Belgrade review meetings.

One should therefore not be surprised, that régimes which at home respond with repression to modest demands for respecting their own commitments, react to genuine concern abroad, with unfounded allegations about interference, revival of the Cold War and the like. One can only be surprised and dismayed, when certain West European statesmen—who might know better—have been willing to advance themselves as the interpreters of Mr. Brezhnev's concerns about the so-called code of conduct of détente.[25] Brezhnev's complaints about the breaking of the code of conduct of détente, presumably refers to the " code " (Final Act) of Helsinki. But who is breaking the code: the government which consistently violates its seventh principle, or the one expressing concern about such violations? Who is compromising the process of détente: the government which

---

[24] See further, K. Birnbaum, " Human Rights and East-West Relations," *Foreign Affairs*, July 1977.

[25] See especially the unfortunate interview given by President Giscard d'Estaing to *Newsweek*, July 25, 1977.

is continuing its massive military build-up, or the one trying to make meaningful proposals towards *significant* nuclear arms reductions instead of merely dragging on with the abortive SALT?

From the two issues, President Carter's emphasis on human rights, has especially produced irritation in the Kremlin and differences of opinion among some Western governments. The Soviet responses to the new American emphasis, however, are clearly unfounded. First of all, the allegation that concern for human rights constitutes inter-ference in internal affairs, is inconsistent with present international law. Secondly, the process of détente in Europe is compromised not by those governments determined to advance respect for human rights, but by those denying them to their own citizens. As former United States Secretary of State, George Marshall, already told the United Nations General Assembly in 1948 [26]: " Governments which systematically disregard the rights of their own people are not likely to respect the right of other nations and other people and are likely to seek their objectives by coercion and force in the international field."

Soviet policy towards Eastern Europe and the resulting crises in the area have always been the principal cause of East-West tension in Europe.

Thirdly, the argument that socialist countries give priority to economic and social rights over political and civil rights . . . " the idea that remuneration for public holidays, however laudable *per se*, should take precedence over the ban of torture, makes nonsense of the whole concept of human rights."

Giving " priority to economic and social rights does not reflect a different political outlook, but is usually merely an alibi for States that practise oppression at home, and whose record even in the economic and social field is anything but brilliant. Among the loudest proponents of the primacy of social and economic rights there is not a single one that permits the existence of free trade unions." [27]

Finally, the opinion—expressed, *e.g.* in *Pravda*—that concern for human rights belongs to the ideological struggle and constitutes an American attempt to revive ideological confrontation, is no less than a negation of the basic conception underlying respect for human rights. It only serves to underline, that universal human rights do not exist according to Soviet ideology.

One cannot therefore but conclude that recent developments have manifested once again, that the Soviet ideological attitude to détente remains the basic impediment to East-West agreement on a code of conduct for détente.

---

[26] Quoted in, W. Laqueur, " The Issue of Human Rights," 63 *Commentary*, Nr. 5, May 1977, p. 33.　　　　　　　　　　　　　　　　　　　　　[27] *Ibid*. p. 32.

## VII—PERSPECTIVES

The CSCE and the Final Act of Helsinki have not, so far, changed the pattern of post-war relations in Europe. The Soviet system is likely to remain an area of instability and concern for the western world. The independence and non-alignment of Yugoslavia is no better assured in the late 1970s than it was in the early 1950s. The western world is no less capable in the late 1970s than before to cope with the uncertainties of détente. What is needed to cope with Soviet power and the barrier of ideology is steadiness and fortitude.

It is a known fact that democratic societies have a tendency to fluctuate "in their attitude towards defence—between complacency and alarmist concern." [28] It is imperative that this fluctuation be restrained by upholding the unity between (especially) the United States and a unifying European Community. At the same time western unity and a continued basic commitment to the values of pluralist democracy are necessary to prevent economic problems from undermining western political institutions and determination. Continued adherence to the values of pluralist democracy and the defensive posture of the North Atlantic Alliance should make clear what the objectives are for a détente policy of the western world: to preserve and promote the recognition and protection of fundamental human rights; and to prevent conflicts from sliding into war, particularly a nuclear war.

The first objective requires a deliberate and persistent effort to promote human contacts across the artificially created line of division in Europe, thus contributing to a gradual breakdown of ideological barriers. The chapter on "Co-operation in Humanitarian and Other Fields" in the Final Act can serve as a frame of reference for continuing such efforts.

The second objective requires a more consistent effort to improve and reassess Western arms-control and disarmament policies alongside their defence policies. Arms-control requires long-term planning in an effort to control arms technology even more than defence requires long-term planning in order to maintain the capacity for technological innovation.

Whatever the setbacks and stalemates in negotiations on the reduction of forces, Mutual Balanced Force Reduction (MBFR) talks should be pressed on, while making clear that parity is not designed as a trick to favour NATO militarily, but reflects a basic political principle of mutual tolerance, which alone can ensure results.

An equally more consistent policy is needed to reduce—through

---

[28] H. A. Kissinger, *loc. cit.* in note 5 above, p. 197.

negotiations—the role of nuclear weapons in the strategies of the two blocs. The protection of the population against the horrors of nuclear war ought to be sought, not by building vast civil defence shelter programmes, but by negotiating the phasing out of nuclear weapons from military strategies.

It is through persistent efforts to build networks of human contacts across artificial boundaries and networks of negotiations between all States that peace in Europe can still be saved. Above all, the demon of ideological confrontation should be exorcised if man wants to prevent the twentieth century from ending even more cruelly than is revealed in the experience of its first 70 years.

# THE NIXON LEGACY
# AND AMERICAN FOREIGN POLICY

By

## M. H. SMITH and R. CAREY

THE analysis of foreign policy has long been bedevilled by questions of constraint and choice. Although there have been many, and determined, efforts to present foreign-policy making as a quasi-mechanical process of input, process, and output (attempts which, let it be said, have often offered valuable insights), eventually any treatment of foreign policy must come up against the question, " How free was the policy maker to act in a given set of circumstances?" Such a question is as much philosophical and psychological in its implications as it is simply descriptive, and it can be avoided least of all if the analyst is concerned, implicitly or explicitly, to *evaluate* the actions or set of actions under review.[1] The attainment of a viable foreign-policy posture depends at least as much on an answer to such questions as it does upon the more positive aspects of foreign-policy study.[2] Questions of voluntarism and determinism, positive and adaptive behaviour, have thus marked the evolution of foreign-policy analysis even where such analysis has set out rigorously to avoid them.[3]

It is the aim of this article explicitly to examine the nature and implications of freedom to act in foreign policy, largely through a study of United States foreign policy in the Nixon and Ford Administrations. We begin with the relatively simple assertion that the Nixon presidency and its legacy—not least its manner of the ending—created problems of constraint and choice for its successor. We hope to explore the nature of these problems, first by setting the Nixon-Ford transition within a set of general ideas about constraints and choices in foreign policy; secondly by applying this set of ideas to the " Nixon legacy " as it was inherited by Gerald Ford; and finally by examining in greater detail two incidents which are especially revealing of aspects of the " Ford inheritance " in foreign policy.

---

[1] For an examination of the evaluation problem in foreign policy analysis see P. Williams and M. H. Smith, " The conduct of foreign policy in democratic and authoritarian states," in this *Year Book*, Vol. 30 (1976), pp. 205–222.

[2] The concept of viability is explored in Williams and Smith, *op. cit.* in note 1 above, at pp. 210–214.

[3] Explicit treatments of these problems can be found (for example) in J. N. Rosenau, *The Scientific Study of Foreign Policy* (1971); J. W. Burton, *World Society* (1972); and J. P. Lovell, *Foreign Policy in Perspective: strategy, adaptation, decision making* (1970).

I—COMMITMENTS AND CHANGE IN FOREIGN POLICY

For the purposes of this paper we are especially interested in two major aspects of constraints and choice in foreign policy—those of commitments and change. Although the posing of such a simple dichotomy is bound to raise important questions we would contend that an analysis of commitments undertaken by governments (and the expectations that they generate) must form a considerable part of any study of constraints and choices; likewise that the impact of these commitments is likely to be understood most clearly when examined in the light of change within the context of foreign-policy making.

(a) *Commitments and expectations*

In dealing with the first part of our analysis—commitments and expectations—three aspects can be seen as important. First, we need to appraise the political orientation of a given régime and the way this finds expression in commitments both declaratory and operational, formal and informal. Secondly, we need to be aware of the style of foreign-policy making identified with a given régime. Thirdly, we must examine the expectations generated at home and abroad by the orientation and style of a government's foreign policy.

A number of scholars have drawn attention to the importance of orientations [4] to a study of foreign policies. Sometimes these have been presented as very broad-brush generalisations about the directions of a particular State's foreign policy; but the idea also has considerable relevance to the more specific character of a given government's activities. Governments, after all, often like to consider themselves as expressing more general directions and traditions within State policy, in addition to adopting, more or less self-consciously, the idea of a national *role* in the international system.[5] Whether such postures are adopted in an ostentatiously declaratory form, or whether they emerge rather more cumulatively and pragmatically, they are of interest to us here precisely because of their frequent translation into commitments. Such commitments need not be solemn, formal and legally binding; they are often the more powerful precisely because they depend upon tacit and informal arrangements, habits of thought, and—as we shall see—shared expectations.

There is an intimate connection between the ideas of foreign-policy orientations, role conceptions, and national governmental *styles* in foreign policy. Indeed, the idea of a national role can be so powerful as to dictate a government's foreign-policy style in line with its

[4] See for example two very different approaches: K. J. Holsti, *International Politics: a framework for analysis* (2nd ed., 1972) Chap. 4; and H. J. Morgenthau, *Politics among Nations: the struggle for power and peace* (3rd ed., 1963), Chaps. 4–7.
[5] National role conceptions are discussed in Holsti, *op. cit.* in note 4 above, Chap. 4.

assumed tasks and obligations.[6] But this is not the sole importance of the idea of foreign-policy style in our analysis. There are, in many ways, two levels of analysis involved—a macro-level which generalises about the foreign-policy style of the country concerned, and a micro-level which interprets these generalised statements in the light of particular governments, particular individuals, and particular decisions.[7] Clearly at the macro-level, the orientations of a State's foreign policy over many years will count for a lot; but at the micro-level we are led more and more to examine individual and group decision-making processes. It is far from impossible that the trends at the two levels will, on occasions, clash and cause difficulties—the more so if the clash is not confined to the foreign-policy area alone.

From these areas of orientation, commitments, and foreign-policy making style are derived—inevitably—a set of expectations about the way in which a State will behave internationally. It is part of the conventional wisdom of foreign-policy analysis that such expectations are bound to be, to a greater or lesser degree, ill-founded in a complex global environment. But it could be argued that the orientation and style of a government play an important role in its determining how reliably its intentions are perceived by others. Uncertainty as to the interpretation of either can be disastrous; yet conversely, it is clearly in any government's interest to build up external and domestic expectations in such a way that they will support, rather than act against, its policies.

## (b) *Change: national and international*

The study of foreign policy has traditionally focused upon the setting within which policy is conducted, in the belief that part of foreign policy's uniqueness lay in the distinctive set of challenges it had to meet. Whilst this is not the place to argue such issues at length, our analysis lays importance upon the nature of *change* within the context of foreign-policy making, as it inter-acts with the commitments, style and perceived intentions of a government. Externally and internally, the dimensions of change can be seen as three-fold—physical and natural; customary and conventional; behavioural and structural—and each dimension can be seen in its own way as having an impact on the demands faced by a given foreign-policy body, as well as its capacity for response.

Traditionally, physical and natural aspects of the foreign-policy setting have been seen as relatively slow to change. Geography and

---

[6] Such a conclusion has, for example, often been reached with reference to British foreign policy since 1945. See A. Schlaim, " Britain's search for a world role," 5 *International Relations* (1975), pp. 838–856.

[7] This distinction is drawn very clearly in Lovell, *op. cit.* in note 3 above.

natural resources, if not immutable, are at least relatively inactive on their own behalf. What gives them their importance in most respects is their interaction with human activity—and this is where their significance for foreign policy undoubtedly lies. In the second half of the 1970s we are conscious as never before of the delicate links between human exploitation of natural resources and international influence, just as we are of the links between poverty and global tensions.[8]

A second dimension of the international setting can be termed " customary and conventional "—the nexus of regulations, practices, and norms which define acceptable behaviour in global affairs, and to which—in at least a substantial proportion of instances—governments feel obliged to defer. Clearly this is not just a dimension applicable to the world outside a State's boundaries; its own population, in various ways and through less formal channels, can often express a set of feelings and opinions which influence government policy. In both domestic and external spheres a government's response to such demands is likely to be conditioned both by its legitimacy and stability, and by its perception of the values embodied in its policies. If a policy is perceived to be in a government's, or a State's vital interest, then it is less likely that customary and conventional constraints will operate—always assuming that the government can make its priorities " stick."

Whether or not a government can get its way is a question which brings us to the third dimension of the foreign-policy setting—the " behavioural and structural " dimension. In most forms of policy-making study there is an implicit and explicit contrast between structures and behaviour, and an assumption that it is the inter-action of structures and behaviour that lies at the centre of policy-making problems. This contrast applies to foreign policy no less than to domestic policy, but partakes of the special qualities of international politics, in ways which modify it importantly. Externally, the " structure " of the international system is expressed only partly through formal institutions, and, indeed, only partly through the distribution of power and concerns among the State population. As a result, much depends upon the activities and interactions of a bewildering variety of State and non-State actors, which impose on any given government (but arguably especially on those of the industrial world) a complex and often unregulated welter of demands. A contrast is often drawn between this picture of semi-chaos and the quiet order of domestic-policy making, backed up, as it is assumed to be, by structures of authority and shared culture. Yet we must not lose sight

---

[8] Three major treatments of this problem in general are: H. and M. Sprout, *Toward a Politics of the Planet Earth* (1971); R. W. Sterling, *Macropolitics; international relations in a global society* (1974); and S. Brown, *New Forces in World Politics* (1973).

of the fact—already mentioned—that the legitimacy and stability of governments, and their relationship to other institutions (legislatures, trade unions, big business) cannot be taken as a constant and that the balance of these bodies may fundamentally affect the capacity of a government to act in foreign as well as in domestic affairs.[9]

Above all, it is now the case that domestic and external affairs are essentially intertwined—that, as James Rosenau has said, " politics everywhere is connected with politics everywhere else." [10] Not only this, but demands emanating from the foreign-policy setting are intimately related to the commitments undertaken—willingly and otherwise—and expectations engendered by a given government's style of operation. No government in foreign policy can be wholly master of its fate—but it can, by its response to the demands it feels and the constructions placed upon its own and others' postures, contribute to the dilemmas facing itself and its successors.

## II—THE NIXON LEGACY AND FORD'S INHERITANCE

It is within the framework of the preceding argument about commitments and change in foreign policy that we can begin to assess the effect of the Nixon legacy on United States foreign policy in the post-Nixon era. We shall first of all examine the nature of the Nixon legacy itself, and the predicament with which its inheritors were confronted; then we shall move to a closer examination of the predicament as expressed through two specific episodes in the diplomatic-strategic sphere of foreign policy, in the Mediterranean and the Middle East.

From what we have said already it should be clear that commitments undertaken, expectations generated and policy-making style established, will be the initial concern of our analysis here. In all of these areas the Nixon Administration from 1968–1974 made distinctive claims and pursued distinctive paths of action. Perhaps more than any other Administration in the post-1945 period, the Nixon White House set store by its reappraisal of foreign policy undertakings, its emphasis on the foreign policy area, and its implied ability to shape perceptions of America's world role.[11]

---

[9] The notion of " capacity to act " in foreign policy—entailing both the ability and the willingness to allocate resources to foreign affairs—is well propounded by D. Puchala, *International Politics Today* (1971), pp. 171–193. For the impact of this consideration on the viability of foreign policies, see Williams and Smith, *op. cit.* in note 1 above.

[10] J. N. Rosenau, " Political science in a shrinking world," in J. N. Rosenau (ed.), *Linkage Politics* (1969).

[11] Nixon's claims in this sphere were also seen by some as the culmination of a long-established trend in the control of American " national security policy." See A. M. Schlesinger, *The Imperial Presidency* (1974), and N. de B. Katzenbach, " Foreign policy, public opinion and secrecy," 52 *Foreign Affairs* (1973), pp. 1–19.

The chief declaratory component of Nixon's foreign policy was undoubtedly the " Nixon Doctrine " as enunciated—but never fully or coherently integrated—in the President's " State of the World " speeches from 1970 to 1973. The set of orientations embodied in the Nixon Doctrine were presented as the basis of a new consensus on the world role of the United States, to replace that shattered by Vietnam, and as a realistic, constructive, response to changing international conditions. Its formal undertakings were three: to maintain adequate national strength; to create new relationships with allies on a basis of partnership, thus making these links more equitable and effective; to move from these foundations to an era of negotiations in place of the preceding era of confrontations.[12] The prize was to be a " generation of peace " ensured by the realistic management of a new global power structure; and in the first Nixon Administration the openings to the People's Republic of China and the Soviet Union seemed to promise the beginning of this more moderate era. By 1974, however, the time of initiatives was long over. In 1972 and 1973 the servicing of those commitments already undertaken, especially towards the Soviet Union, consumed more and more of the energies of the Administration; these energies were further diverted by engagements arising from the Middle East War and Kissinger's " cease-fire diplomacy," as well as the fulfilment of pledges on Vietnam. As a result, the proclamation of the " year of Europe " in Spring 1973 was followed by a resounding silence from the American side; the attentions and energies of both President and Secretary of State were needed elsewhere.[13]

This ambitious and self-consciously innovative foreign policy was pursued in a no less distinctive style. In many ways the manner of Nixon/Kissinger foreign-policy making cannot be separated from the domestic policies formulated simultaneously; but in foreign policy it was possible to view some of the problems which exploded in Watergate at least partly as advantages. The development and consummation of the " Imperial Presidency " and the dominance of the presidential political centre which was cultivated by Nixon and his advisers made in many ways a viable vehicle for the activities of

---

[12] For a serious and thorough appraisal of the Nixon Doctrine and its implications see W. R. Kintner and R. B. Foster (eds.), *National Strategy in a Decade of Change* (1973), especially Chaps. 1–3.

[13] W. R. Kintner, " The emerging Nixon Doctrine: toward a new international system," in Kintner and Foster, *op. cit.* in note 12 above, concludes that the Nixon Doctrine implied *more* commitment to allies rather than less, and that the ambiguities of the " Year of Europe " thus had important implications. See also C. M. Roberts, " Foreign policy under a paralyzed Presidency," 27 *World Politics* (1974), pp. 675–689, and E. M. Kennedy, " Beyond détente," 16 *Foreign Policy* (1974), pp. 3–29.

Kissinger.[14] Assumptions of special competence and unique responsibilities for national security were to lead to disaster elsewhere, but
could be sustained in foreign policy as long as the overseas break-
throughs continued to arrive on schedule. Yet by 1974, as we have
noted, the demands of foreign policy were changing, and the need for
consolidation growing; whilst simultaneously the domestic legitimacy
of the Nixon régime was being undermined. There was no " State of
the World " speech in 1974, and increasingly the style in foreign
policy appeared to be that of the Secretary of State rather than that
of the encircled President.[15]

Failure to sustain the momentum of the first Nixon Administration
can be seen to have had a major impact upon the pattern of expectations which met United States foreign policy from 1972–1974. We
have already mentioned the perceived need to maintain the momentum of détente—a need which was increasingly difficult to meet. In
addition, it became clear during 1973 that the Nixon/Kissinger line
had had a deleterious effect on relations between the United States
and Europe. The need for a " New Atlantic Charter," proclaimed by
Kissinger in April 1973, raised the hope that the Nixon Doctrine
might, at last, be adopted to accommodate the needs of America's
major allies; the lack of any subsequent action created suspicions and
doubts as to United States intentions and commitments. Although
the governments of western Europe had been encouraged to think of
themselves with new confidence as potential partners rather than
clients of the Americans, there appeared to be precious little foundation for their hopes, and substantial reason to fear a new American
isolationism. In the Middle East and South-East Asia also, the
expectations encouraged by Kissinger's highly personal style of
diplomacy were not fulfilled, a dangerous failing in view of the means
by which he had achieved progress in the first place.[16]

The combination of domestic challenges and changing international
conditions produced, during 1974, a virtual paralysis in many areas
of foreign policy. At home, it became increasingly apt to describe
President Nixon, as did Stewart Alsop,[17] as a " paraplegic President,"

---

[14] Schlesinger, *op. cit.* in note 11 above, develops this theme at length. See also A.
Perlmutter, " The Presidential political center and foreign policy," 27 *World Politics*
(1974), pp. 87–106.

[15] Kissinger was seen by one observer as a " surrogate President for foreign affairs,"
especially after the revelation of Nixon's indecisiveness in the " Presidential transcripts."
Roberts, *op. cit.* in note 13 above, at p. 678. See also P. Geyelin, " Impeachment and
foreign policy," 15 *Foreign Policy* (1974), pp. 183–190.

[16] The loss of momentum is well described by Kennedy, *op. cit.* in note 13 above;
by Geyelin, *op. cit.* in note 15 above; and also by L. Stern, " Two Henrys descending,"
18 *Foreign Policy* (1975), pp. 168–76. See also Roberts, *op. cit.* in note 13 above.

[17] Cited by Geyelin, *op. cit.* in note 15 above, at p. 186. One writer observed that in
1973–74 the White House " relinquished all control over policy except for foreign affairs

who could summon the loyalties neither of the people at large nor the predominantly Democratic Congress. Such conditions assumed increasing importance for foreign policy, especially in the light of Nixon's declared aim to secure a new consensus on the United States' place in the world. There were, it is true, attempts to insulate foreign policy from domestic politics during 1973-74—as if it were possible to encourage a collective schizophrenia which might view Nixon as " two presidents in one." [18] But the Congress, which had been ignored in many of the more controversial Nixon manoeuvres—for example, the war in Cambodia—was ill-disposed to allow this kind of duality. During 1973 the passing of the War Powers Act proclaimed the intention of the legislature finally to assert its role, as did the controversy over the Soviet Trade Agreement and the Jackson Amendment. By mid-1974, as one commentator noted: " what is . . . more and more at issue is whether and if so to what degree, Watergate affects both the substance and the conduct of US foreign policy, and whether, and if so to what degree, other nations may have altered, or planned to alter, their postures towards, and dealings with, Washington." [19] Watergate, by consuming the energies and attention of the President —if not of Henry Kissinger—was seen as laying the United States open to exploitation, as well as creating suspicions and uncertainties.

As we have already noted, the decline of Nixon's authority in the light of domestic change was complicated by changing international conditions. Part, at least, of this international change can be attributed to the policies of Nixon and Kissinger themselves. Other aspects of the renewed external turbulence were, however, less directly attributable to their activities. The emergence of new problems which in many cases transcended the bounds of the Nixon/Kissinger " pentagon of power," and which demanded the perception and management of issues outside the strict politico-strategic arena, posed challenges which the faltering Administration was ill-equipped to confront. [20] Most seriously, it was unclear in many cases whether the American leadership could muster the will, or the energy, to confront the challenge; many interested parties seemed consciously to adopt a " wait and see " attitude in the summer of 1974, whilst

and defense programs. Nor could it ever approach control over the central matter that bedevilled it, which was the faith and confidence of Americans in their government . . ."
T. H. White, *Breach of Faith: the fall of Radical Nixon* (1974), p. 243.

[18] Roberts, *op. cit.* in note 13 above, especially p. 675. See also Katzenbach *op. cit.* in note 11 above.

[19] Roberts, *op. cit.* in note 13 above, p. 675.

[20] The Administration's neglect of foreign economic policy was widely noted. For the emergence of clashes between and around the " pentagon of power," see Kintner and Foster, *op. cit.* in note 12 above, Chaps. 2–3.

Nixon, on his trips to the Middle East and the Soviet Union was seen as attempting to enlist external support against his internal enemies.[21]

When the transfer of power did occur, in August 1974, its trauma was little diminished by long standing and widespread expectation of the event. The United States was left with a non-elected President and an Executive that had no mandate except to replace that which had finally become intolerable. In foreign affairs, however, the situation was distinctive, since one half—and the increasingly dominant half—of the Nixon/Kissinger partnership was left in place. Although Henry Kissinger did not escape the wrath of Congress entirely, he had never become a " lame-duck " Secretary of State. Rather he had, in foreign policy, effectively come to wield executive power, to the extent that he had appeared to many an indispensable part of any credible Ford Administration.[22]

At one level, then, the Ford inheritance in foreign policy was one of personnel—an established and highly distinctive Secretary of State who had come largely to determine the style and orientation of America's foreign policy. But it is plain from the preceding discussion that this was not all that the new Administration had to face. The rhetoric of the Nixon Doctrine with its hyperbolic claims of a " generation of peace " had created expectations which remained to be fulfilled, or had gone gradually sour; the practice of Nixon/Kissinger détente diplomacy had equally generated ambiguities and suspicions amongst some of the most important allies of the United States. Some felt that the days of decline had made the United States hostage to, rather than the director of, international events. On the domestic level, it was clear that the Congress, reinforced by the " new generation " of the 1974 mid-term elections, would attempt to assert a newly-realised power, and that Presidential power in general, its legitimacy and its effectiveness, were the object of widespread hostility and cynicism.

In such an atmosphere, it was to be expected that strategic uncertainty and a wide ranging questioning of United States commitments might persist under the new President. There was the possibility that the new Administration might be dominated either by events, or by the Nixon legacy, or by both—with the latter more likely in many people's minds. Such an impression was seemingly confirmed by the

---

[21] See White, *op. cit.* in note 17 above, at p. 306. Others identified a tendency for the United States to become a " hostage " of governments whose support Nixon sought. See, *e.g.* Geyelin, *op. cit.* in note 15 above, p. 188. The inability of Nixon to " deliver " on pledges made in palmier times is described by Roberts, *op. cit.* in note 12 above, p. 679 *et seq.*

[22] See Roberts, *op. cit.* in note 12 above, although Stern, *op. cit.* in note 16 above saw that Kissinger's position was more vulnerable than in earlier days, and that several errors of judgment contributed to its further erosion.

" State of the World " speech delivered by Ford on April 10, 1975. Although the rhetoric was less elaborate, and there was a plea for renewed consensus behind foreign policy, the framework still appeared to be that which was associated with the departed régime.

Within this framework, an area of particular importance—and one which contained many potential problems for the Ford/Kissinger partnership—was constituted by strategic relationships. Much of the Nixon/Kissinger line had been concerned with the management and redefinition of strategic obligations, with both allies and clients, and much of Congress' new-found impact on foreign policy had emerged from its critique of strategic commitments, combined with its financial powers. In addition to the broad commitments of détente and the Nixon Doctrine, there existed for the new Administration a series of potentially damaging areas of uncertainty, in which indications of its ability to slough off the Nixon legacy might be forthcoming. It is to two of these areas of uncertainty—both of them linked with military aid and expenditures—that we now turn for further evidence.

## III—THE IMPACT OF THE NIXON LEGACY: TWO CASES

We have chosen here to examine two cases in the light of the preceding discussion about the Nixon legacy and its potential effects. Both cases—the " aid for Turkey " issue which arose from the 1974 Cyprus crisis, and the issue of missile sales to Jordan—arose in regions where the United States had long-standing interests, and in which the Nixon/Kissinger diplomacy had been closely engaged, with uncertain effect.

### (a) *Military assistance to Turkey*

In the Eastern Mediterranean the Turkish invasion of Cyprus and the ensuing acute hostility between Greece and Turkey—exacerbated by the Aegean oil exploration issue—placed the Administration in an extremely delicate situation from which not even the facility of Dr. Kissinger had been able to extricate the United States. Greece had announced her intention to leave the military side of the North Atlantic Treaty Organisation (NATO)—thereby weakening the Mediterranean flank—and there was intensive activity to bring United States pressure to bear on Turkey over the Cyprus issue, with the inherent danger that Turkey might, for quite different reasons, follow the Greeks out of the NATO military alliance.

The American " balancing " role was under considerable strain. Already, before the Cyprus invasion, the Turks were resentful of the failure of the Nixon Administration to fulfil aid expectations in exchange for the cessation of Turkish opium production in 1972.

This resentment was sharpened by Nixon's failure to include Turkey in his 1974 Middle East tour. As a token of this resentment at the beginning of July 1974 the Turks announced that opium production would resume. Whatever the merits of the resumption of poppy growing, this move enabled the anti-Turkish—mainly pro-Greek— lobby in Congress to call, even then, for the ending of aid to Turkey.

The invasion of Cyprus by Turkey in August 1974 greatly strengthened the hands of the pro-Greek groups, and on September 19, 1974 the Senate voted to cut off aid to Turkey, on the grounds that Turkey had illegally used American-supplied weapons to carry out an aggressive action against Cyprus. Although thought likely to be " killed," the bill was seen by Senator Thomas Eagleton as a severe warning to the Administration. In Turkey there was great certainty that the bill would be reconsidered if only because the " US Executive has expressed its disapproval of any cut in military aid to Turkey." [23]

To the distress of the Administration, however, the House of Representatives took up the anti-Turkish cause. Whilst, perhaps characteristically, Dr. Kissinger was busy at the United Nations seeking a solution to the Cyprus problem, the House of Representatives voted to cut off aid to Turkey " until the President (Ford) certifies to Congress that substantial progress towards a settlement has been made regarding military forces in Cyprus," thereby directly intervening with one party. The Presidential response to this very clear initiative from Capitol Hill was to threaten to veto the spending bill to which the cut-off had been added.[24] Nevertheless, in the second week in October the Senate sent President Ford legislation banning military aid to Turkey.

The Senate—more sympathetic to the Administration—gave President Ford 60 days—until December 15, 1974—to produce " results " over Cyprus, the Democratic leader suggesting that domestic legislation should not be imperilled for the sake of a foreign policy dispute between Congress and the Administration. But the House of Representatives, with a strong pro-Greek lobby, had determined to force a show-down with the Administration, rejected the Senate compromise, and on October 14, 1974 the President vetoed the foreign aid bill containing the Turkish military aid ban. This veto " set the stage for Mr. Ford's first major confrontation with Congress in his two-month-old Presidency." [25]

---

[23] Mr. Baykal, reported in *International Herald Tribune*, September 24, 1974.

[24] It is possible for measures of this nature to be " added " to existing bills—in this case a conferring resolution including foreign aid, and appropriations for health, welfare, and education.

[25] *International Herald Tribune*, October 15, 1974.

As the Congress failed to attain the two-thirds majority necessary
to overthrow the Presidential veto the President nominally " won "
the show-down with Congress. But the House was unrepentant, and
on October 16, ignoring the possibility of a further veto, returned the
legislation to the President, suspending military aid to Turkey from
December 10, or sooner if Turkey sent arms or *equipment* (which
might include truck spares or even food!!) to Cyprus. This resolution
was, predictably, vetoed by the President. But the increasing pressure
on the President led him to accept a compromise that there would be
no aid after December 10 unless there was real progress on the
Cyprus issue, and that, in the meantime, no United States " imple-
ments of war " were to be moved from Turkey to Cyprus. This final
compromise must be regarded as a defeat for the Administration as,
short of a Dr. Kissinger type miracle, they would find it difficult to
evade the prohibition on arms for Turkey. Certainly Senator Eagleton
regarded it as a significant victory because Congress was now placing
its imprint on the United States Cyprus policy.

The Administration took this challenge to its authority seriously.
The State Department refused to rule, publicly, over the legality, or
otherwise, of the use by Turkey of United States arms for the
invasion of Cyprus. Pressure was then put on Congress to amend the
ban, in consequence of which the Senate voted to move the cut-off
date to 30 days after the next Congress convened—a date likely to be
in early February 1975. The House of Representatives initially
refused to comply, and only after intensive lobbying by the President
and Dr. Kissinger—including breakfasts for up to 150 Congressmen
at a time—did the House reluctantly fall into line with the Senate.
Thus, despite the disastrous mid-term election results in November,
President Ford had indicated that he had a capacity to produce
Congressional support if it was felt to be necessary. As *The Times*
suggested, President Ford had " thus survived a major test of his
ability to win essential votes in Congress." [26]

The suspicion of Capitol Hill for the White House was not reduced
by a notification [27] from the Pentagon that the United States was
proposing to sell to Turkey " modernisation kits " for 885 M48 tanks
—a deal worth 229 million dollars. Congress immediately assumed
that this was an attempt to continue arms supply after the new,
February 5, cut-off date, or alternatively that the arms would all go
in a single shipment before the deadline. This suggestion that the
Ford Administration was bent on thwarting the congressional man-

---

[26] *The Times*, December 18, 1974.
[27] Under a 1974 amendment to the Foreign Assistance Act, all arms deals have to be
reported to Congress, and Congress then has 20 working days to disallow any arms deal
worth more than 25 million dollars by a concurrent vote of both Houses.

date indicates the low state of relations between the two arms of Government. In such circumstances it was not surprising that Congress refused to extend its deadline, and that the skilful and vociferous pro-Greek lobby tied the resumption of arms supplies to Turkey to " progress " on Cyprus. In this context, " progress " meant sunstantial Turkish concessions. On February 6, 1975 a statement from the White House indicated that the Administration had complied with the Congressional ruling to halt United States shipments to Turkey. The same statement was highly critical of Congress for thus fettering United States foreign policy, and drew attention, yet again, to the different political requirements of the Congress and the Administration—the former seeking to make their mark on a specific issue—in this case Cyprus—and the latter needing to view not only the Cyprus issue but also the broader context of the security and stability of the Eastern Mediterranean and Middle East regions. The Administration must also have been concerned with the impact such a move against a NATO ally would have on relations with other allies, and on the general credibility of United States foreign policy commitments.

That the nub of this conflict was between the Administration and Capitol Hill became apparent when the Congress refused to make any move in the face of the evidence that the Cyprus situation, far from being resolved because of the embargo, was becoming dead-locked—Turkey not moving because of resentments, and Greece not moving because of the possibility of the United States pressure bringing about a Turkish collapse. Congress, and especially the House of Representatives, was equally unresponsive to pressures from the other members of NATO.[28] But the Administration persisted in attempting to revoke the ban, and in recognition of these efforts the Turks took no decisive actions, though making it clear that the situation could not continue indefinitely without invoking some Turkish response on a " no arms, no facilities " basis. The Senate, where the Greek lobby was weaker, complied with Presidential requests at first, and the leaders of both parties tabled a bill to the effect that arms shipments should be resumed, subject only to a monthly report by the President on the Cyprus negotiations. As a result of further Administration pressure, by the end of March the Senate Foreign Relations Committee had approved a Bill, and Congress was expected to take up the proposal after the Easter recess, in April. Dr. Kissinger's response was to applaud this first favourable response to the Administration's plea for more co-operation, and to

---

[28] This pressure included a threat to give NATO aid to Turkey. This possibility was publicised by Dr. Luns—the NATO Secretary-General—and reported in *The Times*, February 26, 1975.

criticise, yet again, the " unwarranted meddling in his diplomacy " [29] by the pro-Greek faction in the House of Representatives. However, when the Senate voted on the issue it was approved by a majority of only one, thus greatly reducing its significance; doing little to encourage the House to follow suit; suggesting that the Administration might do little to influence the House; and failing to mollify Turkey. Effectively the Administration had been stalemated.

During June the pressure on Congress was increased. The Turkish National Security Council demanded talks on the status of the 26 United States bases in Turkey within 30 days, and after the 30 day period—*i.e.* whilst the negotiations proceeded—the bases would be held by the United States on a temporary basis. Renewed Administration activity resulted. Not only did both President Ford and Dr. Kissinger assure the Turkish Prime Minister that the embargo would be lifted " soon," but President Ford believed that he had found an acceptable compromise with Congress. By this, arms could go to Turkey for NATO purposes only, subject to a review every 60 days, such that Congress would, effectively, " sit in judgment " on Turkish good behaviour, and would be free to reimpose the embargo every 60 days.

Throughout July the Administration pressed for the compromise and a resumption of limited arms sales, aiming their attentions particularly at the House of Representatives. In recognition of this activity Turkey delayed setting up any new arrangements for the American bases in Turkey, but on July 23, 1975 it was reported [30] that the outcome of any vote was uncertain. Both supporters and opponents of the measure saw it as probably the most important vote on foreign policy in the session of Congress. President Ford and Dr. Kissinger were seen to have gone to unusual lengths to get the House of Representatives to follow the Senate. The issue had become highly emotional—the Administration viewing the matter as a test of its ability to conduct foreign policy properly, and the opponents of the measures arguing that if they failed to block the measure the Congress would be surrendering its prerogatives in this area. Opponents also argued that the Administration was twisting arms in a manner that had not been practised since President Ford came into office.

Despite all the pressure, on July 24 the House of Representatives rejected the measure by 17 votes. Within 24 hours the Turkish Government had abrogated all Turkish military agreements with the United States and halted all United States activity on American bases on Turkish soil. Despite the claim that this was a victory " for

---

[29] *Financial Times*, March 27, 1975.
[30] *International Herald Tribune*, July 23, 1975.

foreign policy based on principle," [31] the real significance of the defeat for the Administration was pinpointed by John Brademas, the leader of the pro-Greek lobby in the House.[32] " What was at stake here was not arms for Turkey, or the bases, but the role of Congress in foreign policy. The Secretary of State was bound and determined that Congress should play no significant role at all. He wants Congress flat on its back. But in so doing he has needlessly embarrassed the President and hurt American security interests in the Eastern Mediterranean."

### (b) *The sale of " Hawk " missiles to Jordan*

Although there had been a cease fire and disengagement of forces in the Middle East, the situation in the aftermath of the 1973 Arab–Israeli war was still very tense. These tensions left little room for diplomatic manoeuvre and despite receiving considerable attention from Dr. Kissinger the situation was still " log-jammed " when President Nixon made his 1974 Middle East tour. The tour, like the diplomacy that had preceded it, failed to produce any obvious means of resolving the stalemate. It thus appeared that the Nixon/Kissinger style had failed to produce the desired breakthrough—at least in the short term—and that United States policy to the Middle East would have to confine itself to producing a balance of arms in the area that would lead to a more stable confrontation.

In such a situation Jordan was considerably disadvantaged. The 1973 war had been a humiliation for Jordan who had had to sit on the sidelines for lack of the " hardware " to participate fully and effectively. Accordingly, once it became clear that United States arms deliveries to the Middle East would resume, King Hussein was quick to try and establish his position as one of those States needing armaments in order to produce the " balance " desired by the United States in the Middle East. As early as February 1974, it was being suggested that the Nixon Administration would supply TOW (a wire-guided anti-tank missile) to Jordan via a Military Assistance Grant. This would still leave Jordan with no Surface-to-Air Missile (SAM) —a gap that could be filled if the United States satisfied the Jordanian request for the Hawk missile (an anti-aircraft missile system).

A " closed " meeting of both houses of the Jordanian Parliament in mid-February 1974 was revealed to have approved a plan by King Hussein to seek new, modern, weapons on his forthcoming visit to the United States. Before that visit it was suggested by the Nixon Administration that a program of 245 million dollars might be acceptable—as opposed to the 1·4 billion dollar program drawn-up

[31] *The Observer*, July 27, 1975.
[32] *International Herald Tribune*, August 12, 1975.

by King Hussein. Whether at one or the other figure, the first priority was still the Hawk SAM system. At King Hussein's meeting with Nixon it was reported that there was "considerable reluctance" [33] to supply Hawk, though in general terms it was conceded that sufficient arms should be supplied to ensure a balance with neighbouring Arab States. A meeting with Defence Secretary Schlesinger apparently produced a more positive commitment to send experts to plan the establishment of the Hawk surface-to-air anti-aircraft system.[34]

This commitment " rolled over " to the Ford Administration, but the upheavals of the transition delayed the mission for nearly nine months, and it was mid-January 1975, before a United States military delegation, led by Supreme Commander, United States forces Europe, General G. Eade, arrived in Jordan for a three-day visit. The consequence of that visit was that the Joint Chiefs of Staff unanimously recommended that Jordan be supplied with six Hawk batteries, this number being sufficient for Jordan's needs.[35] Dr. Kissinger is reported as informing King Hussein in February that Hawk would be supplied to him—though in what quantity is not clear, but almost certainly not the 22 batteries that King Hussein originally requested. Details of the deal were, apparently, finalised in late April, but component systems, including the Hawk missile, were not expected to arrive in Jordan before the Autumn of 1975. It was at this point that the Administration's plans *vis-à-vis* Jordan became public. In accordance with the 1974 amendment to the Foreign Assistance Act the Ford Administration announced on July 18 its intention to sell 14 batteries of Hawk to Jordan. In opposing testimonies to the Senate Foreign Relations Committee the Administration claimed that 14 batteries was the minimum for Jordan to have a system, whilst General G. Brown, Chairman of the Joint Chiefs of Staff (JCS) declared that it was the unanimous view of the JCS that six batteries were adequate for Jordan's needs.

This, hitherto, rather private dispute between the Administration, the JCS, and King Hussein now became very public indeed. For on July 10, 1975—the day that the Defense Department informed Congress of the Administration's plans—Dr. Kissinger, the Assistant Secretary for Middle East Affairs, his deputy and the Head of the policy planning staff, and Mr. Joseph Sisco, Dr. Kissinger's chief Middle East adviser, were all in Europe. The disclosure incensed the Israelis—and therefore the Israeli lobby in the United States—as Israel was within striking distance of the proposed Hawk site. The

---

[33] *The Guardian*, March 14, 1974.
[34] *The Daily Telegraph*, March 15, 1974.
[35] *International Herald Tribune* July 28, 1975.

announcement was also in conflict with private information given by the Administration to the Israelis that the program would be for three sites only, and also appeared to contravene the government statement that while the Middle East policy was being reassessed there would be no new commitments.

Dr. Kissinger and the State Department expressed " surprise " at the revelation of the 14-battery sale, as they had expected Congress to be informed of only the first instalment of the development—*i.e.* three batteries. The Defense Department countered by suggesting that to inform Congress of only three batteries was impossible, as in order to arrange contracts and finance, and establish production lines, it was necessary to have a go-ahead for the total deal. As one commentator acidly remarked, there was a feeling that, " If Dr. Kissinger had been minding the store instead of trying to run the State Department from an airplane, he, or one of his chief aides, might have been able to limit the damage." [36]

Within a fortnight it had become apparent that the deal, in its proposed form, would be squashed. The House Foreign Affairs Committee recommended that the House stop the deal, and the Senate Foreign Relations Committee was following a similar course of action. The Administration thereupon withdrew the deal, but announced immediately its reinstatement—a technical manoeuvre to gain time. This second defeat of the Administration within a few days—the first had been the House of Representatives vote to continue the arms embargo to Turkey—led commentators to speculate that the Administration's withdrawal over Jordan allowed it to husband such resources as it had in Congress in order to attempt to overthrow the Turkish vote. Such a manoeuvre also allowed time for compromise, and by mid-September it had arrived. In a letter resubmitting the deal to Congress, President Ford proposed 14 *static* launchers. " The Government of Jordan has informed us that it intends to use Hawk missiles solely for defence of the Amman-Zerka complex and other fixed sites . . . the batteries will be permanently installed at these locations as fixed, defensive, non-mobile anti-aircraft weapons." A reluctant Congress complied with [the wishes of the Administration.

Not surprisingly, Jordan was reported to be " insulted " by the terms imposed on the Administration by Congress, and claimed that the terms undermined Jordanian sovereignty—especially attempts to arrange monitoring to satisfy United States conditions. The plea by Mr. Sisco that the text of the letter had been cleared with Jordan did little to reduce the confusion and embarrassment of the Administra-

---

[36] *International Herald Tribune*, August 4, 1975.

tion. To add to this confusion it was also announced that the price was now 800 million dollars instead of the original 350 million dollars—the missiles cost the same, the difference being accounted for by the cost of training, the software and site construction. This was a factor bound to irritate the Saudi Arabians who were to pay the bill.

The Final Contract, signed in the New Year of 1976 contained only two restrictions, in contradiction to the Ford letter of September —that the missiles be used for defensive purposes only, and that they be not transferred to a third party without United States agreement. Thus the Jordan Government had only these rather nebulous restrictions placed directly on it—though it was likely to remain fully aware of the powers of the Congress.

During the nine months after the signing of the " Final Contract " there was much vacillation—by Saudi Arabia on whether to pay the bill and by Jordan on whether to buy Soviet SAM6s and thus have a common weapon system with its new-found friend in Syria. Jordan having reneged on the initial " Final Contract " a new document of the same name was drawn-up and signed by September 1976, by which Jordan purchased 14 batteries of Hawk missiles at a total cost of 540 million dollars which was to be made available by the Saudi Arabians. These missiles, when installed, would be capable of transport by plane, helicopter, or land vehicle—in other words they would be mobile and have a potentially offensive capacity. No wonder a senior Saudi Arabian official was heard to comment, " What is American foreign policy? The Policy of Congress, or the White House, or the Pentagon; the State Department, CIA, or Zionist lobby? There is no single policy-making body, only a series of different ones, sometimes in contradiction." [37]

In the Administration's Middle East policy with regard to Jordan, it became involved in assisting King Hussein in order to maintain his position and self-esteem. King Hussein needed support *vis-à-vis* his fellow Arabs to participate effectively in the search for Middle East peace—especially as regard the West Bank. Congress was not in a position to make judgments whether this goal could be best achieved with 3, 6, 14, or 22 Hawk batteries, or any other weapons systems combination. The Administration was, or should have been, in a position to make such judgments. But in essence, Congress distrusted the Administration's general purpose and competence to such a high degree that it felt it necessary to question the wisdom of the Administration and directly to challenge it. For the President to call for a " reassessment " in which all arms sales were suspended and then to enter into a deal with Jordan was to invite criticism and conflict.

---

[37] *The Observer*, August 3, 1975.

## IV—Conclusions

What have these two brief case histories revealed about the impact of the " Nixon legacy " on the Ford Administration's foreign policy? Our initial framework for analysis focused particularly on the part played by orientations, style and expectations in the evolution of responses to changing international conditions, and it can be seen that the two examples chosen provide us with a good deal of evidence in these areas. In the " aid to Turkey " case, a set of commitments entered into by the Nixon régime, and later transformed by the events of the Cyprus crisis, provided a challenge which was given extra significance by the role of a resurgent Congress. The Hawk missile sale was significant not only in itself but also in the context of the previous Administration's Middle East policy, and became a painful experience for the Ford régime when it was combined with the need for a wide-ranging reassessment of the military aid policy—a reassessment which again required the concurrence of Congress.

It appears, therefore, that the new Administration suffered a central inability to redefine the commitments accumulated by its predecessor, and was hampered in its attempts both by external change and the shifting balance of domestic forces. Not only this, but it became evident at several points that the style of United States foreign policy under Ford suffered from considerable confusion. As we have noted, it was often unclear by whom—and in the light of which guiding principles—United States foreign policy was being made in the years 1974–76. The persistence of " Kissingerism " and the unassertiveness of the President combined with the renewed vigour of Congress to create a mass of contradictions at the heart of the foreign policy process—contradictions which were especially clear in the two cases surveyed, perhaps because of their financial implications.

As a result, those engaged in the two episodes could rely only spasmodically on their expectations of United States international behaviour. The Turks, the Jordanians, and the Mediterranean and Middle East States generally, often evinced confusion as to the direction of Ford's foreign policy—a confusion due at least partly to failure by Ford and Kissinger to define a consistent mode of policy formation. In addition, the United States NATO allies, interested as they were in the Turkish episode especially, found it difficult to impress their views on the Ford Administration, perhaps as a result of the ambiguities and misunderstandings of the Nixon era.

The ambivalence of the Ford years, indeed, is such that it is not impossible to argue a very different case from that presented here. Two influential commentators lamented in 1975 what they saw as the failure of Congress to establish continuing influence over United

States foreign policy, and the partial resurgence of the " Imperial Presidency " in foreign affairs. [38] As evidence, they cited the " Maya-guez " incident, in which Executive action was unfettered by Congressional control; Congressional acquiescence in an expanded military budget; and the failure of Congress fully to debate the basic issues raised by the new, post-Nixon era. As we have seen, however, such basic debate would have been next to impossible in the absence of positive orientations and initiatives on the part of the Administration. Nonetheless, on limited and specific issues such as those we have examined, the legislature could make its presence felt.

The Ford Administration in many ways was trapped and transitional—unable to escape the commitments of the past, incapable of asserting a distinctive style of operation, fated to disappoint or to confound the expectations of its global audience. Its failure to transcend the Nixon legacy meant that the new Democratic Administration elected in November 1976, had still to confront many of the questions left unresolved by Watergate and the erosion of the " Imperial Presidency," and to redefine America's orientation and role in the international system. [39] The Carter Presidency, however, with a narrow but clear-cut national mandate, and a Democratic Congress, might reasonably have been expected to escape some of the perils experienced by the direct heirs of Nixon and Watergate.

---

[38] L. H. Gelb and A. Lake, " Congress: politics and bad policy," 20 *Foreign Policy* (1975), pp. 232–238.

[39] The problems were well stated by *The Observer*, November 7, 1976, which concluded that " the great doctor (Kissinger) has left behind for Mr. Carter a mixed bag of achievements, mistakes and unfinished tasks," and saw Mr. Carter's main task as identifying those parts of the " Ford legacy " on which he might build a viable future policy.

# CANADA'S INTERNATIONAL CONNECTIONS:

## THE CANADIAN FOREIGN POLICY REVIEW
## IN REVIEW

By

## MARGARET DOXEY

WHEN the government of Pierre Trudeau took office in Canada in 1968, one of its first acts was to launch a fundamental review of foreign and defence policy in the course of which academics, journalists and others, as well as civil servants, were invited to participate in discussion and to offer suggestions and comments.[1] The process led to the eventual publication of two white papers: *Foreign Policy for Canadians* and *Defence in the 70s*.[2]

Two other official statements of policy should be considered in conjunction with these publications in order to obtain a complete picture of official thinking between 1968 and 1972—in so far as it was publicly revealed. These were a major statement on defence and foreign policy made by the Prime Minister on April 3, 1969 (followed by a speech on the same theme in Calgary on April 12)[3] and a survey of Canadian-United States relations written by the Minister of External Affairs and published in the Department's journal *International Perspectives* in October 1972. Thus, the sequence was the Prime Minister's statement, the white paper on foreign policy, the white paper on defence and the article in *International Perspectives*.

In his statement and follow-up speech, which came over a year before the first of the two white papers was published, the Prime Minister inaugurated what was subsequently described as a " process of adjusting the balance between Canadian defence activities to ensure that priorities for defence were responsive to national interest and international developments." [4] The four areas of activity for the Canadian armed forces were listed in order of priority as: the surveillance of Canadian territory and coast lines; the defence of North America in co-operation with United States forces; the fulfilment of

---

[1] As part of the review process, the House of Commons Standing Committee on External Affairs and National Defence held hearings on NATO and Canadian-United States relations. Its report on the latter is to be found in Canada: House of Commons, 2nd Session, 28th Parliament, 1969–70, *Proceedings*, Nr. 33.

[2] Ottawa: The Queen's Printer for Canada, June 1970; Ottawa: Information Canada, August 1971.

[3] Ottawa, Department of External Affairs: *Statements and Speeches*, 69/7, April 3, 1969; 69/8, April 12, 1969.

[4] *Defence in the 70s*, p. 16.

such North Atlantic Treaty Organisation (NATO) commitments as might be agreed upon; and the performance of such international peacekeeping roles as might be assumed.[5] The low rating given to peacekeeping was in contrast to its prominence in the 1964 white paper on defence. Thus defence of the homeland and of the North American continent were to come first in the scheme of things and in line with the lower priority accorded to Europe it was announced that Canadian forces in Europe were to be reduced. The opinion of the Prime Minister, expressed in his speech at Calgary, was that Canadian defence policy had been a product of the NATO commitment, and that foreign policy, in turn, had been the product of defence policy and that this was the wrong order of things.[6] His announcement of a reduction in the number of forces in Europe was not well received by the European members of NATO, but in September 1969, the Canadian strength in Europe was cut by half to 5,000 men.

The foreign policy papers were issued the following year as a package of six booklets in colourful covers: a general introductory survey, which contained the principal exposition of the new aims and directions and criticism of the old, and five " section " booklets dealing in turn with Europe, International Development, Latin America, the Pacific and the United Nations. There was no booklet dealing specifically with the United States.

Foreign policy was described in the first chapter of the general survey as " the product of the Government's progressive definition and pursuit of national aims and interests in the international environment . . . and the extension abroad of national policies." [7] The case for a " renewal " of Canadian foreign policy, instead of continuing " an empirical process of adjustment " [8] was not self-evident; the Liberal party was still in power in Ottawa, although there was a new Prime Minister, and Canada's capacity to change its external orientation was obviously severely limited by the geographical, political and economic imperatives of its international environment. The white paper argued, however, that assumptions on which foreign policy had been based since the Second World War were " crumbling away." [9] Specifically, under the heading of " The Changing World," the following were noted: international institutions—" the focus and instrument of much of Canada's policy "—

---

[5] *Ibid.*

[6] In the course of the foreign policy review, some briefs presented to the government advocated withdrawal from NATO, but this was an extreme view. Material prepared for the Commons Standing Committee and excerpts from its proceedings were published in XXVIII *Behind the Headlines*, Nrs. 1–6, 1969 (Canadian Institute of International Affairs, Toronto).

[7] *Foreign Policy for Canadians*, p. 9.

[8] *Ibid.* p. 8.

[9] *Ibid.* p. 6.

were troubled by internal divergences and criticism of their continuing relevance; world Powers could no longer be grouped in clearly identifiable ideological camps; Third World problems had crystallised into irresistible demands for international action to deal with development needs and to end racial discrimination; science and technology had outpaced political, economic and social institutions; social attitudes had changed, social values were in question, and violence and confrontation politics had become commonplace.[10] Internally, Canada's " changing outlook " was summed up in terms of an overheated economy, regional differences and the quiet revolution in Quebec. Certain external events, such as the ordeal of the United Nations in the Congo, the collapse of the United Nations Emergency Force (UNEF) in 1967 and the frustrations of peacekeeping in Vietnam were seen as signalling the end of Canada's middle-Power role in the world, while the recovery and integrative tendencies of Western Europe and " changes in the Communist world " were said to call into question " the need for continuing Canadian participation in NATO." Moreover, the " renaissance of French Canada, with its direct consequences for relations with French-speaking countries, raised further questions about the fundamentals of Canadian foreign policy." [11]

The white paper also identified an excessive emphasis on role and influence in Canadian foreign policy, which it claimed had obscured policy objectives and actual interests. Canada's internationalist orientation—the attempt to act as " helpful fixer " in world affairs— was criticised as a reactive rather than an active posture. It was asserted that foreign policy should more appropriately seek purposefully to serve national interests, promoting economic growth, sovereignty and independence, peace and security, social justice, the quality of life and a harmonious natural environment—with economic growth, social justice and the quality of life ranked, in that order, as the highest in priority.[12]

The white paper on defence did not break new ground, but followed up on the aims and themes set out in the foreign policy booklet and explained in more detail the decisions announced by Mr. Trudeau's statements. Not surprisingly, in discussing the role of the armed forces, it focused principally on the " sovereignty " and " security " themes.

### I—Shortcomings of the Review

Criticism of the white paper on foreign policy could be directed both at its diagnosis of the state of the world and implications for Canada,

---

[10] *Ibid.* p. 7.      [11] *Ibid.* p. 8.      [12] *Ibid.* p. 14, p. 22.

and at its policy prescriptions.[13] That the world is changing, and at an accelerating pace, is not in question, and the white paper identified a number of important trends, but it would seem to have over-emphasised the waning relevance of international institutions and exaggerated the fading of ideological divisions. Arguably, these " changes " needed heavy official stress in the light of the already announced decision to reduce the Canadian commitment to NATO and the wish to reverse the " internationalist " orientation attributed to previous governments. There are obvious difficulties in publishing official analyses of foreign policy; a government may not wish to " show its hand " in advance and it may also prefer not to stress unpalatable truths. Probably for the latter reason, the white paper did not identify the two striking features of contemporary life of which the foreign policies of all governments must take account: inter-dependence and nationalism. As the twentieth century has worn on, interdependence between nation States has increased.[14] Technological progress has brought a number of " revolutions," in communications and transport, and in weaponry, as well as in agriculture, medicine and a host of other fields. Advanced industrial societies gobble up energy resources and other raw materials; less developed areas of the world must import capital and technical skills. Super-Powers like the United States and the Soviet Union have global " outreach " and intervene overtly or covertly in pursuit of their own interests.

Relationships formerly occurring within imperial boundaries must now be redefined and conducted between sovereign States. Distance is no longer significant either as a barrier to knowledge or as a shield for protection. Likewise, the major social problems of our time are universal, or at least regional in impact. Hunger, poverty, disease, ignorance, overcrowding, environmental pollution, all need far more resources and effort for their alleviation than any single State can muster. It is not surprising that traditional political alliances for security have been complemented by a tremendous range and variety of functional international institutions, both governmental and non-governmental, set up with the object of regulating and co-ordinating international relations and of alleviating international ills.[15]

[13] The Commons Standing Committee held hearings on the general booklet from November 1970 to June 1971, in the course of which some of these criticisms were raised. See Standing Committee on External Affairs and National Defence, *Fourth Report* respecting " *Foreign Policy for Canadians,*" June 23, 1971, Nr. 31 in the *Minutes* of the Committee. See too XXIX *Behind the Headlines*, August 1970 (Canadian Institute of International Affairs, Toronto).

[14] See O. R. Young, " Interdependencies in World Politics," 24 *International Journal*, 1969, pp. 726–750. Young defines interdependence in terms of the " extent to which events occurring in one part of the world system affect—either physically or perceptually—events taking place in other parts " (p. 726).

[15] C. F. Bergsten notes three post-war waves of institution building: the United

At the same time, national self-consciousness is increasing, notably in the Third World, where political independence in many instances is a recent acquisition to be defended and cherished, and economic independence is a goal to be actively pursued. But disintegrative strains are also apparent in older States: for instance, in the United Kingdom, Scottish and Welsh nationalism have gained strength in recent years, while in Canada the distinctive sense of identity of the Québécois has not suffered any eclipse, even if the cutting edge of separatism seemed to be blunted in the mid-1970s.

The fact that these two trends are occurring simultaneously has meant that international bodies have remained subordinate to national governments. " Sovereignty " is jealously guarded and there has been no disposition to create supranational authorities by transference of power centres. Even in the European Economic Community (EEC), the Commission has become increasingly subordinate to the Council of Ministers, and decisions must be made on the basis of unanimity, at least of the major members. Reconciling the interests of very large numbers of States—and the United Nations now has some 140 members—is almost impossible where disparities in size, wealth, ideology and form of government are so great. Although consensus on the need for international organisation is not lacking, consensus on policies to be adopted by existing bodies—and on new régimes to protect assets which have not yet been appropriated by individual States—is usually conspicuous by its absence. In fact, the emphasis on nationalism, national sovereignty and national interests, in the context of growing interdependence, can lead to heightened tension between States, particularly where the relationship with other States is asymmetrical.[16]

Such has been the case in Canada—a medium-sized Power well endowed with territory and resources, though relatively sparsely populated, which shares the North American continent with a super-Power and must continue to do so. The fact that Canada's external relations are primarily relations with the United States was somewhat obscured in the early post-Second World War period when converging interests and habits of co-operation were accepted as the norm, and such phrases as " neighbours taken for granted " and " principles

Nations system and its agencies to deal with economic and political issues; around 1960 a spate of regional bodies, notably the EEC; and beginning around 1973 a series of global agencies such as the World Food Council and the United Nations Environment Programme. " Interdependence and the reform of international institutions," 30 *International Organisation*, 1976, p. 361.

[16] See J. Rosenau, *Linkage Politics* (1969). Rosenau comments that ". . . the world may well be passing through a paradoxical stage in which *both* the linkages and the boundaries among polities are becoming more central to their daily lives " (p. 47. Emphasis in original).

of partnership " were in vogue.[17] In recent years, however, concern about United States dominance in many aspects of Canadian life has become a distinct political issue. This concern has deepened since the United States image as the respected leader of the western world became somewhat tarnished as a product of the Vietnam war, Watergate, revelations of interference by the Central Intelligence Agency (CIA) and multi-national corporations in the affairs of other States, and the obviously undemocratic nature of many régimes supported by the United States, but it also reflects a new awareness of often divergent interests between the two countries.

To the Liberal government of Trudeau, dedicated above all to the preservation of confederation, the sharp internal challenge of Quebec nationalism appeared to underline the need to define an overall Canadian identity which would include French and English Canada. Quebec's efforts to develop its own external relations, highlighted by de Gaulle's " Vive le Québec libre " speech in Montreal in 1967, made it necessary to reassert Ottawa's primacy; but at the same time the Québécois had to be reassured that their interests would be adequately represented and protected by Ottawa. The white paper stressed *national* interest but also the importance of reflecting Canada's bilingual and bicultural nature in all policies, both internal and external. One of the many difficulties is that, in Quebec, English Canada is seen as culturally and economically dominant, whereas for Canada as a whole, the United States presents this image. Another is that Canada's main defence and economic ties are with the English-speaking world; France and La Francophonie do not offer alternatives to existing links, although they are promising areas for developing closer relationships.

The Canadian economy is heavily dependent on international trade and the emphasis on economic growth in the white paper can be understood in this light. Approximately one-fifth of gross national product, which totalled 140·9 billion Canadian dollars in 1974, is accounted for by external trade—a higher proportion than that of the EEC. A typical trade surplus pattern of the 1960s and early 1970s has recently given way to a deficit situation owing to a steady increase in the costs of imported manufactured goods and a decline in the value of Canadian exports.[18] The dimensions of Canadian economic dependence on the United States are well known and need not be spelled out in detail. But statistics which show that over 70 per cent.

---

[17] See for instance, T. Merchant and A. D. P. Heeney, " Canada and the United States: Principles for Partnership," Department of State *Bulletin*, August 2, 1965.

[18] Canada's main exports are motor vehicles, metals and metal ores, timber, wood pulp and newsprint, machinery, wheat, chemicals; major imports are motor vehicles and parts, machinery, petroleum, chemicals, textiles (yarns and fabrics) iron and steel, and fruit and vegetables.

of Canadian external trade is with the United States, that over 80 per cent. of foreign direct investment in Canada comes from the United States; and that foreign control of capital is over 75 per cent. in gas and petroleum, over 65 per cent. in other mining enterprises and over 55 per cent. in manufacturing industry speak for themselves.

There is general awareness in Canada of the unavoidable consequences of having the United States as its only neighbour, with an inevitable, if often unplanned extension of economic, political and cultural influence northwards over the border. But there is growing evidence of a wish to limit this influence, in the interests of Canada, and to achieve a greater measure of Canadian autonomy. Energy resources, in particular, have become a major factor in United States-Canadian relations.[19]

Over the last decade, certain incidents given prominence by the media have heightened the level of concern. In 1969 there was fear of a challenge to Canadian sovereignty in the Arctic, when the United States tanker *Manhattan* forced its way through the north-west passage in order to test the feasibility of this route for shipping oil from Alaska. Under pressure from Parliament and from the public, the Canadian government made a cautious assertion of limited sovereignty in response. It extended Canada's territorial sea from three to 12 miles, effectively closing the entrance to the north-west passage, and it also proclaimed a 100-mile wide pollution control zone in the Arctic, with stiff standards to be met by shipping, and stiff penalties for their contravention.[20] If this could be described as cautious, the establishment of the Foreign Investment Review Agency (FIRA) in 1974 was even more timid, though it did represent some effort to grapple with the thorny problem of foreign ownership.[21] Restraints placed by United States companies on the activities of Canadian subsidiaries, in terms of antitrust and trading with the enemy legislation, have also been greatly resented. There have been several instances of difficulties over selling goods to Cuba, which was subject to United States economic sanctions, and there are recurring problems over antitrust regulations affecting Canadian business operations.[22]

---

[19] There is a growing body of literature on this subject. See particularly K. Levitt, *Silent Surrender* (1970); A. Axline *et al.*, *Continental Community: Independence and Integration in North America* (1974).

[20] Government of Canada, Arctic Waters Pollution Prevention Act 1970, c. 202; Act to amend the Territorial Sea and Fishing Zones Act of 1964, 1970, c. 203.

[21] Government of Canada, Foreign Investment Review Act 1973 (c. 132). The Act was passed in November 1973; Part one, relating to foreign takeovers, was proclaimed in April 1974, and Part two, relating to foreign investment in new business, in October 1975.

[22] A new problem arose with legislation passed in the United States in October 1976 which eliminated foreign tax credits for companies trading with countries observing the

In security, as in welfare, relations with the United States are central to Canadian foreign policy, but in an era of East-West détente and the absence of direct security threats, economic concerns are dominant. It is not the purpose of this paper to examine Canadian-United States relations in detail, but to take their primacy as given, and to consider the white paper's claim to constitute a blueprint for the reorientation of foreign policy, particularly in respect of Canada's participation in international political organisations.

It would have been unrealistic to expect that the government would publish in the white paper detailed policies or bargaining tactics which it planned to employ in dealing with the United States or other foreign Powers. A certain level of generalisation was inevitable. No doubt the desire of a new Prime Minister (particularly one with an academic background and a *penchant* for philosophical discussion) to gain some publicity in a fashionable exercise in " participation " was also important.[23] There was also, perhaps, the sense that the Department of External Affairs was very much the creation and echo of Pearson and his circle, and that extablished views needed to be shaken up. Bruce Thordarson, who has written a good account of the review, suggests that it was " the influence of the Prime Minister, more than any other factor " [24] which determined its course. What is clear enough is that the white paper exhibited serious weaknesses. It was immediately criticised for its failure to place United States-Canadian relations in the forefront of the analysis, which made it seem rather like Hamlet without the Prince of Denmark. The issue was not completely ignored in the white paper; it noted ". . . the complex problem of living distinct from but in harmony with the world's most powerful and dynamic nation . . .," [25] but policy options were not pursued in any detail, and it was two years before this *lacuna* was officially filled. As a result, the review suffered from a general lack of balance and some misplaced emphases, which were accentuated by the government's wish to signal a sharper turnabout in Canada's external orientation than was actually necessary or politically advantageous.

In the first place, its castigation of Canada's internationalist role

---

Arab boycott against Israel. Canadian subsidiaries which have been expanding trade with Arab countries could be affected by this legislation as their parent companies will want to avoid double taxation on their profits.

[23] J. Hyndman described the review as an exercise in " rationalisation " (of directions and priorities already determined), " explanation " (for the general public, the press and the academic community) and " subtle internal fence-mending and bargaining " (within the government). " National Interest and the New Look " 26 *International Journal*, 1970–71, p. 9. This whole issue of *International Journal* was devoted to Canada's foreign policy.

[24] B. Thordarson, *Trudeau and Foreign Policy: a study in decision-making* (1972), p. 16.

[25] *Foreign Policy for Canadians*, p. 21.

and general denigration of international organisation was exaggerated. In a paper published in this *Year Book* in 1975,[26] I suggested that intangible but important benefits of communication, participation, status and role are often associated with membership of international organisations. Communication and participation were not stressed in the white paper, which was the more surprising in that the foreign-policy review was itself designed partly as an exercise in these areas. As for status and role, the review generally condemned them as goals of foreign policy.

Some of the disillusion reflected in the white paper with international organisation was no doubt due to disenchantment with the United Nations where, in the 1950s, Canada had played a leading role earning the designation of a middle Power, which seemed to carry dignified and worthwhile if rather nebulous connotations.[27] Two major achievements of Canadian diplomacy in this period were helping to break the log-jam over membership in 1955 and the establishment of the United Nations Emergency Force in 1956. This peacekeeping initiative not only saved face for the United Kingdom and France and helped to hold the Western alliance together; it also provided the United Nations with a new role to take the place of " collective security " which was out of the question in an era when the two leading members of the organisation saw each other as their main security threat. Lester Pearson, as Canadian Minister for External Affairs, was a prime mover in these initiatives at the United Nations and gained much prestige and a Nobel Peace Prize as a result. But what may have seemed a harbinger of summer for Canada and " middle Powerism " was to be no more than one or two swallows. The circumstances of the 1950s and particularly the Suez crisis, which offered Canada the opportunity to mediate in a United Nations context between the United Kingdom and France on the one hand, and the United States on the other, were not to be repeated. Peacekeeping in the Congo proved to be a disillusioning experience, leaving the United Nations divided and near bankruptcy. Furthermore, the rapid enlargement of the General Assembly meant that the United Nations came to reflect the new majority's concern with decolonisation, self-determination and racial equality in the 1960s, and with redistributive justice and a new economic order in which poorer-countries would get privileged treatment from the rich, in the 1970s. There was no middle role here for Canada. While it could

---

[26] See M. Doxey, " International Organisation in Foreign Policy Perspective " in this *Year Book*, Vol. 29 (1975), pp. 173–195.

[27] See J. Holmes, *Canada: a middle-aged power* (1976) especially pp. 33–34; C. Holbraad, " Middle-Power Roles in Great-Power Triangles " in this *Year Book*, Vol. 30 (1976), pp. 116–132.

support decolonisation without reservation, its own economic interests conflicted with a firm stance over racial inequality in Southern Africa. This was clearly revealed in *Foreign Policy for Canadians* which noted distaste for apartheid alongside " better than normal opportunities for trade and investment " in South Africa.[28] And although it has economic problems of its own—inflation, unemployment, regional inequalities—Canada is clearly a member of the rich, northern group of industrialised States from whom the Third World is demanding concessions.

But even in the area of peacekeeping, in spite of proven limitations, the foreign policy review was perhaps too negative in its attitude. There are still United Nations peacekeeping forces in Cyprus and the Middle East, even if their functions are limited, and the frustrating experiences of peacekeeping in South-East Asia, with Canada's eventual withdrawal from the reconstituted International Commission of Control and Supervision (ICCS), should not be considered as an intimation of a refusal ever to be involved in future peacekeeping operations. One of the main Canadian objections to the ICCS was the failure to make provision for it to report to an international authority such as the United Nations.[29] In suitable circumstances, the Canadian public would probably support further participation in truce supervisory and other peacekeeping exercises initiated under United Nations' auspices.

It is too early to say whether the United Nations will exhaust its credibility by moving further along the route which widens the gap between rhetoric and reality. Canada, as a member of a minority group of members, cannot hope or expect to use the organisation as a means of legitimising foreign policy, but it can still play an active part and, from time to time, as circumstances permit, there may well be special opportunities for action; membership of the Security Council starting in January 1977 is such an opportunity. Modelski has noted the opportunity presented by " parliamentary situations " for " power equalisation " noting that " the ability to determine the agenda or to secure priority for certain resolutions, the timely move to adjourn—in other words, the ability to manipulate the roles of procedure—confers advantages upon those who wield parliamentary skills, and not only upon the powerful." [30] Moreover, one of the consequences of the United Nations has been the instant internationalisation of all issues raised there, so that all States become involved in debate and are obliged to take a position which can be defended. This means that a Canadian policy position must be

---

[28] *Foreign Policy for Canadians*: " United Nations " booklet, p. 19.
[29] See W. Dobell, " A ' Sow's Ear ' in Vietnam," 29 *International Journal*, 1974, pp. 356–392, especially p. 365.
[30] G. Modelski, *Principles of World Politics* (1972), p. 195.

articulated and followed over issues such as the Middle East and Southern Africa. One would not expect the United Nations to be the " main focus and instrument of much of Canada's foreign policy " as the white paper suggested—if indeed it ever was—but it will continue to be a context in which a number of Canadian foreign policy goals can be pursued.

The white paper also questioned Canada's membership of NATO and made little mention of the Commonwealth.[31] Part of the general rationale for NATO had been fear that the economic weakness of Western Europe could make it an easy prey to the spread of Communist ideology as well as to Soviet military strength. The United States and Canada were giving a military guarantee which would bolster European morale and deter Soviet expansion—particularly in West Berlin and West Germany. The North American continent did not seem vulnerable to Soviet attack except by air, and the bilateral North American Air Defence (NORAD) agreement, signed in 1949 between the United States and Canada provided for co-operation in that area.

From the outset, Canada had striven to incorporate a broader set of concerns than the purely military in NATO, and Article 2 of the Treaty which looks to the elimination of conflict in international economic policies and encourages economic collaboration, reflects this concern. Lester Pearson made strenuous efforts to breathe life into this Article, as he relates in his memoirs,[32] but without success. Economic co-operation within NATO has remained a dead letter. A regional focus for European economic co-operation developed among the recipients of Marshall aid, and the EEC and the EFTA were set up in the late 1950s—with an eventual break-up of the latter as the United Kingdom, Denmark and Ireland joined the EEC itself. The Organisation for Economic Co-operation and Development (OECD) which links the original Marshall-aid countries with the United States, Canada and Japan, is now research-oriented, while broader monetary and trade matters are handled multilaterally through the International Monetary Fund (IMF), the World Bank and Associates, the General Agreement on Trade and Tariffs (GATT), and—more recently the United Nations Conference on Trade and Development (UNCTAD). Canada is an active member of these organisations.

The review of the NATO commitment and the decision to cut the Canadian contribution to forces in Europe reflected the easing of

---

[31] The Commonwealth was linked with La Francophonie as international groupings through which social justice could be promoted: see *Foreign Policy for Canadians*, p. 15.

[32] See L. B. Pearson, *Mike: the Memoirs of the Right Honorable L. B. Pearson*, Vol. II (1973) especially pp. 59–62, 68–72, and 99–106.

East-West tension in the middle and late 1960s and a feeling that the economic strength of Western Europe should enable European members of the alliance to play a greater part in providing for their own defence. What the authors of the foreign policy review seem to have overlooked, or under-rated, was the value of NATO membership to Canada as a means of retaining close institutional links with Europe on a basis of a joint commitment to western security.

Canada is peculiarly disadvantaged in that it is not a member of an intermediate regional cluster of States in which group interests are shared. Only the United States shares its " region "; the United Kingdom—the former " mother country "—is no longer the centre of a politically significant Commonwealth but has itself joined the European Economic Community from which Canada is obviously excluded. Western Europe has now coalesced economically to a significant, and politically to a limited degree; Eastern European countries can act as a bloc to counter Soviet hegemony (and can also stress their " Europeanness "); Arab, African and Asian States all have their regional orbits and coalitions of interest. Canada has no such context: the North Atlantic is not a community and in the western hemisphere Canada would share United States rather than Latin American perspectives and would be identified in terms of its own wealth and high level of industrialisation. Thus, it cannot pursue its national interests within a regional group, and this leaves it somewhat exposed in an age of regionalism and caucussing in international bodies.

The white paper was unequivocal in its repudiation of role and influence as goals of foreign policy and this would seem to have been unrealistic. Frankel has noted that " role prescription in international politics is pronounced mainly within international organisations..."[33] and although it would be absurd for Canadian diplomats to neglect their own national interests, while capering about on the international stage on behalf of others, there is no reason why Canadian membership of international bodies should not be used, wherever possible, for the benefit of Canada. As Arthur Andrews has pointed out, " most countries make some effort, conscious or otherwise, to influence the international community's assessment of their position." [34] " Standing " or prestige is akin to international creditworthiness; it enhances credibility and facilitates diplomacy, and it is a normal objective of foreign policy, alongside security and welfare goals.

---

[33] J. Frankel, *International Theory and the Behaviour of States* (1973), p. 83.

[34] A. Andrew, *Defence by Other Means: Diplomacy for the Underdog* (1970), p. 18. See too R. Dore, " The Prestige Factor in International Affairs," 51 *International Affairs*, pp. 190–207.

Prestige based on respect and not just on military might can be particularly valuable for lesser Powers. In fact, Canadian prestige and the reputation of Canadian diplomats stands higher than most Canadians realise. Not only its role in the United Nations, but its role in the Commonwealth have contributed to this status. In the " new " Commonwealth, there is no doubt that Canada has occupied a key position. In welcoming the entry of India, Pakistan and Ceylon as independent members in 1947, Canada gave leadership to the idea of a multi-racial association, and this helped to facilitate its intra-Commonwealth role as conciliator during the Suez crisis, which was paralleled on a wider scale at the United Nations. Again, over the South African membership question in 1961, Mr. Diefenbaker, the Canadian Prime Minister, played a leading role on the side of the new States who were not willing to accept South Africa's continued membership as a republic unless apartheid were substantially modified. The United Kingdom and Australia would have been more accommodating, but the implications for the Commonwealth's future would have been serious had South Africa been allowed to remain.

At the time of the foreign policy review, however, it seems that these perceptions were not sharp among the Prime Minister and his immediate circle. But by 1972 it became necessary to articulate some broad guidelines in the area of Canadian-United States relations and since then there has been a different emphasis in official pronouncements and initiatives regarding institutional links.

In his essay " Canada-U.S. Relations: Options for the Future " published in a special issue of *International Perspectives* in the autumn of 1972, Mr. Sharp, the Minister of External Affairs, set out three possible options for Canadian-United States relations: the first was to proceed as before with the minimum of policy adjustments; the second was to " move deliberately towards closer integration with the U.S. "; the third, and self-evidently, the chosen option, was to " pursue a comprehensive long-term strategy to develop and strengthen the Canadian economy and other aspects of our national life and in the process to reduce the present Canadian vulnerability." [35]

In the wake of the " third option " has come a reaffirmation of interest in NATO which provides Canada with a seat at the Western defence table alongside European governments and a voice in developing a common position towards détente,[36] and also a renewal

[35] *International Perspectives*, October–November 1972, p. 13.

[36] It is interesting to compare the priority for North American defence enunciated by Mr. Trudeau in his Calgary speech with the emphasis accorded to Europe in 1975. See the report in the Toronto *Globe and Mail*, December 19, 1975. See too N. Orvik, " Semi-neutrality and Canada's security," 29 *International Journal*, 1974, pp. 186–215.

of interest in the Commonwealth. The Commonwealth soon re-surfaced in official thinking and in October 1972 Mr. Trudeau declared publicly that he had been " converted " to its usefulness. As early as January 1971, he had found himself cast in a leading role at the Heads of Government meeting in Singapore, where British arms sales to South Africa were a contentious issue, and, as host to the next meeting in Ottawa in August, 1973, he continued to stress the relevance of the association. The Commonwealth offers Canada valuable opportunities to develop close relations with countries in every part of the world on a basis of egalitarianism, relative infor-mality, a common working language, and shared experiences and principles [37] without the oppressive presence of a super-Power as a co-member. Mr. Ramphal, the Commonwealth Secretary-General, has pointed out that the association " can be a catalyst in consensus formation . . . Commonwealth countries occupy places of major significance in nearly all of the world's groupings." [38] While he described the Commonwealth as the " antithesis of a bloc," he suggested that its role in building bridges which are necessary " for the emergence of a planetary community can be of immense value." [39] Canadian participation in the Commonwealth is obviously important as a means of maintaining links with other members and of contri-buting to the reduction of north-south tensions.

Over the last decade, since the establishment of the Secretariat, the functional activities of the Commonwealth have developed rapidly; Canada not only provided the first (highly successful) Secretary-General, Mr. Arnold Smith, but with the United Kingdom, has been the mainstay of the technical co-operation programmes. Canada has also sponsored, with France, a francophone counterpart to the Commonwealth in the area of technical assistance: L'Agence de coopération culturelle et technique.

Before considering relations with Western Europe which clearly form Canada's second most important set of external links after those with the United States, one may note the rather contrived effort in the 1970 white paper to demarcate new " areas " of interest

---

[37] A Declaration of Commonwealth Principles was issued at the Meeting of Heads of Government in Singapore in January 1971. See Report of the Commonwealth Secretary-General 1973, Append. 1.

[38] He proceeded to list the Non-aligned movement, NATO, the Rio Treaty, the ASEAN group, the OAU, the OAS, OECD, the EEC, the East African Community, the Caribbean Community and the South Pacific Forum. S. Ramphal, " The Role of the Commonwealth in the context of the New International Economic Order " quoted in Commonwealth Secretariat: *Commonwealth Record of Recent Events*, January–March 1976, Nr. 17, pp. 11–12.

[39] *Ibid.* See too M. Doxey, " The Commonwealth in the 1970s," in this *Year Book*, Vol. 27 (1973), pp. 90–109; and " The Commonwealth Secretariat," in Vol. 30 (1976), pp. 69–96.

for Canada. A separate booklet on the Pacific, particularly in the absence of one on the United States, was unnecessary. The " Pacific " does not constitute a region in any useful sense of the word and calling it one cannot make it one.[40] The booklet itself revealed the artificiality of the concept, and served only to under-score the very different kinds of relationships which Canada has, or might have, with countries which have Pacific coastlines. For example, different policies are obviously in order for China and Japan. Negotiations to establish diplomatic links with the People's Republic of China began in 1968 and ambassadors were finally exchanged in 1972; China is obviously a major Power and offers great potential for future relations. But, at present, Japan is far more significant in Canadian foreign economic policy. It is Canada's third most important trading partner after the United States and the EEC and accounts for about 90 per cent. of total Canadian trade with Asia. Although the Trudeau government has had great hopes of expanding trade with Japan and of attracting investment, difficulties have persisted. Certainly Japanese investment in Canada has grown rapidly, and was of the order of 260 million Canadian dollars in 1974, but the Japanese are concerned about restraints on foreign investment in Canada and are primarily interested in importing Canadian raw materials, particularly coal, copper and lead ores, nickel and aluminium, while Canadian exporters of manufactured goods find the Japanese market hard to penetrate because of tariff and non-tariff barriers.

Japan's ABC plan, to cultivate closer economic links with Australia, Brazil and Canada in the interests of assured long-term supplies of raw materials, seems to have focused heavily on Brazil with whom a five-year agreement for expansion of trade and investment was concluded in 1976; in contrast the Canadian government was unable to achieve more than a " framework statement," which the Japanese government refused to call an " agreement " when it was signed in Tokyo in October 1976. The statement appears to do no more than give an official nod of approval to efforts which may be made by the Canadian and Japanese private sectors to improve trade and investment links, although Mr. Trudeau is reported to have said it was of some " originality and considerable importance." [41]

Taiwan and Hong Kong are also important sources of imports to Canada, although diplomatic recognition of Taiwan has now been withdrawn. On the other hand, Australia and New Zealand are " old " Commonwealth partners and relations with them have a different character from relations with (say) Chile or Indonesia.

Latin America was also the subject of a separate booklet. Canada

[40] See J. Holmes, *op. cit.* in note 26 above, pp. 161–174.
[41] See reports in the Toronto *Globe and Mail*, October 22 and 23, 1976.

is not and has never been a member of the Organisation of American States (OAS), although a seat at the table has been waiting for it since the pre-war days of the Pan American Union. In the foreign policy review, the pros and cons of joining were frankly set out, and the " balance sheet " suggested that there was no need for formal membership as such advantages as would flow were already available through bilateral relationships.[42] No doubt Canadian governments have not been anxious to be put in a position of " taking sides ": to be pro-United States would mean losing Latin American support; to be pro-Latin American could mean United States disfavour. The OAS has remained largely a political body, concerned with regional security, and for Canada NATO and NORAD (the bilateral air defence agreement with the United States) fill this need. Canada in any case is oriented towards Europe historically and economically, although links with the Commonwealth Caribbean and with other Latin American countries have been growing. In the past, too, the OAS has been an instrument of United States hegemony. It supported the United States quarantine in the Cuban missile crisis in 1962 and voted to impose diplomatic and economic sanctions on Cuba in the same year. Canada would probably not want to be bound by a two-thirds majority vote on such issues.

Recent experience suggests that the OAS is ceasing to fulfil this role, and Canada appointed an official observer to the organisation in 1972. In spite of this, one would not expect an application for membership to follow, partly for the reasons given above, and also in the light of Canada's efforts to define itself outside the American context wherever possible, as a means of offsetting United States preponderance.

A disappointing feature of the Latin American booklet was its failure to discuss the long-established and significant economic links between Canada and the countries of the Commonwealth Caribbean.

## II—Relations with Western Europe

The integration of Western Europe, particularly when the process came to encompass the United Kingdom, was inevitably a major factor in Canadian foreign policy. The United Kingdom's first application to join the EEC in 1961 brought a storm of protest from other Commonwealth countries who anticipated adverse effects on their economies if Commonwealth preference ended and the British market became part of the European market, enclosed by the Community's Common External Tariff (CET). Canada was in the

---

[42] *Foreign Policy for Canadians:* " Latin America " booklet, pp. 20–24.

forefront of those protesting.[43] In fact, the value of Commonwealth preference was already more symbolic than real and the Commonwealth had never been a cohesive trading bloc. Canada's ties were looser than those of others: it was not a member of the sterling area and was always closely linked with the United States. By the time the United Kingdom's second application was made, opposition was less strident but there was an obvious concern that loss of duty free or preferential entry to the British market might harm Canadian exports of manufactured goods and, by removing what appeared to be a lynch-pin of the Commonwealth, weaken the counterweight to United States, influence which the association had provided.

The United Kingdom finally joined the EEC in January 1973, and by then many of these problems had become less acute. Transitional arrangements phased over a five-year period softened the loss of Commonwealth preference and, in any case, Canada's trade with the United States and Japan had increased steadily in the late 1960s and early 1970s. In addition, continuing " rounds " of negotiation in GATT resulted in generally low industrial tariffs for all members. The focus is now more on non-tariff barriers to trade, as well as on privileges and preferences for the exports of Third World countries. By this stage, too, the Commonwealth had taken on its new functional character.

Nevertheless if the " Six " had presented challenges to Canada in their economic unity, the " Nine " obviously became an even more significant factor in Canadian foreign policy. Approximately 12 per cent. of Canada's export trade and 10 per cent. of import trade is with this large and growing market, which through association agreements within Europe and outside it, and through the " Lomé " agreement with 41 Third World States, has far-reaching links beyond its immediate boundaries and accounts for approximately 22 per cent. of all world trade. Furthermore, although prospects for political unity have been dim over the past few years, with disunity over many issues and a tendency to pursue " unilateralism " (particularly in relation to oil supplies) there is no certainty that new life cannot be breathed into the EEC institutions. The inauguration of direct elections to the European Parliament in 1978 could be significant and if a centralisation of external relations does occur in the Community, Canada might find it too late to establish direct links.

For cogent economic and political reasons, therefore, it seemed advisable for Canada to define its relations with the Community as well as with its nine individual members. The Trudeau government recognised this need, and also saw the prospect of breathing some

---

[43] See R. Matthews, " Canada, Britain and Europe: a reappraisal," in P. Uri (ed.), *From Commonwealth to Common Market* (1968).

discernible life into the " third option." Since June 1972, it has energetically and enthusiastically pursued the objective of forging what
was officially described as a contractual link with the EEC. The
Prime Minister himself toured Western European capitals and visited
Brussels twice in 1974 and 1975, and at times it seemed as if the
government was over-anxious for results to the extent that its
initiatives were somewhat hasty.[44]

There was an obvious difficulty in regard to the nature of the
proposed link. The EEC could not conclude a contractual arrangement or trade agreement with Canada which did not also apply to the
United States, or which contravened GATT or other international
agreements. On the other hand, the mere re-enunciation of GATT
most-favoured-nation principles would be superfluous. Canada's
early initiatives indicate that this point had not been fully grasped in
Ottawa. The aide-mémoire presented to the Commission in April
1974 was fuzzy in its proposals and placed heavy emphasis on the
need to affirm the Canadian identity as distinct from that of the
United States—a criticism which could also be levelled at subsequent
official pronouncements.[45] While this goal may be understandable
and laudable in the domestic context, it is not calculated to appeal to
European governments who have no particular interest in soothing
the Canadian psyche, or in boosting the status of Mr. Trudeau and
his government in the eyes of the Canadian electorate. For Europeans, access to Canadian resources was the carrot.[46]

Following an initial period of confusion, matters proceeded more
smoothly and in February 1976, after six months' discussion of a
mandate, the Commission was authorised by the Foreign Ministers
of the Nine to negotiate an agreement with the Canadian government.

What is described as a " framework agreement for commercial
and economic co-operation between Canada and the European
Communities " was signed in July 1976 and came into force late that
year. The agreement is not a contractual link in the sense of a treaty
from which defined economic consequences will automatically flow.

---

[44] See G. Stevens, " Mr. Trudeau Woos Europe," *The Round Table*, Nr. 260, 1975,
pp. 401–409.

[45] See Department of External Affairs, *Transcript* of the Prime Minister's Press
Conference, October 25, 1974. This seems to be a recurring theme in Canadian foreign
policy initiatives. When the Canadian–Japanese " statement " was signed in October
1976, a Canadian official was reported as saying ". . . there has been a past unwillingness
on the part of the Japanese to take us seriously . . . but now I think we have changed
their perceptions about us." (*Ottawa Citizen*, October 22, 1976).

[46] These points were made by officials of the Commission to a group of Canadian
academics, including the writer, who visited Brussels in February 1975 under the
auspices of the Atlantic Council of Canada and the Canadian Department of External
Affairs.

No new preferences or privileges are—or could be—created. They would be excluded by GATT unless extended to all. There is an obligation on both parties to consult at least once a year. In fact, such meetings between Canadian officials and officials of the Commission had already been taking place since 1972, but this process is now formalised by the establishment of a Joint Co-operation Committee.

Co-operation across the whole range of commercial and economic endeavour is envisaged, and access to and processing of resources is specifically mentioned in the agreement which also encourages intercorporate links between industries, especially through joint ventures; increased and mutually beneficial investment; technical and scientific exchange; and joint operations by firms from Canada and the Community in third countries.

Canada had had a mission to the EEC, headed by an ambassador, since the end of 1972, but the Community now has a permanent office in Ottawa offering a press and information service.

The agreement is described in a Community news-sheet as being of an " evolutionary character." [47] At the time of writing it is impossible to forecast in what directions it may evolve. Mr. Trudeau himself described the agreement as " a mechanism that will provide the means (*i.e.* the ' link ') and the obligation (*i.e.* ' contractual ') to consult and confer, and to do so with materials sufficiently pliable and elastic to permit the mechanism to adapt in future years to accommodate whatever jurisdiction the European Community from time to time assumes." [48]

If the Community's disintegrative tendencies continue to dominate, Canada's relations with its individual members will be crucial and the agreement will remain a bloodless, fleshless skeleton. But if the Community moves forward to new levels of integration, it may be important for Canada to have its own lines of communication to Brussels, separate from those operated by the United States in its own interests. And there is no doubt that economic co-operation between Canadian and European business enterprises can be fruitful in many areas.

For the moment, however, although somewhat more formal than the arrangement with Japan noted earlier in this paper, the agreement scarcely qualifies as an institutional mechanism for achieving

---

[47] *European Community*, Nr. 196, 1976, p. 48. It is interesting that in this article, the " third option " is seen as an alternative to the United States and Commonwealth connections, and not as a " third " means of dealing with the United States as a neighbour.

[48] Quoted in D. Humphreys, " Canada's Link with Europe still not widely understood," *International Perspectives*, March–April 1976, p. 35.

collective purposes; informational and promotional functions are not backed up by any concrete areas to be handled collectively.[49]

### III—THE FOREIGN POLICY REVIEW
#### IN RETROSPECT

In seeking to determine how far Canadian foreign policy has changed course or direction since 1970 it is not easy to identify actions in the spirit of the white paper which would not otherwise have been taken. The main charges levelled by the Review against the Pearsonian era of Canadian diplomacy were that foreign policy had been over-reactive, too concerned with " role " and too heavily oriented towards international institutions. But how much has changed? Certainly the reduction of Canadian forces in Europe in 1969, before the Review had been completed, indicated the government's wish to give a new priority to North American defence and to downgrade the NATO commitment. But this posture seems to have been short-lived. Membership in NATO has continued and in the context of maintaining cordial relations with Western European countries and of preserving a Canadian seat at the table in an organisation which brings North America and Western Europe together in pursuit of broad aims of détente and arms control and reduction, as well as mutual defence, it is not likely that it will be played down in the near future, especially as Canada seeks to place its relations with members of the EEC on a firmer footing.

As far as the United Nations is concerned, there has been a general disenchantment in the west with its political role and a growing disinclination to finance its operations. Peace-keeping does not provide solutions to problems and when some members of the United Nations do not pay their share of expenses the burden falls heavily on others. The United Nations has grown too large, and is too divided to take effective action. It is principally a forum for Third World demands and a mechanism for legitimising groups and policies which have their support. The circumstances which were conducive to Canada playing a leading role in the United Nations were peculiar to the 1950s, and will not recur, although other bodies such as the Commonwealth still offer opportunities for role and influence which are not being spurned. And there are many activities in the broad United Nations' framework with which Canada will continue to be heavily involved. Space precludes their detailed consideration, but a good example is the series of Law of the Sea conferences in which Canadian positions and Canadian diplomacy have been prominent.

---

[49] See J. G. Ruggie, " International Responses to Technology: Concepts and Trends," 29 *International Organization*, 1975, pp. 571–572.

This paper has noted the renewed stress on the Commonwealth connection and the eager search for institutionalised relationships with the EEC. It is interesting that when the leaders of the major industrialised nations met at Rambouillet in November 1975, to plan overall economic strategy, the Canadian government was excluded (at French insistence) to its considerable chagrin. On that occasion, Mr. Trudeau is reported to have said that he would not seek revenge.[50] Whether he was in any position to do so is perhaps less important than the intensity of the desire to participate which was clearly revealed. Subsequently Canada accepted, with Venezuela, co-chairmanship of the Conference on International Economic Co-operation between rich and poor countries, which is a by-product of the energy crisis, but has a wider set of concerns on its agenda encompassing finance, raw materials, development and energy.

The intermediate Power which is squarely in the orbit of a super-Power obviously has limited options; and for Canada there is no chance of changing patrons or of becoming a " free floater." [51] And in an age of détente, when super-Powers are talking to each other, there is no middle, interlocutor role for lesser Powers, if indeed there ever was. Mediating roles are more likely to be the product of permanent or temporary office in international bodies, such as Secretary-Generalships or the Presidency of the United Nations Security Council.

Security and the avoidance of nuclear war are still basic goals of foreign policy which must be sought collectively; in addition, the contemporary need to handle many pressing economic and social problems on a multilateral basis, make it inevitable that Canada will not only continue to play an active part in existing institutions, but will join in sponsoring new ones (for instance the United Nations Environment Programme, the World Food Council, and the International Energy Agency). Indeed, the policy themes stressed in the white paper—economic growth, sovereignty, peace, social justice, the quality of life and a harmonious natural environment—if they are to be meaningful, *require* involvement in international organisations; retreat to isolation for Canada, were it feasible, would mean retreat to continentalism.

Moreover, keeping a sharp profile in international organisations can be useful for a country which will continue to be concerned with defining its distinctiveness from the United States.   Were another white paper to be published today, one can be sure that, alongside a more thorough exploration of United States-Canadian relations, these emphases would be made explicit.

---

[50] Reported in the Toronto *Globe and Mail*, November 17, 1975.
[51] A. Andrew, *op. cit.* in note 33 above, p. 33.

# INDUSTRIAL CO-OPERATION
# AND EAST-WEST TRADE

By

## A. NUSSBAUMER

EAST-WEST economic co-operation has been greatly stimulated by the changes in world politics of recent years. Political détente has paved the way for increasing economic exchanges between capitalist and socialist countries, considered beneficial by both groups. Equally, closer economic relations have contributed to a wider appreciation of strategies of general co-operation instead of continued confrontation.

There are so many aspects of economic co-operation that one cannot hope to cover them even summarily within the compass of this paper. Co-operation may take the form of inter-governmental agreements destined to remove existing obstacles to trade and payments, or such agreements may be aimed at establishing common economic institutions and harmonising national economic policies; far-reaching economic integration might even call for limited political integration. Economic co-operation may be concerned primarily with trade, with promoting a freer flow of services, more labour mobility, or easier capital transfers. It may be technical co-operation in research and development, it may be aimed at standardising professional education, acceptable degrees of resource exploitation and of environmental pollution, or it may be concerned with regulating international payments, capital transfers and establishing an international monetary system.

We have to limit the discussion to one special aspect of East-West co-operation which has become increasingly important in recent years: industrial co-operation. It is hoped that industrial co-operation will help in removing still existing obstacles to East-West trade, and that it will help to overcome difficulties resulting from differences between the capitalist and socialist economic systems by providing for a new intermediate level of economic relationships between the inter-governmental one and short-term commercial contracts predominant between independent firms in the West. Finally, independently of East-West relations, industrial co-operation enables industry to take full advantage of modern developments in production and marketing.

## I—THE IMPORTANCE OF INDUSTRIAL CO-OPERATION

As industrial co-operation is not tied to any specific kind of contract

64

and serves many different policy objectives, the term itself does not carry any specific meaning. Any agreement going beyond the traditional forms of international trade may be described as industrial co-operation: it ranges from extended barter trade to joint projects of research, production, design, and marketing; even joint ventures may be included. In an attempt to give a formal definition the Economic Commission for Europe (ECE) has listed the following forms of co-operation [1]; licensing with payment in resultant products, supply of complete plants of production lines with payments in resultant products, co-production and specialisation, sub-contracting, joint ventures, joint tendering or joint construction, or similar projects. In practice the many activities that are covered by the term co-operation can hardly be covered by a neat definition, useful as this may be since co-operating partners frequently ask for exceptions from rules established by international agreements, *e.g.* most-favoured-nation treatment, and national customs legislation.

If the aim is to provide for greater flexibility in international commercial arrangements and, thus, to overcome legal and administrative barriers, especially with regard to East-West trade, a broad interpretation of the term industrial co-operation is preferable. Relying on past experience [2] it appears to be essential that a contract between two firms should be concerned with implementing large complex programmes and/or be of a self-financing nature, generally extending over a minimum of five years.

Attempts have been made at distinguishing between various kinds of co-operation agreements. It has been suggested that the general concept of industrial co-operation should be divided into two main categories: current industrial co-operation including production co-operation and deliveries co-operation, and organic capital co-operation, the most important form of the latter being joint ventures. The packages referred to in a complex co-operation agreement may be characterised as stressing the combination of a traditional contract with a new specially designed element, *e.g.* sale of licences or buy-back clauses, or they may be founded primarily on an element usually not found in East-West economic relations, *e.g.* co-operation in research and development, or more than one element may be organically combined as is the case in co-production agree-

[1] Analytical Report on Industrial Co-operation among EEC countries, United Nations, Geneva 1973, p. 2.

[2] C. H. McMillan (ed.), *Changing perspectives in East–West Commerce* (1974); M. Schmitt, *Industrielle Ost-West Kooperation* (1974); P. Knirsch, *Industrial Co-operation between East and West: the FGR experience*, in J. P. Hardt (ed.), *Tariff, legal, and credit constraints on East–West Commercial Relations* (1975), pp. 56–75; F. Levcik and J. Stankovsky, *Industrielle Kooperation zwischen Ost und West*, in *Studien über Wirtschafts- und Systemyergleiche*, Vol. 8 (1976).

ments.[3] Definitions used for industrial co-operation, including licensing know-how, turnkey and co-production arrangements, and joint ventures, may then be broader than that used by ECE. As suggested above, such agreements should not be concluded for periods of less than five years, and they should provide for prolongation and extension already in the original contracts, for it takes time to create mutual understanding and confidence, collect and utilise information about markets, products, technological possibilities, and credit facilities. Being commercial agreements between equal partners, industrial co-operation agreements have to be mutually advantageous to both partners, and have to be flexible enough to allow for adjustment whenever fundamental inequalities arise.

Industrial co-operation agreements may help to reduce the instability of markets, and barriers to East-West trade resulting from the individual countries being part of different areas of economic integration.[4] They may facilitate access to new technologies, markets, and credit facilities, and Eastern planners might derive from them the additional assurances and safeguards, which otherwise cannot be obtained on basically unstable western markets. Contrary to traditional trade which is predominently market-orientated, co-operation mostly serves technical, production or selling aspects within a partner's unit. It helps directly to utilise better labour reserves and increase labour productivity by technology transfer. But there may also be other complementary advantages such as supply with cheap raw materials or the possibility of establishing a joint organisation for producing and selling a complete set of tools, machines, or products serving the same group of human needs on the world market. Financial and credit problems may be eased by buy-back arrangements, medium-term capital transfers, and, in some cases, even by direct investment in the foreign company or its subsidiary.

Economic motives are not always similar in western and eastern countries. Western companies frequently are interested in raw materials, semi-processed goods, and cheap labour the East can supply; they may also look for additional outlets for their production, especially at times of a business recession. Eastern companies often are interested primarily in access to western technology without complicated and time-consuming licensing processes. Modern technology also may be expensive, and new sources of financing have to be opened. However, its application may demand a continuing

---

[3] See E. Tabaszynski, H. Radice, and P. Marer, in C. T. Saunders (ed.), *Interim Co-operation in East-West Economic Relations, East-West European Economic Interaction Workshop Papers*, Vol. 2 (1977).

[4] Th. A. Wolf, " Progress in removing barriers to East-West trade: an assessment," in F. Nemschak (ed.), *East-West European Economic Interaction Working Papers*, Vol. 1 (1976), pp. 111–124.

flow of knowledge, information, technicians and marketing ability. Sometimes East-West trade is also responsible for new forms of co-operation between industries in the West, since the size of a contract suggested by an eastern partner frequently is too big to be met by any single western company, unless it is a multinational one.

Finally, there are political reasons for East-West industrial co-operation. The doctrine of peaceful co-existence has opened new possibilities for East-West economic relations, even if the ideological struggle continues. Western embargo lists have been shortened, trade discrimination has been reduced, and new credit facilities have been opened. Eastern countries have accepted co-operation with multinational companies. The picture of two monolithic blocs has ceded to a more complex and complicated configuration of the world. The lure of the potentially huge Soviet markets may attract many a western capitalist hoping for big profits. Western technology and capital may be looked on by eastern statesmen as another possibility of speeding up the development of the economic and political potential of their countries. There may even be hopes that industrial co-operation may help to limit the risks of military confrontation, and that populations in eastern and in western countries may learn more about the advantages of their neighbours' way of life.[5]

Even as far as the economic aspects of industrial co-operation are concerned, there is hope that economic barriers erected by the European Community and the Countries of the Council for Mutual Economic Assistance (CMEA) against imports from outside may be lowered, and that problems resulting from the differences between the economic and social systems in East and West can be reduced to a minimum. Special difficulties for negotiations will remain however, but even these might lose some of their importance if standardised patterns and procedures can be worked out. Co-operation may even help to find solutions for ideological difficulties. According to socialist theory the means of production must be nationalised and owned by society at large. But, while this doctrine forbids private ownership of industrial property, co-operation agreements may permit the sharing of some functions of ownership or management with foreign private companies, the most noticeable examples being joint ventures between western companies and State-owned enterprises in Yugoslavia.

## II—RECENT DEVELOPMENTS IN EAST-WEST TRADE

For the last fifteen years the volume of East-West trade has developed

---

[5] For a more detailed analysis see G. Adler-Karlsson, " The Political Economy of East–West–South Co-operation," *Studien über Wirtschafts- und Systemvergleiche*, Vol. 7 (1976), pp. 44–59.

quite satisfactorily. During the period 1961 to 1973 imports of CMEA
countries from western industrialised countries have increased by an
annual average of 13 per cent. and their exports to this group of
countries have grown annually by 11·8 per cent.; this has been faster
than the development of intra-CMEA trade where mutual exports and
imports have only increased by an annual average of 8·7 per cent.
and 9·4 per cent. respectively.[6] Since 1971 these tendencies have been
accentuated, and there has been a sharp upswing in the foreign
trade of CMEA countries, especially with western, industrial countries.
Annual growth rates in the foreign trade of CMEA countries with
market economies have been between 10 per cent. and 13 per cent.
until 1970 and 10·6 per cent. in 1971, but these have increased rapidly
since to 33·4 per cent. (1972), 46·9 per cent. (1973), and 42·7 per cent.
(1974).[7] It will be difficult to maintain the momentum of this development despite the recent economic recession in the West and balance-
of-payments deficits in the East.

Trade between CMEA countries and developing countries has been
increasing nearly equally as quickly from an average annual rate of
growth between 11 per cent. and 18 per cent. before 1970 to one of
40·6 per cent. in 1973 and of 51·6 per cent. in 1974.[8] Intra-European
trade between CMEA countries alone has hardly ever grown more
quickly than by an annual rate of 11 per cent. the only exceptions
being the years 1972 and 1973 when this trade increased by 20·8 per
cent. and 23·7 per cent. respectively.[9]

One cannot escape the impression that, while the share of socialist
countries of Eastern Europe in world trade has fallen short of their
share in world production by a considerable margin, in recent years
they have become increasingly aware of potential gains to be drawn
from trade. They seem to have embarked generally on a policy of
freer international exchanges. This development certainly has been
supported by a lowering of trade barriers erected after the Second
World War by many western nations. However, it may be difficult in
the future to expand East-West trade as quickly as in recent years,
and to put it on a more permanent basis. New methods will have to
be found to make East-West economic relations more independent of
market fluctuations and of temporary balance-of-payments difficulties. Eastern partners of western firms also may need long-term
investment credits from the West if they are to build up the new

[6] B. Askanas, H. Askanas, F. Levcik, " Structural Developments in CMEA Foreign
Trade Over the Last Fifteen Years," *Forschungsberichte Wiener Institut für Internationale
Wirtschaftsvergleiche*, Nr. 23 (1975), p. 55.
[7] United Nations, *Monthly bulletin of statistics*, September 1974 (special table D),
June 1975 (special table B.)
[8] *Ibid.*
[9] *Ibid.*

productive capacities needed for increasing sales in western markets. Industrial co-operation may contribute considerably towards solving these problems.

While one can certainly regard trade between the socialist and the capitalist countries as one of the faster growing sectors of world trade, much remains to be done. Trade between these groups of countries has increased by a factor of 2·7 between 1970 and 1974. Approximately one thousand agreements have already been signed[10] between CMEA countries and western companies providing for various forms of industrial co-operation and showing the great importance attributed to these new and hopeful developments by governments in both East and West. But the average East European share in the West European markets is still as low as only 4·7 per cent. (1974),[11] and the shares in total world trade of West European exports to eastern Europe and *vice versa* were still only 2 per cent. in both directions in 1972. Meanwhile trade between East European countries holds a relatively stable position of not quite 6 per cent. On the other hand, trade between West European countries has increased from what was already 18·5 per cent. of total world trade in 1953 to still higher levels, *e.g.* 31·1 per cent. in 1972.[12] Thus there is good reason to believe that the eastern socialist countries could still draw considerable benefits from increasing trade and closer economic co-operation with the West, and that western industries might be able to develop new markets in the East.

While there has been acceleration in the speed of expansion of East-West trade over the last two decades, it has remained unsteady. Fluctuations may be attributed to the following reasons: large single projects as well as huge imports of food by the Soviet Union in years of bad harvests may upset the balance of trade; as the trade structure is asymmetrical, the West exporting mainly manufactured goods and the eastern countries semi-manufactured goods and raw materials, changes in relative prices will lead to changes in the terms of trade and trade balances (moreover, there is no reason why demand for these groups of goods should develop at the same rate); lastly, fluctuations in the volume of western business activity also exert destabilising influences on East-West trading relations.

Disturbances to trade frequently lead to difficulties for CMEA

---

[10] O. Bogomolow, " General Premises for Economic Co-operation among States with Different Social Systems," in F. Nemschak, (ed.), *World economy and East-West trade, East-West European economic interaction working papers*, Vol. 1 (1976), pp. 66, 71.

[11] See *loc. cit.* in note 7 above.

[12] G. Kohlmey, " Intra-European trade and new trends in international economic relations," in F. Nemschak (ed.), *op. cit.* in note 10 above at p. 27.

countries facing the problem of financing their imports from the West by a steady flow of exports to the West, and consequently having to make increasing demands for international financial assistance. With the exception of 1968, the accumulated balance of trade of CMEA countries with developed market economies since 1965, has been negative, annual deficits fluctuating considerably; for individual socialist countries these fluctuations have been even more serious.[13] Consequently, socialist countries have felt a constant need to finance a steady flow of imports from western industrialised countries. They have drawn on short- and medium-term commercial credits from western banks frequently supported by western export-financing schemes. They have been bargaining energetically for favourable credit conditions, and have sought consolidation of their debts through western central banks increasing their credit margins or by inter-governmental agreements. In addition, imports from the West have sometimes been tied to specific exports to the West. Furthermore, East-West industrial co-operation can be regarded partially as a substitute for western credits and commodity barter.

Frequently today, industrial co-operation is looked on also as an instrument for improving the Eastern countries' export structures and their commodity terms of trade, and for obtaining the best possible conditions when importing capital goods and modern technology; often it is held to be the fastest and cheapest method by which East European enterprises can hope to receive patent rights or licences from large Western multinational companies,[14] and by which they may win wider access to western markets. Industrial co-operation also enables eastern enterprises to make the best possible use of western credit facilities; under co-operation agreements western partners may be expected to take out a higher volume of credit with their own banks in order to cover indirectly the financial needs of their eastern counterparts.

Western companies, on the other hand, hope to benefit from the availability of cheaper, yet well trained, labour in the East, from having easier access to large and unexplored markets, as well as to the huge stocks of raw materials waiting for utilisation in the Soviet hemisphere. It is also hoped that this new method of organising international commodity and money flows might contribute towards bridging differences between the socialist and the capitalist economic systems, which in the past have often proved obstacles to trade and common operations.

[13] G. Kohlmey, *op. cit.* in note 10 above, pp. 36–38, tables 10 and 11.
[14] E. A. Hewett, "The economies of East European technology imports from the West," *American Economic Review*, Vol. 65 (1975), p. 379.

### III—Some Special Advantages
### of Industrial Co-operation

Industrial co-operation provides for a mechanism through which producers can co-ordinate their activities internationally. In this respect its objective is similar to that of international trade or forming a transnational corporation. Since capitalist mergers are scarcely practical in East-West economic relations due to the national ownership of all industrial capital in socialist countries, and trade also faces difficulties as a result of differences between economic systems, industrial co-operation has come to be of foremost importance in the extending of East-West economic relations. Co-operating firms retain their separate identity and essential operational autonomy; but while they continue to conduct some of their relations through the market, they have become quantitatively and qualitatively quite interdependent due to long-term arrangements concerning production, marketing, financing, and the use of property rights. Thus, industrial co-operation provides for a new kind of commercial arrangement between firms profitable for all partners, in ways which otherwise would not be possible.

On the inter-governmental level, too, agreements paving the way for closer direct contracts between firms may be very useful in East-West trade, since these may help to remove administrative obstacles to trade, provide for additional sources of international finance, and give the western partner more influence on the decisions taken by eastern managers and planners. Such inter-governmental agreements create new international legal mechanisms; they are not confined to the limits of traditional trade agreements, but cover wide spheres and extremely diverse forms of co-operation, usually planned for five to 10 years, and offering the possibility of further extension; joint inter-governmental commissions might be established as well, and may be helpful in finding solutions for new problems arising while agreements are in force.[15] By such agreements also new links may be established between capitalist and socialist economic organisations while leaving the functioning of the systems at home unchanged, *i.e.* the market mechanism in the West and central economic planning in the East.[16]

The economic efficiency of co-operating firms, moreover, may be improved by bringing together their economic and technical poten-

---

[15] M. M. Maximova, " Industrial Co-operation between Socialist and Capitalist Countries: Forms, Trends, Problems," in C. T. Saunders (ed.), *Interfirm Co-operation in East-West Economic Relations, East-West European Economic Interaction Working Papers*, Vol. 2 (1977), p. 115.

[16] Yu. F. Kormnov, " All-European production and trade co-operation," in O. T. Bogomolov (ed.), *All-European Economic Co-operation* (1973), p. 122.

tials. This may be essential for tackling large projects especially in developing countries, but also for supplying a sector of the world market for industrial goods with the complete spectrum of products desired by some customers. Partners may also benefit from the common use of existing marketing institutions, their favourable trade connections, service centres, and commission agencies. Even big firms and multinational enterprises may find it expedient to co-operate, and firms in eastern socialist countries have already concluded a large number of co-operation agreements with these western giants despite their being officially branded as imperialist monopolies.[17] Medium-sized firms, on the other hand, frequently fail to find easy access to co-operation agreements, since they are not well enough known, and may be insufficiently powerful by themselves to attract interest. Their chances improve if they form permanent co-production agreements themselves. But, even then, eastern firms may prefer big partners in the West, which are more likely to accept buy-back arrangements and can offer better financing facilities. Regular international conferences for firms interested in industrial co-operation as well as a special information service might in both instances prove useful, particularly if smaller firms are to find easier access to this new form of economic co-operation between East and West.

Industrial co-operation could even lead to integrated joint production. Because it may be necessary for the participating enterprises to work out and apply uniform specifications, standards and technologies, they may have to merge their efforts in the fields of research, the supply of raw materials, financing and marketing. It has been suggested, moreover, that co-operation agreements should be standardised and that the treaty form used by socialist countries in their international industrial co-operation could well be applied even when co-operating with western companies.[18] This is probably true as far as the general outlines of such agreements are concerned, especially if time could be saved in negotiations with government officials by using a standardised outline. But the special characteristics of the individual case will always have to be considered; one should therefore not place too many hopes on attempts to standardise agreements.

Other possible advantages of industrial co-operation between East and West certainly lie in the preservation of scarce resources, the protection of the biosphere and the common fight against pollu-

---

[17] For a listing of the most important co-operation agreements including such firms as Fiat, ITT, Westinghouse and Krupp, see G. Adler-Karlsson, *op. cit.* in note 5 above, pp. 77–79.

[18] Yu. F. Kormnov, *op. cit.* in note 16 above, p. 110.

tion. If humanity is to maintain its present level of exploitation of natural resources, non-renewable ones will have in time to be replaced by substitutes, and renewable resources such as water, the biological resources of the ocean, the soil and the forests will have to be treated with care. For Europe the task of co-operating in these activities is already a pressing one, since a great part of the world's resources are being exploited there and the limited size of nations frequently prevents them from taking efficient action individually.[19]

Finally, one should not dismiss the subject of the special advantages which come from industrial co-operation without again mentioning the financing of industrial development. First, contracts are frequently self-financing, so as to avoid drawing on limited national currency reserves. Co-operation, thus, will be sure to increase the number of international economic transactions, not at the expense of existing trade by absorbing financial resources originally devoted to export promotion. Agreements generally include a long-term financial plan providing for two-way commodity transfers from the beginning, or for the western partner financing initial investments made by the eastern firm. There are basically two kinds of buy-back clauses by which the self-financing principle is being established: the supplied equipment, services, components, licences, and know-how are being paid for in products manufactured from them according to a predetermined schedule, or the supplied components and semi-finished products are matched reciprocally by counter-deliveries. Both clauses force western companies to find new outlets for products produced by their eastern partners.

Secondly, industrial co-operation agreements may be aimed at enlarging credit facilities in the West. Since commercial banks are looking for a diversification of risks, they will not tolerate disproportional expansion of the liabilities of a single debtor; estimation of risks involved in credits to the East raises additional problems, because it always means giving credit to the State. Many western States, therefore, have established special banking institutions, such as the *Osterreichische Kontrollbank AG* in Austria or the Eximbank in the United States,[20] or they have set up special government-sponsored credit schemes in order to provide funds for either long-term credits at reduced rates of interest to developing countries or when exporting to eastern socialist countries. The government will also accept the risk of eventual losses of capital.

---

[19] Ye. K. Fyodorov, " Possibilities of All-European Co-operation in the Field of Environmental Protection," in O. T. Bogomolov (ed.), *All-European Economic Co-operation* (1973), p. 216.

[20] J. C. Cruse and D. C. Wigg, " The Role of the Eximbank in US Exports and East-West Trade," in P. Marer (ed.), *US Financing of East-West Trade: the Political Economy of Government Credits and the National Interest* (1975).

Thirdly, there still is the possibility of direct capital co-operation in which western and eastern partners invest in one common project. These " joint ventures," properly speaking, open the widest range of commercial possibilities. They are, however, also the most difficult forms of common financing. Agreements have not only to be compatible with the political and ideological principles of Marxist socialism, but also to provide solutions for such difficult economic problems as the distribution of profits, international transfer of returns on capital invested, and fluctuations of politically determined rates of exchange.

## IV—TOWARDS A NEW WORLD ECONOMIC ORDER?

Any paper about industrial co-operation would be incomplete, were tri-partite co-operation including developing countries as third partners omitted altogether. There is no exact and comprehensive statistical information available even concerning bilateral co-operation between industries of western industrialised countries or of eastern socialist countries and developing nations, because co-operation, economic aid, and deliveries of armaments cannot be separated easily; however even the volume of bilateral industrial co-operation between North and South is quite limited.[21] Tri-partite co-operation then must be extremely small and only very few cases are known.

Developing countries, meanwhile, might be expected to draw many advantages from industrial co-operation agreements, especially from tri-partite co-operation. It would strengthen their industrial capacities, increase the influx of new technologies and of managerial skills, help them to diversify exports and increase the influx of investment capital. Even so, in relative terms they would remain politically independent of any single one of their partners. If tri-partite co-operation helped developing countries to pay for their imports by increasing their own exports, following the principle of self-financing, it certainly would also be a most important instrument to keep the growth-rates of their foreign debt under control. Because advantages to Third-World countries may be manifold, United Nations agencies, especially UNCTAD, are attributing increasing importance to co-operation agreements.

For the developing nations there are also dangers involved in such agreements. Since it has become customary in trade with these countries that the suppliers of investment goods or of complete turn-key plants not only provide for long-term credits, but also accept full responsibility for the continued operation of the new plant for many subsequent years, industrial co-operation with industries of the

---

[21] G. Adler-Karlsson, *op. cit.* in note 5 above, pp. 94–99.

developing countries may be one way of shifting back part of these new responsibilities. Moreover, commodities supplied to developing countries under tri-partite co-operation agreements at conditions very favourable to them may be selected according to the import and export requirements of their western and eastern partners rather than to fit the special requirements of the developing nation. Tri-partite co-operation in some cases may even be designed so as to direct East European exports to developing countries *via* western enterprises acting as intermediaries, this permitting the eastern exporter to earn hard currency for his deliveries.[22]

Mentioning these possibilities is not to attribute to them any great importance in present tri-partite co-operation, or to suggest that the dangers will ever materialise. But it is good to bear in mind that it is the responsibility of the governments of all industrially developed countries as well as of the enterprises entering into co-operation agreements, to safeguard the poorest countries of the world against losses resulting from such agreements. Bilateral as well as tri-partite industrial co-operation with the South should be designed so as to make the developing nations to the fullest possible degree the beneficiaries of improved economic relations between western and eastern industrial countries.

---

[22] K. Bolz, " Tri-partite co-operation—a Western view," in C. T. Saunders (ed.), *Interfirm Co-operation in East-West Economic Relations, East-West European Economic Interaction Working Papers,* Vol. 2 (1977), p. 121.

# THE INTERNATIONAL OIL COMPANIES IN THE NEW WORLD OIL MARKET

By

## PETER R. ODELL

THE high degree of solidarity of the member countries of the Organisation of Petroleum Exporting Countries (OPEC) has, since the autumn of 1973, steadily become increasingly obvious to and reluctantly accepted by the western industrialised world. Earlier pious hopes—largely based on wishful thinking—that strains and stresses amongst the world's oil producers over questions of price and of levels of production would produce a near future break-up in OPEC [1] have now been generally discarded, and the idea of the oil-producing countries as the dominant element in the international oil system is being accepted—with all the implications that this has for future international relationships.

## I—THE ROLE OF THE INTERNATIONAL OIL COMPANIES

There is thus a much greater willingness on the part of most nations to *consider* ways and means of reducing dependence on the OPEC cartel. Unfortunately, however, this is not always accompanied by a general realisation that this also means either reducing the contribution which the international oil companies make to the world's energy supply or the need for steps to bring these companies under the effective control of the nations concerned. On the contrary, the companies are often still largely believed to be the essential elements needed to ensure the continuity of oil supply and especially for organising the necessary infrastructure of supply arrangements in the event of any further interruption of production and transportation for political and/or economic reasons by the OPEC countries. Such beliefs are, moreover—at the level of analysis concerned with the technicalities of supply problems—justified, for it is a matter of fact that most of the world's oil which is internationally traded continues to flow at the behest of the international oil companies through facilities which they own and operate around most parts of the world.

It is, however, as a result of a recognition of these " facts," that the dangers to the oil-dependent western world are enhanced because this obscures the interdependence and the willing—indeed, the necessary

[1] These hopes were examined in P. R. Odell, " The World of Oil Power in 1975," *The World Today*, July 1975.

—co-operation of the OPEC member countries and the international oil companies which thus jointly constitute a producers' cartel working *against* the real interests of the world's oil importing nations —rich and poor.

### (a) *Oil Company Profits from OPEC Oil*

The motivations of the companies in this respect are not difficult to determine. These are, simply, a recognition of what they have to do in order to ensure that their commercial interests are best served for, in the changed oil supply and price situation, they are able to achieve a higher cash flow by marketing OPEC oil than by seeking to secure alternative supplies from elsewhere. Indeed, throughout 1976, it seems that the companies, on average, achieved a weighted up-stream gross profit margin on crude oil delivered to the refineries in Rotterdam (the world's single most important market for OPEC crude oil) of about 85 cents per barrel.[2]

Table 1, derived from official Dutch government foreign trade statistics and from oil industry publications, indicates the costs of crude oil purchases from OPEC countries and the transportation costs involved in getting the oil to Rotterdam. It thus shows how the up-stream profit margin was achieved in 1976 in respect of this market.

The profit per barrel made on importing OPEC oil to Europe has, moreover, special qualities which enhance its attractiveness. It is virtually an after-tax profit for two reasons. First, as it is earned " off-shore " it can, if appropriate, be accounted for in tax havens. Secondly, under existing legislation in the mother countries of the international oil companies (especially the United States but including also the United Kingdom), profits earned on operations in the traditional producing countries and which are remitted back to the home country are free of additional tax obligations. This is because the taxes already paid in the producing countries (amounting in 1976 to over 10 dollars per barrel) give the companies a substantial tax credit position. This " after-tax " position of the oil companies' earnings on handling OPEC oil makes the apparent per barrel profit " worth "

---

[2] This overall up-stream profit margin for crude oil delivered Rotterdam should be compared with the nominal 25 cents/bbl. profit margin which the companies claim they are allowed on purchases of crude oil in most OPEC countries. It seems that the methods of company operations permit these nominal f.o.b. profits to be multiplied several times before the crude oil is delivered to importing countries. There are, however, weaknesses in some oil-products markets in many oil consuming countries and these necessitate some products being sold below " cost," so reducing the final overall profit level per barrel to less than a 1 dollar per bbl. figure. These calculations have, incidentally, been discussed with representatives of several of the companies involved. They do not accept the results yet; on the other hand, they cannot find any major component in the assumptions on which the calculations are based which would give an upward bias to the per barrel rate of profit.

Table 1

The Cost and Price of OPEC Oil and Oil Companies' Margins at Rotterdam 1976

| Country | Assumed Average A.P.I. Gravity [a] | Imports (mill. metric tons) [b] | % of Total Imported to Rotterdam | Average Value— $ per metric ton [c] | Adjusted Value— $ per Long Ton [d] | Average Freight Cost $ per L.T. [e] | Netback Value $ per L.T. [f] | Netback Value $ per bbl. [f] | Average Cost of Crude Oil to Company $/bbl. [g] | Company Margin $/bbl. |
|---|---|---|---|---|---|---|---|---|---|---|
| Libya | 40° | 1·21 | 2·4% | 98·20 | 99·80 | 2·28 | 97·52 | 12·57 | 12·48 | 0·09 |
| Nigeria | 34° | 8·80 | 17·3% | 99·28 | 100·90 | 3·61 | 97·29 | 13·00 | 12·24 | 0·76 |
| Iran | 32° | 14·49 | 28·5% | 96·96 | 98·54 | 8·05 | 88·91 | 12·23 | 11·31 | 0·92 |
| Saudi Arabia | 33° | 14·36 | 28·2% | 96·16 | 97·73 | 7·83 | 88·33 | 12·06 | 11·04 | 1·02 |
| Kuwait | 31° | 7·04 | 13·9% | 94·86 | 96·36 | 8·12 | 86·74 | 11·99 | 11·08 | 0·91 |
| United Arab Emirates | 38° | 4·90 | 9·7% | 99·87 | 101·50 | 7·80 | 92·07 | 12·08 | 11·56 | 0·52 |

Weighted Average of Company Margin $0·85 per Barrel [h]

*Notes*

*a* Based on the range of crude oils listed for each country in the list of " representative crude oils " per country in the *Petroleum Economist*.

*b* From the Dutch Department of Foreign Trade Statistics, Crude Oils Imports Section, Ministry of Economic Affairs, The Hague. The figures show the volume of crude oil imports for processing in the Netherlands. All such imports reach the Netherlands directly from the exporting countries via the port of Rotterdam.

*c* Calculated for each month from the value of the oil in Dutch gulden and converted into U.S. Dollar values at the middle-rate used each month by the *Foreign Trade Statistical Department—ibid.*

*d* Calculated for a ton of 1016·05 kilograms.

*e* Based on 1976 World Scale rates from the various ports of origin to Rotterdam. For the purposes of the calculation the following assumptions were made on the cost of the VLCCs used for transport: 50 per cent. of volume moved in company-owned tankers operating at WS 55·4 (the rate needed in 1976 to cover the trading and capital costs of an owned tanker—see *Financial Times*, January 24, 1977): 25 per cent. of volume in time-chartered tankers at an average WS rate of 50·0—the average of AFRA freight rates in 1976; and 25 per cent. of the volume in spot-chartered tankers at an average rate of WS 26—the average spot rates for the first half of 1976 as given by Shell Nederland in its publication *Het Tankeroverschot: wat doen we ermee?* (1977), p. 3. This gives a weighted average of WS 47·5 for average freight costs. This is a cost allowance which significantly exceeds the price of tanker transport on the open market and which, to that degree, therefore, overstates the allowance that should be made for freight costs in bringing oil to Rotterdam when viewed from the strictly economic standpoint. See M. A. Adelman, *The World Petroleum Market* (1972), pp. 113–114.

*f* This is calculated from the netback value per long ton by dividing by the appropriate factor for the assumed average API gravity of the crude oil imported from each country.

*g* Calculated from the cost of " Buy Back Oil " and/or " Equity Oil " as given for each country each month—in the list of " Representative Crude Oil Prices " in the *Petroleum Economist*. Where oil at both prices is still available an assumption of a 50/50 split in oil company supplies has been made. Note that " Buy-Back " oil, where available, is now priced at the State selling price, *i.e.* the price of oil to all buyers so that it gives no advantage to the integrated oil companies.

*h* Weighted by the share of each country in the total supply and allowing for losses in transit.

up to twice as much as profit made on the production of alternatives
to OPEC oil in all those countries where such profits are subject to
corporation (and other) taxes at rates which are normally of the
order of 50 per cent.

(b) *Companies' Downstream Investments Tied to OPEC Oil*

The profit situation is, in itself, a powerful motivation for continued
oil companies' collaboration with OPEC countries but, in addition,
there is another—and perhaps an even more important—component
which helps to determine oil company policies towards the new oil
supply and price situation. This is because the companies do not
*need* to make any new investment whatsoever to obtain and to handle
oil from OPEC countries. As far as the production of the oil, together
with the production development facilities required to maintain
and/or increase future output is concerned, the OPEC countries
themselves now largely take care of the investment required, given
their nationalisation of the companies' assets over the period since
1973.[3] And in so far as technical and managerial help is required
from the companies to keep production going and/or to develop new
potential, then the companies collect a fee—either in cash or in the
form of oil at specially discounted prices. These arrangements are in
themselves highly profitable, so adding yet another element favourable to companies' decisions to maintain or even increase their use of
OPEC oil in the world's markets.

A similar situation favouring such traditional flows of oil exists in
respect of the capital investments made by the companies in down-
stream facilities in the oil importing countries—especially in Western
Europe and Japan where almost 70 per cent. of all OPEC oil is used.
In these countries, as a result of the fivefold increase in oil prices
since 1973, demand for oil is running at about 35 per cent. below the
level that was hitherto expected to be in demand by 1977. However,
investment plans made by the oil companies in the early 1970s, in
anticipation of a continued upward trend of over 7 per cent. per
annum in oil demand in these countries, led to projects for terminals,
refineries, pipelines and distribution systems which are only now being
completed. As they come on line they necessarily add further to the
already existing over-capacity of the West European and Japanese oil
industries to handle supplies. Moreover, not only is this additional
capacity not really needed, in light of present and now expected

[3] The one remaining exception to this—at the beginning of 1977—was in the case of
Saudi Arabia, where the proposed nationalisation of ARAMCO had not by then been
effected. In this case, therefore, ARAMCO remained responsible for investment in new
producing facilities. This, however, seems unlikely still to be the case by the time this
paper is published.

future market demands, so increasing the unit costs of supplying oil products to the markets, but most of the new developments are also of a kind and in locations which are related directly to the earlier expectation of increased flows of crude oil from the OPEC countries. [4]

### (c) *Oil Companies must favour the Status Quo*

In light of these facts of oil life at the beginning of 1977, any greater than really necessary changes in the patterns of oil supply—such as would occur if there were too large and too rapid a rate of substitution of oil from traditional sources by oil or by alternative energies from elsewhere—would have a serious adverse effect on the economic viability of the oil companies' operations. This would, moreover, be in a situation in which the much reduced demand for oil has in itself already caused serious problems of retrenchment for the companies in their operations with much increased unit costs in processing and in distribution and, hence, a consequential squeeze of their down-stream profit margins.

In brief, the oil demand situation and outlook in those areas of the world most heavily dependent on OPEC oil, and the fact that the industry's infrastructure in these areas has been developed for hand-ling such OPEC oil, combine to counter any enthusiasm that there might have been on the part of the international oil companies for curtailing their demand for oil from the traditional exporting countries. In other words, oil companies' interests are again bound up with those of the member countries of OPEC. Thus, at the beginning of 1977 one can readily recognise the existence of a set of common interests between the oil producing countries on the one hand and the traditional international oil companies on the other. This situation, however, represents a continuation of the communality of interests which the two parties have shared now since the late 1960s,[5] and thus constitutes a main stabilising element in the changed world of oil power. Its importance for the medium-term future lies particularly in

---

[4] One example is Shell's £60 million crude oil import terminal on Anglesey. This was planned in the late 1960s in the expectation of a continued growth in oil demand in Northern England and a consequential need for a new deep water terminal to handle oil from 500,000 ton tankers. It was only opened in 1976 by which time it was clear that the new capacity was not needed because oil demand had declined. Moreover, the refinery which it was built to serve will increasingly run on oil from the North Sea. This will either be brought to the refinery by pipeline or by small tankers which cannot or which do not need to use the terminal. The terminal could thus become an expensive white elephant.

[5] Co-operation, amounting even to collusion, between the international oil companies and OPEC in the period since 1968 is described in P. R. Odell, *Oil and World Power* (1975). See especially Chap. 9, " The World of Oil Power since 1973." See also J. M. Blair, *The Control of Oil* (1977), for further discussion on this point.

respect of the effect that it must have on the degree to which major oil importing countries are able to develop alternatives to continued dependence of OPEC oil.

## II—INDEPENDENCE FROM OPEC OIL

For the purposes of our analysis we shall assume that a reduction in the degree of dependence on OPEC oil is, indeed, an accepted objective of the national policy-making of importing countries. This, indeed, appears to be the case in respect of countries as different in their economic and political structures as the United States, Brazil, India and the countries of the European Economic Community (EEC).

### (a) *Independence in the Developing World*

For developing countries like Brazil and India the battle for independence from imported oil is, paradoxically, least subject to the influences of the activities of the international oil companies. This is so in spite of the fact that all such countries have significant financial and technical problems to meet and to overcome in their efforts to develop alternative indigenous resources. This relative lack of influence by the oil companies arises because such countries are very strongly motivated, both politically and economically, to achieve energy independence. Such independence is, indeed, seen as an essential element in national policy-making for the immediate future.[6]

Both India and Brazil, which are leading examples of these countries, have, as it happens, a reasonable opportunity for achieving such a policy aim for both have recently had important off-shore discoveries of oil and/or gas along their extensive coastlines and are already in the process of developing them. Furthermore, given their national ownership of and/or control over the petroleum sector of their economies there is no question but that all domestic supplies of oil which become available will automatically be given an absolute position of preference over imported oil. Thus the important outstanding question is the degree to which such countries can successfully pursue policies of indigenous oil exploration and development given their technological and financial limitations. It is not, however, that such limitations are anything like an absolute barrier to such developments because the off-shore waters of the lower-latitudes offer quite modest technical and cost challenges compared with, say, the North Sea or the Atlantic coast of the United States. In the cases of India and Brazil both the water depths involved and the nature of

---

[6] See, *e.g. National Energy Balance,* Brazilian Ministry of Mines and Energy (1976).

the climatic environments are much less unfavourable for the exploitation of hydrocarbon resources.

As a result both India's National Oil Commission and Brazil's Petrobras have already been successful in developing their countries' off-shore resources and they both have continuing and increasing capabilities in this respect. They have, moreover, not unimportant possibilities for the expansion of such nationally-based petroleum developments as a result of help which has been or will be made available to them from State oil entities in other parts of the world. This includes the oil producing countries of the Communist world but help may be sought and given from the growing number of State-owned or State-controlled oil companies amongst West European countries (such as ERAP of France, Statoil of Norway and Hispanoil of Spain, etc.). And one must not exclude the possibilities of financial and even technical assistance for such developing countries from the State oil companies of the OPEC countries.

Although these possibilities do not entirely exclude future projects and ventures in developing countries like Brazil and India by the international oil companies, they obviously limit the openings quite severely. Moreover, they make necessary a willingness on the part of the oil companies to negotiate terms of involvement which will tend to isolate their activities locally almost entirely from their otherwise internationally integrated methods of working. Thus, for example, although Brazil has signed agreements with B.P., Shell and others of the international major companies for their involvement in off-shore exploration, any physical success on the part of the companies in finding oil and/or gas can only be turned into a commercial success within the context of what Petrobras and the Brazilian government wants.

In any such ventures the profitability of the international companies depends on national decisions, and the profitability can, moreover, exist only in Brazil itself which, like most other developing countries, has strong controls on the repatriation of profits and the export of capital assets. Such ventures on the part of the international oil companies are, thus, really high-risk ones—for not only do they have to accept the whole of the risk involved in the exploration and the development effort, but they also have to face the risk of a successful development then being effectively cut off from the rest of the company's international system. In light of this it seems highly unlikely that the international oil companies will be too anxious to get involved on such terms in too many developing countries—except in the case of the very few which, like Brazil, are large enough and with a great enough potential for development to more or less ensure a long-term future for a Shell or B.P. venture isolated from the rest of the companies' activities in the commercial and financial (if not the technical) sense. And, moreover, it must be remembered that the international companies are not even welcome in some countries which fall into this category—including, indeed, India itself.

#### (b) *Can the Oil Companies Trade OPEC Oil in the Third World?*

To a significant degree, therefore, the international oil companies will become cut off from involvement in energising the Developing World unless they are prepared to participate in ways which effectively eliminate most of the usually accepted benefits which flow from the internationally integrated activities of such companies. To make their position even worse, moreover, they seem likely also to be decreasingly involved in trade in oil with such countries—even in so far, that is, as the Developing World's countries still have to import oil from the petroleum exporting lands. On the one hand, the latter have taken over, or are in the process of taking over, the production and associated facilities of the companies. And, on the other hand, the oil importing countries have themselves been nationalising, or bringing under direct government control, the refining and distributing facilities developed in the most part to date by the international oil companies. As a result the necessary infrastructure for direct State-to-State trading between oil exporting and developing-world oil-importing countries is steadily being expanded. Moreover, and perhaps even more important, the political will required for the establishment and development of such activities is emerging—with an additional factor in this being the increasingly firmly expressed wishes of OPEC countries to serve the oil importing countries of the Third World in this way.[7] Before the end of the decade, therefore, it seems likely that the international oil companies will no longer have much opportunity to contribute to this particular part of the international movement of oil.

#### (c) *The United States Market and International Oil*

This much, however, the international companies must already be largely anticipating in their forward planning. Although it means the loss of business which has traditionally been highly profitable (given the oligopolistic position which the companies have generally enjoyed in such international trading activities in most of the developing world), it does nevertheless account for rather less than 10 per cent. of the companies' involvement with OPEC oil exports. Of the remaining 90 per cent. the United States accounted for about one-

---

[7] See, *e.g.* L. Valenilla, *Oil, the Making of a New International Economic Order* (1976), for a clear statement on this development in respect of Venezuela and its neighbouring countries of the Caribbean region.

fifth in 1976. However, because of the growing short-term imbalance between United States demand for oil and its own ability to produce the commodity, both the absolute amounts involved and their percentage contribution to the total quantity originating from OPEC countries, will grow: and this oil will continue to be handled mainly by the international oil companies and a number of other largely American-based enterprises. However, given the general level of acceptance already in the United States on the need to keep a close watch on the delivered prices of foreign oil because of suspicions that the companies otherwise generate oil-price rises for purposes of increasing profits; and, further, given the advent of a Democratic administration led by a President from a State which is heavily dependent on energy imports; then, the companies may well expect their profit margins in respect of their role as suppliers of foreign oil to the United States to be subject to close surveillance.[7a]

Moreover, the companies must also bear in mind that the United States government remains likely to insist on indigenous oil being given preference over imports even in situations where its production and distribution costs make it more expensive to deliver to markets than imported oil—in the interests of as high a degree of energy self-sufficiency as possible. This is a factor which is of particular importance in respect of Alaskan oil which, having been produced, must then be delivered to markets in the continental United States via the West coast. In terms not only of the quantities of oil involved and of its characteristics *vis-à-vis* patterns of oil product demand in California and other west-coast States, but also in terms of the supply/demand patterns of individual companies it seems as though there will be an infrastructure problem which prevents this oil being absorbed in United States markets at a cost below that of alternative patterns of supply based on imports. And this could possibly lead to a squeeze on the profit margins of the supplying companies concerned. The tentative indication by these companies that they might well prefer to sell Alaskan oil to Japan whilst, at the same time, importing OPEC oil into the eastern/southern parts of the United States, in the interests of optimising their own profit opportunities, has been roundly squashed by the new United States Administration which is not prepared to accept the higher-than-necessary degree of dependence on foreign oil that such supply schedule proposals involve.

### (d) *Western Europe and the International Oil Companies*

Thus, the disappearance of opportunities for profitable activities

---

[7a] This has been made clear in Presidents Carter's National Energy Plan (April1977). See Chap. 8 on the role of the government in energy planning.

by the international oil companies in the Developing World, plus the likelihood of increased constraints on their ability to make profits in selling foreign oil to the United States, make it all the more important that the companies concerned should try to defend and consolidate the greatly improved possibilities which they have had in recent years to generate revenues from their activities in exporting OPEC oil to Western Europe. Their opportunity in this respect arises, naturally, from the fact that these companies play a so much more dominant role in energising the Western European economy than in the case of the United States. Their contribution to the energy needs of Western Europe is more than 60 per cent. compared with a less than 40 per cent. contribution to the United States' energy system.

We have already demonstrated above how the international oil companies are now able to supply Western Europe with imported oil at a profit which is higher than that which could be earned as a result of any alternative oil supply patterns—given the limited extent to which the companies concerned have to make investments either in production facilities or in transportation and refining infrastructure in order to enable them to continue to supply oil from OPEC countries. This, however, is *only* possible in the case of Western Europe where the companies continue to enjoy the right to determine the region's oil supply pattern—a right which, as shown, is one that the companies do not enjoy either in respect of developing countries or of the United States: or, for that matter in the case of Japan which, as the single most important importing country of OPEC oil, insists on a high degree of national involvement in the decisions on oil supply patterns through MITI and other official entities associated with the Ministry of Trade. In other words, it is essentially only in Western Europe that the international oil companies still—in 1977—continue to enjoy the uninhibited right freely to trade the oil which they are committed to take, or which they prefer to take, from their OPEC suppliers at over 14 dollars per barrel (landed at a West European port). This is not only one of the main—or even perhaps the main—factor which ensures the maintenance of the OPEC system. It also has two other consequences which are specifically European in their importance. First, it means that Western Europe remains—and will continue to remain— unnecessarily over-dependent on insecure and expensive supplies of oil. Secondly, it means that there is an effective barrier to the rapid development of Western Europe's own indigenous energy sources— most notably those of North Sea oil and gas which constitute immediate, or near-immediate, and directly substitutable resources for imports of OPEC oil.

## III—North Sea Oil and Gas
## as Alternatives to OPEC Oil

The exploitation of North Sea oil and gas is placed in jeopardy because so many of the developmental decisions belong to exactly the same international oil companies which, as shown above, have a strong commercial interest in maintaining the level of oil imports to Western Europe. Or perhaps it would be more correct to say that the development of the North Sea's recoverable reserves has been placed in jeopardy because the companies are still allowed to take supply, production and refining decisions in Western Europe that are virtually free of relevant and meaningful government or inter-governmental control.

And matters must remain like this until action is taken by the governments, the EEC and other relevant institutions in Western Europe to secure the divorce of the indigenous oil and gas industry from this degree of external control over its affairs. Such a divorce can only become absolute as the international oil companies are required to take their decisions on the provision of energy in Europe in the light of the best interests of the countries of the region rather than in the context of maximising profits for the member companies of the international oil system together with the continued enrichment of their OPEC partners.

### (a) *The Resource Base—and its Exploitation*

Unfortunately, misunderstandings—arising partly out of deliberately misleading statements [8]—on the nature and probable size of the Western European off-shore oil and gas resource base, and on its possibilities for determining the medium-term outlook for the Western European energy economy, have detracted attention away from the fundamental issues involved in securing the full exploitation

---

[8] It is, for example, inconceivable that the October 1973 statement of Sir F. S. McFadzean, the Chairman of Shell, that the North Sea oil and gas could not possibly provide more than 15 per cent. of Western Europe's energy was made for other than political reasons; *viz.* to awake Europe from its lethargy over its energy supplies in the light of the deteriorating situation in the Middle East. Similarly with the comment in his Chairman's speech in April 1976 that Britain will not be energy self-sufficient for more than 10 years " because all the big North Sea fields have already been found." This seems to be a McFadzean effort to stop the United Kingdom relying on North Sea oil to solve its economic problems and is as unlikely as his 1973 statement to be based on the knowledge that Shell has about the probability of North Sea oil and gas production potential. It must, moreover, have been written only a short time before the Brae field was discovered in the British sector. This has been declared as a big field for certain and there is a high probability that it could prove to be the biggest field yet in the North Sea. It is the coincidence of events like this that make the major oil companies non-credible in their pronouncements about the North Sea. Such pronouncements indicate that the companies are motivated by other considerations—perhaps those related to their role in the international oil system.

of the already known resources of the North Sea fields. Thus, whilst much effort has been directed by the United Kingdom, Norway and the Netherlands to ways of toughening up the conditions under which the companies have been allowed to operate in the North Sea (so that the countries concerned could secure a larger share of the economic rent arising from the recovery of each barrel of oil or gas that the operating company decided to produce), no European country has yet taken any action which obliges the international companies to produce all the recoverable oil and gas from each field as quickly as possible to substitute for imported oil. And neither have the three producing countries (the Netherlands, Norway and the United Kingdom—in order of importance at the beginning of 1977), nor, indeed, any West European oil importing country, yet offered to guarantee profitability on the oil that could be produced by the oil companies as a means of getting them to develop their fields more intensively than they will do in the light of their own calculations of their optimal strategy in the open-market conditions of the West European energy economy.

Indeed, the very opposite has been happening—from two points of view. First, the main potential customers for North Sea oil—*viz.* France and West Germany—appear to view with suspicion the idea that they should underwrite or guarantee the production of high-cost North Sea oil. Instead, they prefer to keep their energy supply options orientated in two other directions: first, to the protection and the financing of extraordinarily expensive and very large programs of nuclear power development; and secondly, to special deals and or greatly enhanced trading relationships with the Arab oil producing countries of the Middle East seen, in terms of such trading potential, " as a natural extension of Western Europe." Thus, special relationships with these countries to try to secure essential oil supplies seem to be preferred to the alternative of special arrangements with the oil and gas producing countries of Western Europe.

Secondly, the oil and gas producing countries of Western Europe have not themselves done very much to persuade their neighbouring countries to change their policies in this respect. Indeed, the Netherlands, Norway and the United Kingdom all appear to be convinced that their resources of oil and gas are so scarce that they need to be protected against the rapacious demands of their neighbours. Such resources, these countries argue, are better left unproduced now for the sake of future generations. The validity of such arguments of inevitable scarcity are very much open to question and appear to emerge mainly out of too unquestioning an acceptance of oil companies' sponsored views on the size of the reserves (ignoring the fact that the companies do have a good commercial motivation to minimise rather than maximise their estimates as to how much oil is recoverable) and out of a serious misinterpretation on the nature of the resource base. Here we are not concerned with the validity or otherwise of the scarcity hypothesis as such, but only with it in terms of the impact that it has on the way governments look at the development decisions on North Sea oil and gas reserves.

(b) *The Optimal Development of North Sea Fields—Conflict between Companies and Governments*
A development decision which involves the installation of fewer platforms and/or fewer wells on a field than are needed to produce all the technically recoverable oil from a field in an economically relevant time-period is likely to be counter-productive in terms of national policy concern for the conservation of resources. In a multi-field province such as the North Sea there may be something to be said on grounds of conservation (if not of economics) for not producing some of the fields which have been discovered or, even better, for not discovering so many of the fields in the first instance. But neither on grounds of conservation nor on grounds of national economic considerations is there any reason to allow, let alone encourage, a field which is in the process of development not to be developed to its maximum possible extent—to a degree of development, that is, which lies beyond that which is optimal for the oil company.[9]

This is so because a decision which means the development of a field only up to the level of investment, and hence of production, which is optimal for the company concerned, instead of to the maximum possible level of recovery (at or approaching the level of the technically producible reserves), will have an adverse effect on the degree to which the exploitation of the oil benefits the economy of Western Europe. In the short-term, this will arise because jobs and profits which could be generated from oil development related activities will be less than they could be. In the medium- to the longer-term, the benefits to the country concerned will be reduced in terms of the size of the government revenues arising from oil production, of the contribution of the production of oil to the Gross National Product (GNP) and to the balance of payments. It also affects the degree to which oil imports to Western Europe can be substituted by North Sea production.

One must thus hypothesise an *inevitable* and *normal* divergence of international oil company and West European interests in the development decisions on North Sea oil production. On the one hand, one has to recognise the validity, from the oil company's point of

---

[9] The technico-economic background to this is presented in full in P. R. Odell and K. E. Rosing, *Optimal Development of the North Sea Oil Fields* (1976).

view, of the strictly commercial methods used by a company to calculate the optimum recoverability of the oil in light of competing alternative opportunities *at the international level* for its available investment funds. On the other hand, the European government has an interest in maximising the returns to the country from a field's development by ensuring that it contributes as much as possible to the growth of the GNP, to the creation of employment and a local as well as regional multiplier effect, to the balance of payments' situation, to government revenues and to substituting insecure supplies of foreign oil.

(c) *Government Action to Secure Optimal Developments of Indigenous Oil*

If a government's interest thus lies in maximising the recoverability of oil, then, in order to persuade the company concerned to do what the government believes to be necessary, flexibility in the arrangements for taxing the production of oil from the field and/or the possibility of the government contributing to the financing of the field's development will be necessary. Such a government contribution is necessary in order to create conditions in which the company concerned will be at least no worse off when it is obliged to install a production system which aims to maximise the degree to which the technically recoverable oil is recovered, than it will be if the company's preferred less complex system is employed, which—on the basis of the company's own evaluation of costs, prices and taxes—appears to provide it with its optimum investment strategy as far as the development of the field is concerned.

A full analysis by government of each of the several possibilities for developing each field is thus necessary in order to establish the " best " solution from the point of view of the government and country—and then there must be the means to " impose " this solution on the company concerned—though this means that the company has to be assured of a minimum acceptable level of return on its investment. Agreements between government and companies to produce this kind of result seem to be possible based on appropriate calculations of the contrasting risks and present values which are attached to the possibilities of the future production of oil from North Sea fields by the international companies, on the one hand, and by European government interests, on the other.

## IV—REDUCING UNCERTAINTY
### IN WESTERN EUROPE'S ENERGY OUTLOOK

It is only by divorcing decisions on the production of the North Sea's oil and gas reserves from the control mechanism of the international oil companies that there is a chance to reduce the uncertainties in the energy sector of the European economy to manageable proportions. This is because it is only in this way that it is possible to maximise the production of indigenous resources. The essential element in achieving this is an effective co-operative effort between governments of European countries and the international oil companies. Such co-operation ironically, however, can only be possible when the latter have been brought under control—in respect, that is, of eliminating their continuing opportunity to exercise, jointly with OPEC, the right to determine the supply and price of energy in Western Europe. Only when this has been done—within a necessarily interconventionist framework of the kind that Europe has built up over the years in respect of other, and less-important, sectors of the economy and as other countries are, as shown, already building up in respect of their oil sectors—will it be possible effectively to realise the opportunities for independence from the international oil system which have been generated by the oil and gas resources of the North Sea province—now generally accepted to be a major one by world standards. This is a development which is as important to the United Kingdom, Norway and the Netherlands—the important producing countries of Europe—as it is to the other nations in Western Europe, whose energy needs can also be more securely and more cheaply met out of the North Sea's resources than they can from their continued reliance on insecure and increasingly expensive oil from the OPEC countries.[10]

*A New Role for the Oil Companies in Western Europe*

This analysis of the European future of the international oil companies may be construed as a criticism of them. But this is not so, for these companies justifiably, from the point of view of their own interests, seek to achieve the most profitable set of operations possible. And they have to do this in relation to governments and to inter-governmental organisations around the world. On the one hand, they have to deal with OPEC which, in its wisdom and as a result of many years of experience with the international oil companies, has created very effective constraints on the companies' activities. OPEC has, however, also ensured the continuity of highly profitable operations

---

[10] A possibility finally recognised by the EEC at the very end of 1976 when the then out-going Commissioner for Energy, Mr. H. Simonet, at his final press conference on, December 22, 1976, spoke in terms of the Community developing a guaranteed market for British and other nations' oil in return for EEC participation in the decisions on the exploitation of the resources. See *Europe*, Nr. 2120 (New Series), December 23, 1976, pp. 6–7. More recently (July 1977), the new Energy Commissioner, Dr. G. Brunner, has suggested that a fixed upper limit should be set on the EEC's oil imports from OPEC, so implying guarantees for indigenous production.

for the companies. In Western Europe, on the other hand, it is the lack of the *right* sort of governmental constraints on the companies which enable the latter to pursue policies which lead to the inevitable divergence of what they do from what they should be doing for Europe's well-being and security. And this occurs without the companies, in their turn, really knowing if and how they are going to be able to make adequate profits out of activities in Western Europe.

In no way is this gap between governments and companies of more importance in 1977 than in respect of decisions which affect the speed and the degree of development of the North Sea's considerable resources of oil and gas. Too many of the province's known or expected recoverable reserves remain unnecessarily unexploited basically because the international oil companies and European governments have not yet found a *modus vivendi* which makes the development of them a top priority of common interest to both parties. As a result, the energy supply potential from the indigenous oil and gas resources of Western Europe remains much more limited than it need be, with the consequential dangers of a continued too high a degree of dependence on imported OPEC oil and/or the need for an economically unsustainable and environmentally unacceptable degree of development of nuclear power. The companies, in their turn, do not really know where they stand in relation to the medium-term development of the European energy market. Perhaps one way of clarifying the issues involved—such that appropriate solutions could then be sought—would be a European take-over of all the European-located subsidiaries of one of the American-based major international oil companies, say Exxon. Shares in the resultant large oil company— with producing, refining and marketing activities throughout the continent—could well be placed with Europeans (*en masse*) in order to form a kind of European Peoples' Oil Company (EPOC Ltd.). The efforts of this could then be centrally directed to ensuring that its activities maximise returns in and for Europe rather than, as hitherto, being employed to achieve what is acceptable to OPEC's member countries and in order to ensure as high as possible a rate of return on the investment involved for the benefit of the American parent company. For a sector as important as oil to the welfare of its inhabitants, West European policy towards the international oil companies and their activities cannot afford to be any the less interventionist and nationalistic than in the case of countries like Brazil—or the United States.

# THE ECONOMIC COMMUNITY
# OF WEST AFRICA

By

## T. O. ELIAS

### I—BEGINNINGS OF THE WEST AFRICAN
### ECONOMIC COMMUNITY

THE Treaty of Lagos establishing the Economic Community of West African States (ECOWAS for English-speaking and CEDEAO for French-speaking) was signed in Lagos on May 28, 1975, after 12 years of gestation. For it was in November 1963, some six months after the founding of the Organisation of African Unity in May of the same year, that, under the auspices of the United Nations Economic Commission for Africa, the Lagos Conference on Industrial Co-operation in West Africa was held. This first attempt at discussing possible economic co-operation was followed by the agreement to create an Interim Organisation with a view to the establishment of a Permanent Organisation for West African Economic Co-operation. The agreement was signed at Freetown on May 28, 1965, and was then followed, in October 1966, by the Niamey Conference on Economic Co-operation and, in April 1967, by the Accra Conference at which a document entitled " Articles of Association for the Establishment of an Economic Community of West Africa "[1] was signed (May, 1967). One of the provisions envisaged the setting up of an Interim Council of Ministers to which was entrusted the main task of preparing the draft treaty for the proposed Community.

The Interim Council of Ministers held its first and only meeting in Dakar in November 1967 when it was agreed that the inaugural meeting should be held soon after at the level of the Heads of State and Government, who should be approached for the purpose. Fortunately, a little earlier in the same months, the four Heads of State of the Organisation of Senegalese River States had met in Bamako and had recommended the creation of a regional grouping which should embrace the whole of West Africa. The Head of State of Mauritania was accordingly mandated to go on a mission to all the Heads of the 14 States of West Africa.

---

[1] Published in E/CN. 14/399, Annex IV. Reprinted in 6 *American Journal of International Law* (1967), pp. 776–781. See also H. M. A. Onitiri, " Towards a West African Economic Community," 5 *Nigerian Journal of Economic and Social Studies* (1963), pp. 27–53.

As a result of this mission, these Heads of State held a conference in April 1968 and the Protocol establishing the West African Regional Group was signed. There were two important decisions taken at the meeting: one was that Nigeria and Guinea should prepare priority studies of possible areas of co-operation between and among the member-States of the proposed community, and the other mandated Liberia and Senegal to prepare a draft treaty and an accompanying protocol on a customs union. Although the expert officials of both Nigeria and Guinea held two meetings, one in Lagos and another at Conakry in June and November, 1968, and submitted their report to the 14 States for study pending its consideration by the Interim Council of Ministers, the latter never met. It is not clear whether the Liberia-Senegal Study Committee also submitted its own report on the draft treaty and protocol on customs union. These worthwhile initiatives were thus frustrated and, between 1968 and 1972, the community idea was allowed to lapse.

Then, in April 1972, a fresh initiative was taken, this time by Nigeria and Togo. Both met and agreed to revive the project of establishing a West African economic community which would cut across linguistic and cultural barriers and would be based on a pragmatic approach. The aim was that " the door of the community would be left wide open so that other countries in the sub-region might join as and when they were ready." As a first step, a joint Nigeria-Togo official delegation had previously toured all the West African countries during July and August, 1973. The committee of expert officials of both countries thereafter prepared a detailed draft, which was later submitted to the 14 Heads of State and Government and tabled under the title of " The Evolution of a West African Economic Community " at their summit conference held in Lomé from December 10 to 15, 1973.

Dr. A. Adedeji, the leader of the Nigerian delegation to the Conference and Federal Commissioner for Economic Development and Reconstruction in Nigeria, pointed out in his opening address that the proposals placed before the conference were not final in any sense, but constituted a working paper which was subject to changes and modifications as the conference saw fit. The community was conceived as an organic entity which should be allowed to evolve over a number of years. The document appeared to be a continuation or even the culmination of the study assigned to Nigeria and Guinea at the 1967 session of the Monrovia conference in 1967. Dr. Adedeji said: " It must start modestly and achieve some successes. The following areas in which there is reasonable hope of achieving success—trade liberalisation, customs and immigration, industrial harmonisation, agriculture, monetary and financial matters, and infrastructural links

—have been identified in the document before you." [2] It is interesting to note the realism and caution which animated the draft proposals. No one was more aware of the problem of their undertaking than the officials themselves. Dr. Adedeji continued: " The reasons for the failures of the past attempts have been due to the fact that we have hitherto tried to build a closely-knit economic community when we have not yet acquired the experience of working closely together. We have adopted a ' wholistic ' approach which has required all the 14 countries to be members at one go and for all levels and types of economic co-operation to be embarked upon at the same time. . . . But we have now learnt our lessons. In all the countries we visited every one wanted pragmatism in our approach. Every one emphasised the need to identify areas of co-operation which are urgent and where we can achieve some measure of success." [3]

One of the results of the Togo conference in December 1973 was the meeting of official experts and jurists held in January 1974. At this meeting the draft (already considered in Lomé)—after full revision by the Nigeria and Togo experts appointed for the purpose— was tabled for further study and referred to a later meeting of officials held in Monrovia in January 1975. It was then finally agreed that Nigeria, Liberia, Togo and Dahomey should put the finishing touches to the various texts in readiness for the summit of Heads of State and Government scheduled for May 1975, at Lagos.

## II—Certain Problems Facing the Community

### (a) *The Colonial Heritage and its aftermath*

The first and probably the most important single hurdle that the Community has had to surmount has been the historical fact that all the 15 countries (the original 14 having been recently joined by Guinea-Bissau) have had a common experience of colonialism under British, French and in the case of the latest member of the fold, Portuguese rule. The creation of a common market for the 124 million people spread over 6,500,000 square kilometres of territory is certainly a huge task. Within the national boundaries populations are often too small, and incomes too low; it has been said by the United Nations that 16 out of the 25 countries classified as the least developed of the so called developing countries of the world are to be found in Africa.

The countries of West Africa have or had until recently, monetary systems and institutions linked to those set up in the colonial era; and, although there have been notable modifications in some of

---

[2] At p. 9 of the Address, Federal Government Printer, 1973.
[3] *Ibid.* p. 10.

them, the links to ex-colonial currencies are still strong in many cases. In the case of the four ex-British territories of Gambia, Sierra Leone, Ghana and Nigeria, there used to be a British West African Currency Board which issued a common currency linked to sterling.[4] In the closing years of the 1950s, each territory acquired independent currencies issued by their respective Central Banks which made its own clearing arrangements. Although the strength of the economy of each depends on its level of foreign-exchange reserves and its balance of payments, each country still maintains its sterling link since it is yet to become an international trading currency.

In the case of the ex-French countries the monetary system is very closely linked to the French franc.[5] The original *Colonies Françaises d'Afrique* (CFA), even in spite of the nominal change to *Communauté Financière Africaine*, enjoys a measure of guarantee of parity and convertibility of their respective local francs into their French equivalents at a fixed rate. Ivory Coast, Senegal, Upper Volta, Niger, Dahomey and Togo belong to the group of West African Monetary Union having one and the same Central Bank (BCEAO) between them; their foreign exchange reserves are kept in a deposit account at the French Treasury. In effect, France guarantees their foreign exchange commitments. More recently, however, there have been some changes. The Central Bank now has its headquarters in Dakar, and no longer in Paris, and up to 45 per cent. of the foreign exchange reserves could be held in other than French francs. It must be admitted that advantages of parity and convertibility with the French franc are so great that the Francophone African countries in West and Central Africa could be expected to break away from the system. Fortunately, no one expects them to do so, any more than the ex-British countries would be expected to give up sterling. The proposed West African economic Community is, therefore, being planned on realistic and flexible lines.

The co-existence of both the ex-British and the ex-French monetary systems, no doubt, have obvious disadvantages some of which ought to be removed or at least minimised by a new arrangement such as the proposed economic community envisages. The problem is that the artificially high level at which parity and convertibility with the French franc has kept the whole price structure higher in French-speaking than in their English-speaking neighbours. The results have

---

[4] The headquarters of the Board was located in London and the Accountant-General of Nigeria was the local Currency Officer. It was constituted in November 1912 " to provide for and to control the supply of currency to the British West African Colonies and Protectorates...."

[5] A useful introductory note, followed by a detailed bibliography is contained in L. B. Sohn, " Regional Groups in French-speaking Africa," I *Basic Documents of African Regional Organization* (1971), pp. 251–269, 271–307.

been a great increase in smuggling of goods across frontiers and also other trade distortions, especially in the case of cocoa, coffee, and oil palm for which French producers receive far higher prices from their local marketing boards than their ex-British counterparts.

It was towards removing these and similar economic and financial disadvantages that a series of meetings were held in Lagos in March, 1975, between the governors of the Central Banks from both groups in West Africa. It was agreed to set up a West African clearing system with a Secretariat in one of the Francophone States, probably Abidjan, in order to offset all intra-West African payments and settle the outstanding balances in a mutually acceptable hard currency at regular intervals.[6]

## (b) *Regional Economic Sub-Groups*

There is a regional economic sub-group, *La Communauté Economique de l'Afrique de l'Ouest* (CEAO) of which account must also be taken. It replaced *L'Union Douanière des Etats de l'Afrique de l'Ouest* (UDEAO), which was a customs union formed on the eve of independence in 1959 grouping Senegal, Ivory Coast, Mali, Upper Volta, Niger and Mauritania. Despite the 1966 revision of the terms of the customs union, it became clear to the member-States that it had failed to level their economic disparities or to promote economic growth. A re-fashioned CEAO was finally instituted in Abidjan in 1973 consisting of the same group of States with the stated aim, in Article 3, " to promote harmonised and balanced development of member-States' economies in order to improve the living standards of their citizens." The completion of the formation of the customs union is to be achieved by 1986 when the six States will have established a common external tariff with regard to imports from third countries. As most of the institutions established within the framework of the organisation will be found in the ECOWAS arrangements on a larger and more detailed scale, we need not set them out here. The volume of intra-community imports and exports as between the member-States is growing steadily, although some of the poorer members like Upper Volta and Mali benefited reasonably well from the richer and better-endowed ones like Ivory Coast and Senegal, which obtained a good measure of compensation from the Community Development Fund. When the Dakar conference of Senegal River States decided to send its mission to all the West African territories in November 1967, so that a larger and wider customs union could be established, they showed considerable foresight and courage. By 1975, it was no longer possible for an exclusively French-speaking

---

[6] This has since been formalised into a Community Committee of West African Central Banks by Art. 38 of the Treaty.

economic grouping of States to exist. The trend all over West Africa was clearly in the direction of both the English-speaking and the French-speaking groups of States coming together inevitably and irresistibly into one customs union.[7]

But it must not be thought that ECOWAS would be incompatible with existing sub-groupings, like the Entente, the Organisation of Senegal River States, the River Niger Commission,[8] and the Chad Basin Commission; or bilateral institutions or arrangements like the Liberia-Sierra Leone, Ghana-Togo, Nigeria-Niger, Niger-Dahomey Joint Commissions, which have all been set up on a bilateral basis for the promotion of specific projects of mutual assistance and development. Their purposes and objectives are not inconsistent with those envisaged for the all-embracing economic community.

It is also useful to mention in parenthesis that, supplementing all the various bilaterial and multilateral economic and financial efforts within West Africa which we have outlined above, is the encouraging start already made by business communities in 11 countries in the region by establishing the Federation of West African Chamber of Commerce, Industry, Agriculture and Mines. This, like ECOWAS, cuts across cultural and linguistic boundaries, and it is rapidly growing.

## (c) *Summary of the Prelude to ECOWAS*

The foregoing analysis is sufficient to the nature of the problems with which the West African States are confronted in their endeavour to create an all-embracing economic community. It points to the need for them to pool their resources in order to develop their agricultural and industrial potentialities with a view to raising the standards of living of their peoples. As one of the consequences of colonial administrative and economic arrangements over fairly long periods, the patterns of development of the several countries have been vertical rather than horizontal. The various units were developed as more or less disparate entities the economies of which were tied to London and to Paris. Until after independence, there was little intra-State trade, little attempt at co-operation and co-ordination of their economic efforts across frontiers.

---

[7] Both the Prime Minister of Senegal speaking for President Senghor and President Houphouet-Boigny when replying to General Gowon's address at the Lagos Conference, urged that membership of ECOWAS be made open to other African States because of the wider economic and other ties involved. It is clear, however, that membership is restricted to West Africa by Article 2 of the Treaty which provides that " the member-States shall be the States that ratify this Treaty and such other West African States as may accede to it." See *Daily Times* (Nigeria), May 29, 1976, p. 2.

[8] T. O. Elias, " The Berlin Treaty and the River Niger Commission," 57 *American Journal of International Law* (1963), pp. 873–882.

We can, therefore, see why both the English-speaking and the French-speaking States of West Africa have in recent years been coming together in various groupings in order to increase mobility of productive resources by forging infrastructural links to facilitate communications and mutual co-operation. They will, no doubt, continue to work with Europe and other areas of the world for the development of their economies, but the need for a much greater economic self-reliance has never been more urgent or more necessary. No longer must they look upon themselves as perpetual suppliers of raw materials for the factories of Europe and America. The growing interdependence of the world especially in the economic sphere, requires that the various parts of the world should develop along mutually beneficial and economically competitive lines. As the present writer once observed: " Whereas about 78 per cent. of the export trade of the developing countries is with the industrialised ones, only 22 per cent. is with each other. This means that they are becoming more and more dependent on the industrialised countries for their foreign trade, whether as suppliers of raw materials for their industries or as markets for their manufactured goods. There can be no doubt that the overall expansion of trade among the developing countries is much slower than the rate of growth of the trade between the developed ones." [9]

It is against this background that we may now turn to a considera-tion of the treaty so painstakingly prepared over many years and finally signed at Lagos by all of the 15 Heads of State and Govern-ment in West Africa. Eleven Heads of State and four Heads of Government attended the two-day conference held in the Federal Palace Hotel on May 27 and 28, 1975. The treaty has rightly been described abroad as one of " the most ambitious projects of its kind in the world " [10] and, in West Africa itself as " by far the most momentous and far-reaching economic treaty since its component parts won independence." [11]

In their final communique,[12] the Heads of State and Government and the plenipotentiaries affirmed their " determination to make the Community a pragmatic, dynamic and effective institution which will take into account the realities prevailing in the member-States "; they recognised the existence of inter-governmental organisation and other economic groupings within the region; they expressed their " determination for the early ratification of the treaty so that the aims

[9] See T. O. Elias, " The Association Agreement between the European Economic Community and the Federal Republic of Nigeria," 2 *Journal of World Trade*, Nr. 2, March–April 1968, pp. 189–209, at p. 204.
[10] *The Times* (London), June 30, 1975, Supplement on West Africa, p. IV.
[11] *Daily Sketch* (Nigeria), May 27, 1975, Editorial page.
[12] See *Daily Times* (Nigeria), May 29, 1975, p. 3.

and objects could be realised without delay "; they recognised " the need to accelerate the preparation of the protocols of the implementation of the present treaty," and entrusted the Governments of Nigeria and Togo to take all necessary measures towards that end.[13]

### III—The Main Characteristics of ECOWAS

The principal Institutions of the Community are as follows:

(a) *The Authority of Heads of State and Government.* This is the principal governing institution of the Community, responsible for the general direction and control of the performance of the executive functions of the Community, for its progressive development and the achievement of its aims. It is the supreme body and, therefore, its decisions and directions are binding on all the institutions of the organisation. It meets once a year and regulates its own procedures, including convening of meetings and annual rotation of the office of chairman. All the decisions and directions of the Authority and of the Council are disseminated according to procedures determined by the Authority.[14] This emphasis in Article 7 of the Treaty on the supremacy of the Community over the Council of Ministers seems necessary in order to avoid any situation in which the Council might take the Authority for granted by regarding a resolution of its own as binding upon member-States merely because it has been adopted by the Council of Ministers.[15]

(b) *The Council of Ministers.* This consists of two representatives of each member-State and is responsible for keeping under review the functioning and development of the Community in accordance with the Treaty, making recommendations to the Authority on policy matters aimed at its efficient and harmonious development, giving directions to all subordinate institutions of the Community, exercising such other powers conferred on it and performing such other duties assigned to it by the Treaty. Subject to any contrary direction of the Authority, the Council's decisions and directions are binding upon all subordinate institutions of the Community. It meets twice a year, and one of such meetings is held immediately preceding the annual meeting of the Authority. It may convene extra-ordinary meetings.

---

[13] In the preamble, be it noted, is recalled the Declaration of African Co-operation, Development and Economic Independence adopted by the Tenth Assembly of Heads of State and Government of the Organisation of African Unity (OAU) at Addis Ababa in 1973.

[14] Arts. 4, 5 and 7 of the Treaty.

[15] This happened once under the OAU: See T. O. Elias, " Legality of the OAU Council of Ministers' Resolution on Rhodesia in December 5, 1965," 3 *Nigerian Law Journal*, 1969, pp. 1–12.

Like the Authority, it regulates its own procedures, including the annual [16] rotation of the office of chairman.

Any objection which a member-State may raise against a proposal intended for a decision by the Council must be forwarded to the Authority for a ruling.[17]

(c) *The Executive Secretariat (under an Executive Secretary)*. The Executive Secretary is appointed by the Authority for a four-year term and is eligible for only one further term. He is removable from office on the recommendation of the Council of Ministers. The Executive Secretary is the principal executive officer of the Community, and is assisted by two Deputy Executive Secretaries appointed by the Council of Ministers. A Financial Controller and other Secretariat officials are also appointed by the Council. There are staff regulations to govern the conditions of service of all the Secretariat officials, including the Executive Secretary, and these are made by the Council.

In the seventh paragraph of Article 8 is to be found a clear restriction on this freedom of appointment of the Secretariat staff: " In appointing officers to the Executive Secretariat due regard shall be had, subject to the paramount importance of securing the highest standards of efficiency and technical competence, to the desirability of maintaining an equitable distribution of appointments to such posts among citizens of the member-States." [18] This is a key provision of the Treaty because upon its faithful observance may depend the success or failure of the Secretariat or, indeed, of the Community itself.

The Executive Secretary is responsible for the day-to-day administration of the Community and all its institutions, including their servicing and assisting with the performance of their functions.[19] It keeps the functioning of the Community under continuous examination, reports the results to the Council, submits reports of all Authority and Council activities to all sessions of both bodies, and undertakes " such work and studies and perform such services relating to the aims of the Community as may be assigned to him by the Council of Ministers and also make such proposals thereto as may assist in the efficient and harmonious functioning and development of the Community."

---

[16] There would seem to be a slip here, since at least two meetings a year are envisaged and there may be more, unless it is intended that the same chairman is to preside at all meetings every year.

[17] Arts. 4 and 6.

[18] These provisions should be compared with those in the United Nations Charter, Art. 101 and the OAU Charter, Art. XVIII.

[19] The Executive Secretary and all the Secretariat staff " owe their loyalty entirely to the Community."

(d) *The Tribunal of the Community*. This has two main functions:
(i) To ensure the observance of law and justice in the interpretation
of the provisions of the Treaty; and (ii) To settle such disputes as may
be referred to it in accordance with Article 56 of the Treaty, which
provides that " any dispute that may arise among the member-States
regarding the interpretation or application of the Treaty shall be
amicably settled by direct agreement." It is further provided that, in
the event of failure to settle such disputes, the matter may be referred
to the Tribunal by a party to such disputes and " the decision shall be
final." [20] It remains to be seen the exact organisation and powers of
the Tribunal when the details are known.

There are two notable departures from the usual formula: the first
is that either party to the dispute may go to the Tribunal, and the
second is that the decision is final as between the parties to the
particular dispute.

(e) *The Technical and Specialised Commissions*. The fifth-named
group of institutions of the Community comprises the following four
Technical and Specialised Commissions: (i) The Trade, Customs,
Immigration, Monetary and Payments Commission; (ii) the Industry,
Agriculture and Natural Resources Commission; (iii) The Transport,
Telecommunications and Energy Commission; (iv) The Social and
Cultural Affairs Commission. The powers and functions of the four
commissions and of any others that may subsequently be established
by the Authority for other specific purposes are as set out in the
Treaty and in the various protocols to be affixed to the Treaty.

Under Article 9, each commission consists of representatives
designated one each by the member-States, and these representatives
may be assisted by advisers. Each commission is under a duty to
submit from time to time reports and recommendations through the
Executive Secretary to the Council of Ministers either on its own
initiative or upon the request of the Council or of the Executive
Secretary. Each commission may perform such other functions as
may be assigned to it under the Treaty. These commissions may
meet as often as necessary for the proper discharge of their functions
and have the power to determine their own procedures.[21]

An External Auditor is provided for in Article 10 to function
outside the Executive Secretariat and the Technical and Special

---

[20] Arts. 11 and 56. Compare the Court of Justice of the European Economic Community in this respect. It seems that the Tribunal of the Community of ECOWAS looks
like the Court of Arbitration set up to settle disputes between European Economic
Community (EEC) members and those of the African Associated States.

[21] There are Committees of the Community which are provided for in Arts. 38
(Committee of West African Central Bank) and 39 (Capital Issues Committee). These
will be discussed later.

Commissions. He is appointed and removable by the Authority on the recommendation of the Council of Ministers which is given the power to make regulations governing the terms and conditions of service as well as the powers of the External Auditor.

It is not clear how an external auditor will be able to cope with the huge and complicated organisation which ECOWAS promises to become in a relatively short time. It could not be long before each of the technical and specialised commissions would require an auditor for its accounts. Other institutions of the Organisation might soon follow suit.

## IV—AIMS AND OBJECTIVES OF THE COMMUNITY

These are set out with reasonable fullness in Article 2 of the Treaty as follows: " It shall be the aim of the Community to promote co-operation and development in all fields of economic activity, particularly in the fields of industry, transport, telecommunications, energy, agriculture, natural resources, commerce, monetary and financial questions and in social and cultural matters for the purpose of raising the standard of living of its peoples, of increasing and maintaining economic stability, of fostering closer relations among its members and of contributing to the progress and development of the African continent."

In order to achieve these purposes the Community is enjoined to ensure *by stages*: (i) the elimination as between the member-States of customs duties and other charges of equivalent effect in respect of the importation and exportation of goods; (ii) the abolition of quantitative and administrative restrictions on trade among the member-States; (iii) the establishment of a common customs tariff and a common commercial policy towards third countries; (iv) the abolition as between the member-States of the obstacles to the free movement of persons, services and capital; (v) the harmonisation of the agricultural policies and the promotion of common projects in the member-States notably in the fields of marketing, research and agro-industrial enterprises; (vi) the implementation of schemes for the joint development of transport, communication, energy and other infrastructural facilities as well as the evolution of a common policy in these fields; (vii) the harmonisation of the economic and industrial policies of the member-States and the elimination of disparities in the level of development of member-States; (viii) the harmonisation, required for the proper functioning of the Community, of the monetary policies of the member-States; (ix) the establishment of a Fund for Co-operation, Compensation and Development; and (x) such other activities calculated to further the aims of the Community as the member-States may from time to time undertake in common.

These grandiose schemes have, in the words of the penultimate preambular paragraph to the Treaty itself, as the ultimate objective the " accelerated and sustained economic development of their States and the creation of a homogeneous society, leading to the unity of the countries of West Africa, by the elimination of all types of obstacles to the free movement of goods, capital and persons." This idea is, however, tempered by a note of realism sounded by the Treaty provision itself which at the very outset emphasises that the various items listed will be tackled stage by stage, not all at once, not in any pre-ordained order of priority, but attempted singly or in groups after careful deliberation and conscious planning.

## V—The Basis of the Customs Union

The Community envisages a gradualist approach to the establishment of a Customs Union within a transitional period of 15 years beginning immediately after the coming into force of the Treaty.[22] This takes place when a minimum of seven signatory States have ratified it " in accordance with the constitutional procedures applicable for each signatory State." [23] Within the 15-year period, customs duties or similar charges on imports must be eliminated. As a further incentive towards liberalisation of trade, quota, quantitative or similar restrictions or prohibitions and administrative obstacles to trade among the member-States must also be removed. There will be introduced a common customs tariff in respect of all goods imported into the Community from third countries.

During the first two years, a member-State may not be required to reduce or eliminate import duties, nor may impose any new duties and taxes or increase existing ones, and all information on import duties must be submitted to the Executive Secretariat for study by the relevant institutions of the Community. Between the end of this two-year period and the next eight years, member-States must progressively reduce and ultimately eliminate import duties, due account being taken of the effects of such reduction or elimination on the revenue of member-States concerned.[24]

After the end of this period of eight years, and during the last five years of the transitional period, member-States agree to introduce a common customs tariff in respect of all goods imported into the Community from third States, and gradually abolish existing differences in their external customs tariffs. Common customs and statistical nomenclatures will also be established for all the member-States by the Trade, Customs, Immigration, Monetary and Payments Commission.[25]

[22] Art. 11.   [23] Art. 62.   [24] Art. 13.   [25] Art. 14.

Goods will be accepted for Community tariff treatment if they originate in one member-State and have been consigned to another member-State; but they must be primary products or wholly produced by enterprises wholly owned by a member-State or owned by such a State to the extent of at least 51 per cent. although goods partly produced in third countries may be accepted if the conditions previously laid down by the Community have been complied with.[26]

The Council of Ministers is required to keep under review the question of deflection of trade and its causes, to take such decisions as are necessary to deal with it. If such deflection results in detriment to a member-State in consequence of the abusive reduction or elimination of duties and charges levied by another member-State, the Council must study the question and arrive at a just solution.[27]

Within three years that the Treaty comes into force, all internal taxes and other internal charges for the protection of domestic goods must be eliminated and within 10 years of the Treaty's coming into force, all revenue duties imposed for the same purpose must similarly be progressively eliminated.[28] The same 10-year period is set for the removal of all quota restrictions or prohibitions.[29] Member-States must not impose fiscal charges upon goods imported from any other member-State in excess of those charged on domestic goods for their effective protection.

## VI—RIGHT OF ESTABLISHMENT
### AND SERVICES WITHIN THE COMMUNITY

In order to encourage the free movement of persons as a complement to that of goods within the Community, it is necessary to liberalise the existing legal and administrative regulations regarding movement across frontiers.

Under Article 27, member-States are to enter into agreements with one another to exempt Community citizens from having to possess visitors' visas and residence permits. Such agreements are to provide that Community citizens have the right to work and to undertake commercial and industrial activities within the territories of the member-States. Hitherto citizens from member countries have required visas and residence permits to visit and stay in some West African countries. In some cases, notably Ghana, the setting up of enterprises by citizens from other countries within the region has been barred by law. In Nigeria, the law on indigenous enterprises grants an exemption to citizens from all OAU member-States on a basis of reciprocity.

Another related provision of the Treaty is contained in Article 31

---

[26] Art. 15.     [27] Art. 16.     [28] Art. 17.     [29] Art. 18.

according to which member-States are free to exchange skilled, professional [30] and managerial personnel in the operation of projects within the Community. They are also expected to provide places for training in their educational and technical institutions for Community citizens. They can engage, where appropriate, in joint development of projects, including those that entail the execution of complementary parts in different member-States. Under Article 32, the Council of Ministers may, as a result of their periodic reviews or otherwise, make recommendations for the taking of remedial measures to rectify or ameliorate disparities in the levels of industrial development as between member-States.

## VII—Co-operation in Agricultural and Natural Resources

In this very important area, the Community relies heavily on the Industry, Agriculture and Natural Resources Commission. Member-States undertake to work towards the harmonisation of their internal and external agricultural policies in their relations with one another, and to co-operate in the development of their natural resources, especially in agriculture, forestry, animal husbandry and fisheries. They also undertake to exchange information on experiments, results of research being carried on in their respective territories and on existing rural development programmes. It is also provided that they should formulate, as appropriate, joint programmes for both basic and in-service training in existing institutions. [31]

Member-States also undertake to take all measures necessary for the creation of a common policy especially in the fields of research, training, production, processing and marketing of the products of agriculture, forestry, animal husbandry and fisheries. The Commission is, as soon as possible after its establishment, to meet to make recommendations to the Council of Ministers for the harmonisation and exploitation of the natural resources of the member-States. [32]

## VIII—Co-operation in Monetary and Financial Matters

The Trade, Customs, Immigration, Monetary and Payments Commission has responsibility, among other things, for (i) making recommendations on the harmonisation of the economic and fiscal

---

[30] The difference between the English-speaking and the French-speaking States in professional fields like law makes an interchange of personnel a difficult matter until the citizens from both acquire the necessary competence later.

[31] Arts. 33 and 34.

[32] Art. 35.

policies of the member-States; (ii) giving its constant attention to the maintenance of a balance-of-payments equilibrium in the member-States; (iii) examining developments in the economies of the member-States.[33] All its recommendations go to the Council of Ministers.

As regards the settlement of payments between member-States, Article 37 provides that the Commission shall make recommendations to the Council of Ministers on the establishment, in the short term, of bilateral systems for the settlement of accounts between the member-States and, in the long term, of a multilateral system for the Community as a whole.

A Committee of West African Central Banks consisting of the Governors of the various central banks of the member-States or such other persons as may be designated by the member-States, has been established for the purpose of overseeing the system of payments within the Community. It is to be recalled, as explained earlier, that the Francophone countries do not yet all have their own central banks, and that the CEDEAO members share only one between them. The provision for alternative representation by designation is, therefore, a necessary one. The Committee idea has, as we have also seen, arisen from the first informal meeting of bank representatives which was held in March, 1975, in Lagos.

The Committee is to make recommendations to the Council of Ministers from time to time on the operation of the clearing system of payments and on other monetary issues of the Community.[34]

In this type of organisation, the provisions made in respect of movement of goods, persons and services must be completed by another relating to movement of capital and capital issues. There is accordingly established, under Article 39, a Capital Issues Committee consisting of a representative, designated by a member-State, who is a person with financial, commercial, banking or administrative experience or qualifications.

In the exercise of its functions, the Committee shall: (i) seek to achieve the mobility of capital within the Community through the interlocking of any capital markets and stock exchanges; (ii) ensure that stocks and shares floated in the territory of a member-State are quoted on the stock exchange of the other member-States; (iii) ensure that nationals of a member-State are given the opportunity of acquiring stocks, shares and other securities or otherwise investing in enterprises in the territories of other member-States; (iv) establish a machinery for the wide dissemination in the member-States of stock exchange quotations of each member-State; (v) organise and arrange the quotation of prices, timing, volume and conditions of

---

[33] Art. 36.           [34] Art. 38.

issue of securities of new enterprises in the member-States; (vi) ensure the immediate flow of capital within the Community through the removal of controls on the transfer of capital among the member-States in accordance with a time-table to be determined by the Council of Ministers; (vii) seek to harmonise the rates of interest on loans prevailing in the member-States so as to facilitate the investment of capital from a member-State in profitable enterprises elsewhere within the Community. The Capital Issues Community will determine the movement within the Community of all capital other than that of the member-States and of their citizens.

## IX—INFRASTRUCTURAL LINKS IN THE FIELDS OF TRANSPORT AND COMMUNICATIONS, ENERGY AND MINERAL RESOURCES

In order to improve and expand their existing transport and communication links [35] and to establish new ones so as to promote greater movement of persons, goods and services within the Community, member-States undertake to evolve common transport and communication policies. These will include the formulation of plans for a comprehensive network of all-weather roads traversing the territories of the member-States.[36] The Transport, Telecommunications and Energy Commission, which will be in charge of all these, will do the same to railways and to shipping and international waterways within the Community. Member-States undertake to do their utmost to form multinational shipping companies for both maritime and river navigation.

They also undertake to form a merger of their national airlines in order to promote efficiency and profitability in the air transportation of passengers and goods within the Community. Efforts will be directed towards the co-ordination of the training of their nationals and the standardisation of their equipment.

The various national telecommunications networks will be reorganised and improved in order to meet the standards required for international traffic. The Commission will ensure the gradual establishment of Pan-African Telecommunications network through the creation of links for the economic and social development within the Community fostered by the mobilisation of national and international financial resources. Steps will also be taken to achieve speedier, cheaper and more frequent postal services within the Com-

---

[35] Arts. 40–48.

[36] ECOWAS should undertake to strengthen its road links with such great projects as the Lagos trans-Sahara and the Lagos to Mombasa highways connecting with the Maghreb States and the East African Community States.

munity. The Commission will in this connection establish a system of postal remittances and preferential tariffs which are more favourable than those envisaged by the Universal Postal Union.

The Commission will promote consultation on and co-ordination of the policies and activities of the member-States in the field of energy and mineral resources.

It must be recalled that the OAU has done some spadework in many of these fields through the studies undertaken by its various committees within the past 10 years.

## X—SOCIAL AND CULTURAL MATTERS

Essential as these are, the Treaty rightly contains a somewhat summary provision in Article 49 to the effect that the special Commission established on the subject should examine ways of increasing exchange of social and cultural activities among the Community members and of developing them, provide a forum for consultation generally on social and cultural matters, and make necessary recommendations to the Council of Ministers.

## XI—FUND FOR CO-OPERATION, COMPENSATION AND DEVELOPMENT

A Fund of this name is established [37] and will derive its sources from member-States' contributions to be determined in accordance with the Ministerial Council's schedule, from income from Community enterprises, from receipts from bilateral and multilateral sources as well as other foreign sources, and also from subsidies and contributions of all kinds and from all sources duly authorised and approved by the Community. A Protocol annexed to the Treaty will contain the details relative to the method of determining the members' contributions, the regulations governing the payment and the currencies in which the contributions are to be affected, the operation, organisation, management, status of the funds and matters related and incidental thereto. [38]

According to Article 52, the Fund will be used to finance Community projects as well as to provide compensation to member-States which have suffered losses as the result of the location of Community enterprises or of the application of measures for the liberalisation of trade. The Fund will also be used to guarantee foreign investments made in pursuance of the promotion of the harmonisation of industrial policies and to provide appropriate means to facilitate the sustained mobilisation of internal and external financial resources for the Community and its members. Finally, the

---

[37] Art. 50.

[38] Art. 51.

Fund will be used to promote development projects in the less developed member-States of the Community.

This is a key provision of the Treaty and it is specifically designed to remove doubts and anxieties of the smaller and less developed member-States of the Community, while at the same time attempting to do real equity by providing reasonable compensation for the richer ones that will suffer losses as a result of the reduction of duties and other concessions made to favour the former. The whole scheme of the Treaty may prove to depend on the satisfactory functioning of the delicate complementary system of equitable adjustments.

## XII—The Community Budget

Different and distinct from the Fund is the Budget. Under Article 53 on Financial Provisions, the Budget will have chargeable to it all expenditures of the Community other than those in respect of the Fund. The draft annual budget must be prepared by the Executive Secretary and approved by the Council of Ministers which will determine the respective amounts of the annual contributions payable by each member-State as well as the other sources of contribution. Special budgets may be established to meet extraordinary expenditures of the Community. A Protocol will set out the method by which members' contributions are to be determined and the currencies in which the contributions will be paid.[39] There is statutory undertaking that each member-State will pay its annual contributions regularly. The penalty for failure to pay the annual contribution is suspension from participation in the activities of the institutions of the Community. There is, however, a dispensation where a member-State is in arrears for reasons caused by public or natural calamity or exceptional circumstances that greatly affect its economy. Suspension, where it is to be imposed, requires a resolution of the Authority of the Community.

Financial Regulations will be established by the Council of Ministers for the application of the provisions relating to the Fund and to the Budget.

## XIII—Relations with Other Regional Associations and Third Countries

In the introductory part of the present study, we have referred to this matter more than once. Conscious of its importance, the Founding Fathers of the Community have made the following provisions in Article 59: (1) Member-States may be members of other regional or sub-regional associations, either with other member-States or non-

---

[39] Art. 54.

member-States, provided that their membership of such associations does not derogate from the provision of this Treaty.[40] (2) The rights and obligations arising from agreements concluded before the definitive entry into force of this Treaty between one or more member-States on the one hand, and one member-States and a third country on the other, shall not be affected by the provisions of this Treaty. (3) To the extent that such agreements are not compatible with this Treaty, the member-State or States concerned shall take all appropriate steps to eliminate the incompatibilities established. Member-States shall, where necessary, assist each other to this end and shall, where appropriate, adopt a common attitude. (4) In applying the agreements referred to in paragraph 1 of this Article, member-States shall take into account the fact that the advantages accorded under this Treaty by each member-State form an integral part of the establishment of the Community and are thereby inseparably linked with the creation of common institutions, the conferring of powers upon them and the granting of the same advantage by all the other member-States.

There are three important principles enshrined in this provision. The first is the over-riding principle that membership of any regional or sub-regional association must not in any way derogate from the provisions of the Treaty. It therefore follows that rights arising from and obligations assumed under treaties or agreements setting up bilateral or multilateral institutions like CEAO and WARG are automatically void. Secondly, rights and obligations arising from treaties or agreements between one or more member-States on the one hand and one member-State and a third State on the other are not affected by the Treaty provisions, provided that such treaties or agreements have been concluded *before* the Treaty comes into force. If there is any incompatibility between such treaties or agreements and the Treaty, the member-States concerned must take necessary steps to eliminate it, if necessary by the adoption of a common attitude. Thirdly, stress is laid on the importance of the mutuality of the rights and obligations arising from membership of the Community. It would seem to follow that the provision must be deemed not to affect member-States, membership of the African, the Caribbean and the Pacific (ACP) group of States and the EEC under the Lomé Convention signed on February 28, 1975, in Togo and brought into force on April 1, 1976.[41]

---

[40] Art. 103 of the United Nations Charter prescribes that in the event of a conflict between the obligations of United Nations membership and those imposed by any other international agreement, the Charter obligations prevail.

[41] The ACP, a 46-nation Third-World bloc, has a joint agreement with the EEC on trade, aid and co-operation. The objectives of the group include: (a) To ensure the reali-

Finally, it is to be recalled that Article 3 of the ECOWAS Treaty enjoin member-States to " make every effort to plan and direct their policies with a view to creating favourable conditions for the achievement of the aims of the Community " and, in particular, " to take all steps to secure the enactment of such legislation as is necessary to give effect " to the Treaty. Thus, this positive obligation to assure the efficacy of the organisation is counterbalanced by the negative provision of Article 59 not to frustrate or hamper its effectiveness and integrity.

## XIV—MISCELLANEOUS PROVISIONS

Under this heading may be mentioned the provision of Article 60 which endows the Community, as an internal organisation, with legal personality in respect of the discharge of its functions under the Treaty.[42] The Community has the capacity to acquire, hold or dispose of movable or immovable property and to be represented by the Executive Secretary in the exercise of its legal personality.

The privileges and immunities to be granted to the officials of the Community at its headquarters and in the member-States are the same as those accorded to diplomatic persons under international diplomatic law [43]; and the same apply to the Community's Secretariat. Other privileges and immunities are to be prescribed by the Council of Ministers.[44]

## XV—ESTABLISHMENT OF THE INSTITUTIONS
## OF THE COMMUNITY

At the first meeting after the entry into force of the Treaty, the Authority is to appoint the Executive Secretary, determine the headquarters of the Community, and give such directives to the Council

---

sation of the objectives of the Convention of Lomé; (b) To contribute to the development of greater and closer trade, economic and cultural relations amongst the ACP States and among developing countries in general, and to the end to develop the exchange of information amongst the ACP States in the fields of trade, technology, industry and human resources; (c) To contribute to the promotion of effective regional and interregional co-operation among the ACP States and among developing countries in general, and to strengthen links between the respective regional organisations to which they belong; and (d) To promote the establishment of a new world economic order. The main organs of the ACP group are a Council of Ministers, a Committee of Ambassadors, and a Permanent Secretariat based in Brussels. This constitutional structure contained in the Georgetown Agreement was approved on Saturday, June 7, 1975, at the meeting held in Georgetown, Guyana. See also W. Briggs: " Negotiations Between the Enlarged European Economic Community and the African, Caribbean and Pacific (ACP) Countries," in 1 *Nigerian Journal of International Affairs*, July 1975, pp. 12–32.

[42] Similar to Art. 104 of the United Nations Charter.

[43] Modern international diplomatic law is to be found mainly in the Vienna Convention on Diplomatic Relations 1961, and the Vienna Convention on Consular Relations.

[44] Compare Art. 105 of the United Nations Charter.

of Ministers and other institutions of the Community as are necessary for the expeditious and effective implementation of the Treaty. Within two months of the entry into force of the Treaty, the Council of Ministers must hold its first meeting to appoint the Secretariat staff and give necessary directives to other subordinate institutions and to the Executive Secretary in respect of the implementation of the provisions of the Treaty.[45]

## XVI—ENTRY INTO FORCE, RATIFICATION AND ACCESSION

As provided under Article 62, the Treaty and the annexed Protocols as an integral part of it will enter into force *provisionally* upon the signature by Heads of State and Government, and definitively upon ratification by seven signatory States in accordance with the constitutional procedures applicable for each signatory State.

Access to the Treaty may be had by any West African State on terms and conditions to be determined by the Authority itself. The instrument of accession may be deposited with the Government of Nigeria which must then notify all other member-States. The Treaty enters into force in relation to an acceding State on the same date as its instrument of accession is deposited.

The government of Nigeria is the depositary for the Treaty and all instruments of ratification and accession, and should transmit certified true copies of the Treaty to all member-States. It should notify them of the dates of the various deposits, and should thereafter register the Treaty with the Organisation of African Unity, the United Nations and other organisations determined by the Council of Ministers.[46]

## XVII—AMENDMENTS AND REVISIONS

The Treaty may be amended or revised at the instance of any member-State which submits proposals to that effect to the Executive Secretary who must communicate them to other member within 30 days. The Authority will consider the proposed amendments or revision after giving one month's notice of them to member-States.[47]

The rule of immunity governs the adoption of any amendment or revision, which then comes into force upon such adoption. Article 63, paragraph 3 provides: " Any amendment or revision of this Treaty shall be by agreement of all the member-States and shall thereupon enter into force."

---

[45] Art. 61.
[46] See Art. 25 of the Vienna Convention on the Law of Treaties.
[47] Art. 65.

## XVIII—WITHDRAWAL FROM ECOWAS

In order for a State to withdraw from membership of the Community, two conditions must be satisfied: one is that the State must give one month's written notice to the Executive Secretary, and the other is that a period of one whole year must elapse thereafter, during which the notice of intention to withdraw has remained in force.[48] Thereupon, the State ceases to be a member of the Community, although it must during that one year continue to observe the provisions of the Treaty and remain liable for the discharge of its obligations thereunder.

Thus, unlike the Treaty of Rome, the ECOWAS Treaty permits of withdrawal from the Community upon these stated terms. The member-States, given their present cautious mood, would require to be assured of a right of withdrawal from a commitment to an organisation of the absolute value and advantages of which they are not yet persuaded. It may be that, in time, the necessary confidence will grow to the point that the great majority of them will agree to a renunciation of the right of non-withdrawal.[49]

The pragmatic approach adopted by the signatory States in making the establishment of a customs union as gradual and easy as possible is designed to encourage reluctant members to join, and the setting up of the Fund for co-operation and compensation should leave no one in any doubt that member-States, rich and poor alike, are compensated for possible losses in revenue incurred as a result of membership of the Community. The lessons of the less sophisticated arrangements of the West African Regional Group (WARG) would appear to have been well learnt.

## XIX—HEADQUARTERS AND OFFICIAL LANGUAGES

The Headquarters of the Community will be determined by the Authority.[50] The official languages are English and French, and other African languages may also be so declared by the authority.[51]

## XX—EPILOGUE TO THE ECOWAS TREATY

It will be recalled that, after the signing ceremony of the Treaty in Lagos on May 28, 1975, Nigeria and Togo were assigned the task of ensuring that all unfinished business relating to the Treaty should be put in hand as speedily as possible. Officials of both countries

---

[48] See Art. 64.

[49] The United Nations Charter contains no provision for withdrawal of member-States. The San Francisco Conference merely contented itself with the adoption of a Declaration admitting the right of withdrawal: See UNCIO, Documents, I, pp. 616–617; also L. M. Goodrich, *The United Nations* (1960), pp. 87–88.

[50] Art. 57.                                                                   [51] Art. 58.

prepared the drafts of the five protocols to the Treaty and the Community experts thereafter conducted a preliminary examination of them at Abidjan on June 7, 1976.[52]

At a Conference held on Tuesday, July 20, 1976, General Archeampong, Ghana's Head of State, addressed the opening session of the Council of Ministers of the Community in Accra [53] and urged member-States to implement speedily the Treaty establishing the Organisation. He expressed the hope that the Community would lead to a vast homogeneous society linked together by a network of roads as proposed through common ventures in agriculture, industry and other economic efforts. Member-States were urged to strengthen their capacity for " collective self-reliance." The restructuring of the new economic world order would be a painfully slow process for the developing countries if these placed reliance on the developed countries. Collective self-reliance is the answer. There should be greater attention paid to trade and economic co-operation among members of the Community and with other developing countries " if we desire a change in the pattern of north-south commerce which is dominated by the giant multi-national corporations." The power of the multi-national corporations could best be countered not by appeals to consciences but by the establishment of competing multi-national enterprises owned by the developing countries themselves. General Archeampong further observed that, even when as a result of constraints on capacity, the developing countries required assistance from the developed nations, they would be likely to succeed if they confronted the latter as an economic bloc rather than as fragmented units.

The three-day conference reviewed the activities of ECOWAS since it was set up in May 1975. It prepared for a summit of the Heads of State and Government which would decide, *inter alia*, on the appointment of the Executive Secretary and the designation of the Headquarters. The main task of the Accra Ministerial Conference was to discuss and put finishing touches to the five draft protocols which elaborate the modes of implementing some of the important provisions of the Treaty.[54] The Protocols are as follows: (1) Protocol relating to the definition of the contents of products originating from member-States; (2) Protocol relating to the re-exportation within the Community of goods imported from third world countries; (3) Protocol on the assessment of loss of revenue by member-States; (4) Protocol relating to the Fund for Co-operation, Compensation and

---

[52] See *Daily Times* (Nigeria), Monday, June 7, 1976, p. 3.

[53] *The Nigerian Observer*, Saturday, July 24, 1976; *The Nigerian Herald*, July 21, 1976, p. 1.

[54] *The Nigerian Observer*, July 16, 1976, p. 1; also July 24, 1976, p. 3.

Development of the Community; and (5) Protocol relating to contributions by member-States to the Budget of the Community.

Nigeria and Togo have played a leading role in establishing ECOWAS and it is gratifying to note Ghana's recent voice being added to those of the pioneers.[55] Ghana's latest appeal to the member-States to sign the protocols, appoint the Executive Secretary and determine the Headquarters of ECOWAS as well as its proposal that the Community adopt the Naira and the CFA Franc as possible currencies deserves careful and urgent attention.

---

[55] Liberia and Ivory Coast have also played noble roles.

# SOUTHERN AFRICA:

## *FROM DÉTENTE TO DELUGE?*

By

## TIMOTHY M. SHAW

SOUTHERN Africa has come to be perceived as an international sub-system because of a tradition of regional co-operation and South Africa's regional dominance.[1] Paradoxically, however, the demise of regional integration and the decline of South Africa's local hegemony, combined with an escalation of violence, have served to increase awareness of the interdependence of the sub-continent: " the very conflicts themselves have caused more people to think in regional terms about Southern Africa than ever before."[2] So whilst its dominant motif has been transformed—from co-operation to conflict —Southern Africa can still usefully be considered to be a sub-system in world politics. This essay analyses its transformation—focusing especially on the tension between confrontation and co-existence— and also examines the alternative future political economies projected for this important region.

The notion of co-existence has always been controversial but nonetheless appropriate when applied to Southern Africa, as regional co-operation has been neither voluntary nor irreversible. Indeed, the pervasiveness of co-existence in its historical setting has largely been a function of South African power and the primacy of white interests. Nevertheless, taking a wider perspective co-existence has charac-terised the region in several ways and at several levels. First, it has been enforced amongst the races *within* the States of Southern Africa, especially inside those with white régimes. Secondly, it has been perpetuated *between* the States themselves; the white régime of South Africa has advanced these two basic forms of co-existence. Further, the region while under South African dominance, had co-existed with other regional and international organisations, at least until the rise of the Third-World majority. But black government in Africa has not of itself led to change in the sub-continent because another type of co-existence—that of interests and perceptions—

---

[1] L. W. Bowman, " The Subordinate State System of Southern Africa," 12 *International Studies Quarterly* (1968), pp. 231–261 and T. M. Shaw, " Southern Africa: Cooperation and Conflict in an International Sub-System," 12 *Journal of Modern African Studies* (1974), pp. 633–655.

[2] J. Barratt, " Southern Africa: a South African View," 55 *Foreign Affairs* (1976), p. 150.

has developed between élites of whatever colour. As is suggested below, the co-existence of interests among rulers in Africa has cut across lines of race and ideology in response to extra-continental threats; the perpetuation of some forms of co-operation in the region is one expression of shared interests and perceptions among some of the ruling classes of Africa.

Finally, then, a further variety of co-existence is that of patterns of interaction: conflict and co-operation have co-existed in Southern Africa, albeit in varying proportions and intensities. Nevertheless, neither of them has been excluded in regional politics to date, perhaps because of the continued presence of the other types of co-existence—especially inter-racial, inter-State, and inter-élite—and the complex set of interactions to which they give rise.

The development of novel forms of co-existence in Southern Africa is one result of the increased complexity of regional politics. Several of the new forces in world politics—transnational relations, new States and issues, and the erosion of the distinction between internal and external interactions—have had an impact on Southern African affairs. Further, current debates about a new international economic order affect both the perceptions and status of actors in the region as the politics of oil and gold, inflation and indebtedness, modify established relations. But the co-existence of continuities as well as change in Southern Africa make it premature to speak of a " revolutionary situation." [3] Rather, orthodox patterns of interdependence are under challenge from several sources and the future political economy of the region is now more problematic than before. Nevertheless, the greater incidence of violence in recent months takes place in a sub-system still characterised by a considerable potential for co-existence, given its inheritance of regional integration. [4] But to assess the prospects for the continued co-existence of co-operation and conflict in Southern Africa we first need to identify the range of actors and associations involved.

## I—The Actors in Southern Africa

The complex regional politics of Southern Africa may be usefully approached through an analysis of coalitions of actors with interests

---

[3] N. Shamuyarira, " Revolutionary Situation in Southern Africa," 4 *African Review* (1974), pp. 159–179. *Cf.* J. E. Spence, " Southern Africa's Uncertain Future: adjusting to a new balance of power," 258 *Round Table* (1975), pp. 159–165.

[4] On recent changes in the structure, texture and scope of the subsystem see C. P. Potholm, " The Limits of Systemic Growth: Southern Africa Today," in T. M. Shaw and K. A. Heard (eds.), *Co-operation and Conflict in Southern Africa: papers on a regional subsystem* (1976), pp. 118–143, and " The Effects on South Africa of Change in Contiguous Territories," in L. Thompson and J. Butler (eds.), *Change in Contemporary South Africa* (1975), pp. 329–348.

in the region.[5] Given the continuities of regional exchange and confrontation, along with South Africa's local hegemony, contemporary change has altered the texture but not the structure of the sub-system. The kaleidoscopic changes in the region can, then, be viewed as shifts within and between these coalitions rather than substantive developments in the regional structure itself. Although the content of regional co-existence has changed, it has not yet been superseded by a new political order.

*(a) The Diversity of Actors*

The politics of Southern Africa involve the formulation and expression of interests on at least five levels—subnational, national, regional, continental, and global—and conflict and co-operation among actors and coalitions at each of these levels. Any understanding or prediction about the region requires reference to this rich

*Figure One*
*The Multinational Politics of Southern Africa*

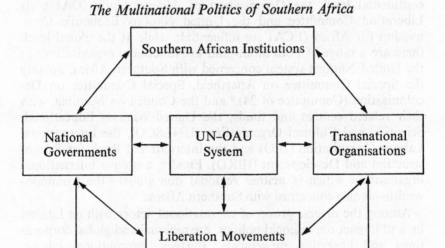

N.B. There are few and irregular direct links between Southern African institutions and either the United Nations–Organisation of African Unity (UN–OAU) System or the liberation movements, although indirectly they do respond to each other. (Adapted from T. M. Shaw, *Prospects for International Order in Southern Africa: conflict and co-operation in a regional subsystem* (unpublished Ph.D. dissertation, Princeton University, 1976, p. 127).)

---

[5] See T. M. Shaw, " International Organisations and the Politics of Southern Africa: towards regional integration or liberation? " 3 *Journal of Southern African Studies* (1976), pp. 1–19, and K. W. Grundy, *Confrontation and Accommodation in Southern Africa: the limits of independence* (1973).

diversity of actors, which is much more diverse than just States situated or influential in the sub-system. Regional interactions also involve a wide group of multinational actors, from liberation movements to multi-national corporations, from support groups to United Nations committees, and from political factions to the super-Powers. Some of the important types of relationship which affect the politics of Southern Africa are illustrated in Figure One.

The major actors which affect the politics of Southern Africa are the States located in or around the region along with a few " intrusive " Powers with significant political, economic and/or strategic interests in the area. The former include white " neutral " and " frontier " States; the latter, African, western and socialist States. In addition to these types of States, there are several non-State actors continuously involved; these include regional, continental and global international organisations, and transnational organisations with interests and associations at each of these levels. The most important regional organisation is the Southern African Customs Union; at the continental level, the Organisation of African Unity (OAU), its Liberation Committee and the United Nations Economic Commission for Africa (ECA) are influential; while at the global level, there are a range of both multi- and uni-functional organisations in the United Nations system concerned with Southern Africa, notably the Special Committee on Apartheid, Special Committee on Decolonisation (Committee of 24),[6] and the Council on Namibia, with their related centres and funds, the United Nations Educational, Scientific and Cultural Organisation (UNESCO), the International Labour Organisation (ILO) and the International Bank for Reconstruction and Development (IBRD). Finally, a unique international organisation which is neither regional nor global—the Commonwealth—is also concerned with Southern Africa.

Among the diverse group of transnational actors with an interest in, and impact on, regional politics, are regional and global corporations and liberation movements. Further, international labour, church, educational, legal and humanitarian movements retain an interest in Southern Africa. The most important transnational actors are, however, multinational corporations and the nationalist parties in the region, the latter with their support groups throughout the world. In addition to this diverse set of actors there are important coalitions and conflicts amongst them which affect the nature and outcome of regional issues. Their actions determine the pattern of co-existence and the contemporary trend towards confrontation.

---

[6] See J. H. Mittelman, " Collective Decolonisation and the UN Committee of 24," 14 *Journal of Modern African Studies* (1974), pp. 633–655.

(b) *Coalitions Among Actors*

The major cleavage between the actors and coalitions is whether they advocate integration or liberation in the region. South Africa has been at the centre of attempts to secure regional co-operation among the present group of States and institutions. In opposition to this " minor coalition " is the " major faction " based on the liberation movements and African States; this grouping demands liberation and perceives any attempt to secure regional integration before political change to be " counter-revolutionary." The minor faction advocates co-operation among actors to control violence and increase growth. In contrast, the major multinational coalition demands majority rule within all the States of the region and opposes moves to limit the activities of the liberation movements; it is critical of any progress towards regional integration which perpetuates white rule and uneven development in Southern Africa. So the minor faction seeks to protect the current regional order whereas the major coalition advocates a " revolution " in both the texture and structure of Southern Africa.[7] Given their antagonistic bases and goals any co-existence between them is likely to be tenuous and tactical.

South Africa has been anxious to play a " peace-keeping " role to protect the regional *status quo*, whereas the majority coalition advocates a controlled form of " peace-breaking " to advance racial and economic justice in Southern Africa. Incremental change sponsored by South Africa may yet prevent a more fundamental social revolution in the region. Its economic dominance and military capability pose significant obstacles for the liberation movements and the major coalition, although, as is noted in Section IV below, its " sub-imperial " role no longer goes unchallenged. The détente and Kissinger initiatives are, then, the latest in a series of attempts to divert support away from the dominant faction and towards collaboration with South Africa, to achieve regional co-existence without a significant redistribution of resources. They may also serve to divide the dominant coalition into more complex patterns of support over the troubled conflicts in Angola and Zimbabwe, as well as over the issue of South Africa itself.

South Africa's recent advocacy of regional integration has historical antecedents but it was revived after the Second World War in response to new opportunities in Africa and to express the Afrikaners' interest in the continent rather than in Empire. Its Africa

---

[7] See T. M. Shaw, " Southern Africa: dependence, interdependence and independence in a regional subsystem," in Shaw and Heard (eds.), *op. cit.* in note 4 above, at pp. 81–97; S. C. Nolutshungu, *South Africa in Africa: a study of ideology and foreign policy* (1975), and K. Woldring, " South Africa's Africa Policy Reconsidered," 5 *African Review* (1975), pp. 77–93.

policy has always been ambivalent because of a continued hope that it would become acceptable as a member of the western alliance, despite apartheid. As this unlikely prospect receded, so it has come to emphasise its national interests in the region.[8] But its several grand schemes for regional economic and political integration or federation have never been realised and even the long-established Southern African customs and currency areas have undergone substantial change. Dreams of a South African-dominated " co-prosperity sphere " in Africa have remained elusive because of the combination of internal inequalities and external dominance. Internal " decolonisation " through the Bantustan scheme will not now win much international support in either the West or Africa, so wider conceptions of a " multinational " confederation in Southern Africa are unlikely to be realised.

Through its interrelated policies of regional co-existence and national " decentralisation," South Africa hoped to perpetuate the dependence of both the black States and Bantustans. It sought to maintain white control and affluence by encouraging the creation of a group of actors which were disinterested in liberation and would oppose (or at least not support) the nationalist parties and the majority international faction. South Africa mobilised its considerable economic, as well as military, forces to advance an alternative regional structure to that advocated by the dominant coalition. Its aspirations for continued white power and regional dominance inform the reluctance of actors in that coalition to enter into a dialogue with it over the future of Southern Africa. Continued co-existence requires a greater degree of confidence for diplomatic overtures to mature and flourish.

(c) *Confrontation Between Coalitions*

The liberation movements, and most actors in the dominant coalition, have opposed South Africa's designs for regional integration because (i) national independence has always preceded integration on the continent, and (ii) white South Africa's existence, let alone its leadership role, is unacceptable whatever the short-term economic benefits or military costs. The majority coalition is divided not so much by offers of détente, but because of several continuing sources of friction which exist largely within and between the liberation movements. This factionalism has been based on several factors: ethnicity, race, leadership, strategy, ideology, and external influences, both African and global. Despite repeated attempts by influential

---

[8] See *ibid.* and D. Venter, " South Africa as an African Power: the need for a purposeful détente policy in Southern Africa," 8 *South African Institute for International Affairs Newsletter* (1976), pp. 7–12.

African Presidents and the OAU Liberation Committee to force factions and parties together into united fronts, divisions persist, leading to civil war in Angola and complicated and protracted bargaining over Zimbabwe.

Moreover, the movements have become bureaucratised, partially to administer the liberated areas, but mainly to secure the continued flow of funds, *matériel* and support from and through the dominant coalition. This has led to further divisions between the military and political/diplomatic wings of the movements, with the latter seeking finance and legitimacy from African States and organisations, the Socialist countries and the United Nations system. Larger international divisions have been reflected in the pattern of extra-African support with the Soviet Union generally being associated with the bigger, more established and non-racial groups, and China helping the other parties.

The core of the majority faction—the liberation movements and the front-line African States—has received significant support and legitimacy from the OAU and the United Nations and from transnational groups with relations both with the movements and international organisations. Indeed, the compatibility of the OAU with the United Nations is largely based on mutual interests in Southern Africa [9]; the OAU has come to act as an intermediary between the United Nations and the movements. The numerical and rhetorical dominance of this coalition in the United Nations has led to the isolation of South Africa and to the alienation of some western States, especially over its critique of the role of western alliances and corporations in the white south. This, built on earlier critiques of capitalism by Hobson and Lenin, has consisted of blaming corporations for the perpetuation of white rule. Its over-simplification and exaggeration of the role of foreign business fails to take into account Hobson's earlier defence of the Afrikaners against imperialism and the contemporary impact of local white capitalism in resisting some forms of dependence.

Because of the challenges, both internal and external, to white government and to their own interests, multinational corporations have maintained a certain distance from the ruling white elites. Although they have advocated regional integration and have supported activities such as the South Africa Foundation and the United States–South Africa Leadership Exchange Programme, it is not clear

[9] See Y. El-Ayouty, " Legitimization of National Liberation: the UN and Southern Africa," in Y. El-Ayouty & H. C. Brooks (eds.), *Africa and International Organization* (1974), pp. 209–229; L. T. Kapungu, " The OAU's Support for the Liberation of Southern Africa," in Y. El-Ayouty (ed.), *The OAU After Ten Years: comparative perspectives* (1975), pp. 135–151; and B. Andemicael, *The OAU and the UN: relations between the OAU and the UN* (1976), *passim*.

that they share all interests. Indeed, given the prospect of change in the region and also the ability of corporations to collaborate with States elsewhere on the continent, they are likely to encourage moderate black rule rather than white intransigence, especially if an escalation of regional conflict leads to increased military expenditures and casualties, and to a decline in the rate of economic growth.

South Africa's economic dilemmas—always present due to apartheid—have intensified because of inflation, the falling price of gold, increasing costs of labour and energy, and escalating expenditures on coercion. But the majority coalition has been unwilling to enter direct negotiations with the minority faction, either with the white régimes or the multinationals. The United Nations–OAU coalition has chosen not to exploit the increasing opportunities to support progressive groups within the white-ruled countries; rather it has intensified its association with the liberation movements and its rhetorical commitment to violent change. It has not adopted a more sophisticated policy of incentives as well as coercion but has maintained its strategy of isolation and sanction against South Africa,[10] whilst recognising that it cannot effectively challenge established economic exchange with the West.

In addition to an economic crisis, South Africa has—since the initial Soweto riots of June, 1976—faced a profound political crisis. The intransigence of the Vorster régime to the escalating deaths and destruction stands in contrast to its relative flexibility over regional issues. *Verligtheid* is practised externally but still only contemplated internally.[11] Black unrest has spread both between races and locations and from the townships into the " white " city centres; yet Mr. Vorster asserts that there is no crisis. This *verkrampte* " granite response " refuses to admit the different intensity and potentiality of Soweto compared with Sharpeville and the changing regional environment. The pleas of sensitive South Africans like Alan Paton for rapid change away from inequalities and discrimination and towards a majority-ruled unitary State will likely fall on deaf ears. Paton demands generous rather than grudging change: " Internal change is imperative if we are going to avoid external intervention and internal unrest." [12] Failure to heed the sage, informed advice of such persons will almost inevitably lead to the termination of the remaining forms of regional co-operation and an escalation of

---

[10] See R. E. Bissell, " The Ostracism of South Africa," in this *Year Book.*

[11] See R. Hodder-Williams and P. Hugo, " Verligtheid and Change in South Africa: stirrings in the Afrikaans intellectual community," 263 *Round Table* (1976), pp. 261–270; and J. de St. Jorre, " Inside the Laager: white power in South Africa," 55 *Foreign Affairs* (1976), pp. 169–186.

[12] A. Paton, " The Beloved Country Today," 7 *South Africa International* (1976), p. 26.

conflict, both within and between the States of Southern Africa. The decline of internal inter-racial co-existence as well as external inter-State co-existence together threaten any moves towards dialogue and détente. The re-creation of stability is increasingly problematic as assumptions about national and regional politics are shattered.[13] Nevertheless, even if integration and federation are elusive, more modest forms of regional co-existence are still sought, especially by South Africa itself.

## II—FROM DIALOGUE TO DÉTENTE

South Africa has tried to advance co-existence and co-operation in both the sub-continent and the continent through its advocacy first of dialogue and then of détente. However, the temporary successes of these foreign policy tactics have had a very fragile basis because of the different interpretations of white and black Africans about the meaning of such inter-State co-existence. On the one hand, South Africa advocated dialogue and détente to secure its acceptance on the continent, and hence in the international system; it also hoped to secure markets and raw materials in Africa whilst making Africa safe for apartheid. On the other hand, most of the African leaders who engaged in dialogue did not intend to legitimise, or even moderate their criticism of, apartheid; rather they saw talking as merely an alternative tactic to fighting. Many of them were anti-Communist and pacific as well as non-racial in their preferences; they shared some values with the white élites but did not abandon their demand for majority rule throughout the sub-system. Given these very different sets of perceptions and intents, dialogue and détente might lead to co-existence; they were unlikely to generate other more substantive forms of co-operation.

Moreover, the interests and stances of the two international coalitions suggest different time scales and political economies for Southern Africa: the minority group centred on South Africa seeks continued and enhanced political order and economic growth whereas the majority faction demands economic redistribution and political change, believing these to be inevitable at some stage in the future. The United Nations–OAU coalition advances confrontation because it fears that co-existence and compromise now will jeopardise majority rule later. It insists that peace and integration in Southern Africa can be achieved only *after* justice has been secured, whereas South Africa asserts that peace is necessary *before* regional relations can be normalised and economic co-operation advanced.

---

[13] See R. Butterworth, " The Future of South Africa," in this *Year Book*, Vol. 31 (1977), pp. 27–45.

Confrontation between the two coalitions has produced intransigence and escalation as well as co-existence. The majority coalition has successfully tried to exclude South Africa from international organisation and competition while South Africa has been unprepared to negotiate directly with the liberation movements, recognising instead only a few Bantustan or " acceptable " black leaders.

However, despite the intensification of guerrilla struggle, some indirect and even bilateral contracts and negotiations have occurred. These have increased again lately because of changes in the regional balance of power and the imperative of minimising violence. Clearly there is a complex relationship between confrontation and compromise, conflict and negotiation, both within and between the coalitions. African leaders have continually advanced peaceful change rather than armed struggle, but their offers had largely been ignored until regional politics began to change in 1974. As one South African scholar has since recognised, " the Republic has made a serious mistake in its foreign-policy planning by not at least capitalising on the positive aspects of the Lusaka Manifesto—the rejection of violence to solve disputes between States—at an earlier stage." [14] Since then intermediaries, both regional and external, have been able to bring the two sides together over particular territories, but these diplomatic flurries have yet to lead to substantive change either international or internal. Both sides recognise the advantages and dilemmas of co-existence, but also acknowledge the dangers and wastefulness of conflict: hence the cycle in regional politics of confrontation, escalation and then a return to co-existence and tentative forms of co-operation. Substantive progress is likely to remain a mirage until the two sides begin to agree not only on the jorm of co-existence, but also on the bases of co-operation and the future regional political economy.

## (a) *Co-existence Between Coalitions*

The foreign policy of the Republic of South Africa has long recognised the interrelatedness of its regional, continental and global relations. After becoming resigned to not incorporating the High Commission Territories into its territory, it was then able to exploit their dependence on it to advance its continental and global image. But opposition to apartheid has always been the one issue that has maintained Africa's tenuous unity and over which a consensual continental foreign policy has usually been sustained.[15] So despite

---

[14] Venter, *op. cit.* in note 8 above, at p. 10.

[15] See C. Legum, " The OAU: success or failure?," 51 *International Affairs* (1975), pp. 208–219; and J. Mayall, " Black–White Relations in the Context of African Foreign Policy," in P. Jones (ed.), 1 *International Yearbook of Foreign Policy Analysis* (1974), pp. 181–205.

South Africa's attractions as a source of trade, technology and capital, few African States had even informal contact with it in the 1960s. To reduce its diplomatic isolation, to maximise its markets, and to undermine Africa's cohesion, South Africa advanced in the 1970s on a policy of " dialogue," [16] in part as a perverse and belated response to the conciliatory overtures of the Lusaka Manifesto (1969).

Africa's rejection of this early continental initiative, along with the upsets in the regional balance in 1974, led to a more limited South African response of détente in the mid-1970s.[17] Once again, the objects were external issues and respectability, with apartheid itself being largely excluded as a subject for negotiation. However, Namibia, as well as Zimbabwe, became a topic for discussion and a few leading and influential African statesmen were involved such as President Kaunda, rather than somewhat discredited figures like President Banda; significantly President Houphouet-Boigny was supportive of both attempts at negotiation rather than confrontation and the exclusion of the supposed " communist " threat.[18]

Because of Africa's collective adherence to confrontation with the white South, for " *détente . . .* to hold, it would have to be endorsed by the OAU: it was therefore necessary to reopen the question of *dialogue* with African States to the north." [19] In other words, regional co-existence was dependent on a degree of continental co-existence; this in turn was affected by the current state of global co-existence. Clearly, such understandings were highly vulnerable, open as they were to different interpretations and nuances at each stage.

(b) *Differing Perceptions of Dialogue and Détente*

Just as global détente has a variety of meanings for members of the two blocs, so regional détente has had very different implications for the two sets of parties or coalitions. For South Africa it meant time, respectability and influence, whereas for most African States it implied merely the same fight by other, or several, means. However, for a few diplomats on both sides the stylish motif secured legitimacy for contact and talks about talks. It also led to the further radicalisation of guerrilla groups in the region who were supported by a few

---

[16] See C. Legum, *Dialogue: Africa's Great Debate* (1972); and Y. Tandon, " South Africa and the OAU: the dialogue on the dialogue issue," 3 *Mawazo* (1971), pp. 3–16.

[17] See C. Legum, " Southern Africa: the Politics of Détente " in this *Year Book*, Vol. 30 (1976), pp. 14–29. For further, representative analyses see J. Barratt, " Détente in Southern Africa," 33 *World Today* (1975), pp. 120–130; O. Geyser, " Détente in Southern Africa," 75 *African Affairs* (1976), pp. 182–207; and D. Hirschman, " Southern Africa: Détente?," 14 *Journal of Modern African Studies* (1976), pp. 107–126.

[18] See B. Charles, " The Impossible Dialogue with ' White ' Southern Africa: francophone approaches," *International Perspectives* (1976), pp. 11–16.

[19] J. Mayall, " Foreign Policy in Africa: a Changing Diplomatic Landscape," in P. Jones (ed.), 2 *International Yearbook of Foreign Policy Analysis* (1975). p, 200.

African States and their Socialist associates. Both dialogue and détente threatened, then, to split not only the OAU but also the "radical caucus" within the Organisation; only the continued intransigence of the white régimes prevented deeper and longer fissions, although the cohesion of the five "front-line" Presidents remains tenuous.

South Africa had two major objectives in advancing these twin initiatives—the "normalisation" of relations with black Africa and the "non-violent" resolution of regional conflicts: "The détente policy was conceived as a means of normalising inter-State relations and of working for stability in a region threatened by sudden and uncontrollable change." [20] In other words, the revival of co-existence would limit change, hardly an attractive proposition for the majority coalition which sought black rule before regional order was re-established. South Africa's unacceptable terms for détente included an unwillingness to let apartheid itself be one subject of negotiation—the very issue that lies at the heart of black Africa's concerns. Further, if a related goal was to secure continued western support for itself then intransigence over its own policy of "separate development" would tend to be counter-productive. Moreover, the *débacle* of South Africa's hasty intervention in Angola indicated for the West that "any attempt to enlist South African support in stemming a supposedly 'Communist' challenge to white-ruled states is dangerously counter-productive." [21]

### III—THE DEMISE OF DÉTENTE

The combination of African antagonism and western ambivalence adds up to a failure of South Africa's foreign policy. Its self-appointed historic mission to make Africa safe for the Afrikaner and for anti-Communism failed because it rested on the untenable domestic system of apartheid; white power cannot be exercised externally with particular force because it is considered to be unacceptable and illegitimate. South Africa's successive attempts to overcome collective African opposition failed, then, because of a fundamental misperception. While the OAU States saw détente as compatible with other pressures on apartheid and white rule, South Africa hoped that it was an alternative (not a supplement) to further and intensified confrontation. The Dar es Salaam Declaration of April 1975, is flexible on means but not on ends; Afrikanerdom in contrast saw détente as postponing the need for change for decades. Africa may have divisions both within and between States and liberation movements, but over majority rule—if not a Socialist political economy—

---

[20] Barratt, *op. cit.* in note 2 above, at p. 151.
[21] C. Legum & T. Hughes, *After Angola: the War over Southern Africa* (1976), p. 5.

for Southern Africa there has always been considerable unity.
Tactics have been variable and multiple but the goal has remained
consistent and non-negotiable. From the Lusaka Manifesto, through
the Mogadishu Declaration and the Accra Strategy to the Dar
statement, Africa's voice and direction have been clear and consistent.

Thus far, the domino theory has worked quite well to advance and
explain the progress of change in Southern Africa, and Africa's
leading frontier States have skilfully implemented the logic of such a
geo-political strategy as expressed in this set of declarations. But
South Africa itself poses problems of quite a different order to those
of Rhodesia or Angola, let alone Mozambique or Namibia. This is
not to suggest that politico-economic change will not occur in the
white redoubt; rather the timing, direction and processes of change
remain problematic. In particular, South Africa is a much more
complex political economy than the other units. Moreover, its very
dominance in the sub-system makes its future orientation of substantial interest to other States in the region (as well as for the OAU
as a whole and the wider world economy): " As the dominoes fall, in
fact, the real (as opposed to the mythic) problem of African relations
with the Republic will have to be faced by both sides." [22] It is the
appreciation of the difficulties of bringing about change within the
*laager* that has made some African States prepared to co-exist at an
inter-State level whilst regretting its implications for inter-racial affairs
within South Africa. Further, there are emerging common interests
among some of Africa's rulers which encourage a revival of co-
existence among them.

(a) *Co-existence Among the Ruling Élites of Africa*
Increasing concern about the future orientation of the region
among certain African ruling classes may help to explain why they
were more responsive to the offer of détente than to the earlier
" outward-looking " initiative of dialogue. In particular, Zambia's
acceptance of détente—in an apparent reversal or shift in its policy of
disengagement—may have been motivated by the common interest of
its leadership with that of South Africa in avoiding radical change in
Southern Africa. The understanding reached between these two
States in 1974/5 over the desirability of moderate régimes in Zimbabwe (Rhodesia), Namibia and Angola cannot be explained without
reference to their respective political economies, which are the bases
of this new form of co-existence.[23]

---

[22] Mayall, *op. cit.* in note 19 above, at p. 205.
[23] See T. M. Shaw & A. T. Mugomba, " The Political Economy of Regional Détente:
Zambia and Southern Africa," 4 *Journal of African Studies* (1977/8); and " Zambia:
Détente or Disengagement?," in J. Seiler (ed.), *Southern Africa Since the Portuguese
Coup* (1978).

Zambia had always displayed an ambivalence over its continuing links with South Africa and over its conditional, and often partisan, support for the liberation movements. Given its continued dependence on copper and the world economy, and reflecting its own ruling class interest in the maintenance of affluence and control,[24] Zambia entered into a tacit coalition with South Africa which largely cut across established regional cleavages. Zambia has always been attracted by the prospect of acting as a regional core in Central Africa, but this ambition would require the establishment of moderate régimes around it: the Zambia–South Africa " axis " reflected a common interest in regional integration within the capitalist world economy.[25]

Détente and co-existence offered the prospect of turning the problem of land-lockedness into a geopolitical advantage and the potential for upward mobility in the global hierarchy. Zambia had already acted as midwife at the birth of Mozambique by chairing negotiations between the Front for the Liberation of Mozambique (FRELIMO) and Portugal in 1974. It then participated in a round of regional " shuttle diplomacy " with President Kaunda's Assistant for Foreign Affairs travelling between Lusaka and Pretoria, with occasional safaris to Salisbury and Lisbon. This contemporary form of statecraft—which occurred two years before Kissinger's own characteristic personal intervention—produced the Lusaka Agreement of December 1974 and the Pretoria Agreement of August 1975 over change in Rhodesia. It led to the historic meeting between President Kaunda and Prime Minister Vorster at the otherwise abortive Victoria Falls Bridge talks on the future of Zimbabwe in August 1975.

### (b) *Détente Between Zambia and South Africa*

The *rapport* established between these two leaders enabled the co-existence between their States to weather some of the storms produced by the vacillations of the Smith régime in negotiations and the spill-over of guerrilla war in Zimbabwe. The " mission " of these two leaders, their foreign ministers and special advisers to peaceful change in the region appeared hopeless when the Smith régime terminated the Victoria Falls meeting and then refused to seriously negotiate with Joshua Nkomo. So in 1976, the escalation of guerrilla struggle

---

[24] See T. M. Shaw, " Zambia: Dependence and Underdevelopment," 10 *Canadian Journal of African Studies* (1976), pp. 3–22; and *Dependence and Underdevelopment: the Development and Foreign Policies of Zambia* (1976).

[25] See T. M. Shaw, " Zambia's Foreign Policy," in O. Aluko (ed.), *The Foreign Policies of African States* (1977), pp. 220–234. *Cf.* D. G. Anglin, " Zambia and Southern African ' Détente '," 30 *International Journal* (1975), pp. 471–503.

in Zimbabwe (Rhodesia) [26] and Mozambique's closure of its border with Rhodesia, along with the failure of South African intervention in Angola, all pointed to the demise of détente and diplomacy. However, Kissinger's African safari of April 1976, and his regional shuttle of September 1976, may have revived the prospects for negotiation and co-existence as well as Zambia's own diplomatic credibility on the continent.

Zambia's support for moderate movements and governments is, then, an expression of the dominant interests in its political economy. Along with the white oligarchy in South Africa it opposes any radical restructuring of the sub-system other than the colour of its rulers. Given the vagaries of the production and price of copper and its continuing dependence on foreign exchange and capital, Zambia's implementation of State-capitalism could be advanced by association with South Africa. The resistance to a Socialist definition of Humanism in Zambia is indicative of the strength of those forces which also advocate regional détente.[27]

The debate within Zambia over its future political economy and regional strategy is indicative of tensions within and between other actors over the emerging structures of Southern Africa. The consensus within the majority coalition has largely been against negotiation, and the front-line Presidents have taken some risks in even considering the possibilities of negotiations, especially as their Socialist partners have opposed Kissinger's activities. Nevertheless, they recognise that America's declared new commitment to change in Southern Africa might overcome the regional stalemate of white intransigence and black disunity. Yet they remain fearful of the West's naïvety and the possibility of it again being lured into a position of supporting the remaining beleaguered white régimes.[28] They also insist that Africa would prefer to fight its own battles without any Great-Power support or intervention. Whether such aspirations will be realised depends on the continuing dialectic between the two international coalitions and the response of extra-regional Powers to South Africa's dominance or demise. The continued co-existence of actors and patterns of relations remains problematic, in part because South Africa's regional dominance is now less assured.

---

[26] See A. R. Wilkinson, " From Rhodesia to Zimbabwe," in B. Davidson, J. Slovo, A. R. Wilkinson, *Southern Africa: the new politics of revolution* (1976), pp. 211–352; and K. Maxey, *The Fight for Zimbabwe: the Armed Conflict in Southern Rhodesia since UDI* (1975).

[27] See T. M. Shaw, " The Foreign Policy of Zambia: ideology and interests," 14 *Journal of Modern African Studies* (1976), pp. 79–105.

[28] On the problems of western policy being based on the assumption of continued white power, see Legum, *op. cit.* in note 17 above, at pp. 14–19, and A. Lake, *The " Tar Baby " Option: American Policy Toward Southern Rhodesia* (1976).

## IV—THE DILEMMAS
## OF SOUTH AFRICAN SUB-IMPERIALISM

Although South Africa has had a somewhat ambiguous relationship with the West, until the early 1970s they shared many common interests. By not opposing, and often supporting, South Africa's regional power western actors—both State and non-State—encouraged it to play a " sub-imperial " role. A sub-imperial, " go-between " State advances the interests of itself and other actors in a particular regional " sphere of influence." It is at the " centre " of the " periphery," a " client " which advocates and exploits regional integration itself while remaining dependent on external Powers. A sub-imperial State exerts a regional hegemony akin to the global dominance of an imperial Power, but at a sub-systemic level. Clearly, South Africa is dominant in its region and has advanced its own growth and status as well as certain western interests in the region. At times it has been able to insist on some integration as well as co-existence in Southern Africa,[29] but it now faces a combination of economic and strategic difficulties.

### (a) *Economic Difficulties*

There are limits to South Africa's regional hegemony. One indication of the decline of South Africa's dominance and influence is the revision of the long-established regional customs union and the fragmentation of the rand currency area. The Southern African Customs Union was altered in 1969 in an attempt to reflect the uneven economic development of Botswana, Lesotho and Swaziland (BLS) and in a belated and ambiguous effort to reduce some of the gross inequalities between the other member-States and South Africa. Moreover, formal co-operation with South Africa is an increasingly controversial policy for even the small black States of the region to follow especially as their choices gradually increase with the independence of Mozambique and Angola; indeed, their control over crucial flows of labour, water and other resources may enhance their bargaining power and also the leverage of the Bantustans. In restructuring regional monetary arrangements, Botswana has introduced its own central bank and currency, the *pula*, and Swaziland has introduced its own currency, the *emalangeni*, although this is backed by, and freely exchangeable with, the rand. Also, the two major commercial banks in the region—Standard and Barclays—now have separate branches in BLS. The continued and future participation

---

[29] See Venter, *op. cit.* in note 8 above; and T. M. Shaw, " International Stratification: Sub-imperialism in Eastern and Southern Africa," *International Political Science Association* (1976).

of Namibia and the Transkei in these regional arrangements remain somewhat controversial, especially as they relate to schemes for a federal " solution " to racial inequalities.

The established multilateral institutions in Southern Africa are only part of the larger set of relations within the sub-system involving trade, capital, labour, energy, water and several forms of communications. But the problems of these two formal regional institutions help to illustrate the increasing resistance in Southern Africa to both co-operation and co-existence with white power for reasons of nationalism, race and development. The checks on South African dominance are particularly salient in the military issue area, not just because of successful guerrilla struggle, but also because any occupation by South African forces would be particularly hard to sustain. In the regional arms race South Africa still has the largest and best-equipped forces, supported by a burgeoning national " military-industrial complex." However, its jet-fighters, tanks, missiles and submarines constitute an impressive, but not impregnable, arsenal. The logic of guerrilla war upsets its apparent military supremacy, with South Africa being peculiarly vulnerable to a simultaneous external attack and internal uprising. South Africa's " power " would quite quickly be exhausted if it had to contain guerrillas along its borders and internal acts of sabotage. Moreover, its possession of nuclear weapons would not be helpful unless it was intent on large-scale genocide and it still relies on external supplies and technology, especially from France and Israel.[30] Military aid to Malawi, Swaziland and the Transkei might be a more subtle and profitable use of its power than sending troops to the Zambesi or the Cunene. The latter disturbed the pattern of co-existence as well as undermined South Africa's image of invincibility.

(b) *Strategic Defeats*

The considerable constraints on South Africa's regional foreign policy have been clearest in the cases of Angola and Rhodesia. In the 1960s it helped in both to perpetuate white régimes and provide anti-guerrilla support along with investment, infrastructure and technology. But political change in Portugal and the region upset its geo-political calculations. South Africa has, since 1974, become resigned to black governments in the two States which would terminate its white *cordon sanitaire*. However, it has consistently advanced the

---

[30] On the possibility of an Israeli–South African alliance in response to their shared rejection by Africa and the United Nations, see R. E. Bissell, " Africa and the Nations of the Middle East," 71 *Current History* (1976), pp. 158–160; and T. M. Shaw, " Oil, Israel and the OAU: an introduction to the Political Economy of Energy in Southern Africa," 23 *Africa Today* (1976), pp. 15–26.

claims of moderate black leaders rather than radical ones and it has also tried to gain respectability and time for itself by being associated with western diplomacy in Southern Africa. Further, the Nationalist Party has had to play an ambivalent diplomatic role because of the imperatives of white politics and Afrikaner nationalism. Given the dominance of FRELIMO in Mozambique there was no alternative strategy to consider in this case other than co-existence.

In Angola, however, the complexities of the liberation movements provided the opportunity for military intervention. Clearly some of the more " moderate " guerrilla leaders and front-line Presidents (despite their general association with the dominant faction) along with certain western actors encouraged active South African support for UNITA. However, the rapid push from the south to Luanda served to activate long-established associations between MPLA and the Socialist States, leading to an escalation of the internal conflict. The anti-MPLA forces could take, but not hold or pacify, Luanda. Their defeat-*cum*-retreat to their base areas in front of the Cuban-backed MPLA revival is indicative of the divisive nature of Angolan politics.[31] It is not yet clear that internal and external opposition to the Neto régime has ended; UNITA has so far prevented the re-opening of the Benguela Railway and guerrilla groups continue to harass the MPLA. Moreover, there is considerable debate within MPLA itself on the desirability of over-dependence on Cuba and the Soviet Union. The instability of Angola affects the factional conflict in Zimbabwe.

The nationalists in Rhodesia have always been plagued by divisions but these have become more numerous and acute in the last couple of years as the Pearce Commission was followed by two successive Pretoria agreements, leading to talks at Victoria Falls and in Geneva. South Africa's military and economic support for the Smith régime has been an issue in these negotiations: South Africa withdrew its forces to advance détente in 1975 and to revive co-existence threatened to end economic assistance in 1976. Clearly these moves to undermine a neighbouring white régime have involved difficult and protracted decision-making for the Vorster government. They were made in response to changes in the sub-system which affected the ability of South Africa to use its power effectively; they were also part of a continuing quest for respectability and association with the West. But their primary objective was to replace white régimes with accep-

---

[31] See C. Stevens, " The Soviet Union and Angola," 75 *African Affairs* (1976), pp. 137–151; and C. K. Ebinger, " External Intervention in Internal War: the politics and diplomacy of the Angolan Civil War," 20 *Orbis* (1976), pp. 669–699. *Cf.* J. Saul, " Angola and After," 28 *Monthly Review* (1976), pp. 4–15; and T. H. Henriksen, " Angola and Mozambique: intervention and revolution," 71 *Current History* (1976), pp. 153–157.

table black leaders. Race is only one part of the equation: the other is to achieve a non-socialist political economy.

Clearly a continuation and escalation of the conflict in either Angola or Zimbabwe would jeopardise the prospects of moderate African governments being established in the region. South Africa's foreign policy and power failed to maintain the white *entente*; it has now concentrated largely on economic and diplomatic rather than military instruments to secure moderate régimes and an acceptable regional political economy. The demise of détente has not helped to secure a new pattern of co-existence. Indeed, the debate over the future political economy for Southern Africa by introducing new, extra-regional interests may undermine any tentative and fragile steps towards regional co-existence in the future. It is these wider concerns that make the talks over Zimbabwe so crucial and have led to new patterns of alignment—as in the Patriotic Front—which reflect differences in ideology rather than ethnicity or personality.

## V—Towards a New Regional Political Economy

The wind of change that is now blowing in Southern Africa is of particular importance not just because it will bring " independence " to the region but also because it may overturn an established and apparently entrenched regional political economy. Formal decolonisation in Africa has rarely meant much more than a change in *dramatis personae*; roles and relations have remained largely dependent, prescribed by external actors and associations. However, there has been a tradition of resistance to foreign values and exchange in Southern Africa among both blacks and whites and this may yet provide the basis for a more radical restructuring of its political economy. The continuation and escalation of guerrilla war and violent urban demonstrations may make majority rule merely one among a set of demands for a new order. These might include a rapid redistribution of property and opportunity, introduction of socialist structures and even the prompt emigration of most " settlers."

### (a) *Ideology as the Basis of New Coalitions*

The possibility of radical black régimes being established in Southern Africa has led to determined moves to head-off such change by both black and white States and the strengthening of the tacit alliance between these " moderate " régimes, which cuts across established international coalitions concerned with the region. This new form of " ideological " co-existence has different bases and structures than previous inter-State or inter-racial types; it also increases the prospect of more overt and insistent extra-regional involvement. It was this wider ideological concern—in addition to

" cold war " perspectives—that led to Kissinger's Southern African shuttle in September 1976: " We are facing a situation now in which a so-called ' armed struggle ' is already taking place in Rhodesia and is beginning in Namibia. The history of these struggles is that they lead to escalating violence, drawing in more and more countries, and have the danger of foreign intervention and the probability of the radicalisation of the whole continent of Africa, in which moderate governments will find it less and less possible to concentrate on the aspirations of their people and becoming more and more focused on events in Southern Africa. For this reason, we want to provide a non-violent alternative to this prospect." [32]

Although some wars of liberation in Africa have not produced " progressive " régimes (Kenya, for example), most have done so (as in Algeria); and the three Lusophone States established on the African mainland—Guinea-Bissau, Mozambique and Angola—all have become radical Black governments. Revolution in Southern Africa, then, may not only upset the radical/moderate balance in the OAU; it may also prove to be contagious, especially among the poorest African States. The prediction of Arrighi and Saul made in 1969 remains pertinent, and coincides with contemporary State Department fears: ". . . a successful socialist revolution in Southern Africa would radically restructure neocolonialist relationships on the whole continent since, after a necessary (and admittedly difficult) period of reconstruction it would act as a powerful pole of politico-economic attraction for the less developed and less wealthy nations of tropical Africa." [33]

The impact of such a radicalisation of the majority of African States would also affect Euro-African relations as well as the quality of global co-existence; hence the willingness of the EEC to support Kissinger's diplomacy and the establishment of a moderate African–European–American coalition to advance gradual change in the region: ". . . all European countries recognise the interests that they have in a moderate evolution of events in Africa . . . the consequences of the radicalisation of Africa would be serious in many other parts of the world. We have been urged, not only by the States of Southern Africa but by all the moderate leaders in Africa, to engage in this enterprise, because they understand what is at stake for the future of their countries. And, therefore, we believe that the national interest of the United States is involved." [34]

---

[32] United States Department of State, *The Secretary of State Press Conference*, September 11, 1976, p. 2.

[33] G. Arrighi and J. S. Saul, " Nationalism and Revolution in Sub-Saharan Africa," in their *Essays on the Political Economy of Africa* (1973), p. 37.

[34] *Op. cit.* in note 32 above, at p. 2.

The dominant United Nations–OAU coalition was created to advance black rule in Southern Africa in opposition to the minority faction. Moves towards dialogue and détente have cut across this established pattern of international coalitions; regional co-existence has changed its nature away from inter-racial and inter-State affairs and towards issues of an inter-élite and ideological nature. The question of what type of political economy has led to such new and more complex regional and global associations, in which the black-versus white-rule conflict is replaced or juxtaposed with socialist versus non-socialist alternatives. Because of wider international concerns, this may introduce into Southern Africa " cold war " symbolism of a type which African leaders have striven to avoid.[35] The complexities of race and class add to the imponderables of the region and further complicate the issues of integration and liberation, justice and order already present in Southern Africa. They also make the balance between conflict and co-operation more problematic and the achievement and maintenance of co-existence less likely.

### (b) *The Balance Between Confrontation and Co-existence*

The prospects for regional co-existence in Southern Africa cannot be separated, then, from two wider forms of co-existence—those between the super-Powers and between the two " global " ideologies of capitalism and communism. International détente enhances the chances of regional détente, but does not guarantee it. Indeed, one implication of a regional perspective is that extra-regional (as well as national) politics are treated as less salient. If the focus is on regional relations, then non-regional issues tend to move out of focus and become blurred, constituting the " background " to the scene. So, while they cannot be taken out of the picture, they are relevant only while the major images or actors are viewed. They are influential in an indirect way, through their participation in the two major coalitions. So regional co-existence could develop despite the wider global situation but this is unlikely until a consensus is formed within Southern Africa over its future political economy. The interests —both strategic and ideological—of the two super-Powers in the outcome of the issue, open the sub-system to increased, and more direct, extra-regional influence, and so undermine the possibility of a regionally-defined form of co-existence, both between States, races and ideologies.

The prospects of increased violence reinforce the attentiveness of

---

[35] For " cold-war " perspectives on contemporary regional conflict, see C. A. Crocker, " The African Dimension of Indian Ocean Policy," 20 *Orbis* (1976), pp. 637–667; and P. Vannemann, " Soviet National Security Policy in Southern Africa and the Indian Ocean: the Case of Mozambique," 3 *Politikon* (1976), pp. 42–50.

external interests,[36] and further reduce the chances of change without either conflict or interference. Until a new pattern of co-existence is created in Southern Africa, based on democratic, non-racial and egalitarian principles, the region is unlikely to co-exist with the changing world system. A new regional political economy is an imperative in order to re-establish the several varieties of co-existence and inter-dependence which are themselves prerequisites for real development in the future. Compatibility between races and States, ideologies and interests in Southern Africa may yet lead to fruitful forms of co-existence and détente within the region.

---

[36] See Stockholm Peace Research Institute, *Southern Africa: the escalation of a conflict* (1976); and P. Janke, *Southern Africa: new horizons* (1976).

# THE OSTRACISM OF SOUTH AFRICA

By

## RICHARD E. BISSELL

THE international effort to alter South Africa's racial policies has employed forms of political and social sanctions on a wide scale. South Africa has certainly not been the only international pariah in this age of contending ideologies, but it has clearly been more isolated diplomatically, over a longer period of time, than any other State challenging the international majority. Major and minor examples of diplomatic isolation can be found in all parts of the world: Franco's Spain, Israel, Trujillo's Dominican Republic, Castro's Cuba, Yugoslavia, junta-ruled Greece, post-revolutionary China, and others. All have been subjected to social sanctions of varying intensity since 1945, and indeed, could profitably be compared with the South African case. None, however, has experienced isolation in universal and regional organisations in a comparably escalating fashion.

The developing ostracism of South Africa in international organisations forces the observer to pose questions on two time scales. In the short run, have the social sanctions levied against South Africa accelerated the developments of the last few years in southern Africa? In the long run, more systemic questions must be asked. Can social sanctions be useful in affecting the behaviour of even the most intransigent societies, such as South Africa? And what impact does the expulsion of a member have on international organisations in their attempt to fulfil their mandates on a universal basis? The South African case can offer, at least, some tentative answers as the experiences of the post-war world would indicate.

## I—NATURE OF THE DISPUTE

The anti-apartheid forces in the United Nations were concerned with human rights until the late 1950s.[1] All resolutions were recommendatory in nature, originated principally in the United Nations

---

[1] Human rights as a concept can be elusive; Africans tend to limit it to the struggle against racial discrimination, as pointed out by A. Mazrui, "The United Nations and Some African Political Attitudes," in R. W. Gregg and M. Barkun (eds.), *The United Nations System and its Functions* (1968), pp. 47–51. More conventional views are reflected in H. Lauterpacht, *International Law and Human Rights* (1950); E. Luard (ed.), *International Protection of Human Rights* (1967), esp. pp. 249–85; E. B. Haas, *Human Rights and International Law* (1970); and R. B. Bilder, "Rethinking International Human Rights: A Current Assessment," 1 *Wisconsin Law Review* (1969), pp. 171–217.

Economic and Social Council (ECOSOC) and the General Assembly, and asked only for a negotiated end to apartheid; force, at that time, did not appear to be the solution. As leadership of the anti-apartheid forces was taken over by the African States, however, the dispute was altered in terms of tactics (by approaching the Security Council) and goals (by protagonists publicly and actively working for the overthrow of the South African Government). The dispute was thus highly politicised, in jeopardising the future of the South African polity, and attempting to invoke the extraordinary powers of the Security Council. It is interesting to note, at the same time, that the Africans continued to invoke human rights provisions of the Charter to justify the competence of jurisdiction of the United Nations; they also insisted that it was a serious political dispute, because they could then involve the Security Council with the problem: the Charter provides far greater powers for the Security Council than for human rights organs.

The South Africans have an equally interesting quirk in their logic, which has done nothing to de-politicise the dispute. They have maintained from the beginning that it is a political question, but purely internal, and therefore of no concern to the United Nations. It is additionally clear from the internal legislation of South Africa that they regard the anti-apartheid forces as a political problem, and have used extraordinary powers to deal with the threat to the existence of the régime. The South Africans, indeed, have refused to admit the jurisdiction of the United Nations organs concerned with human rights, thereby ensuring that the Africans would eventually seek aid from the Security Council through its powers under Chapter VII of the Charter.

The upshot of this gradual transformation into a political dispute has been a significant escalation of the stakes involved. The initial stakes in this particular game comprised simply the apartheid policy of South Africa, on one side, and the diplomatic prestige of the black Africans on the other. Through successive " raises " by each side, the existence of the present South African governmental structure has become imperilled, and the black African States have committed much of their political capital to a game with long-shot odds. In the investment, commercial, and strategic fields, too, the interests of outsiders are considerable; States such as France, the United States, and Japan have a large vested interest in the present government, while officially opposing apartheid.

The question of South African racial policies was first raised in the General Assembly in 1946, in connection with India's complaint concerning the discriminatory treatment of South African residents of Indo-Pakistani origin. Resolution 44 (I) of December 8, 1946, recommended that South Africa treat Indo-Pakistanis in conformity with " international agreements " and the United Nations Charter. South Africa adamantly held, however, that the question lay within South Africa's domestic jurisdiction, and that, in any case, India refused to negotiate in good faith. South Africa thus refused to co-operate with the General Assembly. As a result, no progress was made in negotiations, and the question remained on the agenda of the General Assembly until 1962, when it was combined with the apartheid question.

The question of the Indians in South Africa represented one of the first disputes between Commonwealth members taken to the United Nations. This violation of the tacitly accepted *inter se* doctrine of the Commonwealth set the stage for later recourse to the United Nations over the apartheid issue itself.[2]

Placed on the agenda of the United Nations General Assembly in 1952, " the question of race conflict in South Africa resulting from the policies of apartheid of the government of the Union of South Africa " [3] could not be treated in the same delicately legal manner as the situation of the Indians. The case of apartheid and its effects on the black population of South Africa was basically an issue between the black and white citizens of that country. Hitherto, the black-white issue had not been introduced at the international level, and many members of the United Nations, therefore, were reluctant to become involved. The precedent that it might establish for United Nations handling of violations of human rights was also disturbing to nearly all members, since few could honestly say that they had removed the beams from their own eyes.

The year 1952 was a time of high tension in the Cold War, which complicated third parties' views of the situation even further. As a vociferous opponent of the Communist bloc and a contributor to the Allied forces in Korea, South Africa had a claim on the United States and the West European members of the North Atlantic Treaty Organisation (NATO). Only in the votes of 1958 and the years following, did the United States depart from its English-speaking allies in voting with the majority attacking South Africa's race policies.[4] Thus the atmosphere into which India introduced the apartheid question in 1952 was not particularly friendly. It was,

---

[2] J. E. S. Fawcett, *The Inter Se Doctrine of Commonwealth Relations* (1958), pp. 36–37.

[3] Agenda Item 66 of the 7th Session, placed on the agenda by a letter from 13 States (A/2183), September 12, 1952. The result of deliberations was General Assembly Resolution 616, December 5, 1952, in GAOR, 7th Sess., *Resolutions*, Supp. Nr. 20 (A/2361), p. 8.

[4] For full voting figures, see D. Kay, *The New Nations in the United Nations, 1960–1967* (1970), pp. 200–205.

however, perhaps a typical situation in the United Nations, where one issue carries implications for other far more political questions, and thus becomes a victim of larger super-Power disputes.

The most striking common element of the nations pushing hardest for action against apartheid in the 1950s was their professed non-alignment. In the voting bloc that appeared each year for the debates on the apartheid issue one could see the growing power of what was in time to be called the Afro-Asian bloc, a misnomer for a group of nations that coalesced only on certain issues, especially apartheid.

Of greater importance to the future treatment of the apartheid issue was the establishment of a permanent African group at the United Nations.[5] As New York was the only city where all independent African States were represented, it was logical that the permanent machinery be located there.[6] What may have been unexpected was the impact the existence of the African consultation machinery might have on the United Nations. Given the general mandate of co-ordinating " all matters of common concern to the African States," the co-ordinators soon shaped the newly-emerging African States into a force to be reckoned with on every vote in the General Assembly. Of greatest importance to South Africa, the African bloc took the leadership of the anti-apartheid campaign away from the Afro-Asian group by 1962, and carried it to a point unimagined by early advocates.

The inability of the anti-apartheid movement to achieve its ultimate goal in the early years (1952–59) reflected several factors whose reversal would be important in the succeeding decade. Hesitant leadership by the Asians meant that the apartheid dispute was not widely discussed outside the General Assembly. The cold-war climate, which pervaded the United Nations, was also detrimental to progress on the apartheid issue. The killing of the United Nations Commission on Apartheid in 1955 at the insistence of South Africa was only one instance of that country parlaying its anti-communism into political capital at the United Nations. There was also an honest unwillingness of many members to continue the Commission without the co-operation of South Africa.

## II—THE GROWTH OF AFRICAN MILITANCE

The apartheid conflict grew during the period 1960–62 as a result of

---

[5] Conference of Independent African States, *Confidential Report* (April 15–23, 1958), Resolution XI, p. 117.

[6] There was, in addition, the opposition of the United Arab Republic to the existence of a headquarters in Africa, the complex reasons being explained by W. S. Thompson *Ghana's Foreign Policy, 1957–1966* (1969), p. 38.

two principal factors: the dramatic events of Sharpeville, and the upbeat of African organisational efforts. The crisis of 1960 is a turning-point in the apartheid dispute for a number of reasons. Most superficially, it blew open the ivory curtain for a moment to give the world a glimpse of the nature of apartheid. For the United Nations, the crisis jerked the issue out of its rut that ran from session to session of the General Assembly, and dumped it on the table of the Security Council. Inevitably then, the Secretary-General became involved, with the combination of these elements giving the apartheid dispute a new impetus.

The apartheid dispute received its second major impetus with the appearance of serious African organisational efforts. These efforts were apparent on the African continent and, even more importantly, in African caucuses at the United Nations, the International Labour Organisation (ILO), and the World Health Organisation (WHO).

The initial stages of the conflict between South Africa and the African States developed naturally from the policy decisions of the Conference of Independent African States and the easy publicity obtained by the Security Council meetings on Sharpeville. Important support for the African cause appeared periodically, often unpredictably: the exclusion of South Africa from the Commonwealth and its effects on British votes in the United Nations; the publicity of the South-West Africa issue; and, in 1962, the combining of the " Indian " and " apartheid " issues in the General Assembly. These random events never affected the basic African strategy, which depended on a large amount of good luck for implementation. Only gradually was the African group able to impose its interpretation of events on organisations: first, on the Special Political Committee and, eventually, the General Assembly. The process culminated with the creation of the Special Committee on Apartheid. Obtaining a secure " base of operations " was essential to the African cause if success were to be achieved in prodding other organisations into action. This was a time, after all, when no African continental organisation existed.

The Africans utilised two primary tactics, punishment and isolation of South Africa, much as though the Africans regarded it as a criminal. Punishment was represented by a movement to institute economic sanctions against South Africa. This tactic encountered significant opposition, even among African States, for nearly every State had something to lose by breaking economic ties with South Africa. Other opposition came from States concerned about possible violence that could ensue from enforcement of sanctions. The latter objection raises the question of whether economic sanctions would have helped, in this case, to control violence or merely to exacerbate the situation.[7]

Isolation of South Africa, on the other hand, was essentially a social sanction, and did not necessitate the ending of economic and political relationships. The theme, instead, was exclusion from international organisations, as though it were the international equivalent of exile.[8] Social sanctions, in contrast to economic sanctions, were easily voted, since they cost little and South Africa had been an international recluse since the coming to power of the Nationalist Party in 1948. The use of social sanctions had more " positive " elements than other forms of sanctions, in that South Africa withdrew from as many organisations as she was ejected from in the course of the dispute. In other words, South Africa understood the norm of behaviour that required termination of membership when basic values were in conflict.

What is most striking about 1961–63, perhaps, is the extraordinary naïvety with which the African group pursued its quarry in organisation after organisation, without an overall plan, but confident as long as South Africa was on the defensive. In the game of diplomatic poker, the Africans could place their bets without other players knowing whether they were bluffing. The result was success in many arenas, as measured by the diplomatic setbacks suffered by South Africa.

The General Assembly Special Committee on Apartheid, established in late 1962, became an essential weapon in the hands of the group trying to combat apartheid on the battlefield of the United Nations.

It remained a useful focus of the scattered anti-apartheid forces, even some non-governmental forces being brought into the fracas. In addition, it took the burden of the apartheid issue off the General Assembly and its regular committees, which was helpful to the General Assembly but, in a sense, also weakened the anti-apartheid movement in isolating it in a committee of its own.

Within the United Nations the Africans looked beyond the General Assembly and ECOSOC to the Security Council, where the real power lay. On a broader scale the Africans could see easy targets in the specialised agencies, where one country had one vote, giving them a solid bloc even before the debate began. Perhaps most importantly, however, the African diplomatic scene was reaching a maturity that would permit the formation of the Organisation of African Unity,

---

[7] See the excellent discussion by Margaret Doxey, "International Sanctions: A framework for Analysis with Special Reference to the UN and Southern Africa," 26 *International Organization* (1972), pp. 527–550.

[8] See A. Mazrui, "The United Nations and Some Political Attitudes," 18 *International Organization* (1964), pp. 507–508.

giving the anti-apartheid effort a new basis of public support as it fought South Africa on a broader front of international organisations.

### III—THE ORGANISATION OF AFRICAN UNITY AND THE RETREAT OF SOUTH AFRICA

The direction of the apartheid dispute during 1963–64 is notable for the role of the Organisation of African Unity (OAU), formed in Addis Ababa, Ethiopia in May 1963. The new organisation was an important force in affecting the apartheid issue in international organisations, but only as long as African diplomats remembered the spirit of Addis Ababa. Thus in this period one saw not only the most impressive successes of the anti-apartheid drive, but also the flow and ebb of OAU strength. As the Africans achieved success, and occasionally met failure, the lesson they learned was that only Africa could lead the fight against apartheid. This realisation led, by the end of 1964, to a realignment of tactics: a de-emphasis of the sometimes unwieldy OAU in favour of institutionalising the anti-apartheid effort in the United Nations.

International organisations were forced into a posture of reaction, in which the results only occasionally contributed to dampening the dispute. One frequent response, given the unwillingness of either side to compromise, was flat rejection of African demands—a move that could be sustained only in certain organisations not governed by the majority vote. This brutal form of socialisation of the Africans eventually produced the desired results in some organisations, in the sense that violent disruptions of existing programs ceased.

During 1963–64, the South Africans showed little ability to deal imaginatively with the new radical environment in which they were being pressured in organisation after organisation to withdraw. Such universal application of a diplomatic weapon had rarely been seen before, and certainly the South African government, which habitually responded slowly to international events, had a difficult time understanding the nature of its enemies. South Africa had not yet conceded the legitimacy of international concern with race problems in Southern Africa, and its response was generally to retreat in the face of diplomatic adversity, leaving the field to the enemy while attempting to devise a counter-strategy. In this case, it meant withdrawal from a number of specialised agencies before being expelled, in order to avoid having to meet the arguments of the anti-apartheid forces. South Africa's psychological posture was still weak in the wake of the Sharpeville incident and the resulting outflow of western capital. A more liberal wind, too, was emanating from the United States, carried by the rhetoric of the Kennedy Administration. South Africa was thus uncertain of western attitudes towards continued Nationalist rule, causing it to take a passive response to African attacks.[9]

The strangest element of the continuing debate over South Africa in the specialised agencies was that the opposing sides could not agree on the central question. The Africans asked whether any member could be tolerated in their ranks who practised racial discrimination. For their antagonists, primarily the West Europeans and Americans, the essential question was the possible effect of apartheid on the effectiveness of international programs. Through 1963, there had been no damage; when the Africans insisted on making an issue out of it, however, thereby crippling the African services, it became a choice as to which part of the program would have to be sacrificed: South Africa or the rest of the continent. Its withdrawal from the World Health Organisation (WHO), for example, was mentioned in terms of who would make up the $200,000 dues that it had paid annually into the WHO.[10]

The African States, in subsequently taking their campaign to the International Atomic Energy Agency (IAEA), were faced with a tricky problem. They had to face up to the fact that when a State is expelled from an international body, it not only loses the privileges attached thereto, but it is also freed from most responsibilities that are involved with belonging to the organisation.[11] The issue was quite important in the case of the IAEA, since South Africa was the only African country capable of producing nuclear weapons within a short time. In addition, one project of continuing concern to African leaders was the denuclearisation of the African continent, and one useful way of achieving that goal would be through the IAEA.[12] It

---

[9] See D. C. Watt, *A Survey of International Affairs 1962* (1970), pp. 497–498.

[10] See *20th World Health Assembly*, May 8–26, 1967, Pt. II, pp. 432–437.

[11] See C. W. Jenks, " Some Constitutional Problems of International Organizations," 22 *British Yearbook of International Law* (1945), pp. 11 and 25; in the case of the IAEA, under Article XVII.E, when a State ceases to be a member, " a State cannot denounce its contractual obligations to the Agency with respect to projects—*e.g.* it cannot escape any safeguard controls it agreed to on receiving assistance from the Agency." See P. C. Szasz, *The Law and Practices of the International Atomic Energy Agency* (1970), p. 102. The degree of South Africa's obligation to the IAEA in regard to specific projects is not available in public documents.

[12] Adding to the OAU dilemma was the position of the United Arab Republic and Tanganyika, who argued unsuccessfully in the OAU that denuclearisation had to be achieved through the IAEA or the United Nations: unilateral renunciation of nuclear weapons would be opening Africa to " a danger from outside Africa." Their position was, in effect, supported by African tactics at the IAEA. See *OAU, Council of Ministers*, Lagos Conference, February 24–29, 1964, pp. 330–335. Attempts to denuclearise the African continent were also occurring in the United Nations, where the history of unsuccessful efforts seemed to be plagued by a testy relationship with the OAU. All resolutions urged the OAU to undertake studies and initiate the process of drawing up a denuclearisation treaty. Progress was clearly impossible because of disagreements among African States. See United Nations, *The United Nations and Disarmament, 1945–1970* (UN Sales Nr. 70.1X.1), pp. 159–160.

was, therefore, a crucial decision as to which tactics to follow in the IAEA, since expulsion of South Africa would place it beyond the restraining reach of the organisation.

At the seventh session of the General Conference in 1963, the African States contented themselves with submitting a joint statement that condemned South Africa's policy of apartheid, and asked for a review of South Africa's role in the IAEA.[13] No further action, however, was taken at that time. By the 1964 Conference, the Africans felt somewhat more confident, and submitted a declaration that South Africa could not represent Africa on the Board of Governors and asked for its removal.[14] Again, however, it was treated as a mere expression of sentiment, allowing South Africa to remain a prominent member of the atomic energy community. The Africans seemed to realise, in the case of the IAEA, that they had plunged in over their heads, and were just barely treading water. Because of the OAU's vested interest in the IAEA, they did not dare splash too much, for South Africa might quit if it got too wet, which would be worse than having it remain in the organisation.

Africa, in any case, was moving into turbulent times, to be successively plagued by the second Congo crisis, the Rhodesian Unilateral Declaration of Independence (UDI), and finally the Nigerian civil war. In this atmosphere, the anti-apartheid campaign moved hardly at all, with resolutions of the OAU strictly ritualistic. The meeting of the foreign ministers in Nairobi early in 1965 once again asked African States to implement the sanctions voted two years before. But there were no new proposals, and the escalating rhetoric on apartheid was temporarily at a plateau.[15] The African offensive had reached its high point.

## IV—THE SOUTH AFRICANS COUNTER-ATTACK

By the mid-point of the 1960s, international organisations were ranged across a whole spectrum of policy responses to the apartheid conflict. Those taking the African line in resolutions, including the United Nations General Assembly, the International Labour Organisation (ILO) and Educational, Scientific and Cultural Organisation (UNESCO), continued their efforts to reverse South African policies. In other organisations such as the World Bank group or the

---

[13] Declaration on the Incompatibility of the Policies of Apartheid of the Government of South Africa with the Membership of the IAEA, September 30, 1963 (GC(VII)266), in IAEA, 7th General Conference, Agenda Item 10, mimeo.

[14] *Official Records of the International Atomic Energy Agency*, 8th General Conference, 84th Plenary Meeting, September 15, 1965 (GC(VIII)OR.84), p. 2.

[15] *OAU*, CM/RES. 48 (IV); text in A/AC.115/L.127, April 26, 1965. There was no resolution on apartheid at the Fifth Extraordinary Session of the Council of Ministers, June 10–13, 1965, Lagos.

IAEA, on the other hand, African initiatives were rejected, not so much as an expression of alignment with South Africa, but out of a belief that these latter organisations should not be used as battle-fields for African conflicts.

The greatest disappointment for the African diplomats, however, and the greatest implicit support for the South African position came from the unwillingness of key international groupings to pass mandatory sanctions: the Security Council in the political-military field, and the World Bank in economic affairs. Without those two institutions adopting policies in favour of mandatory sanctions, the tactic was clearly in trouble.

Some natural forces were also at work. By 1965, the African States had been around long enough to lose friends; endemic tensions existed between the Africans and Latin Americans, especially over trade matters after the United Nations Conference on Trade and Development (UNCTAD) of 1964, as well as competition for political spoils in the General Assembly.

A more complete explanation, however, would have to include the change in South Africa's posture. No longer passive, it even demanded to be admitted to the western caucus in 1965, and was admitted. It made increasingly successful overtures to black African countries for economic agreements and, implicitly, political agreements to " live-and-let-live." South African foreign policy, which had always been formulated as an extension of domestic policy, began to be formulated in a fashion that envisioned " national interests " that lay outside its national boundaries.[16] In the case of Rhodesia, for instance, South Africa undertook a complex policy of supporting the Smith régime at the same time it pressed for a negotiated solution.[17] Faced by a changing environment, therefore, the Africans found that the militant tactics of the early years did little to achieve the end of apartheid, the substance of what they sought. They still needed international organisations to implement their policies, and with the downgrading of social and economic sanctions as a tactic, the role of education became foremost.

Education, as implemented by the Special Committee on Apartheid with the aid of several other United Nations organs, became diffuse both in terms of methods and target groups. Propaganda, public testimony, travelling committee meetings, international conferences,

---

[16] For a contemporary South African critique of its "passive" foreign policy, see G. G. Lawrie, "South Africa's World Position," in 2 *The Journal of Modern African Studies* (1964), pp. 41–54.

[17] See R. Hall, *The High Price of Principles: Kaunda and the White South* (1970), pp. 143, 232. The same conclusions were reached by A. Mazrui, *On Heroes and Uhuru-Worship* (1967), p. 237, and Rosalyn Higgins, in S. M. Schwebel (ed.), *The Effectiveness of International Decisions* (1971), p. 45.

issuing of postage stamps, and publication of tracts on apartheid all became a part of the effort to " educate " the general public on the African view of apartheid. The educational campaign, in fact, had become too disorganised by 1969, and the United Nations was unable to evaluate its effectiveness; its repudiation of any plans to expand funding for education was clear in a decision of the Economic and Social Council (ECOSOC) not to fund another commission on apartheid, designed primarily to produce more propaganda.

A second emerging trend after 1965 was continual testing of the effectiveness of violence against the South African government. Violence was sanctioned by the Special Committee on Apartheid, but had to be implemented elsewhere, presumably by the OAU.[18] That which was still useful to the African cause in international organisations had been institutionalised: the Secretariat Unit on Apartheid for education; the Special Committee on Apartheid for liaison with the United Nations; and the fact of South Africa's expulsion from most international organisations.

The question of South African participation in international-sports competitions is important in illustrating the impact of non-governmental, transnational factors in international politics. The exclusion of South Africa from various sports groups, in fact, is important only in part in terms of social sanctions; sport is also an area of tremendous visibility to the general public, and the measures taken against apartheid, through exclusion of South African teams, had an enormous impact on the public.[19] The Africans felt that South Africa was not " playing fair " in the international system, and therefore deserved to be ejected from the game.

The role of the South African government in slowing down the campaign against apartheid appeared to be only indirect. Certainly many diplomatic initiatives were undertaken by the South Africans to strengthen ties with West European States and those African States willing to talk to them. By the late 1960s, South Africa had so little remaining presence in international organisations that, virtually by definition, its diplomatic goals had to be pursued through separate bilateral ties.

The period of retrenchment, therefore, was a sobering time for the OAU. It reached the apparent limits of its powers, direct and indirect, to implement sanctions at that time. Equally difficult to budge were the remaining international organisations that kept South Africa as a member. The campaign for ostracism was virtually

---

[18] For the OAU response, see reports of the OAU Heads of State meeting in Rabat, June 1972, where pledges to the Liberation Committee were doubled.

[19] See R. E. Lapchick, *The Politics of Race and International Sport: The Case of South Africa* (1975).

ended. Even the educational campaign, institutionalised by the Secretariat and the Special Committee, offered few challenges and showed few results. Symbolic conflict had run its course; some innovative thinkers turned to violent tactics, understandable in a time of despair. Whether violence would occur depended to a large degree on the strength of the institutional channels of protest established by the OAU, the UN, and other organisations during the stormy decade of the 1960s.

## V—THE DIPLOMATIC PLATEAU

The descriptive use of cyclical or linear paths for international history would be misleading in this case, for what had occurred by 1970 was a stalemate—not at the same level of tension as in 1952–59, and with somewhat greater understanding of the stakes of the conflict by both sides. The black Africans had forced South Africa into a new diplomatic posture, but the relative strengths of white and black Africa resulted in a reasonably static situation, a diplomatic plateau of uncertain duration.

The decade of the 1970s has so far witnessed the return of stability to most international organisations. Disruptions by Africans in protest against a South African role in the specialised agencies have occurred within the framework of constitutional instruments. The confrontation tactics of the previous decade have lost favour with the majority, as South Africa has used various diplomatic manoeuvres to keep the African States in disarray.

International organisations, by the 1970s, demonstrated predictable responses to demands for action against apartheid. The issue has been examined so often that there are few surprises for the intergovernmental organisations. The responses are quick, the secretariats know their powers, and the issue is handled with dispatch. Where severe conflicts appeared in the previous decade, they are largely ignored, and few efforts are made to prod the World Bank group or the IAEA into action against South Africa. Realism pervaded much of the African camp, and they chose to point their cannon where the projectiles might do some damage.

Events in Southern Africa in the course of 1974 led to a dramatic testing of South Africa's position in the United Nations. The changes of government in Portugal, and the subsequent independence for Angola and Mozambique indicated to the Africans and South Africans that the situation was once again fluid.[20] For the South Africans, the historic changes under way led them into dialogue over

---

[20] See C. Legum, " Southern Africa: The Politics of Détente," in this *Year Book*, Vol. 30 (1976), pp. 14–29.

Rhodesia and Namibia with the Africans and the United Nations. For most African States, however, the new fluidity in Southern Africa meant that they saw an opportunity to place greater pressure, perhaps the final push, on South Africa's apartheid policies. The results of that confrontation indicated to the world how solid the continuing stalemate in Southern Africa was.

The 29th Session began with a mild slap at South Africa, when the General Assembly voted not to accept the credentials of the South African delegation. Such a move had been somewhat routine in recent years, so the decision by the General Assembly on September 30, 1974, caused little stir. The only concern on the part of the South Africans was the presence of Algeria's Abdelaziz Bouteflika in the President's chair, a position that gave him the theoretical power to enforce the credentials decision. Such a choice for Bouteflika was delayed while the Africans pressed the Security Council to remove South Africa from the organisation entirely.

In the Security Council, where the debate ran through the last half of October, stated positions of delegations gave rise to a sense of predictability. The United States was unwilling to accept the expulsion of a member, and cited the goal of universality to buttress its case. The Africans demanded with greater fervour the removal of a moral cancer from the United Nations, and cited the opinion of the General Assembly in their favour. Compromise efforts on resolutions were not successful, and when the African resolution providing for the expulsion of South Africa was put to a vote on October 30, 1974, it was vetoed by the United States, the United Kingdom, and France. Such a united response by the western States was not entirely expected, and it underlined the profound division in the United Nations over South Africa.

Having achieved no satisfaction in the Council, the Africans returned to the Assembly, and urged Bouteflika to enforce the decision on credentials. He did so, in a decision on November 12, 1974, and was upheld in a vote of 91–22.

The United Nations and other organisations have continued to pass resolutions condemning South Africa's policies. In the autumn of 1976, the United Nations General Assembly passed ten separate resolutions on apartheid, calling for a complete economic boycott, an arms embargo, the exclusion of South Africa from all international events, and so forth. South Africa's response was categorical rejection of the resolutions as irrelevant and unconstructive. South Africa, in any case, had not attended the General Assembly nor submitted credentials for its delegates since the 29th session (1974). It has not paid any financial commitments since that date either, since the only penalty for not doing so is the loss of voting rights in the General

Assembly. The dispute over apartheid has thus arrived at a remarkably stable condition: freedom for the General Assembly to pass any and all resolutions, and the freedom for South Africa to ignore them. The Africans won the battle for social sanctions in international organisations, and apartheid remains.

# SINO-SOVIET CONFLICT AND RIVALRY IN SOUTH-EAST ASIA IN THE POST-VIETNAM PHASE

By

USHA MAHAJANI

THE end of the Indochina War removed the most important phenomenon that had dominated South-East Asia for three decades, overshadowing others including the budding Sino-Soviet rivalry. It originated in the late 1950s,[1] became noticeable in South-East Asia after 1965 and came into a sharper focus after the end of the Indochina War when the last tenuous bond between the People's Republic of China and the Soviet Union in support of Indochina's struggle against " American aggression " had been snapped. Now there is no need to maintain even a simulated unity of Communist ideology in defence of that struggle.

## I—BACKGROUND TO THE CONFLICT

The Sino-Soviet conflict can best be studied against the backcloth of the post-Vietnam War situation in South-East Asia: Peace has descended on Indochina where three independent States, Laos, Cambodia, and Vietnam, have emerged. Burma continues its strict neutrality, but the Association of South-East Asian Nations (ASEAN) —comprising Indonesia, the Philippines, Malaysia, Singapore and Thailand—has evolved since its formation in 1967 into a strong anti-Communist, pro-United States, pro-capitalist organisation.[2] Therefore a certain polarisation has developed between ASEAN and the countries of Indochina which share Laotian charges that ASEAN is an " instrument of neo-colonialism," an outgrowth of the South-East Asian Treaty Organisation (SEATO), and continues to serve the war policy of the United States.[3]

---

[1] J. G. Stoessinger hypothesises that the Soviet Union had come to appear as a threat to the Maoist leadership group in 1959. " China and the Soviet Union: Retrospect and Prospect," in Francis Wilcox, *China and the Great Powers* (1974), p. 17. Alfred D. Low traces the " seeds of the disagreement " to 1956–59 and the development of the dispute to the 1960–62 period. A. D. Low, *The Sino-Soviet Dispute, An Analysis of the Polemics* (1976), Chaps. 3 and 4. The Soviets claim that " in the late 1950s negative tendencies began to increasingly manifest themselves in China's relations with the Soviet Union— through no fault of the latter." O. Borisov, *Soviet-Chinese Friendly Ties, A Historical Review* (Moscow: 1974), p. 76.

[2] See Usha Mahajani, " Sino-American Rapprochement and the New Configurations in South-East Asia," in this *Year Book*, Vol. 29 (1975), p. 119.

[3] Editorial in *Sieng Pasason*, official Pathet Lao (People's Revolutionary Party of Laos) Newspaper, September 17, 1976, quoted in *The Asian Student*, October 9, 1976.

South-East Asia is now free of wars and decolonisation has been almost completed with Portugal's departure from East Timor.[4] Domestic insurgencies, however, continue to rage. The military *coup* in Thailand has disturbed the regional peace threatening an armed confrontation with Indochina.

The region moreover is by no means free of the intervention, influence and interest of foreign Powers. Contrary to the impression of an impending American withdrawal from Asia, Nixon's Guam Doctrine of 1969 reaffirmed United States treaty commitments in Asia asking the local governments to supply greater manpower while the United States would provide arms.[5] Ford's Pacific Doctrine reiterates: " America, a nation of the Pacific Basin, has a very vital stake in Asia and a responsibility to take a leading part in lessening tensions, preventing hostilities, and preserving peace. World stability and our own security depend upon our Asian commitments." [6] The United States has tightened its military commitments to its formal allies and consolidated ties with its South-East Asian semi-allies, Singapore, Malaysia and Indonesia. Since the *coup* in Thailand, the United States airbase at Takli has been reopened. The United States military mission in Bangkok remains active. ASEAN's call for South-East Asian neutralisation is not directed against the pre-eminent United States influence and military presence.[7]

Japan is an economic, if not a military or political, giant in South-East Asia. With a vital stake in it as a source of raw materials and a market for Japanese goods and with an equally vital interest in keeping the Malacca Straits open for international passage, Japan cultivates close economic ties with both Communist and non-Communist States in the region.

The end of the war has brought to an end the United Kingdom's Co-Chairmanship of the Indochina Conference. The dismantling of SEATO has further reduced its role.[8] But the United Kingdom has

---

[4] Whether Indonesia has invaded or liberated East Timor is a different question.

[5] The Nixon or Guam Doctrine refers to these points which President Nixon made in his remarks in July 1969, at Guam. Partial text in Sudarshan Chawla, M. Gurtov and A.-G. Marsot, *South-East Asia Under the New Balance of Power* (1974), pp. 124–126.

[6] Speech in Honolulu, December 7, 1975; text supplied by the State Department.

[7] At a speech honouring Vice-President Nelson Rockefeller, Singapore's Prime Minister, Lee Kuan Yew, expressed a hope on behalf of ASEAN nations that the United States " will continue to be a force in Asia." He firmly supported the right of the United States to " make big decisions to achieve a durable balance of power and peace all over the world especially in the Indian Ocean, the Pacific, East and South-East Asia and Australasia." See Government of Singapore, Ministry of Information, 12 *The Mirror*, Nr. 15, April 12, 1976, p. 1. Indonesia has also moved closer to the United States and like Singapore had long urged Thailand to go slow on its declared eagerness to dismantle United States bases: See *Victoria Times* (Canada), June 21, 1975.

[8] The British military adviser used to serve as SEATO's Chief of Defence Staff since 1971.

economic interests in the area, a protectorate in Brunei and some influence in Malaysia and Singapore through the Commonwealth association and the ANZUK (Australia, New Zealand and United Kingdom) force in Singapore. As a staunch ally of the United States, the United Kingdom is likely to continue to support American interests in South-East Asia.

India has no strategic interests in South-East Asia and its ideological solidarity of non-alignment with certain South-East Asian nations as in the 1950s and early 1960s has considerably weakened owing to the shifting international scene and the change of governments in these countries. But India has resumed vigorous diplomatic and economic relations with South-East Asian nations and constitutes one of the foreign Powers with an interest in their region.

The Soviet Union is not a predominant Power in South-East Asia. In addition to not having any military bases in the region it has suffered heavy political setbacks in Indonesia and Cambodia since the *coups* against Sukarno in 1965 and Sihanouk in 1970. But, as a super-Power, the Soviet Union seeks influence in the region, and needs to keep the Malacca Straits open for its ships.

China has re-emerged in South-East Asia. With the Sino-American reconciliation the United States has encouraged its allies and friends to let China play a " constructive role." [9]

The rivalry between China and the Soviet Union is only one among these several geo-political contours of South-East Asia.[10] But it merits attention as a part of their current global cold war. The Soviet-American Cold War has abated, and in any case their conflict of interest is not as sharp in South-East Asia as in Europe and the Middle East. The Sino-American hostility has been replaced by a congruence of interests. The United Kingdom, Japan and the United States are allies in South-East Asia, although the latter two are economic rivals. Thus the Sino-Soviet conflict is an outstanding, externally introduced, irritant in South-East Asia.[11]

At the outset it should be noted that South-East Asia is not pivotal to the basic " conflict " or " vital " to the security [12] of China and the

---

[9] See Usha Mahajani, " U.S.-Chinese Détente and Prospects for China's Rehabilitation in South-East Asia," III *South-East Asia—An International Quarterly*, Nr. 2, Spring 1974, pp. 713–739.

[10] See Usha Mahajani, *op. cit.* in note 2 above, pp. 106–120.

[11] Low's major study of the polemics of the Sino-Soviet disputes does not even touch on South-East Asia, nor discusses its impact on individual countries there, except Vietnam to which nine out of a total of 343 pages of the text are devoted. See Low, *op. cit.* in note 1 above, pp. 65, 66, 84, 228–302, 310, and 338–339.

[12] *Current Digest of Soviet Press* [*CDSP*], compiled in the United States, does not even have a heading " South-East Asia." Individual countries are occasionally mentioned under Far East, with scattered references to Indochina and nonaligned countries. The *Peking Review* during 1976 covered very few South-East Asian countries. The best

Soviet Union as Europe is to the United States and the Soviet Union.[13] Their conflict in South-East Asia is not an explosive issue likely to lead to a war. Neither Power has military bases or troops in that region or any deterministic influence. The confrontation of their forces, unlike that between the United States and the Soviet Union, is strictly along their mutual border.

The subject merits academic enquiry because China and the Soviet Union have extended their conflict into wider global and non-military areas [14]: Latin America, especially in Chile, Brazil and Cuba; Africa, especially in Angola; Europe where China opposes détente; the Indian subcontinent; East Asia and finally South-East Asia. Each uses obverse accusations to persuade various countries to regard the other as their deadly enemy.

## II—BROAD ASPECTS OF SINO-SOVIET CONFLICT

Both China and the Soviet Union claim themselves to be truly Marxist and each other to be heretics. The ideological conflict affects their relations with Communist governments and movements. Each accuses the other of being the enemy of the world.

China brands the Soviet leaders as " the new Tsars "; and the Soviet government as " an out and out social imperialism " engaged in global aggression, control, subversion and colonial expansion." [15] In October 1972 it declared the Soviet Union as its chief enemy and set out to " expose Soviet expansionism." [16] Its attacks on " United States imperialism in Indochina " tapered off, and the invectives, earlier reserved for the United States, were directed against the Soviet Union.[17] After the Indochina war, China has intensified the frequency and stridency of innovative invectives against Soviet " social imperialism " as being " the worst of its kind," a " growing menace," " a most

---

source to study Sino-Soviet rivalry in South-East Asia is *USSR and Third World, A Survey of Soviet and Chinese Relations with Africa, Asia and Latin America*, compiled by Central Asian Research Centre, London.

[13] Elsewhere each has shown readiness to fight with its adversary: the Soviet Union in East Europe; China in Korea and along the Sino-Soviet border.

[14] This point has been made in Wilcox, *op. cit.* in note 1 above, p. 26.

[15] For the remarks in the Security Council by Ambassador Huang Hua, December 5–6, 1971, and Peking radio domestic broadcast, December 15, 1971, see Sub-committee on National Security and International Operations of the Committee on Government Operations of the United States Senate, *International Negotiation, Chinese Comment on Soviet Foreign Policy* (1972) pp. 1 and 3. These charges are repeated endlessly as on August 15, 1976, by the official New China News Agency [NCNA] and the Communist Party journal, *People's Daily*.

[16] Editorial in *Renmin Ribao, Honggi, Jiefangjun Bao*; see *Peking Review*, Nr. 40, October 6, 1972.

[17] Between 1972 and 1975 *Peking Review* published countless articles and quotes from foreign sources on Soviet " imperialism and attempts at hegemony." See Mahajani, *op. cit.* in note 9 above, p. 735.

dangerous source of war," and an " arch enemy of the world people, more dangerous than classical European colonialism and post-Second World War American imperialism " bent on a global offensive. The Soviets are accused of seeking hegemony by, *inter alia*, expanding their naval fleets, oceangoing fishing vessels, merchant ships, so-called scientific research ships and engaging in espionage activities in order to step up plunder of maritime resources.[18]

Both China and the Soviet Union accuse each other of seeking global hegemony, but the former has made it a special pejorative charge against the latter and the term is understood as such in international parlance. To boost its self-image as a " socialist developing country " whom other Third-World nations admire, China reiterates that the latter are winning new victories in their joint struggle against hegemony.[19] The willingness of a nation to " oppose hegemony " has become a measure of China's success.

Non-alignment and economic development being primarilyThird-World concerns, and since the Soviet Union has built friendly ties with many non-aligned countries, China warns that the Soviet Union is only " the other super-Power " and no better; the " New Tsars " of Russia are a " ferocious enemy of the non-aligned movement "; and Soviet aid is as exploitative as western aid. Commenting on the United Nations Conference on Trade and Development (UNCTAD) in Nairobi, China violently denounced the Soviet Union as a " self-styled ' natural ally ' of the developing countries that shamelessly demands a special most favoured nation treatment." [20]

### III—RELEVANCE OF SOUTH-EAST ASIA
#### IN THE RIVALRY

South-East Asia thus easily fits into the framework of the implacable Sino-Soviet hostility and suits their Third-World diplomacy. Moreover, China would like to prevent Soviet encirclement through South-East Asia just as it previously tried to break United States encirclement. There is also the old international game (proven futile several times) to try to exclude one's enemy from a particular region. The United States played it against China in the 1950s and the 1960s. Now the Soviet Union and China are playing it against each other.

In early 1976, China fired a major salvo to warn the South-East

---

[18] For a few samples, see 19 *Peking Review*, Nr. 1, January 2, 1976, pp. 24–25; Nr. 2, January 9, 1976, pp. 20–22; Nr. 5, January 30, 1976, pp. 9–13; and Nr. 6, February 6, 1976, pp. 8–9, 21.

[19] *E.g.*, Premier Hua Kuo-feng's speech in May, 1976, in honour of Prime Minister Lee Kuan Yew of Singapore; *ibid.* Nr. 20, May 14, 1976, p. 7; and Nr. 24, June 11, 1976, pp. 19–21.

[20] *Ibid.* Nr. 24, June 11, 1976, pp. 19–20; and Nr. 36, September 3, 1976, pp. 15–16.

Asian States to beware of the Soviet " tiger " now that the American " wolf " had been repulsed. In the usual style of " noting " developments abroad, China observed that the South-East Asian governments were aware of Soviet attempts to fill the vacuum; that they were struggling against Soviet bids for military bases and that they repeatedly uncovered the KGB's attempts at subversion and plots to sow discord among South-East Asian countries. Philippine officials and a Thai newspaper were quoted to that effect.[21]

China also denounces Soviet aid on the following grounds: (i) Moscow forces down prices of raw materials and raises those for its own products; it " gangs up " with the western capitalist countries to monopolise the rubber market and force down rubber prices as in Malaysia in 1974 when it also raised the price of urea exported to Thailand; (ii) Moscow uses " trade repayment " as a new form of foreign trade link to satisfy its own insatiable greed for exploitation. A recipient has to ship products from a Soviet " assisted " project to the USSR; and (iii) through joint enterprises, the Soviets export capital to plunder other countries' mineral resources and control their production.[22]

China's influence in South-East Asia would not be a military threat to the Soviet Union but a blow to its image as a super-Power which needs friends especially if there is a strong rival to contend with. Failure to win South-East Asian support would partially jeopardise the validity of Soviet international stands. As a professed friend of the Third World, the Soviet Union presents its assistance as being true " socialist aid " in contrast to " western neo-colonialism " and is offended when China equates the two as " exploitative." [23]

The Soviet Union therefore has also taken the offensive. In 1975 it welcomed the " defeat of the Pentagon and reactionary régimes in Indochina " and the hopeful signs of demands for United States military withdrawal from Thailand and the Philippines, but warned of Peking's pressure on them and added that diplomatic ties would only increase Chinese interference in South-East Asia to the advantage of the United States. The Soviet Union greatly fears Sino-United States collusion. It now claims that China is " a dangerous enemy not only of the Socialist countries but also of all peace-loving peoples and States "; that China's dangerous influence on Asian politics cannot be ignored; that Chinese leaders, well aware of the risks of direct military confrontation with the Soviet Union, are

---

[21] " Guard Against Tiger at the Back Door While Repulsing Wolf at the Gate," *ibid.* Nr. 2, January 9, 1976, pp. 21–22.

[22] *Ibid.* Nr. 24, June 11, 1976, pp. 19–21; and Nr. 36, September 3, 1976, p. 14.

[23] In a long article, *Pravda* deplored the speeches made by some delegates at the non-aligned conference in Colombo, blaming both socialist and capitalist aid and trade policies; XXVIII *CDSP*, Nr. 3, September 15, 1976, p. 19.

trying their luck elsewhere; and that now they are seeking outlets to the sea via Pakistan, Bangladesh and Burma.[24]

The Soviet Union warns of the " great-Han hegemonism " of the Maoists who play a two-faced game with South-East Asia, promising non-interference and doing just the opposite. For example, the Soviet's charge: in June 1975, Burmese separatist elements, aided by Chinese instructors from Yunnan, revolted; China has sent thousands of guerrillas to Burma and Thailand which has not even received Chinese guarantees against interference; China gives support to the seccessionists operating in the Malaysian jungles, calling these " declassé elements " revolutionaries, and openly congratulates the terrorist organisations of Malaysia and Indonesia.[25]

Given South-East Asian anxiety over borders, the Soviet Union denounces China as a violator of boundaries. A Soviet book published in late 1975, *The People's Republic of China: Political and Economic Development in [since?] 1973*, charged that China " ignores existing State frontiers " and precipitates disputes: for example, China's claims of 70,000 kilometres of Burmese territory are a part of its massive territorial claims against India, Mongolia and the Soviet Union; to press these claims China provokes border conflicts, as in Burma in 1955. In one of its sharpest attacks, Moscow has charged that Peking is expanding southward. It produces expansionist maps designating international waters adjoining the territorial waters of the Philippines, Indonesia, Malaysia and Vietnam as Chinese inland waters; and claims as Chinese territory those islands there which since times immemorial have been used by these people. China's " seizure " of the Paracel Islands from South Vietnam in 1974 would enable it to establish complete rule over the entire South China Sea and shows that China asserts its claims by force. It also claims the Spratley Islands lying about 1,000 kilometres to the south. All this shows that Peking aims to become a hegemonic Power in Asia rather than to improve relations with its neighbours.[26]

### IV—ASIAN COLLECTIVE SECURITY SYSTEM

In June 1969, Mr. L. Brezhnev proposed a collective security system for Asia and other regions where the threat of a new world war or a regional one was centred. He also called for stable borders and

[24] *Izvestiya*, July 11, 1975: see V *USSR and Third World*, Nrs. 6–8, July 7–December 31, 1975, p. 275; *Soviet Weekly* (London), September 20, 1975, p. 6; and Moscow radio, reported by D. Davis, *Far Eastern Economic Review*, July 9, 1976, p. 21.

[25] M. Gavin, " Peking Smoke Screen," *New Times*, Nr. 30, 1975, p. 23; *Soviet News* (London), December 16, 1975; report on the 25th CPSU Congress, *Far Eastern Economic Review*, March 19, 1976, pp. 22–23.

[26] *Soviet News*, December 16, 1975.

peaceful co-operation among States. China has scorned the move which was undoubtedly made to neutralise its border claims. The Asian Collective Security System (ACCS) is not a proposal for a military pact but for a Helsinki-type agreement. The Soviet Union would like nothing better than China's endorsement which would also signal a Soviet victory in the territorial dispute. China's refusal prompts it to seek wider Asian support and to expose China as an enemy of Asian countries that rejects the sanctity of existing borders.

Undaunted by a negative response from South-East Asia, the Soviet Union now presents ACCS in terms of the principle of territorial integrity and inviolability of borders incorporated in the Helsinki agreement: (i) participants must not demand or seize or usurp each other's territory; (ii) State frontiers should be changed according to international law, by peaceful means or agreement; and (iii) force is renounced in settling international disputes. The Soviets stress that ACCS is particularly suited to South-East Asia where many conflicts might provoke world conflagration.[27]

To allay small nations' concern over China's reaction and retaliation and their weariness about being hustled into a Soviet-inspired project, the Soviet Union reiterates that ACCS is not anti-China but " must be a result of the efforts of *all* Asian States without exception"; it is a long process of creating regional zones of peace and bilateral and multilateral agreements. Far from exacerbating their conflicts with China, ACCS would help promote an area of peace and harmony which, after all, is the self-proclaimed goal of South-East Asian countries themselves. The Soviet Union claims " something hopeful is happening " and points to settlements in the Indian subcontinent. But in South-East Asia it can only hope that Soviet-Philippine diplomatic relations " will foster creation of a favourable climate in this region." [28]

China attacks the Soviet Union for " peddling " ACCS and cites local comments to prove how the South-East Asians have rebuffed ACCS as " a Soviet tool to contend for hegemony in Asia and to disintegrate and control Asian countries." It taunts the Soviet Union as a European country waxing eloquent about Asian security with a mania. Thus, China has invoked its own Monroe Doctrine and echoed the Japanese catch-phrase, " Asia for the Asians." [29] The

---

[27] *Izvestiya*, August 28, 1975: see *USSR and Third World, op. cit.* in note 24 above, p. 276; U. Mahajani, *op. cit.* in note 9 above, pp. 737–39; D. Muraka, " Soviet Plan for an Asian Collective Security Pact," *South China Morning Post*, October 9, 1975.

[28] V. Kudryavtsev, " Asia's Pressing Problem," *Izvestiya*, July 16, 1976: see XXVIII *CDSP*, Nr. 28, August 11, 1976, p. 14.

[29] See 19 *Peking Review*, Nr. 1, January 2, 1976, p. 25; Nr. 15, April 9, 1976, p. 18; and Nr. 47, November 19, 1976, p. 30; the South-East Asian sources cited are: a Thai paper, *Chia Pao Daily News*; comments by former Thai Foreign Minister; and a Philip-

Soviet Union claims that China's suspicion of ACCS as a scheme to encircle and isolate China is " ridiculous " and counters that the Chinese leaders violate the Bandung spirit and all other principles of peaceful co-existence, and oppose ACCS simply because it " conflicts with China's designs to grab Asia for its own domain." [30] So far China is the winner.

## V—THE ASSOCIATION OF SOUTH-EAST ASIAN NATIONS

Despite initial scepticism towards the Association of South-East Asian Nations (ASEAN) the Soviet Union became encouraged by ASEAN's proposal for South-East Asian Neutralisation in 1970 and grew tolerant towards the Association after 1971.[31] Soviet hopes were shattered by growing evidence in 1975 that Indonesia wanted ASEAN to become " a military bloc " of anti-communist countries through a Council of Defence Ministers and development of military co-operation. Fearful that this " anti-communist orientation " would be anti-Soviet and anti-Indochina, the Soviet Union has urged ASEAN to concentrate on regional co-operation.[32]

China, though gratified, cannot publicly praise the " anti-Communist " nature of ASEAN, but has warmly commended its efforts to " oppose economic plunder and exploitation by imperialism." It now hails ASEAN for gaining new victories in defence of national rights, strengthening regional economic co-operation, and for jointly struggling against hegemony and the super-Powers who are shifting their economic crisis on to others.[33] A curious praise since ASEAN is closely integrated into the western capitalist system. China sees in the ASEAN summit meeting in Bali in February 1976, a triumph in its own cause, and claims that the meeting " spurned " ACCS, " hawked by the Soviet Union." [34]

## VI—COMMUNISM IN SOUTH-EAST ASIA

As leading communist countries, each claiming true inheritance of Marxism, China and the Soviet Union strive for support from South-East Asian Communists. Neither has exclusive domination, but each has a sphere of influence. In Laos and Vietnam where Communism

---

pine paper, *The Orient News,* which have violently criticised ACCS: see *ibid.* Nr. 1, January 2, 1976, pp. 24–25.

[30] *Izvestiya, op. cit.* in note 27 above: see *USSR and Third World, loc. cit.* in note 27 above; *Izvestiya,* July 16, 1976, and XXVIII *CDSP,* Nr. 28, August 11, 1976, p. 14.

[31] Comments in *Izvestiya,* July 27, August 21, September 27, 1975, and in *Pravda,* July 29 and September 26, 1975: see *USSR and Third World, op. cit.* p. 275.

[32] *Pravda,* August 31 and November 14, 1975: *ibid.* pp. 276, 292.

[33] *New China News Agency,* August 26, 1975: *ibid.* p. 277; *Asahi Evening News,* July 4, 1975; 19 *Peking Review,* Nr. 4, January 23, 1976, pp. 54 and 56.

[34] 19 *Peking Review,* Nr. 10, March 5, 1976, p. 20.

gained power after prolonged national liberation wars, the Soviet Union has retained ideological solidarity. To the still struggling Communist insurgents elsewhere, and to Cambodian Communists who won a victory after a short but fierce struggle, China appears a true Marxist model. The Thai, Malaysian and Burmese Communist leaders are pro-China. The latter visited Peking twice in 1976 and affirmed " continuous growth of revolutionary friendship and military unity " with the Chinese Communist Party.[35]

The Soviet Union has sought ideological links with Burma's left-wing Marxist-oriented government. In December 1975 a delegation of the Communist Party of the Soviet Union (CPSU) toured Burma at the invitation of the ruling Socialist Party, which, for the Soviet Union, is the next best thing to a purely communist solidarity.[36] In the Philippines China supports the New People's Army which is still engaged in an armed revolt, while the 25th Congress of the CPSU was attended by a Philippine Communist Party delegation led by Jesus Lava who scorned Maoism for joining imperialism and undermining the alliance of anti-imperialist forces.[37]

The Sino-Soviet rivalry has torn apart the remnants of the *Partai Kommunist Indonesia* (PKI). After the carnage of the anti-Sukarno *coup* in 1965, some Indonesian Communists took refuge in eastern Europe and some, led by Jusuf Adjitorop, went to China. The latter has accused the Soviet Union of trying to take advantage of the United States failure in Indochina to expand its own influence in South-East Asia. He also has charged that the Soviet armies are " ganging up with the Indonesian revisionists to split the PKI and sabotage the Indonesian revolution," and that the Soviet Union controls the renegade revisionist Indonesian clique in Moscow and gets it to issue revisionist documents in the name of Marxist-Leninist Group of the Communist Party of Indonesia.[38] Peking also strongly supports the Fretilin movement in East Timor.[39] Ideologically China has won solidarity with the major faction of Indonesian Communism because its hands are not tied by the restraints of preserving amity with Indonesia's anti-Communist military government.

## VII—RELATIONS WITH INDIVIDUAL COUNTRIES

The end of the Indochina war has also intensified the bilateral diplomacy of China and the Soviet Union towards South-East Asian

[35] *Ibid.* Nr. 5, January 30, 1976, p. 14; Nr. 48, November 26, 1976, p. 3.

[36] *Izvestiya*, December 12, 1975, and *Pravda*, December 21, 1975, gave glowing accounts of the tour; *USSR and Third World, op. cit.* in note 24 above, p. 283.

[37] *Far Eastern Economic Review*, March 19, 1976, p. 23.

[38] 19 *Peking Review*, Nr. 7, February 13, 1976, pp. 28–29.

[39] *NCNA*, December 31, 1975: see V *USSR and Third World*, Nrs. 6–8, July 7–December 31, 1975, p. 288.

countries. The times appear propitious for China because the anti-Communist governments, having become uneasy at the Soviet-Vietnamese friendship and a possibility of further Soviet influence, are collectively welcoming China to enter their region. Their contacts with China have considerably increased since 1974 when Malaysia recognised Peking and Imelda Marcos, wife of the Philippine President, visited China.

## (a) *Burma*

As Burma moved closer to China in 1974, the Soviet Union tried to ingratiate itself with General Ne Win by praising him and denouncing China for giving clandestine support to the Burmese insurgents. The tactics failed, and, during 1974–1975, the Soviet role in Burma —especially in terms of economic aid—was reduced to nil. In 1974 Burma even declined a Soviet offer to build an oil refinery and then invited China to make a feasibility study on a project first studied by Soviet experts. The Soviet Union, in turn, has bitterly attacked the " Maoist intrigues ": China has adopted a " Great-Power " approach to Burma more than to any other country in order to turn it into a stronghold of Chinese influence in South-East Asia; the " Maoists " team up with the reactionaries in Burmese cities and, with subversion and " escalation of armed provocation," seek to keep Burma " in a state of permanent tension "; the sub-units of the Chinese army are giving " direct and all-round support " to the " rebels," preventing Burma from having peace.[40]

The Soviet Union, however, cannot fight geography nor block Burma's increased contacts with China. In August–November 1975, several Burmese leaders and delegations went to China to " affirm friendship," and in December the Chinese Foreign trade minister visited Burma.[41] Soviet-Burmese contacts have been scanty except for the CPSU delegation's visit. The Soviet Union however, realises that Burma is not a Chinese satellite and, therefore, continues to befriend it by offering aid and by expressing gratification when it is accepted.[42]

## (b) *Indonesia*

Indonesia is in no hurry to restore diplomatic relations with China. On August 17, 1975, the 30th anniversary of Indonesian independence, President Suharto ruled them out because " foreign support " for the PKI was interference in Indonesian affairs. In November of the same year, Foreign Minister Adam Malik echoed these sentiments at a

[40] *Soviet News*, July 22, 1975 and January 20, 1976.

[41] *USSR and Third World, op. cit.* in note 24 above, p. 284.

[42] *Izvestiya*, November 12, 1975: see *USSR and Third World, op. cit.* in note 24 above, p. 283. *Peking Review* had no coverage of Burma in 1976.

press conference pointing to widespread anti-Chinese feeling among the people.[43] China too, therefore, feels free to attack Indonesia without reserve—especially its " naked aggression " and " massive invasion " of East Timor.[44]

The Soviet Union is on the horns of a dilemma because it wants to cultivate further its cordial diplomatic relations with Indonesia. China's failure raises hopes, but the growing United States–Indonesian military ties cause alarm.[45] The Soviet Union therefore blends cajolery and mild admonition in its comments on Indonesia. Its concern over Indonesian " armed intervention " in East Timor [46] is alleviated by President Suharto's assurances in his 1975 independence speech on developing economic co-operation with all States, including socialist ones. The Soviets claim that this speech and the exchange of Parliamentary delegations confirm the possibilities for co-operation in the economic and international affairs.[47]

### (c) *The Philippines*

In June 1975, President Marcos visited Peking and profusely flattered China as " the leader of the Third World and a moral inspiration " to all. Acting Prime Minister Teng Hsiao-peng promised non-interference. The two countries announced their " opposition to any attempt by any country or a group of countries to establish hegemony or create spheres of influence in any part of the world." Marcos claimed to be completely satisfied with Chinese intentions.[48]

The Philippines is, however, cautious in its approach to Peking and, before Marcos' visit, had established diplomatic relations with the Soviet Union in 1974. China, aware that its policy towards the Filipino Chinese is still suspect, is letting the matters remain quiet.[49]

---

[43] *USSR and Third World, op. cit.* in note 24 above, p. 292.

[44] *NCNA*, December 7, 1975, *ibid.* pp. 287–88. During 1976, all references to Indonesia in *Peking Review* were in terms of violent denunciation of Indonesian actions in East Timor: see Nr. 1, January 2, 1976, p. 22; Nr. 15, April 9, 1976, p. 21; Nr. 25, June 18, 1976, p. 21; Nr. 31, July 31, 1976, p. 11.

[45] Moscow radio expressed concern at the United States–Indonesian talks during July 1975 for increased United States military aid to Indonesia: see *USSR and Third World, op. cit.* p. 292.

[46] *Tass* report, October 24, 1975; *Pravda*, December 12, 1975: see *USSR and Third World, op. cit.* in note 24 above, pp. 286–87.

[47] *Pravda, Izvestiya* and Radio Moscow, August 17, 1975: *ibid.* pp. 287–88. *Izvestiya* carried a long article on October 23, 1975, by its special correspondent who visited Indonesia on a tourist visa. He " found " warm popular friendship for the Soviet Union in the light of many years of Soviet assistance: *ibid.* pp. 291–92.

[48] Joint communiqué, July 9, 1975; See " Asia, A New Tripolar Balance," *Time*, June 23, 1975, p. 37; D. Bloodworth, " Chinese Win Friends and Influence," *Asahi Evening News*, July 4, 1975.

[49] *The Asian Student*, San Francisco, May 8, 1976. During 1976 *Peking Review* made only one brief reference to the Philippines in connection with China's relief aid to the Filipino flood victims: See Vol. 19, Nr. 24, June 11, 1976, p. 7.

(d) *Singapore*

After Vietnam, Prime Minister Lee Kuan Yew urged all South-East Asian countries to make peace with China and not show favours to the Soviet Union which would provoke the Maoists into stoking the fires of Communist insurgency. Singapore struck off the official record the visit of a single Soviet destroyer made in 1971 as being " unexpected " and without permission.[50]

Lee Kuan Yew's " goodwill mission " during May 1976, was used by China to launch a tirade against " the other super-Power " and to praise Singapore and ASEAN for opposing hegemonism. He evidently did not appreciate the attack but merely welcomed China's support for ASEAN and hoped for better Sino-Singapore relations without referring to imperialism and hegemonism.[51] The Soviet Union is content that China has not won a total victory although Singapore has established close, extensive trading relations with China and permits Chinese financial institutions to operate in Singapore.

(e) *Thailand*

During the brief civilian period [October 1973–October 1976] Sino-Thai relations were consolidated. In July 1975, Premier Kukrit Pramoj visited China and joined his hosts in opposing hegemony. He called the Soviet Union just another super-Power contending for hegemony and declared that it would not be allowed to fill the vacuum created by United States withdrawal. The Chinese " broadly hinted " their support for continued United States military presence in South-East Asia (including Thailand) as a counter to the Soviet Union and its new victorious ally, Vietnam.[52]

The Soviet Union, stung by this camaraderie, retaliated by propaganda and charged that China was trying to undermine the Thai government by manipulating Thai overseas Chinese and disrupting the Thai economy, and that it would use diplomatic relations to interfere in Thai affairs, through about 400,000 Chinese with " influential economic positions." [53] But the Soviet Union had also welcomed the Thai policy of relaxing restrictions on the left wing, closing down United States military bases and promoting amicable relations with Indochina.

---

[50] Bloodworth in *Asahi Evening News*, July 4, 1975, *op. cit.* in note 48 above.

[51] 19 *Peking Review*, Nr. 20, May 14, 1976, pp. 3–4, 7–8. Its 1976 issues contain no reference to Malaysia which remains equally cordial to China and the Soviet Union, and has warned China not to support Malaysian communists: See *Asahi Evening News*, June 23, 1975.

[52] 19 *Peking Review*, Nr. 2, January 9, 1976, p. 21; editorial in *Asahi Evening News*, July 4, 1975 and Bloodworth, *op. cit.* in note 48 above, in the same issue.

[53] *Pravda*, June 23, 1975, reported in *Asahi Evening News*, June 24, 1975.

The Soviet Union has now expressed concern over the " anti-Communist " and " anti-progressive " developments since the Thai military *coup* in October 1976 and over the " reported " role of the CIA but, wishing to keep a foothold in Thailand, it has not denounced the Thai military rulers.[54] In fact, it agreed in October 1976, after several years of sticky negotiations, to sign a Cultural and Scientific Agreement with Thailand, like the one it signed earlier with Malaysia, in which, owing to their anti-Communist sensitivity, a special clause was incorporated that both parties have the right to take measures to maintain internal peace and security. The concession stems from what observers call Soviet " keenness " to counteract China's influence in Thailand.[55]

China reported the official Thai version of the events leading to the *coup* without criticising the Thai military or even expressing concern over its " anti-Communism." [56] China apparently is not disturbed by the suppression of those left-wing forces that are not exclusively pro-China; it probably welcomes the return of the United States and of Thai hostility towards Laos and Vietnam. Before the *coup* China often gave coverage to the " splendid victories " of the Thai Communist forces and their following " the correct (*i.e.* pro-China) political line." [57] It remains to be seen how it will pursue its diplomacy in Thailand.

### (f) *Indochina*

In Indochina the rivalry between China and the Soviet Union combines ideological struggle and diplomatic competition to win over independent States. The pattern of their aid policy and diplomatic support during the Indochina war has greatly affected their relative success or otherwise. Some patterns of alignment are discernible.

### (g) *Cambodia*

During the war China gave asylum to Sihanouk. The Soviet Union, swayed by calculations of its dispute with China, kept a diplomatic mission accredited to Lon Nol. Indignant at this betrayal, Cambodia now rebuffs Soviet offers of diplomatic relations. China has exploited this situation to attack the Soviet Union. The latter has hit back by trying to convince the Cambodians that it really did support the Khmer liberation forces and backed their representation in the United Nations as Sihanouk himself acknowledged in November 1974. These efforts have been to no avail. In August 1975, Cambodian

[54] *Pravda*, October 8, 1976, p. 5: See 40 *CDSP*, November 3, 1976, p. 19.
[55] *The Asian Student*, October 23, 1976.
[56] 19 *Peking Review*, Nr. 43, October 22, 1976, pp. 45–46.
[57] *Ibid.* Nr. 29, July 16, 1976, p. 1; Nr. 34, August 20, 1976, p. 23.

leaders, including Premier Khieu Samphan, received a grand-victory welcome in China and signed an agreement of economic co-operation. In a major shift on foreign policy, Khieu Samphan, who until then had not criticised the Soviet Union, signed a joint communiqué endorsing China's line on all international issues including an attack on both super-Powers for seeking world hegemony. His visit was followed by that of Deputy Premier Ieng Sary in September and a Cambodian journalists' delegation in October.[58]

Since then China and Cambodia have moved in unison. They boycotted the World Congress of Women in East Berlin in October 1975, because the Soviet bloc had a major role in hosting it, and, more importantly, the 25th Congress of the CPSU. To keep Cambodia in its orbit China often gives, in addition to aid, supportive publicity to Cambodia's constitutional and reconstruction achievements.[59] In the hope of getting reciprocity, the Soviet Union also heaps praise on Cambodian reconstruction and harps on Soviet " moral and material support " which helped liberate Cambodia as well as Laos and Vietnam.[60] It is a feeble effort.

Like Cambodia, Laos and Vietnam profess non-alignment but have moved closer into the Soviet fraternal-friendship periphery and maintain only formal " friendship " with China.

Soon after the war, China and the Soviet Union gave aid to Vietnam, especially food assistance in October 1975. But as during the war, Soviet aid was swift and more substantial. In May, the Council for Mutual Economic Co-operation (COMECON) formulated plans for aid. In June, the Soviet Union signed an aid agreement with the Provisional Revolutionary Government in South Vietnam, and, in November, with North Vietnam.[61] At the same time a mammoth Soviet-Vietnam friendship rally was held in Moscow. Soviet leaders profusely praised the successful Vietnamese struggle against " foreign interventionists and their henchmen " and promised to " go on consistently taking sides of the South-Vietnamese patriots." [62]

---

[58] *People's Daily*, March 19, 1975, charged that the Soviet Union gave aid and " encouragement " to the Lon Nol clique. *Soviet News*, April 15 and 22, 1975; *New York Times*, July 11, 1975; *USSR and Third World, op. cit.* in note 24 above, pp. 285–86; *Christian Science Monitor*, August 21, 1975.

[59] 19 *Peking Review*, Nr. 2, January 16, 1976, p. 37; Nr. 10, March 5, 1976, p. 20; Nr. 11, March 12, 1976, p. 13; Nr. 12, March 19, 1976, p. 4; Nr. 14, April 2, 1976, p. 21; Nr. 17, April 23, 1976, p. 6; Nr. 23, June 4, 1976, p. 23.

[60] Moscow radio broadcasts mentioned in *Pravda*, July and August 1975; Kosygin's article in *Kommunist*, Nr. 14, September 1975, pp. 3–20, quoted in *USSR and Third World, op. cit.* in note 24 above, pp. 273 and 285.

[61] *Soviet News*, May 6, June 10, and November 8, 1975.

[62] Speeches by L. Brezhnev, May 8, 1975: See *New York Times*, May 9, 1975; and by Kosygin, August 28, 1975: See *Soviet News*, September 3, 1975; *ibid.* June 10 and November 8, 1975.

The Vietnamese have been profoundly grateful to the Soviet Union for " valuable and effective assistance " and have hailed Soviet shipments arriving soon after the war as a " real contribution to healing the scars of war suffered by our people." The joint communiqué in November 1975 called for peace in South-East Asia, withdrawal of all United States troops and dismantling of United States military bases there and overall congruity of views on major issues.[63] Le Duan, First Secretary of the Vietnamese Workers' Party, led a large delegation to the 25th Congress of the CPSU. Both there and at a major rally, held in Hanoi in March 1976, to celebrate the Vietnamese uprising against the Chinese invasion 1,936 years ago, he hailed the Soviet Union as " the world's mightiest socialist State," which had supported national liberation wars in Asia, Africa and Latin America and praised the Soviet policy of peace in Europe. In May, Premier Pham Van Dong reiterated these sentiments, stressed the need for " socialist solidarity and fraternal co-operation between our people " and concluded: " We shall always be loyal to our unbreakable friendship." [64]

Thus, without denouncing China as a deviationist or a great-Han hegemonic Power, Vietnam has unequivocally supported the Soviet Union both as a leading socialist State and a true friend of small countries. It has openly broken with China in supporting India, on Bangladesh in 1971 and the emergency in 1975. Vietnam has stoutly defended Soviet socialist assistance while attacking western " capitalist " aid. Pham Van Dong has declared: " Our (non-aligned) countries should be interested in developing relations with the Socialist countries on the basis of the principle of mutual respect, equality and mutual advantage " in order to destroy the old economic order and help create a new, more just one.[65]

The reasons for this defiance of China are related more to Vietnam's experience than to the Sino-Soviet dispute. During the Vietnam War China refused co-operation with the Soviet Union in sending aid to the embattled Vietnam.[66] Soviet assistance, moreover, was about 80 per cent. of total foreign aid. Vietnam therefore finds that China's accusations about Soviet hegemony and aid-policy have a hollow

[63] *Soviet News*, June 10, and November 8, 1975.

[64] Elizabeth Pond, " Hanoi Praises Moscow," *Christian Science Monitor*, March 9, 1976; Pham Van Dong's interview to Moscow Radio to mark the 30th anniversary of defeat of Germany, excerpts in *Pacific Tribune*, Canadian Communist Party organ, May 30, 1976.

[65] Speech at the Non-aligned Nations' Conference in Colombo, August–September 1976, quoted in *Pravda*, August 19, 1976: See XXVIII *CDSP*, Nr. 3, September 15, 1976, p. 19.

[66] H. Hinton, " China and Vietnam," in Tang Tsou (ed.), *China in Crisis: China's Policies in Asia and America's Alternatives*, II (1968), pp. 208–222.

ring. Moreover, with the war over, Vietnam has reverted to the unalterable geographic reality: territorial disputes with China, against whom as a close neighbour in the past, Vietnam waged a liberation struggle for over a thousand years. In 1974, China seized the Paracel Islands from South Vietnam in a pre-emptive manner. In April 1975, North Vietnam captured the Spratley Islands which, too, China claims. So grave is their dispute that Hanoi is reportedly building its navy with Soviet assistance. In March 1976, both the Vietnams published maps showing the disputed islands as their territory and in August a stamp to that effect was issued. Vietnam has also made radio broadcasts on the claim.[67]

This element has created a major Sino-Vietnamese rift which introduces a new dimension of Soviet-Vietnamese alignment into the Sino-Soviet conflict. By February 1976, the Chinese presence in Vietnam had tapered off to become unnoticeable. Observers note that China's virulent charge that the Soviet Union wanted " to swallow South-East Asia in a gulp," made in July 1975, was actually directed against Hanoi.[68]

The Soviet Union is not taking things for granted and shows its sympathetic interest in Vietnam by giving aid and publishing voluble articles. *Peking Review* by contrast completely omitted coverage of Vietnam in 1976 except for a brief reference to production in South Vietnam and " warmest congratulations " on the reunification, reaffirming " revolutionary friendship " with Vietnam. This reference, too, was couched in terms of attacks on hegemonism.[69]

### (h) *Laos*

Laos, like Vietnam, cannot ignore China's détente with the United States in 1971 and perfunctory support for its struggle since 1973,[70] and has therefore moved closer to the Soviet Union. Prime Minister Kaysone Phomvihan led a large delegation to the 25th Congress of the CPSU. Nor can Laos provoke the powerful giant next door. China, too, needs Laotian friendship as a model of its good neighbour policy. The result has been a Sino-Soviet aid competition in Laos. In 1975, China donated 10,000 bicycles, while the Soviet Union flew in a cargo aircraft during the Thai blockade in December

---

[67] " Periscope," *Newsweek*, February 16 and August 2, 1976, and *The Asian Student*, March 27, 1976.

[68] *New York Times*, July 11, 1975, and February 15, 1976.

[69] " Sun of Freedom," *Pravda*, July 13, 1976, p. 4; one on unification was published on July 4, 1976. XXVIII *CDSP*, Nr. 28, August 11, 1976, pp. 13–14; 19 *Peking Review*, Nr. 25, June 18, 1976, p. 21; Nr. 28, July 9, 1976, p. 22.

[70] China welcomed the Laotian political settlement of September, 1973, without echoing Pathet Lao's attack on " United States imperialism." *Renmin Ribao*, editorial, " A Major Step towards National Accord in Laos," text in *Peking Review*, Nr. 38, September 21, 1973, p. 8.

of that year to complement the Vietnamese airlift of goods from Soviet ships unloaded in Haiphong.[71]

In March 1976, Kaysone Phomvihan signed an aid agreement in China. But the two countries are not on the same ideological wavelength. Peking called his visit an " official, friendly " visit—a cool term. Although Chinese leaders declared that they would carry on a struggle against hegemonism, Kaysone pointedly omitted reference to it, but praised " China's influence on the struggle against imperialism, colonialism and neo-colonialism." No joint communiqué was issued.[72] American visitors to Laos in May 1976 saw a large number of Soviet and Cuban aid experts, but very few Chinese. China's recent coverage on Laos has been scanty.[73]

Soviet-Laotian fraternal ties have become consolidated. In September 1976, Kaysone Phomvihan made a " goodwill visit " to Moscow, and held talks with Mr. Brezhnev in an atmosphere of " cordiality, comradeship and complete mutual understanding," and expressed deep gratitude for Soviet aid in the past and in the current Laotian stage of development. The two countries decided to expand co-operation, and, more significantly, the two Communist parties reaffirmed their " fraternal ties in a spirit of Marxism and Leninism and proletarian internationalism." [74] Howsoever small, Laos is an important ally to the Soviet Union in its international diplomacy and in the Sino-Soviet rivalry.

## VIII—CONCLUSIONS

China and the Soviet Union are compelled to conduct their rivalry in South-East Asia from a position, not of strength, but of weakness and poor manoeuvrability. Neither has a staunch, reliable ally there. Vietnam, though pro-Soviet, must remain strictly neutral in the Sino-Soviet conflict. It has mastered the art of walking on eggshells in developing affinity with the Soviet Union without provoking open retaliation by China, which is geographically too close for comfort.

The two antagonists evidently are aware of this situation and, even while hurling mutually shrill, vitriolic recriminations, are more

---

[71] J. Everingham, " Mekong Blockade Rebounds," *Far Eastern Economic Review*, January 16, 1976.

[72] Text of speeches in 19 *Peking Review*, Nr. 12, March 19, 1976, pp. 3, 6–7. A ceremonial audience with Mao Tse-tung was granted to the Laotians. See also *ibid.* Nr. 13, March 26, 1976, pp. 3–5.

[73] *Ibid.* Nr. 26, June 25, 1976, p. 18, for a brief reference to Laotian achievements. Laos applied for a Chinese loan in April: see *Far Eastern Economic Review*, April 23, 1976, pp. 24–25.

[74] *Pravda* published a long article on September 4, 1976, on " Republic's First Year," praising Laotian recovery efforts. This news item and Kaysone's visit were considered important enough to be included in XXVIII *CDSP*, Nr. 36, October 6, 1976, pp. 17–18.

cautious than rash. They can only woo the regional nations and not threaten them with either economic or military sanctions and have not even tried to do so.

What is the reaction of the anti-Communist South-East Asian governments to this uninvited foreign-Power rivalry in their area? They have many problems and preoccupations and powerful western friends to assist them, so that Sino-Soviet aid is not vital to their economic development especially since the ASEAN governments have chosen a capitalist and pro-western path. Nor are they interested in even trying to play off China and the Soviet Union against each other. They might welcome assistance but free of intra-donor rivalry. They still view China and the Soviet Union with suspicion and ponder how each of them would exploit Communist movements in order to assert its own authority as the leader of world Marxism.

Neither China nor the Soviet Union can be said to have gained an upper hand over the other in the anti-Communist South-East Asian countries, except in a minor manner. In Burma China seems to be holding out. Indonesia's hostility towards China has become aggravated over East Timor, but that is cold comfort to the Soviet Union which has not gained much ascendancy in Indonesia. Thailand, Singapore, Malaysia and the Philippines have developed warm ties with Peking, but their flattering gestures and comments on China —including acceptance by some of them of China's stand on hegemony—are balanced with a careful preservation of friendly relations with the Soviet Union. The latter, in fact, has diplomatic relations with all South-East Asian countries except little Cambodia. China does not have diplomatic relations with Singapore and Indonesia.

In Indochina, as noted above, the Sino-Soviet rivalry has produced some discernible alignments. Laos and Vietnam have distinctly nudged closer to the Soviet Union but preserved cordial relations with China. Cambodia's exclusive alliance with China, and her marked coolness towards the Soviet Union, seem more a reflection of the ideological stridency and national pride of the Cambodian leaders than a case of choosing sides. Whatever the case, the Soviet Union is, at least for the time being, the loser in Cambodia and China in Laos and Vietnam.

Outwardly both China and the Soviet Union are constrained to put a brake on their mutual invectives when dealing with Indochina. Neither can afford to lose the friendship of a Communist country, howsoever small, which excessive, clumsy propaganda can easily bring about. Both need more Communist allies as feathers in their ideological caps. That is why Cambodia's open rebuff of the Soviet Union is not matched by Soviet admonishments, let alone retaliatory denunciations, but by perseverant cultivation of Cambodia's friendship. The Chinese have refrained from attacking " Soviet social-imperialism, hegemony and expansionism " when dealing with Laos and Vietnam.[75]

Where does the United States stand? Officially it assumes a posture of disdainful disinterest in the Sino-Soviet rivalry in South-East Asia, but insofar as it has built a global congruity of interests with China while retaining an adversary posture towards the Soviet Union, the United States cannot be considered a neutral bystander, especially in South-East Asia. Even before the announcement in July 1971 of Nixon's projected visit to China, it had openly favoured China's re-entry into South-East Asia.[76] SEATO since then has ceased to exist as an anti-China grouping, being disbanded in 1976. China too had stopped attacking United States military bases in East and South-East Asia and had not backed Thailand's desire to dismantle American military bases on its soil. In fact, China has welcomed a strong United States presence in Asia to counter Soviet influence.[77]

In the post-Vietnam phase, the Sino-American community of interests in South-East Asia against the Soviet Union has been strengthened. The United States is too sophisticated for its spokesmen and leaders openly to voice this view, but it has found expression through a kind of journalism which in the United States has an authoritative aura. Mr. Joseph Alsop, a well-known " establishment " columnist, has raised a question: " As North Vietnam steps up its march to empire, in alliance with Moscow, will Peking risk a major confrontation with the Soviet Union to try to stop it?" His answer is: " As the Soviets are effectively allied to the North Vietnamese, so we, in an odd way, are at least the silent partners of the Chinese. If Hanoi's drive for conquest is stopped where it is, things will go on much as they are today. But if China fails to halt the North Vietnamese, one can foresee an early and really thunderous fall of many more dominoes. Malaysia, Indonesia and Singapore will be deeply affected, and the whole hard-won American position in the Western Pacific will begin to founder." [78] This then is another version,

---

[75] During his visit to China, the Laotian leader, Kaysone Phomvihan, prudently refrained from praising the Soviet Union, while China's acting Premier, Hua Kuo-feng, also made no derogatory reference to " Soviet social imperialism." See *Peking Review*, Nr. 12, March 19, 1976, pp. 6–7.

[76] In a speech to a SEATO Council Meeting on April 27, 1971, in London, Secretary of State William Rogers stated that the United States policy was not to deny China a growing role in Asia but to encourage it to be constructive rather than destructive. See State Department, LXIV *Bulletin*, Nr. 1667, May 31, 1971, pp. 682–684.

[77] See Mahajani, *op. cit.* in note 9 above, p. 735, and *op. cit.* in note 2 above, p. 120.

[78] Alsop is also strongly sympathetic with China's ally, Cambodia, as a victim of North Vietnamese " aggression " and claims: " Whereas the Cambodian Communist Party is solidly dominated by passionate nationalists, the reverse is true of the Lao Communist Party, the Pathet Lao " whose real leaders long ago gave their full allegiance to Hanoi, and who have allowed Laos to be " under what amounts to a military

or rather a perpetuation, of the discredited domino theory with a new tacit alliance between the United States and China pitted against the Soviet-Vietnamese alignment. The recent military *coup* in Thailand —which destroyed all prospects of civilian democracy there as well as dashing any hopes of reconciliation between Thailand and its Indochinese neighbours, and in which a United States supportive role has been detected [79]—has an element of an anti-Vietnam, anti-Laos as well as a domestic anti-left move.

Unless President Carter drastically alters the Nixon–Ford South-East Asian policy, the United States would probably do nothing to alleviate Sino-Soviet rivalry in South-East Asia, but would probably consolidate its relations with China to further isolate Vietnam from the rest of South-East Asia. It is also likely to encourage expansion of China's role in South-East Asia as a check to the Soviet Union and Vietnam. The United States has neither created nor aggravated the Sino-Soviet conflict. That as an actor in international politics it would use that rivalry to further its interests is another matter.

Being a result rather than a cause of the basic feud, the Sino-Soviet rivalry in South-East Asia will not end until that stubborn conflict itself is resolved, their relations normalised, and their mutual fear of encirclement and collusion with each other's enemies is reduced. Hopes for this appear dim although the Soviet Union apparently desires it. At the 25th Congress of the CPSU, Mr. Brezhnev declared: " We are ready to normalise relations with China in line with these principles (equality, respect for sovereignty and territorial integrity, non-interference in each other's internal affairs and non-use of force) of peaceful co-existence. More than that . . . we stand for the restoration of good relations in line with the principles of socialist internationalism." [80] China's response even after Mao Tse-tung's death

occupation by the North Vietnamese." See J. Alsop, " Showdown Over South-East Asia?" *Reader's Digest*, December 1975, pp. 137–142. *Reader's Digest* may not be a " scholarly " journal but it is an important popular vehicle of expression of the American Government's thinking. It may be called, amongst other things, the American common man's *Foreign Affairs*. For a similar analysis, see M. Woollacott (of *The Guardian*), " Dominoes Piling On Vietnam," *Victoria Times*, March 29, 1976.

[79] E. T. Flood, *The United States and the Military Coup in Thailand: A Background Study*, published by Indochina Resource Center, Washington, D.C. (1976). Several close observers suspect that the United States role came through the Office of the United States Military Attaché. While the Thai left-wing and neutralist elements have endorsed the demand of the Indochina States to end what the Cornell University's scholars call " the huge American military and intelligence presence on Thai soil," the Thai military leaders strongly desire its retention which has produced for them and for the " bureaucratic cliques " of Thailand " an intimate, immensely profitable relationship with Washington." (Background material supplied by Thailand Information Project, Cornell University, Ithaca, New York, October 1976, headed by Professor George McT. Kahin.)

[80] Excerpts in *Pacific Tribune*, November 12, 1976, p. 6.

has been negative. Vice-Premier Li Hsien-nien has violently attacked the Soviet Union as " wildly ambitious " and guilty of " criminal action " in Africa.[81] With no let-up in the Sino-Soviet global conflict, their rivalry in South-East Asia too is likely to become more irritating and irrational in the foreseeable future.

---

[81] A speech at a banquet in November 1976. The undiplomatic violence of the language prompted the Soviet bloc ambassadors (but not those of Vietnam and Laos) to walk out. A western reporter, R. Munro, writes: " China has categorically rejected the conciliatory gestures Moscow has been making to Peking since the death of Chairman Mao Tse-tung on September 9." *Victoria Times* (Canada), November 16, 1976. Huang Hua, in a United Nations speech on November 8, 1976, denounced United States-Soviet rivalry for hegemony as being irreversible and " exposed " Soviet " pretensions of détente." *Peking Review*, Nr. 47, November 19, 1976, pp. 28–29. Li Hsien-nien also told the *Le Figaro* correspondent that China was preparing for the " inevitable war " with the Soviet Union: see *Victoria Times*, November 4, 1976.

# PROBLEMS OF THE MEDITERRANEAN:
## A GEOPOLITICAL PERSPECTIVE

By

## ROBERT A. FRIEDLANDER

" NORTH Africa must trade with Europe, right across the board. The
Arab countries must have a stake in Europe's well-being. The economics must link, otherwise Africa will let Europe die of inflation." [1]
This comment by a fictional character in a contemporary best-selling
spy-novel well illustrates the recent shifting of traditional political
and economic relationships that has taken place in the Mediterranean
basin. A new economic alignment and possible political transfigura-
tion have begun to emerge in the Mediterranean area. Their consequence is the formation of a tripartite association between countries in
need of industrial and technological development, countries technologically developed, and the oil-producing States. Thus, the Arab
governments on the southern rim of the Mediterranean are attempting
closer ties with the more industrialised northern States, which have
been historically dependent upon North African energy resources.

### I—THE EMERGING NEW ECONOMIC ALIGNMENT

The economic gravitation of Southern Europe towards North Africa
is due in part to the effects of the 1973-74 oil embargo, partly to the
oil pricing policies of the Organisation of Petroleum Exporting
Countries (OPEC) cartel, and partly to the growing reserves of
Arab petrodollars and their investment in the more advanced European economies. A likely consequence of the above factors is a newly-
developing partnership between technological resources of Western
Europe and the natural resources of the oil-producing Arab States.

The changing economic interests of the South European countries
at present portend a weakening not only of Europe's military ties
with the United States, but also a possible weakening of the impetus
towards European unity with a fragmentation of ties previously
binding Northern Europe and Southern Europe. On the other hand,
if the current international economic dislocation merely proves to be
a temporary displacement and not a permanent configuration, then
Europe's predominant economic interests will still be pointed in the
direction of the Common Market and the European Community,
where the European States in combination constitute a potential
economic super-Power.

---

[1] L. Deighton, *Yesterday's Spy* (1976), p. 12.

These presumptions, however, are based on the existence of a unity of interest among the South European States. Recent events in Portugal, Spain, France, and Italy, particularly the declining strength of their majority political parties, indicate that domestic politics in the northern rim of the Mediterranean may adversely affect the future of both the European Economic Community (EEC) and the North Atlantic Treaty Organisation (NATO). Moreover, there are those who claim that oil has become an international dissolvent, especially " for disintegration of the Western alliance." [2] If South European unity does erode, then inevitably the oil problem will take on an entirely new dimension. Yet, there is no indication that the European States have even begun to conceive of a common energy policy. [3]

Caution should also be exercised in viewing the Arab south shore of the Mediterranean as a monolithic bloc. In actuality, a wide variety of institutions and many disparate interests exist in the Maghreb countries. Similarly, differences abound in their respective economic postures *vis-à-vis* the outside world. Viewing the Arab States as a monolithic entity often leads to overgeneralising about what is in actuality a very large and diverse area. In Algeria, for example, there has been a great deal of experimentation and a great deal of striving for new ideas and experimentation with new positions. [4]

The 18-nation conference of consuming States held in Paris during the first week of April 1975, provided a fitting symbol of the shifting power relationships in the Mediterranean basin. The American Secretary of State, Dr. Kissinger, adopted the position that the United States should not enter into dialogue with the producing countries until an agreement had been reached between the Organisation of Petroleum Exporting Countries (OPEC) and the consuming countries to hold a general meeting of both groups. However, efforts to establish a mutually acceptable agenda failed, for not one of the 17 other countries represented at the Paris conference shared the United States' view. It may well be that the United States was the real loser in economic and political terms, for the question still remains as to whether the United States ever really needed that conference which had been called primarily on its own initiative. [4a] Here, as elsewhere, the inevitable consequence of Secretary of State Kissinger's person-

---

[2] E. Friedland, P. Seabury and A. Wildavsky, " Oil and the Decline of Western Power," 90 *Political Science Quarterly* (1975), p. 444.

[3] The comments of West German Chancellor, Helmut Schmidt, " New Tasks for the Atlantic Alliance," in this *Year Book*, Vol. 28 (1975), pp. 29–30, are illustrative of the problem.

[4] R. Brace, *Morocco, Algeria, Tunisia* (1964). See also R. Brace and J. Brace, " Algeria," R. Starr (ed.), 1976 *Yearbook on International Communist Affairs* (1976), pp. 558–560.

[4a] See the comments in I. Shihata, " Arab Oil Policies and the New International Economic Order," 16 *Virginia Journal of International Law* (1976), pp. 286–287.

alisation of the diplomatic process had been to divert the real focus of American interest.

The purpose of the meeting was actually to enable Dr. Kissinger to secure an improved United States negotiating position before entering into a dialogue with the producing States. Of the 18 consuming States in attendance, only the United States possessed alternative sources of energy,[5] and her group bargaining position was therefore inherently suspect. Ironically, another loser in Paris was the French government which had hoped to become a moderator between the producer and consumer groups. The net result was that OPEC was not obligated to have any future meetings with consuming countries, and the western nations were henceforth forced to deal with OPEC by other means. An International Energy Agency (IEA) has been created by the oil-consuming States as a crisis-oriented mechanism to deal with OPEC policies, but its influence is minimal.

Moreover, the uncertain future of Dr. Kissinger's step-by-step diplomacy in the Middle East, along with the forced withdrawal of the American presence from South-east Asia, and the election of a Democratic President, have altered some of the fundamental positions of the United States in the world arena. The decline of American power and prestige has likewise altered, perhaps significantly, the traditional political-strategic power relationships in the Mediterranean. In the eyes of many, " [energy] is enervating NATO. Each member is poorer than it was. . . Europe needs energy which America cannot supply." [6] One might argue that the Arab-Israeli conflict and the Arab oil boycott were merely the tip of the iceberg.

Beneath the surface are the basic forces of change in the Arab world: nationalism, modernism, and revolutionary ideology. Present trends indicate that there is indeed a revolution now occurring in Arab thought based upon the interaction of Arab socialism, Islamic ideology, and Middle Eastern nationalism. The influence of the Palestinian Liberation Movement must also be taken into account, particularly in its effect upon the internal political structures of other Arab States.[7] In some Islamic countries, there has been a radical transformation of the role of the masses, and popular values have begun to challenge those ideas previously imposed from above by Arab élites.[8]

---

[5] The North Sea oil discovery has made the United Kingdom a potential producer for the European market.

[6] Friedland, Seabury and Wildavsky, *op. cit.* in note 2 above, p. 445.

[7] E. Dawn, " The Arab-Israeli Confrontation: An Historian's Analysis," 5 *Denver Journal of International Law & Policy* (1975), pp. 378–383.

[8] See B. Lewis, *Islam in History* (1972); B. Lewis, *et al.* (eds.), *Islam and the Arab World* (1976); T. Kiernan, *The Arabs: Their History, Aims and Challenge to the Industrialized World* (1976).

An essential difference between the North African countries and those of Southern Europe is that of commonality. Throughout the Arab world there exists a common language, a common cultural experience, a common religion, a common experience of colonisation, similar economic structures, and a similar historical development.[9] There is even a common enemy to replace the hated western imperialists—Israel. Middle Eastern nationalism is the defence of an injured self-view reflecting the history of the past 150 years. Thus, it is not surprising that the current Moslem political leadership is now seeking to recapture lost greatness, lost power, and lost glory. The emotional element of the new Arab nationalism is of vital importance to understanding the North African world view. According to French President Giscard d'Estaing, the contemporary economic crisis was induced by " the revenge on Europe for the nineteenty century." [10]

Nevertheless, strong cultural factors already exist which bind the North African States to the South Mediterranean, such as the continuing ties between France and her former Maghreb colonies. Even the Arab concept of nationalism is a descendant of its West European predecessors. The possibility is growing that in time the separate evolutionary process of the two regions will give way to a mutual affinity, and thereby diminish still further the influence of the United States and the Soviet Union in the Mediterranean basin. If one adds to these factors the new economic tripartite arrangement, the seeds of co-operation and interdependence may already be in full germination. According to Saudi Arabia's King Khalid, " [i]t's obvious that there is an interaction between the western industrialised economies and the oil-producing nations. And if the European nations don't take the necessary steps to put their affairs in order, then their economic problems will continue and will indeed affect other nations. . . We have contributed more than our share in alleviating Europe's difficulties." [11] Thus, the current attitude and policies of the former western colonial governments are of fundamental importance in the redistribution of resources and the realignment of economic interests. So far the Palestinian question has blocked further progress in negotiations for closer economic ties between the Arab countries and the EEC, but there can no longer be any doubt of the European desire for a restrengthening of old bonds with North Africa and the Middle East.

The basic question, as yet unresolved, is whether the Mediterranean

---

[9] Brace, *op. cit.* in note 4 above, takes careful note of the wide variations among non-religious institutions in the Maghreb countries, and of the different approaches towards economic development and social change in Morocco, Algeria, Tunisia, and Libya. On the latter see especially, R. First, *Libya: The Elusive Revolution* (1976).

[10] Quoted by R. Brace and J. Brace, *op. cit.* in note 4 above.

[11] Quoted in *Newsweek*, November 22, 1976, p. 88.

countries have sufficient commonality among themselves to emerge as a new grouping. Though cultural incompatibility may be overcome through a mutuality of commercial interests, there are limits to the identification of underdeveloped societies in change with those of developed technologies. And other questions have yet to be resolved. What will be the future role of education, since most of the Arab teachers on the secondary and university levels have been educated in the western world? What will be the impact of the rise in population as opposed to the increase in petrodollars? (Both Egypt and the Maghreb have increasing birth rates.) Who now has the dollars and how will they use them? What of the many-faceted problems of food production and distribution? What of future investments in the oil consuming States by the oil-producing States? (The United States Treasury estimate of OPEC income derived from oil exports in 1975 was between 100 and 114 billion dollars.) It is now self-evident that there has been a world-wide redistribution of dollars with the new moneys looking to stable national economies such as the United States for potential investment.[11a] But what of the contingent and the unforeseen, such as new unanticipated supplies of natural resources which may create further disruptions in current patterns of supply and demand, commonality, and cultural affinity? The answers to these questions as they unfold during the next decade will provide the key to the future of the Mediterranean and to the future of the world community.

The focus now has to be on interdependence, and to have interdependence there must first be equality. It should not be forgotten that oil-producing countries are also developing countries. Therefore, the most important thing from their vantage point is co-operation. Because of this factor, during the past several years, particularly as a result of conservative Saudi Arabian influence, OPEC has attempted to allocate production. There is common agreement that the current price of crude oil is unreasonably high, and that an additional 10 to 15 per cent. raise in price for 1977 is likely, but there really is no way of predicting the course of events. According to Saudi figures, oil consumption has increased by 4 per cent. annually and likely to rise this year to 5 per cent. Since OPEC prices have been in effect stabilised since 1974 and consuming nations have increased consumption, the lack of reciprocity has played a considerable role in melting the current price freeze. What the conservative oil-producing States fear most are the political results of a sharp increase in world oil prices. The Saudis recognise that a more aggressive OPEC pricing policy may not only provide a severe setback to economic recovery in the

[11a] Arab investment in the United States has been currently estimated at 25 billion dollars. See *Chicago Tribune*, April 18, 1977, sec. 6, p. 8.

West, but also increase the chances of a Communist takeover in the
South European countries.[12]

There are four major factors that tie the level of economic activity
in Europe to that of the Middle East. They include: (1) Exports by
Europe to the Middle East; (2) Partial financing of Europe by the
Middle East (*e.g.* Italy and the United Kingdom by Iran); (3) Middle
East exports to Europe; (4) Dependence of the Middle East on
European labour and technology. As the Middle Eastern Countries
increase their level of economic development, they will inevitably
approach the more advanced stages of developed countries, though
admittedly in lesser degrees. If this does indeed happen, a natural
economic partnership will develop between North Africa and South
Europe, and the economic focus of Europe will consequently shift
from the United States (now importing 50 per cent. of its oil by CIA
figures) to the oil-rich, industrially developing Middle East.[12a] In the
coming years, the question of the importation of industrial skills and
foreign labour should become an important factor in modernising
Middle Eastern countries. Diversification will become a key factor in
building a European–Middle Eastern economic axis.

Does co-operation necessarily mean equality? How can interdependence work when the United States has always insisted, at the
very least, on being the first among equals? This has been an American condition precedent to any international co-operative enterprise
(which General de Gaulle was never able to comprehend). American
foreign policy had been crisis-oriented prior to Dr. Kissinger,
continued to be during his ascendancy, and will probably be after his
departure. To propose American-style national economic solutions
for international economic problems is in legal terminology a useless
act. Autarchy is not compatible with interdependence, and like it or
not, from an economic viewpoint it is an interdependent world. The
underlying problem is that single-commodity States require a condition of interdependence if they are to develop viable economies.

Several basic issues present themselves with respect to the above
analysis: (1) Does a global surplus of oil and natural gas really exist
given the technological demands of the modern world? (2) Is a
solution to the Arab-Israeli conflict a necessary prerequisite to any
resolution of the on-going energy crisis, and if the Arab-Israeli
dispute ended tomorrow, would this alleviate causes underlying the
recent quadrupling of oil prices in the world market? (3) How much
significance should be attached to the fact that the United States

---

[12] *Ibid.* pp. 88–90. See also E. Rouleau, " Saudi Arabia's Burgeoning Power," 24
*Atlas World Press Review* (April 1977), p. 22 (Reprinted from *Le Monde*).

[12a] In December 1976 the Libyan Government acquired a 10 per cent. interest in the
Fiat Corporation for 415 million dollars. See *Newsweek*, December 13, 1976, pp. 80 and
83. For CIA Report, see *Chicago Tribune*, April 19, 1977, sec. 1, p. 10.

receives most of its oil from non-Arab OPEC countries? [13] (4) What is the definition of a surplus, if it is not supply over demand?

In the long run almost every expert agrees that no surplus of fuel resources actually exists. Not only will there be a severely diminished supply throughout the world in the coming decades, but in addition the oil-producing countries themselves are attempting to allocate production much more restrictively than in the past and to conserve their known reserves. To the oil producers petroleum is both a national resource and their economic heritage. Saudi Arabia, in the words of its monarch, will not " accept an invitation to deplete its prime source of wealth just because others are unable to conserve it or use it reasonably." [14] Thus, escalation of oil prices by the producing States is actually a conservation mechanism designed to bring into balance the competing forces of supply and demand.

Historically, petroleum is also the one global natural resource that has supplied energy at a lower cost to a greater market than any other raw material. The recent sudden increase in petroleum pricing has often resulted in difficult adjustment and periodic dislocation. During March 1975, French national television ran programs picturing landing operations being practised somewhere in the Mediterranean by the United States Sixth Fleet and quoted an admiral to that effect. Several American commentators wrote of seizing Arab oil, and the American Secretary of State in a now famous interview implied the possible use of American arms if another oil embargo should bring about " some actual strangulation of the industrialised world." [15] Certainly, the emotional and political elements in oil production and distribution cannot be overlooked.

The Middle East produces one-third of the western oil imports and the United States share is somewhat less than half of that. In 1974–75 Venezuela, which had been providing over 50 per cent. of America's oil imports, reduced its production by 12 per cent. and eventually plans to turn off the tap altogether. (Abu Dhabi has by itself about double the known reserves of Venezuela.) Similarly, Canada is inaugurating a Canada-first policy for all natural resources and specifically with reference to oil. By 1983 the Canadian Government intends to stop sending oil to the United States. Thus, even if the new Alaskan field eventually produces at a level commensurate with the present production rates of Venezuela and Canada, within a decade the United States will be in the same position as present.[16] Western

---

[13] Nigeria is now the primary supplier to the United States.

[14] *Newsweek, op. cit.* in note 11 above, p. 89.

[15] *Business Week*, January 13, 1975, pp. 66–69.

[16] *Cf. Oil and Gas Journal*, December 2, 1974, p. 23, and *ibid.* December 30, 1974, p. 94. Simply put, " Canada offers no solution to American dependence on OPEC oil."

Europe will still have to shift for itself. That is the hard reality of the immediate future.

One therefore is reluctantly drawn to the inevitable conclusion that a peaceful settlement in the Middle East will not necessarily change the overall oil picture. Whether or not Arab unity would be seriously affected by a Middle East peace accord is secondary to the economic problems that would still remain. On the other hand, what forecasts can be made if war resumes? The best guess is that another Arab-Israeli encounter would encourage Arab countries to use every weapon at their disposal—political, military, and economic—especially oil, if the military hardware made available to them by the United States and the Soviet Union is not enough for victory. The current price of oil gives to the Arab States huge revenues which are used to purchase up-to-date military equipment from European debtor countries, while the latter in turn use petrodollars to remedy their balance-of-payments deficits. France is probably the best example of this whipsaw effect, and the net result has been to make the South European industrialised economies doubly dependent upon the Arab oil producers.

The first stages of modernisation and technological development as applied to the Arab world will be a vertical expansion of petroleum production techniques. For the last three years the Arab States have invested heavily in expansion of their oil tanker fleet with the intention of giving preference to their own vessels in the transportation of crude oil. During the next six years, these same producing States will invest more than 67 billion dollars in oil refineries, petrochemical plants, and liquid natural gas facilities, in addition to another 25 billion dollars in ships, pipelines, and heat exchangers.[17] The integration of production and distribution techniques will thus provide the Arab OPEC countries with an even greater stranglehold over the western energy lifeline. The geopolitical implications are self-evident. In the words of one observer, " [t]he next embargo, if it comes, will be more effective than the last." [18]

## II—THE ARAB BOYCOTT, THE OIL EMBARGO, AND ARAB-ISRAELI CONFRONTATION

Another difficulty in strengthening economic ties between the Middle East and the industrialised West is the current Arab economic boycott of Israel. Actually, there is not much that is new in the existing boycott, for it has been much the same since its inception at Damas-

P. Trezise, " The Energy Challenge," H. E. English (ed.), *Canadian-United States Relations* (1976), p. 116.　　　[17] *Chicago Tribune*, November 19, 1976, s. 4, p. 11.
[18] V. H. Oppenheim, " Arab Tankers Move Downstream," 23 *Foreign Policy* (1976), p. 117.

cus by the members of the Arab League Council in May 1951. It differs from the boycott of Cuba by the Organisation of American States (OAS) and the earlier United States boycott of the People's Republic of China in one major respect. The American boycotts were direct and did not include third countries, nor were they applied in an indirect fashion. The Arab boycott of Israel does both. Its underlying rationale is that the Arab League is at war with Israel, and therefore the use of economic as well as military means to achieve its political objectives should be expected. It is a logical extension of the military campaign to destroy Israel.[19]

From the American perspective, the real issue is whether or not there is also a secondary boycott directed against United States business instead of a primary boycott against Israel alone. The Arab reply is that the boycott is considered to be a means of self-defence against a hostile people. " In numerous instances, companies have had to decide between investing in Arab nations or in Israel. It is beyond dispute that many of these firms have had to choose one market and forgo the other. . . ." [20] From the Arab perspective, the problem is a simple one. Israel ultimately will have to choose between continuing as a client State of the United States and an agent of International Zionism or becoming part of the Middle East.

The ramifications of this still volatile situation (which was a focus of contention in the recent American presidential debates) extend south of the Sahara to black Africa, where as a result of petrodollar diplomacy and the October War, almost all of Sub-Sahara Africa came to support the Arab cause and the anti-Israeli boycott. Already Arab petrodollars are reaching black Africa, and new ties are being fashioned, while old ones are being further extended. The Sahara is no longer the political and economic barrier that it had been in past history. Black Africa and North Africa are becoming joined, and the Organisation of African Unity (OAU) which officially favoured the Arab States during the October War, has similarly favoured the Arab boycott of Israel. In point of fact, the OAU not only has offered its good offices to help resolve tensions in the Eastern Mediterranean, but also seeks investment of petrodollars in the development of its own considerable natural resources.[21]

The legality of the Arab oil embargo, fashioned as an instrument of war in October 1973, and thereafter applied as a political weapon, has been the source of considerable disagreement.[22] Oil was " the

---

[19] R. Weigand, " The Arab League Boycott of Israel," *Business Topics* (Spring 1968), p. 75.  [20] *Ibid.*
[21] C. C. Mojekwu, " African Perspectives on Issues in the Mediterranean Basin," 13 *The Globe* (August 1975), p. 4.
[22] *Cf.* J. Paust and A. Blaustein, " The Arab Oil Weapon—A Threat to International Peace," 68 *American Journal of International Law* (1974), pp. 410–439; and I. Shihata,

most powerful sanction the Arab world had against the industrialised powers, led by the United States, on the Palestine issue." [23] Implementation of the embargo depended on three different categories of national behaviour: (1) Friendly States which were permitted to obtain all their petroleum requirements; (2) Neutral States, such as the United States, which were allowed to obtain the average level of imports during the first nine months of 1973 or at the rate of the month preceding the October War; and (3) Embargoed States, such as Portugal, South Africa, and Netherlands whose imports were completely cut off.[24] The net result has been to make the western democracies hostage to Arab oil. " Petroleum blackmail is the only weapon the Arabs have thus far found which has promised them any chance of success." [25] Israel and Arab oil remain intimately connected, and shuttle diplomacy should be seen as the by-product of the western energy crisis.

Customary international law does not prohibit the right of a sovereign State, or a group of States, from disposing of their natural resources in accordance with what they deem to be their legitimate national self-interest. Economic coercion has in fact been applied by both the League of Nations and the United Nations against those States found to be in violation of the prevailing norms of international conduct. Regional organisations have likewise employed economic boycott as a means of political coercion, the OAS sanctions against Cuba and the OAU sanctions against Rhodesia being two recent examples. It is the realisation that the Arab oil embargo did not violate international law which led to the veiled threat by some American officials that United States national interests must not be challenged by the petroleum producing States.[26]

If indeed the past is prologue, then the problems of the Eastern Mediterranean cannot be fully understood without reference to the Arab-Israeli conflict and the aftermath of the October War of 1973. Super-Power pressures, and the frenetic efforts of the American

---

"Destination Embargo of Arab Oil: Its Legality under International Law," *ibid.* pp. 591–627; J. Paust and A. Blaustein, " The Arab Oil Weapon: A Reply and Reaffirmation of Illegality," 15 *Columbia Journal of Transnational Law* (1976), pp. 57–73; " A Symposium on the New International Economic Order: Commentaries and Discussion," 16 *Virginia Journal of International Law* (1976), pp. 289–295.

[23] First, *op. cit.* in note 9 above, p. 212.

[24] Shihata, *op. cit.* in note 22 above, pp. 597–598.

[25] H. Cahn, " A High Stakes Game," 12 *Skeptic*, March/April 1976, p. 48. *Cf.* K. Knorr, " The Limits of Economic and Military Power," 104 *Daedalus* (1975), pp. 229–243.

[26] See note 15 above. The then Secretary of Defense, J. Schlessinger, warned in May 1975, that the United States might " conceivably " take " military measures " in response to another embargo. *U.S. News & World Report*, May 26, 1975, pp. 24–27. *Cf.* United States, 94th Congress, First Session, Oil Fields as Military Objectives: A Feasibility Study, Committee on International Relations (1975).

Secretary of State, were the primary reasons for the termination of that conflict. The rationale was a simple one: " the danger that the Middle East may become a Balkan-like situation involving the super-Powers in a nuclear confrontation. . . ." [27] The United Nations had at best a supportive role, along with its sponsorship of a Geneva Peace conference (reluctantly approved by Dr. Kissinger). Substitution of step-by-step diplomacy for the December 1973 Geneva negotiations was a short-run expedient that sacrificed long-term solutions. The replacement by Secretary Kissinger of the aeroplane shuttle for the conference table was due in part to the domestic pressures of American politics and the impeachment crisis, and also to his emphasis upon personalism as the prime technique of Great-Power diplomacy.

In retrospect, though the Arabs and Israelis might have denounced each other openly in the conference room, they would also have had the opportunity for private talks among all parties and to engage in serious negotiations out of the glare of the media lights. The Palestinian issue had a much better chance for resolution in the hallways of Geneva than in the trenches of Syria and Lebanon.[28]

Ironically, the Lebanese civil war and its awful human toll has been able to effect what Secretary Kissinger's diplomatic pyrotechnics could not accomplish. The Palestine Liberation Organisation (PLO) has been severely and perhaps fatally weakened as a political force, while military necessity and strategic considerations have led Syria and Israel to come to a temporary and possibly meaningful accommodation. Rumours of their private contacts are a far better harbinger of Middle Eastern peace than Airforce One. In geopolitical terms, the human cost notwithstanding, a divided Lebanon may lay the foundation for an era of reconciliation in the Eastern Mediterranean.

Every Middle Eastern State is aware that some day its most precious natural resource will be exhausted, if oil continues to be exploited at its present rate. Looking towards the inevitable future, the Arab world hopes to utilise the income from this non-replaceable natural resource to develop economic independence in its own right through both agrarian and industrial development. Thus Europe, if it is willing and able, can participate in a new petrodollar partnership with the Middle East. The United States, because of its technological

---

[27] G. Ball, " The Looming War in the Middle East and How to Prevent It," *The Atlantic*, January 1975, p. 11.

[28] It is not surprising, therefore, that President Anwar Sadat of Egypt on November 13, 1976, renewed his call for a resumption of the Geneva Peace Conference: "It's time and we are ready and I hope Israel is ready too." *Chicago Tribune*, November 14, 1976, s. 1, p. 3. This call was echoed by Israeli Premier Begin during late July 1977. See *Newsweek*, August 1, 1977, p. 27.

and industrial superiority, also has the opportunity of forging new economic ties and political bonds with the Arab States, if it is ready to pay the price.

One thing is certain. The old international economic structure of the post Second World War generation no longer exists. The United States no longer dominates the international economic scene, the political base of the old global economic system has been permanently eroded, and a new multipolar economic framework is now slowly emerging.[29] Peaceful and reasonable compromise provides the only means to achieving effective and meaningful solutions to the vexing problems of the Mediterranean in the modern world.

## III—NATO AND THE MEDITERRANEAN BASIN

" Energy is enervating NATO." [30] The threat of NATO becoming a non-entity is a serious one, and nowhere are the implications more serious than in the Mediterranean basin. The hard fact and cold reality is that the power of both the United States and NATO is undergoing a precipitate decline, and Southern Europe seems to be heading towards greater neutralisation. Détente, if it does continue, will most likely be in the area west rather than east of Suez. Both the North African and South European States are growing suspicious of super-Power motivation. American promises, policies, and objectives are closely scrutinised and are being subjected to increased questioning. From the South European perspective, the underlying rationale of Soviet-United States détente is to partition the world between the super-Powers into spheres of influence in both economic and political terms. There is little demand from the States of the Mediterranean basin for either United States or Soviet domination of the area. The United States particularly may become gradually excluded from the newly developing economic and political configurations, and it may well be that the Mediterranean countries will be glad to see the United States depart altogether.

Throughout the 1960s and into the 1970s there has been a constant shift of strategic and military power in the Mediterranean basin towards the Soviet Union. A decade ago, the NATO Council of Foreign Ministers noted the particular importance of the Southeastern Mediterranean as an " exposed " area, and admitted that the Mediterranean in general " presents special problems. . . ." [31] Today,

---

[29] See C. F. Bergsten, *The Future of the International Economic Order: An Agenda for Research* (1973), pp. 2–8; R. Vernon, " The Distribution of Power," 104 *Daedalus* (1975), pp. 245–256.

[30] Friedland, Seabury and Wildavsky, *op. cit.* in note 2 above, p. 445.

[31] " Annex to the Final Communiqué of the Ministerial Meeting," December 1967, reprinted in *NATO Facts and Figures* (1970), p. 335. One will search in vain through Dr. Kissinger's study of *Nuclear Weapons and Foreign Policy* (1957), written two decades ago, for any mention of the Mediterranean or its strategic problems.

the United States Sixth Fleet has already been outflanked by Soviet naval influence in that region and is no longer able to show the flag in most Mediterranean countries. The Soviet naval presence is at least equal to that of the United States, and perhaps has greater staying power for the future.[31a] It is even possible that the Soviets, given recent internal developments in the South European countries, and its own still considerable influence in North Africa, may become so entrenched politically and strategically that NATO interests simply will no longer be meaningful.

" The Middle Eastern crisis is a NATO crisis, not an Arab-Israeli quarrel." [32] There are strong indications that the ultimate objective of the Soviet Union in the Middle East is to keep the Arab-Israeli conflict simmering, and, at the very least, to utilise the Palestinian cause to secure for itself a major role in any resumptive Geneva negotiations.[33] But the clear lesson of the October War of 1973 is that the interests of NATO's European members are not necessarily those of the United States, and that the dangers posed to Israel and her American protector are not a matter of common concern for the alliance.[34] Indeed the NATO countries of the southern flank may be in the process of transferring their own interests and priorities from a European towards a Mediterranean policy.

The implications of these shifting economic and political realities are, first, a terminal weakening of NATO's role in the Mediterranean basin, and, secondly—despite the forthcoming election of a European parliament—a possibility that the South European countries may be about to forgo the long-sought post-war goal of a United Europe. More than a quarter-century after its creation, to use the two-decades-old words of Dr. Kissinger, " NATO is still without a force sufficient to prevent its members from being overrun by the Soviet Army." [35] Three months before the October War, the Chairman of the United States Joint Chiefs of Staff, Admiral Thomas Moorer, testified that " [t]he Soviet Mediterranean squadron is the most formidable and largest group of Soviet naval ships and submarines continuously deployed out of home waters, and together with the

---

[31a] See testimony of Admiral James L. Holloway III, United States Chief of Naval Operations, United States, 94th Congress, Second Session, Department of Defence: Hearings on Appropriations for 1977, Committee on Appropriations (1977), pp. 184–186.

[32] E. Rostow, *Peace in the Balance* (1972), p. 250.

[33] *Cf.* the excellent analyses of A. R. Norton, " Moscow and the Palestinians: A New Tool of Soviet Policy in the Middle East," in M. Curtis (ed.), *The Palestinians: People, History, Politics* (1975), pp. 228–247; and R. O. Friedman, " Soviet Policy Toward the Middle East Since the October 1973 War," 29 *Naval War College Review* (1976), pp. 61–99.

[34] N. Graebner, " United States Policy and NATO's Southern Flank," 13 *The Globe* (August 1975), pp. 3–4.

[35] Kissinger, *op. cit.* in note 31 above, p. 271.

Black Sea Fleet, constitutes the primary naval threat against NATO's southern flank." [36] It is acknowledged that the Soviets are considerably ahead of United States naval technology (and thereby of NATO as well) in the categories of ship design, propulsion technology, and anti-ship missiles, though France and Italy have successfully deployed anti-ship missiles.

In mid-November 1976, two American Senators who serve on the Senate Armed Services Committee returned from a visit to major NATO countries with an ominous report. NATO, they declared, is in effect a paper tiger, while Warsaw Pact conventional forces have the " ability to initiate a potentially devastating invasion of Europe with as little as a few days warning." [37] Present NATO defence plans assume that there would be warning signs of up to one month before an attack, and—once hostilities had broken out—that the war itself would last from one to six months, thereby allowing the NATO forces to regroup. But in actuality, the Soviets have the ability to be on the Rhine within several hours, compelling the NATO allies to choose between nuclear weapons on their own territory or accepting defeat at the hands of improved Soviet conventional forces. [38]

Small wonder, then, that there is a growing belief among the South European States that the naval presence of either super-Power in the Mediterranean may not be at all necessary. More than ever, questions are being raised on both sides of the Atlantic about NATO as a potentially effective military deterrent force, and the concomitant disintegration of United States power and prestige around the globe may presage a breakup of the NATO alliance in its present form.

There has already been an indentifiable erosion of United States influence in the Eastern Mediterranean. Greek, Turkish, American, and NATO interests have collided rather than coincided, and this was dramatically demonstrated by the July 1974 Greek-sponsored *coup* on the island of Cyprus, and by the Turkish invasion and occupation which followed. First the Greeks, angered over what they considered to be insufficient United States support, removed Greece from the military base sector of the NATO alliance in the fashion of General de Gaulle. Then, the Turkish government, angered by the cut-off of military aid to Turkey by the United States Congress in December 1974, threatened to end its military participation in NATO

---

[36] United States, 93rd Congress, First Session, U.S. Forces in NATO, *Hearings before the Committee on Foreign Affairs* (1973), p. 217. *Cf.* testimony of Admiral Holloway, United States, 94th Congress, Second Session, Hearings on Military Posture, Committee on Armed Services (1976), pp. 745–746.

[37] United States, 95th Congress, First Session, NATO and the New Soviet Threat: Report of Senator Sam Nunn and Senator Dewey F. Bartlett, Committee on Armed Services (1977), p. 4.

[38] *Ibid.* pp. 4 and 9. " NATO's Southern Flank," the Report adds, " can be regarded as little more than a shambles," *ibid.*, p. 3.

and pressured the United States into renegotiating its military base agreements. Today, Cyprus, to all intents and purposes, has been partitioned into a Greek sector and a Turkish sector, with the Greek sector prospering and the Turkish sector stagnant and completely dependent on the motherland.[39] Moreover, Greece and Turkey are now engaged in a bitter dispute over the Aegean seabed, and the International Court of Justice, in denying Greece's claim of right on August 10, 1976, sternly warned both parties " to do everything in their power to reduce the present tensions in the area " and " to resume direct negotiations over their differences." [40] Since both countries apparently fear no aggression from outside Powers other than themselves, they now feel free to direct their historic animosities against each other. The real loser is the NATO alliance.

The greatest concern for the preservation of stability in the Mediterranean basin during the latter third of the 1970s is centred on Yugoslavia and the possibility of Soviet intervention when President Tito gives up the reins of power. Immediately after the American presidential election, President-elect Carter felt it necessary to issue a corrective statement to prior remarks made during the presidential debates that his administration would never get militarily involved in keeping the Soviets out of Yugoslavia,[41] thereby avoiding a possible repetition of Secretary of State Dean Acheson's famous January 1950 statement that South Korea was outside of the United States defence perimeter. For their part, the Soviets, perhaps seeking to assuage the new Carter administration, joined with the Yugoslavs in a declaration of common partnership which seemed to imply a hands-off pledge by the Soviet Union from any military or political intervention in Yugoslavia after Tito's passing.[42]

## IV—MEDITERRANEAN POLITICS
## AND THE UNCERTAIN FUTURE

Conflicting and competing interests in the Aegean, the Adriatic, and the Western Mediterranean indicate an outmoded NATO structure and the transformation of the United States into a geopolitical factor of secondary significance. Simply stated, the United States has failed to maintain a constructive and workable international policy which serves to define and to implement its own national interests.

---

[39] *Chicago Tribune*, November 14, 1976, s. 1, p. 38.
[40] 13 *UN Chronicle*, October 1976, p. 35. The frustrations and convolutions of American foreign policy are carefully examined in T. Couloumbis, " Five ' Theories ' Regarding Kissinger's Policy Toward the Cyprus Crisis," 2 *International Studies Notes* (Spring 1975), pp. 12–17. *Cf.* United States, 94th Congress, First Session, Greece and Turkey: Some Military Implications Related to NATO and the Middle East, Report for the Committee on Foreign Affairs (1975), pp. 14–18.
[41] *New York Times*, November 5, 1976, s. A, p. 14.
[42] *Chicago Tribune*, November 18, 1976, s. 1, p. 24.

The Cyprus controversy has not abated, Greece and Turkey are continuing their politics of confrontation, the Middle East still boils, and—if it grows stronger—a leftward political trend in South-west Europe are factors which will all combine to neutralise the existing NATO Mediterranean defence system. The narrow victory of the Christian Democrats and their tenuous majority in the Italian parliamentary elections of June 1976, has already provoked a strong response from the new United States President: "Italians cannot expect continuing aid from the United States towards their development and at the same time turn the peninsula's political boat to the left. . . . Now the time has come to ask something from Italy. What? The political loyalty that keeps together two allied countries." [43]

That "loyalty" has already been severely strained by several French presidential régimes. The new democratically elected Spanish Cortes will be much less favourable towards the American presence in Spain. And the urgent Portuguese request for a 300 million-dollar loan in late November 1976, is placing the same kind of financial pressure on the United States, that the United States had sought to put on Italy before her parliamentary elections. To threaten Portugal with expulsion from NATO and economic collapse (and to issue the same threat for Italy), as Dr. Kissinger's policies (and President Carter's statements) indicate, is to invite the very disintegration that the United States has historically sought to avoid. [44]

It is by now commonplace to say that the traditional political and economic relationships in the Mediterranean are in disarray. The future is at best uncertain. There are far more questions to be raised than are there answers to be given. In the final analysis, the future of the Mediterranean and the very survival of humanity itself, " depends on the co-operation, interdependence and understanding among all classes of human beings—the rich and the poor, the industrialised and the developing nations." [45] Without a willingness to begin anew, the Mediterranean basin will once more fall victim to the turbulence of its past.

---

[43] Quoted by *Gioia* (Milan) and reprinted in the *Des Moines Register*, November 6, 1976, s. A, p. 13. This was a much harsher statement than his pre-election posture. See the interview in *Playboy*, November 1976, p. 77.

[44] On the Portuguese Revolution and its NATO impact, see T. Szulc, " Lisbon & Washington: Behind Portugal's Revolution," 21 *Foreign Policy* (1975), pp. 3–62.

[45] Mojekwu, *op. cit.* in note 21 above, p. 6.

# RETURN TO DEMOCRATIC GOVERNMENT

By

## FERDINAND A. HERMENS

OURS is a world of contradictions, in the political field more than in any other. On the one hand, non-democratic governments have, for two generations now, been collapsing all over the globe. On the other hand, too many of the democratic governments instituted to replace them have failed to function.

### I—THE FAILURE OF DEMOCRATIC CONSTITUTIONALISM

The failure of democratic constitutionalism is largely based on a type of mismanagement which fundamentally arose out of non-management. Years ago, Leon Trotsky said that the Bolshevists had won out during the Russian Revolution because they knew what to do " the day after." Similarly, in later years Communist groups all over the world did know what to do whenever a chance opened up for them. For decades their representatives in Moscow made plans for their return; their opponents were inclined to ridicule them, feeling that their day would never come. It did, however, come in the wake of the events accompanying the collapse of the Axis Powers. The Communists had plans for all contingencies, beginning with cases permitting their immediate assumption of power, continuing with those where intermediate solutions seemed necessary, and ending with preparations for conditions in which the survival of " bourgeois democracy " was to be expected for some time.

The strength of the Communists is based on three assets: They have a viable political structure, they use a popular terminology, and they know how to make the democratic Left co-operate with them in promoting institutions which tend to keep " bourgeois democracy " weak when this suits, or seems to suit, Communist purposes.

The political structure which the Communists have to offer is a tightly controlled political party which, in the words of Phillip Selznick [1] constitutes an organisational weapon. When Lenin laid down its intellectual foundation he did so in a way which combined clarity in his own thought with a terminology apt to confuse his opponents. When he considered himself a " socialist," this meant that in the context of the social and economic structure certain goals had to be pursued. In this respect the difference between Lenin and

---

[1] P. Selznick, *The Organizational Weapon: A Study of Bolshevist Strategy and Tactics* (1952).

true Social-Democrats lies in the choice of the means to be employed; this is one of the cases in which the choice of means was to determine the ends actually achieved.

Lenin scolded the Social-Democrats and the trade unionists because they used, in the main, peaceful processes which, he felt, induced them to make so many compromises with the existing order that, in the end, they were bound to be assimilated and absorbed by it. Only a new type of political party would be able to resist such tendencies. The emphasis on the party (rather than on a mere social class) as the primary political tool of action made Lenin a strong believer in the primacy of the political. In his words: " The essential and ' decisive ' interest of classes can be satisfied *only* by radical *political* changes." [2] This primacy of the political—so hard to grasp for the modern western intellectual [3]—Lenin connected immediately with emphasis on something even more difficult to grasp in this day and age: the primacy of political form.

The problem which arises in this connection was formulated succinctly by Rudolph Hilferding in a paper on which he was working when the Nazis arrested him in southern France: ". . . Economic conditions require transformation (*Umsetzetung*) into the political. This transformation is a process in which interests and motives of an immediate economic nature undergo a change." [4] For a socialist of the Second International it was quite a step forward to recognise this much and formulate it so forcefully. Hilferding failed, however, to see the implications of his views in regard to political form, as do most other democratic socialists to this day. Lenin's answer to these problems was simple: a party based on " democratic centralism " and characterised by the criteria laid down in *What Is To Be Done?* was all that mattered. All " socialist " States (and " people's democracies ") are, indeed, dominated by this type of party; all additional arrangements as to the nature of the political structure are of minor significance.

The developments after the Portuguese Revolution of April 1974, demonstrate what the existence of such a party means for " the day after." Its structure enabled it to survive under the type of " authoritarian " dictatorship which the Salazar-Caetano government repre-

---

[2] V. I. Lenin, *What Is To Be Done?* (1941), p. 47. For details and additional literature, see Ferdinand A. Hermens, " Totalitarian Power Structure and Foreign Policy," 3 *The Journal of Politics* (1959), and *Der Ost-West Konflikt: Gruende und Scheingruende* (1964).

[3] It might be mentioned in passing that, during his 1934 conversations with Stalin, H. G. Wells found it necessary to tell Stalin that, perhaps, he believed more strongly in the economic interpretation of history. Stalin retorted that Wells underestimated political power, which seemed to escape him completely. (*Stalin-Wells Talk, The Verbatim Record and a Discussion* (1934), pp. 7–11.)

[4] Published under the title, " Das Historische Problem," 4 *Zeitschrift fuer Politik* (1954), with Introduction by B. Kautsky.

sented. After its collapse, Communists quickly moved into the
" commanding heights " of the trade union movement, of the media
of mass communication and, surprisingly, of significant segments of
the armed forces. General Spinola had thought in terms of making
Portugal into a parliamentary democracy on the western model; at
first, most of the young officers supporting him held similar views.
The Communists, however, moved into the battle with their organisation as well as with their terminology, thereby making it possible for
them both to reveal and to veil their intentions. The aim of " socialism " appealed to many, and " capitalism " no one felt like defending.
At first only a few became aware of the political goals hiding behind
this economic terminology: When the Communists rejected " capitalism " they also rejected " bourgeois democracy," and the rule of the
proletariat which they professed to promote also included the rule of
its " vanguard," the Communist party; they were willing to accept
allies but claimed the right to lead them toward their own goals,
which included a new dictatorship to take the place of the old one.

Communists, meanwhile, are not 10 feet tall. They make mistakes,
and sometimes their opponents know how to take advantage of these
mistakes. At first, however, the leaders of the Communist Party had
it all their own way, and one of their achievements consisted in
forcing their " socialist " terminology into the Portuguese Constitution. Its first Article declares Portugal to be a " sovereign republic
engaged in a transformation into a society without classes." According to the second Article the country's ultimate goal is " to assure a
transition to socialism by creating the conditions for the democratic
exercise of power by the working classes." These aims are restated
repeatedly, in particular in the constitution, a second section of which
deals with the economic organisation. Finally, " the principle of
collective appropriation of the principal means of production and
natural resources as well as the elimination of monopolies and
Latifundia " are among those exempted from the possibility of a
constitutional revision. It is true that the constitution is equally
characterised by its emphasis on fundamental rights, on pluralism,
and on other vital aspects of democratic government. The provisions
concerning " socialism " will, however, always lend credence to
Communist charges that whatever government is not to their liking
is not " socialist " and, therefore, lacks legitimacy.

Communist awareness of the requirements of political form also
makes it possible for them to avail themselves of the indirect and
largely involuntary support of those who sincerely desire a State
based on " councils of workers, soldiers and peasants." When the
first " Soviets " developed during the Russian Revolution of 1905
Lenin was afraid of them. They might have been close to Marx's

own political thought, but they certainly were opposed to the political monopoly of a party based on " democratic centralism." By 1917, Lenin had come to realise how well " Soviet " ideology suited his purposes. Spontaneously formed councils lacked a viable principle of political integration. The Communists, on the other hand, found it easy to fill the resulting political vacuum. At the same time, " Soviets " could effectively disrupt the social and political structure of both the Tsarist and the provisional government. Lastly, after the Bolshevists had won out, " Soviet " terminology admirably served the purpose of camouflaging their monopoly of political power. To this day every western country co-operates in this process when (as diplomatic custom makes inevitable) it deals with the Soviet Union as if that country were governed by freely-elected councils and as if the nationalities constituting it formed a voluntary " union."

## II—PORTUGAL AND PROPORTIONAL REPRESENTATION

In Portugal, General (later returned to his permanent rank as major) Otelo Saraiva de Carvalho became the leader of those who believed in a " second road to socialism." As in other countries, his followers constitute a motley group. In the elections of 1975, many of them were members of the Portuguese Democratic Movement (MDP/CDE), which, closely allied to the Communists, polled slightly more than 4 per cent. of the votes; in 1976 they preferred to vote for the Communist lists because, on account of the technical aspects of the system of Proportional Representation used, half of the votes cast for them in 1975 were wasted. In the Presidential elections of June 1976, however, Carvalho competed with the rather colourless Communist, Octavio Pato, securing 16·52 per cent. of the votes to Pato's 7·58 per cent. Carvalho was, as the weekly, *Expresso*, put it, hardly more than an exponent of " heroic populism " with a " romantic halo," capable of being for some time " a Don Quixote of discontent." [5] The superior power of organisation of the Communists soon reasserted itself, in particular in the local elections of December 1976. Groups like Carvalho's were useful in the fight against the Socialist government headed by Mario Soares.

It is, at any rate, significant that in the debates of the Constituent Assembly [6] the Communists as well as the MDB proposed extensive sanctioning of *poder popular*. This met with the opposition of the Socialists as well as of the other parties, and the major remnant of the demands for a recognition of " basis groups " is found in Article 118, in which these groups, " formed according to the consti-

---

[5] " Otelo e o futuro," *Expresso*, June 5, 1976.
[6] For some excerpts see Victor Silva Lopes, *Constituicão da Repubblica Portuguesa 1976 (anotada)* (1976).

tution, have the right to power within the forms determined by law." This will mean little as long as the government is reasonably effective, but whenever the government is weak Communist support for extra legal actions by " basis groups " may result in considerable damage.

In addition to the " organisational weapon " and an effective, if confusing, terminology, Communists can bring to " the day after " concrete plans as to the new constitutional structure—although we shall see forthwith that in this respect the Portuguese introduced a measure of flexibility, ill-advised as it turned out to be. Let it also be added that the views in question can be, and usually are, stated in an entirely non-Communist language.[7] Some of them are held by a variety of democratic groups; others are more closely associated with the views of those who, in the terminology of Max Weber, basically want freedom *from* the State rather than freedom *within* the State.

The first demand is for proportional representation (P.R.),[8] so popular again in our day. Its most immediate effect is a " shift in the constitutional order." [9] Instead of parliament deciding as a whole, a number of political parties takes over, none of which either has, or ever expects to have, an overall majority. Governments are, as a rule, no longer determined by the voter himself but in the negotiations between parties which take place *after* the elections. Inevitably there is mutual jealousy among the coalition partners, none of which cherishes responsibility for policies not entirely its own. Furthermore, new types of parties are likely to develop or be strengthened, in particular in times of economic difficulty; extremists of the Right and of the Left may be among them, as well as parties representing a narrow economic interest.

In the second place, Communists appreciate the fact that under P.R. they can secure seats without co-operating with more moderate groups. Palmiro Togliatti, in an article entitled, " On the Possibility of Using the Parliamentary Path for the Transition to Socialism," [10] stated that under majority voting the representatives of the " popular masses " might " splinter into small groups and sometimes disappear

---

[7] This was done for the first time when, early in 1944, Georges Cogniot developed the Communist idea on the political structure of a " bourgeois democracy " in the, then clandestine, *Cahiers du Communisme.* On the historical setting see Gordon Wright, *The Reshaping of French Democracy* (1948), p. 36 *et seq.*

[8] For theoretical aspects of the problems involved see the first part of the author's *Democracy or Anarchy? A Study of Proportional Representation,* 2nd ed. (1972). For the current British discussion see his review article entitled, " The English Malady and English Political Thinking," *Verfassung und Verfassungswirklichkeit,* with the English sub-title, *The Living Constitution* (1976).

[9] R. Smend, "Der Verschiebung der konstitutionellen Ordnung durch die Verhaeltniswahl," first published in 1919; here quoted from *Staatsrechtliche Abhandlungen* (1955), p. 55 *et seq.*

[10] The Moscow *Pravda* of March 7, 1956.

completely." That was an exaggeration; Italian Communists were already strong enough to be a serious factor under a majority system. However, after the regional elections of 1975, when the PCI reached one-third of the total vote, Enrico Berlinguer and Georges Marchais still insisted, in a common declaration, on P.R. The reason may be the experience of the French Communists who continue to suffer from the fact that, strong as they may be, they need Socialist, and even centrist, support, in particular in a second ballot.

The other major plank in the Communist constitutional platform (somewhat ignored in Portugal) is " parliamentary sovereignty." Even under the conditions created by P.R., there exist possibilities of endowing the executive with certain rights, such as that of parliamentary dissolution and, under certain conditions, with the right of legislating by decree. Once the results of P.R. begin to be serious such provisions may prove to be two-edged swords; the dissolution of the Reichstag by Dr. Bruening in 1930 weakened the moderate parties, and executive law-making can, as Bruening's successors proved, be grossly abused. Still, during the periods of relative calm, for which the friends of a " consociational democracy " based on P.R. must always hope,[11] provisions for the strengthening of executive power may be useful and, as a rule, the Communists want none of it.

In Portugal the Communists did insist on P.R.; they deplored the fact that the d'Hondt system for distributing seats was adopted. But, so far as the executive is concerned, they expected to control the military, and through it, both the President and the Cabinet. The failure of the *coup* of November 25, 1975, created a new situation. Still, the Communists accepted the structure of the executive in the new constitution as shaped by the agreement between the military and the parties. This meant a directly elected President who, with the approval of the Council of the Revolution, may dissolve parliament. Contrary to Communist expectations, General Eanes, an " operational " officer, was elected; he is interested in an orderly functioning of constitutional processes, which would permit the army to " return to the barracks." Similarly, the Cabinet was accorded the right to issue decree laws in certain areas; parliament may empower it to do so even in fields normally reserved to itself. The first Prime Minister, Dr. Mario Soares, found these rights most helpful, and the Communists must be asking themselves why they ever deviated from the constitutional prescription issued by Georges Cogniot in 1944.

In Portugal the d'Hondt system of P.R., associated with a number of comparatively small constituencies, gave the Socialists, in 1975,

---

[11] Max Weber was aware of the difference in the effects of P.R. during " normal times " and during stormy periods. See *Gesammelte Schriften zur Politik* (1921), p. 367.

46·77 per cent. of the seats with 37·86 per cent. of the votes and, in 1976, 40·68 per cent. with 36·59 per cent. With such a strong plurality Dr. Soares decided to form a homogeneous one-party government rather than seek a coalition. In that way he minimised the danger of alienating either the right or the left wing of his supporters; for the time being, the moderate parties at his right were willing to endorse his major measures. Still, whether he entered into a coalition with one or both of the centrist parties or whether he led a homogeneous minority government, he had to conduct a two-front war, with opponents at both his left and right ready to denounce his policies. This is an essential aspect of many governments now existing in countries with P.R. electoral systems.[12]

The second aspect of this situation consists in economic troubles which, differing in severity from country to country, may be expected to be substantially greater than those characteristic of the (unprecedented) boom which most of the world experienced between 1948 and 1973. Portugal's post-revolutionary governments inherited a strong financial position from the dictatorship, but were hit immediately by the oil crisis, the return of workers from Western Europe and the influx of more than half a million people from the former colonies. Some of the resulting difficulties could have been mitigated by a rational economic policy. Instead, there was the popular view that liberation from dictatorship meant liberation from economic constraints. Demands for enormous wage increases were no rarity; even after they had been scaled down there remained more than the economy could absorb. Haphazard measures of socialisation, sanctioned by the government or not, cast a pall of insecurity over vast areas of the nation's economic life.

A French correspondent [13] discussed the anguished reflections of the then Socialist Minister of Finance who was trying to explain to the workers that any willingness to meet their continually rising wage claims would simply reduce the production from which their own needs were satisfied. The correspondent added that, in the denunciation of " capitalist profits," the essential notion of rentability had been lost. Even a Marxist analysis could have shown what was wrong. When Marx discussed " accumulation " he mentioned that if the enterprise was successful " Geld " (money) would be exchanged against " Ware " (commodity), in the expectation that when this was sold it could again be exchanged for money; if at all possible

---

[12] The government of the Federal Republic of Germany is the major exception which confirms the rule, as was discussed by W. Kaltefleiter, *Verfassung und Verfassungswirklichkeit—The Living Constitution* (1977), where he deals with the 1976 elections and their aftermath.

[13] Danièle Liger, " Comment consommer 30 per cent. de plus qu'on ne produit? " *Le Monde*, December 3, 1975.

" G1 " had to be larger than " G." Marx might have added what this
process meant from the social as well as from the individual point of
view: As long as " G1 " is larger than " G " the process of investment
can be repeated on a higher level. Output is, in that case, again from
the point of view of society, larger than input. As long as this process
is kept up there is a chance for more employment and higher wages.
If, however, output is less than input, there is a loss for society as well
as of the individual " capitalist." [14] In his analysis Marx never fully
grasped the significance of money as a standard of value. Only
during this century have Socialist economists emphasised the fact
that simple rationality requires a monetary basis for comparing
demand with input and output. They are now logical enough to
insist that some kind of a " market " is necessary in a Socialist
society.

The simple worker emerging from a generation of dictatorship
may be forgiven if he does not understand these relationships, but too
often his leaders do not understand them either. This applies to
most groups of the extreme Left. Communists, in addition, want to
demonstrate that they are the " vanguard " of the proletariat and,
therefore, tend to endorse any popular demand even if, once they
have taken over, they are likely to impose heavy sacrifices on the
workers in order to restore production. In our day, orthodox
Communists may nevertheless be more responsible than what German students called the " Chaotiker," people who may call themselves
Trotskyists, Maoists, anarchists, or even populists. As long as the
goal is to bring down a moderate government like that of Dr. Soares,
the impact of the attacks on it is cumulative, whatever the ideological
shades of the groups from which they proceed. A responsible
economic policy is most difficult.

If we now ask what lessons can be derived from the Portuguese
experience the first is the need for terminological clarification. The
word " socialism " covers too much ground to be a reliable guide to
anything. Any realistic analysis must begin by an awareness of the
primacy of politics as well as of political form. After the Salazar-
Caetano dictatorship had collapsed the people wanted freedom. The
way to secure it was to establish a functioning democracy. If some
want to disparage it as " bourgeois," let us remind them that there is
also the " citoyen ": what we want is a democracy based on " citizens "
over and above all class divisions.

Secondly, in any country a functioning democracy becomes
difficult even if only a part of the Communist prescription, as laid

---

[14] There are the well-known exceptions to this rule: hidden " social costs " or social
benefits, such as savings in unemployment compensation and increased tax returns,
items which do not show up in a private employer's accounts.

down by Georges Cogniot in 1944 is followed. Thus with a strongly watered-down P.R. system Socialists and Popular Democrats (the latter now calling themselves Social Democrats) could secure an impressive lead in terms of seats. Even so, Portugal seemed about to become a " democracy without a safety valve." [15] All, or most, of the moderate parties had to share, directly or indirectly, in the responsibility of government, which had to fight enemies on its right as well as at its left. Whenever there develops a protest vote it cannot, as it does in the Anglo-Saxon countries, strengthen the opposition *within* the system; it has to coalesce around the opposition *to* the system. In latter-day Italy, the Communists won that race against the neo-Fascists; it is well to recall that in both pre-Fascist Italy and in Weimar Germany the extremists of the Right carried the day.

Even under an extreme form of P.R. (which, as mentioned repeatedly, Portugal does not have), the victory of a dictatorship is only one of several possibilities. Nonetheless, in the inter-war period this was the experience of 198 million people living in countries where P.R. operated, whereas democratic institutions survived in such countries for no more than 40·6 million people.[16] A major reason for this trend was the predominance of highly adverse economic conditions. They constitute quite a contrast to the boom period of 1948 to 1973, during which the word " Wirtschaftswunder " came to be spelled in a variety of languages, including Italian, Japanese, Spanish (Mexico) and Portuguese (Brazil).[17]

During this period governments in countries with P.R. were able to do better than their predecessors of the earlier period.

Even when coalitions formed by parties shaped by P.R. manage to last, they suffer, during boom periods as well, from the fact that they are not considered " legitimate " in the same sense as governments resulting, under majority voting, from a direct popular verdict.[18] Furthermore, even if the number of parties needed for a majority is as low, and the parties themselves are as moderate as is the case in

---

[15] See F. A. Hermens, " Demokratie ohne Sicherheitsventil," 2 *Vierteljahrshefte fuer Zeitgeschichte* (1955). This article deals with Italy after the 1953 elections.

[16] For details see *op. cit.* in note 8 above, p. 356.

[17] The relationship between economic and political conditions is spelled out, with a wealth of statistical detail, in: W. Kaltefleiter, *Wirtschaft und Politik in Deutschland: Konjunktur als Bestimmungsgrund des Parteiensystems*, 2nd ed. (1968). An English edition of this book is long overdue.

[18] If such decisions become as questionable as they did in the United Kingdom, the reasons mentioned in the publications cited in note 8, above, have to be taken into account. The same goes for the opposite case when, as happened in the Federal Republic of Germany, coalitions are known to the voter beforehand and approved by him. Such engagements may, as happened in Lower Saxony in 1976, break down. The entire complex of problems involved was discussed in W. Kaltefleiter, *Verfassung und Verfassungswirklichkeit—The Living Constitution* (1977) in which he analysed the 1976 Bundestag elections in the framework of the German political system.

present-day Germany, a cabinet may not be easy to form or to hold together.

Portugal benefits from an electoral system even less proportional than that of Germany and from provisions concerning the constitutional structure which, on the whole, may be considered more favourable to executive stability than those of the *Grundgesetz*. On the other hand, the Soares government began with economic conditions which were as adverse as those accompanying the inauguration of the Federal Republic had been propitious.[19] A few months after the formation of the Soares government, the Communists, in the local elections of December 12, 1976 fully made up for their decline in the presidential elections, while the Socialists lost slightly. Dr. Soares can always fall back on a formal coalition with the " Social Democrats " or with the " Social Democratic Centre," and even with the Communists, but in that case the advantage of homogeneity would be lost, while the battle with economic adversity would remain.

Similar battles, though not nearly as severe, may dominate the balance of this century in more or less all countries. Economic interest groups have begun to supplant parliaments and governments, making workable decisions harder to reach. The claims for welfare benefits grow and budget deficits reach unprecedented heights. Wages increase in most years by greater proportions than productivity. These and other factors combine to foster a willingness to promote, or tolerate, inflationary policies. Will coalition governments, faced by internal difficulties, find it easier to cope with such problems than one-party-majority governments? In Iceland, which has P.R. coalitions, the rate of inflation, now somewhat reduced, reached a peak of 50 per cent. Even the comparatively well placed coalition government of the Republic of Ireland is no more successful in its fight against inflation than is that of the United Kingdom. In Denmark a Socialist minority government finds it difficult to get any policy adopted. The cabinets succeeding one another in Italy, the country which, at the time of writing, has the most consistent type of P.R.,[20] have the most trouble making an anti-inflationary policy stick.

The basic economic problems of our time now exist, in spite of all

---

[19] Basically, the " Wirtschaftswunder " begins with the currency reform of June 20, 1948, and the subsequent scrapping of restrictive regulations by the Minister of Economics, Professor Erhard. Its perception becomes, however, as Kaltefleiter (*op. cit.* in note 17 above) emphasises, politically effective only in 1952. This time lag caused considerable political fragmentation in the 1951 *Land* elections in Hesse, Lower Saxony and Bremen.

[20] There is not only P.R. between the parties but also P.R. within the parties; the preference votes cast for individual candidates on a list encourage the formation of *correnti* to such an extent that the coherence of the major parties is threatened; it is said that a *correntocrazia* has taken the place of what is supposed to be a *democrazia*.

variations in their intensity, in all countries. They do not permit us to expect anything like the 1948–1973 boom during the next quarter of a century. Recessions may be quite extensive and economic growth slower. Therefore, countries in which new democracies are to be established may do well to ask themselves whether their power to handle such problems will be enhanced if P.R. is adopted and typical coalition governments are formed.

### III—THE TRANSITION IN SPAIN

If we now turn to Spain's unique and, so far, successful attempt to provide for a peaceful transition from a dictatorship to a democracy there are, in the first place, points of similarity to developments in Portugal. Both dictatorships had built up a strong financial position. The Portugal of Salazar and Caetano used its resources conservatively, without a substantial effort to foster economic development. In Spain there began, in 1959, a period of rapid expansion, fostered by the planning of the " technocrats," headed by Lopez Rodó. When, in October 1976, King Juan Carlos visited France, President Giscard d'Estaing gave an interview to the Spanish news agency, EFE,[21] in which he emphasised that during the last ten years Spain's production had increased at an annual rate of 7 per cent., higher than that of all other countries of the Organisation for Economic Co-operation and Development (OECD) except Japan, with average income reaching the Italian, and almost the British level.

Spain is, indeed, a much changed country, by comparison with the time after the Civil War. There is a strong urban middle class, proud of its refrigerators, television sets, cars, and, in some cases, country houses. Skilled workers find themselves in a similar position. Overall, industrial employment has risen substantially; this must be borne in mind when recent increases in unemployment are emphasised. Spain, then, is no longer a " semi-feudal " but an almost modern country. Certain segments of agriculture remain a problem, and measures of agrarian reform are overdue. But, then, agriculture is no longer of overriding importance. A rational policy would face up to the need for changes as part of an overall plan, and proceed deliberately, without the spasms characterising Portugal's agricultural policy. Similarly, there are good reasons for increasing income and estate taxes in the higher brackets; within a certain range differences in income distribution can be reduced without jeopardising production. The Chilean experience, however, suggests that when too much pressure is put on the members of the middle class they can be alienated from the democratic order, with serious consequences.

---

[21] See *Sol de Espana*, October 29, 1976.

The favourable aspects of Spain's economic and social development are partly offset by negative ones. The recession brought about the return of Spanish workers from Western Europe and affected tourism as well; the oil crisis also hit hard. Spain's dying dictatorship exhibited a marked weakness in dealing with the problems arising from these events. Even during the years of expansion inflationary tendencies were not controlled as effectively as in most industrialised countries; economic growth was valued more highly than economic stability.[22] This may be the reason why the full force of the recession did not develop until 1975.

One of the results of a lenient economic policy was the failure to curb oil imports; while in the other industrial countries imports declined up to 10 per cent., in Spain they increased by 7 per cent. Similarly, there was comparatively little resistance to pressures for increases in wages. Strikes continued to be illegal, but they were frequent, without much regard for economic consequences. Tourists will remember the flight controllers' " work to rule "; the controllers had their reasons but their actions contributed to the difficulties of an industry on which Spain had to rely for substantial foreign exchange earnings. When, in other cases, demands for increases in the hourly rate of wages [23] were made which were clearly in excess of the increase in productivity, there were all the excuses derived from a primitive version of the purchasing power theory—or from " Keynesian " theories which caused Lord Keynes to state, a generation ago, that he was not a " Keynesian."

In Spain a responsible wages policy was rendered difficult by the atmosphere of transition. As in Portugal, some workers seemed to believe that the end of a dictatorship removes all economic con-

---

[22] For details see W. Haubrich and C. R. Moser, *Francos Erben: Spanien auf dem Weg in die Gegenwart* (1976), pp. 44 *et seq.* and 177 *et seq.* See also *OECD Economic Surveys, Spain* (1976).

[23] Nominal hourly earnings increased in 1973 by 19·7 per cent., in 1974 by 26·7 per cent., and in 1975 by 30·2 per cent. Real hourly earnings increased in 1973 by 7·4 per cent., in 1974 by 9·5 per cent., and in 1975 by 11·4 per cent. Few pointed out the difference between increases in the hourly rate of wages and the total income of the workers in a given industry or, for that matter, of all actual and potential workers. When the elasticity of the demand for workers is greater than one, the total amount of wages paid to the group in question will decline. It is surprising that so few students of econometrics venture forth with calculations aiming at determining the approximate elasticity of the demand for workers. Calculations of a similar nature were made before the oil-exporting countries increased their prices, the aim being to fix a rate which would be as high as possible without leading to a substantial reduction in demand and/or the encouragement of large-scale substitutions. The economists in question (supposedly located in Cambridge, Massachusetts) did their work well enough—even if their results may have been more aptly interpreted by Sheik Yamani of Saudi Arabia than by the Shah of Iran. Similar attempts could be made to help workers and employers in a given industry to identify the optimum wage; a further attempt could be made to put such calculations into a national framework.

straints. The dictatorship was evidently to blame for the absence of responsible trade unions.[24] When members of recent cabinets declared that they were aiming at, and to some extent getting close to, a " social contract " with the workers, this evoked the reply by one of the academic leaders of the opposition that what existed constituted a " *political* contract "; the workers were granted almost any wage settlement as long as they remained quiet in the political field. This rejoinder contains an important element of truth. Restraint in wage settlements is a *conditio sine qua non* for the control of a rate of inflation which, in the fall of 1976, independent observers placed at 20 per cent. Inevitably, there developed a sizeable gap in the balance of payments; the latter led to an increase in the foreign debt which may, in a year or so, approach the level of 20 billion dollars, beyond which creditors are not likely to go. As matters stood at the end of 1976, the Suarez government was given excellent marks for its handling of the political side of its tasks, but poor ones for the way in which it allowed matters to drift in the economic field.

That Spain's economic situation has improved so much since the early 1960s makes it particularly urgent to come to grips with current troubles. An advanced economy is so complex that it cannot stand much experimentation. At the same time, the increase in well-being (which has its limits) was followed by a " revolution of rising expectations." Under such conditions only a free government can make the people accept the sacrifices needed in order to set matters right. To do this, however, a free government needs authority. Thus, in Spain, too, the question arises whether the required combination of the complementary (rather than contrary) principles of freedom and authority will be secured.

If an answer is attempted in the brevity required, it must first refer to the political structure contemplated by the " Reform Law " as passed by the old Cortes on November 18, 1976 and approved by the voters in the referendum of December 15, 1976. Its (brief) provisions leave the King in the possession of executive power; a Senate intended to be a kind of second Chamber is flanked by a " Congress of Deputies." The Cabinet depends upon the King rather than upon the Cortes. The overall result is that of a " constitutional monarchy " (on the model of, let us say, pre-1918 Germany) rather than of a " parliamentary monarchy " on the British model. Evidently, this was the best the King could make the old Cortes accept. It may also be a good solution for a more extended period of transition; the parties need time to reduce their number, estimated as

---

[24] How responsible free unions will be depends, in part, on whether extremist groups (not only Communists but also Trotskyists, anarchists and the like) will be able to substitute their political goals for rational economic considerations.

higher than 200, and to bring some clarity into their thinking. If, however, an attempt should be made to perpetuate the " Constitutional monarchy " [25] the first question is whether any government would have enough power to put Spain's economic house in order. In the second place, the institution of monarchy might rather quickly erode together with the entire " constitutional " system. Monarchs no longer dispose of the stable " intermediate powers " needed in order to make such a system last; even in the short run attempts to that end would require all kinds of manipulation.

Let us then assume that there will, eventually, be a fully-fledged parliamentary government. Will it develop enough force to act? That depends on the coherence of the parties in back of it; this, in turn, depends in part on the system of voting.[26] There is always the possibility that the characteristics of a country's political " matter " exclude the optimum solution, the plurality system of voting. They clearly do in the sense that Spain, with its bewildering multiplicity of parties, requires, for the time being, something on the order of the French second ballot [27]; otherwise, there might be too many accidental results.

Then there are the objections to majority voting which arise out of the possible influence of the old " caciques " and out of parochial interests. These are common fears in Latin countries; French experience since 1958, however, seems to indicate that voters are of late more inclined to vote according to national rather than local considerations. On the other hand opposition leaders are on firm ground when they insist that the administrative and political remnants of the dictatorship must be removed, or at least neutralised, before free elections are possible.

Then there is the fear of polarisation; the Socialists and other left-wing parties might, it is said, react to the introduction of majority voting by agreeing to a Popular Front, prepared to bring Communist ministers into the Cabinet. If, however, the Communists are as weak as most public opinion surveys indicate, the Socialists do not need them; they could be of help in but a limited number of constituencies. On the other hand, the Socialists plus the " Social Democrats " (provided that the various brands unite at least for a second ballot) could, with the help of majority voting, keep the number of Com-

---

[25] M. Duverger, " L'Espagne au moment de Verité," *Le Monde*, November 27, 1976, in which the writer seriously discusses such a possibility.

[26] The problems involved are discussed in more detail in: F. A. Hermens and P.-H. Koeppinger, " Der Uebergang von der Diktatur zur Demokratie: Die Beispiele Spaniens und Portugal," *Verfassung und Verfassungswirklichkeit—The Living Constitution* (1977).

[27] Arrangements like the alternative vote could also be considered, perhaps even run-off elections limited to the first two candidates.

munist seats so low that they would not endanger the moderate Left. In the long run the bulk of those now inclined to vote for the Communists might realise that, as the Socialist Leader Felipe Gonzalez said, Communism is an outdated ideology. Absorption of the bulk of these people in a Social Democratic grouping [28] would certainly be preferable to permitting even the most moderate " Eurocommunist " group to prosper with the help of P.R.

Actually, when discussing such problems with Spanish proponents of P.R. one is reminded of what Walter Lippmann said in his discussion of stereotypes: " We do not first see and then define; we define first and see then." The most effective arguments advanced are standard components of all advocacy of P.R., regardless of time or place. The first is the claim that P.R. alone is just and fair. Jacques Maritain [29] disposed of it succinctly when he said that just as the common good is not the mere sum of individual goods, the common will is not the sum of individual wills.

If such brevity is permitted (in an issue which touches on central elements of political philosophy), it could be said that the justice of P.R. follows the maxim: To everyone his due; to the whole nothing.

To Madrid's Left and Centre it is now simply axiomatic that P.R. is just: the perception of all aspects of political reality passes through this screen; whoever dares to disagree finds himself under a moral shadow. Similar considerations apply to the claim that majority voting would lead to " polarisation " and civil war. It is of little use to refer to the facts mentioned above, namely that if available opinion polls are even halfway reliable, neither the extreme Right nor the extreme Left could by themselves wrench the moderates away from the decisive influence of the centre. If, however, people persuade themselves so firmly that majority voting does not mean what Rudolf Smend termed it a generation ago—a " Kampf mit Integrationstendenz," a " struggle with a tendency to integration "—but a bloody revolution, that may become a fact; the day of self-fulfilling prophecies is not over. [30]

Such is the resulting situation that opposition to P.R. is now virtu-

---

[28] After some hesitation the Communist Party was legalised. Its democratic opponents rightly refer to the fact that in Portugal nothing helped as much to deflate the Communists as their open participation in free elections.

[29] *La République Française*, December 1943. See also *op. cit.* in note 8 above, pp. 78–85.

[30] In his conversations in Madrid the author repeatedly encountered a terminology strongly reminiscent of recent British pro-P.R. literature. This is quite a contrast to the situation prevailing a decade ago when the thought of French writers, in particular of Maurice Duverger, drawing the lessons from the failure of the Fourth Republic, clearly predominated. See, for example, a volume produced by a group presided over by G. Robles, *Cartas del Pueblo Español* (1967), p. 95.

ally limited to the Right, in particular the " Alianza Popular," headed by the former Minister of the Interior, Manuel Fraga Iribarne. At first the members of the old " Cortes " friendly to them threatened to block the " Ley de Reforma Politica " unless majority voting was adopted. They yielded when the government agreed to measures against " extreme fragmentation." Among these a clause which, on the German model, keeps a party with less than 5 per cent. of the votes (which presents its problems in a country with substantial regional parties) may be of minor significance.

It is more important that every one of Spain's 50 provinces is to have a minimum number of seats. When the campaign for the elections took shape the hopes of the minor parties faded. The leader of the " Spanish Socialist Workers Party " (PSOE), Felipe Gonzalez, attracted a surprisingly large amount of support. Prime Minister Suarez prevailed upon various groups to unite in the " Union of the Democratic Centre," placing, in the end, himself at the head of its list in Madrid and supporting it to the hilt. The result was that this coalition, with 34·71 per cent. of the votes, secured 47·14 per cent. of the seats.[31] The PSOE taking, with 29·24 per cent. of the votes, 33·71 per cent. of the seats, also benefited from the concentrating effects of the d'Hondt system in small constituencies. The parties at the left and at the right of the political spectrum paid most of the freight: The Communists with 9·24 per cent. of the votes had 5·71 per cent. of the seats; Fraga's " Alianza Popular " with 8·39 per cent. of the votes secured but 4·57 per cent. of the seats. The strongest group of the Christian Democrats, headed by Alvarez de Miranda, became part of the " Union of the Democratic Centre " and did well; those running independently fared disastrously. The minor Socialist groups did not do much better; Tierno Galvan's combination obtained 4·48 per cent. of the votes and 1·71 per cent. of the seats—six in all—of which three were secured in the large constituency of Madrid where there was almost complete proportionality.

The logical result of this outcome was a tendency towards a two-party system. The PSOE began to attract the minor Socialist groups, and Premier Suarez took steps to change the loose coalition of the centre (" Suarez's 12 tribes ") into a political party. A change in the electoral system could greatly strengthen the tendency towards *bipartidismo*. The majority system would do so most forcefully and, in the long run, most securely. If objections to it persist, the d'Hondt system of P.R. in small constituencies, which would only have to be extended to the large provinces, might do—as long as no prolonged

---

[31] The figures are not yet official, and are quoted from the daily *El Pais*, July 17, 1977.

depression or something similar basically shakes the voting pattern established in the first elections.[32]

Measures of this kind would logically be part of an explicit constitutional consensus between the two major parties, which is possible provided there is an adequate understanding for the requirements of democratic government and of the present situation. Such a consensus would be greatly assisted if clear explanations of the essential aspects of the democratic process emanated from the older democratic countries; as yet there is but little indication that this might be forthcoming, current British P.R. literature being particularly unhelpful.

A measure of economic consensus is equally important. Mr. Suarez's reconstructed government had to take matters into its own hands with a reform plan which may, or may not, go far enough, but which cannot succeed unless the trade unions, now in the process of formation and reformation, co-operate. The prospects for this are as uncertain as those of a constitutional consensus. Meanwhile, the new Suarez government, while stronger than that of Soares in Portugal, is still a minority government, a fact which has its consequences for the organisation and the operation of the Chamber as well as for the substance of the measures to be approved. Still, the near majority system of voting for the Senate elections helped; the Centre took 106 of the 207 directly elected Senators and is supported by the majority of the 41 appointees of the King. There is, then, a chance for matters to turn out right in Spain.

### IV—CONCLUSIONS

Whatever conclusions may be drawn in regard to the overall aspects of a controlled transition from dictatorship to democracy three imperatives are clear. First, there must be a clear recognition of both the primacy of both politics and political form. Secondly, a reasonably clear terminology must prevent people from talking in ambiguous economic terms when overriding political issues are involved. Thirdly, no country trying to establish a new democracy can dispense with a minimum of economic literacy. That applies to long-established democracies as well.

---

[32] Some observers have taken issue with the assumption that a two-party system would necessarily mean the type of polarisation which preceded the Civil War. Julian Marias in his article " La politica de la elipse," *El Pais*, July 10, 1977, does so in a manner which constitutes a brilliant contribution to the analysis of electoral systems.

# RECONCILING THE IRRECONCILABLE:

## THE QUEST FOR INTERNATIONAL AGREEMENT OVER POLITICAL CRIME AND TERRORISM

By

## NICHOLAS N. KITTRIE

THE international community has witnessed in recent years a growing number of unorthodox political activists and movements. Their tactical arsenal has ranged from civil disobedience to *coups d'état*, from tyrannicide to guerrilla war and terrorism. Their proclaimed goals have emphasised self-determination and human rights. But unorthodox activism is not to be equated with exclusively liberal and humane pursuits, for history, both recent and earlier, has demonstrated that reactionary and oppressive goals may also be furthered by resort to extra-legal or violent means.

Despite terrorism's challenges to the basic institutions of the world community, newly coupled with fears of potential exposure to nuclear or other high-risk blackmail, the family of nations has not produced a comprehensive plan of anti-terrorist action. The inability to define the contours and objectives of an " international " approach to the problem of terrorism transcends even the difficulties which customarily attend attempts at developing solutions to transnational problems. Lack of consensus affects not only the willingness of governments to respond to the manifestations of violence, but also their ability to classify and differentiate among various types of politically motivated offenders. In the face of these disagreements, the two major international attempts of the past forty years—by the League of Nations in 1937 and by the United States in 1972—to define and control terrorism have not proven successful.[1]

The prevalence of transnational violence places the topic once again on the international agenda and revives attempts to seek new and acceptable solutions. Previous world efforts have failed, largely because they have not adequately recognised that international legal solutions must be founded on a basic understanding of the particular nature of the so-called " community of nations." Not truly a " community," these nations may be more properly characterised as a

---

[1] The convention prepared by the League of Nations in 1937 was ratified by only one State, and the United States draft convention presented in 1972 to the United Nations languishes in committee. See Bassiouni (ed.), *International Terrorism and Political Crimes* (1975), Appendix Q, p. 546; and M. Hudson, *International Legislation* (1941), p. 862.

" decentralised " society marked by a plurality of widely differing political and social values. Any proposal for the international control of terrorism must recognise, therefore, the need to reconcile widely differing views on the acceptability of violence as a tool to achieve political change and to resist perceived injustice.

Even the rather limited objectives which underlie the United States Draft Convention on Terrorism have been anathema to a significant part of the international community.[2] Opposition comes from those who see most efforts towards defining and curbing international terrorism as status quo oriented. Any international agreement on terrorism would, they fear, neglect the claims and needs of the politically abused to pursue their internationally recognised rights.

Self-determination [3] and other advancements of fundamental human rights and freedoms have been a major purpose of international law in the post-United Nations Charter era. Attempts to develop wider agreement on the means of controlling and diminishing international terrorism must minister to two conflicting purposes: an increase of political rights as well as the preservative of world tranquillity. The imperative, therefore, must be to seek a reduction in the international climate of violence without ignoring the other cogent objectives of the international community.

How can the irreconcilable be reconciled? Is there a possible international formula which, while increasing international co-operation towards control of terrorism, will solidify the growing body of internationally recognised political and human rights? The premise advanced in the subsequent pages is that the pursuit of exclusively anti-terrorism agreements is a sterile enterprise. It is proposed, instead, that the older and broader body of international law, which deals with political offenders generally, could be fashioned into a more effective tool with which to reconcile the diverse view-points on the acceptability of violence to achieve political goals.

## I—The Measure of the Threat

Political activists, in recent times, have attracted an inordinate degree of public attention. More square inches of newsprint have been devoted in the United States, and in many other countries of both East and West, to the adventures and trials of Ulrike Meinhof, Rose Dugdale, Patricia Hearst, and Lynette " Squeaky " Fromme than to

---

[2] See below, section V.

[3] General Assembly Declaration 2625 (XXV), " Declaration on Principles of International Law Concerning Friendly Relations and Co-operation Among States in Accordance with the Charter of the United Nations." Under the declaration an existing State complies with the principle of equal rights and self-determination where the State is " possessed of a government representing the whole people belonging to the territory without distinction as to race, creed or colour."

any other topic in the field of criminal justice. Uniquely common to all four was not simply their feminine gender but rather the political character of their crimes. As one adds to these domestic-headline leaders the coverage of such transnational violence as the skyjacking to Entebbe, the South Moluccan train hold-up in Holland, the kidnapping in Vienna, of the ministers of the Organisation of Petroleum Exporting Countries (OPEC), and world-wide speculations regarding the mysterious Carlos, it is apparent that political crime and terrorism have become the decade's favourite "cops and robbers" stories.

Like crime generally, terrorism and other political offences used to be domestically based. It was in Moscow and St. Petersburg that Russian anarchists and revolutionaries fought their war against the Czars; it was in the streets of Germany that the Nazis sought and gained power. Only in rare instances was violence carried to more distant theatres. But the past two decades have seen a spill-over effect of political violence. Victims and offenders are now drawn in on a world-wide basis. Like other types of modern criminality—the drug traffic, corporate corruption and environmental abuse—terrorism and other political crime are no longer confined within national boundaries.

It is not the sheer number of those killed, injured or otherwise affected by political crime and terrorism, which accounts for the widespread public attention given to this phenomenon. In the four recent years of domestic political turmoil in the United States (1965–1968), a grand total of 214 were killed and 9,000 were injured as a result of terrorism, and other mass violence. This compares with a national total of approximately 12,000 murders and 250,000 aggravated assaults annually. During the height of the skyjacking epidemic (1968–1972), the number who lost their lives or were injured in all domestic and international flights did not exceed 200. In the same period the number of internationally protected persons subjected to attack, kidnapping or threat of violence did not exceed 46, with 16 eventually meeting death. A recent statement issued by the Director of the Federal Bureau for Investigation, Clarence Kelley, pointing to the growing threat posed by terrorists, lists 11 victims killed and 72 injured through bombings and other terroristic violence in the United States during 1975.[4] Worldwide, it is estimated that during 1975 at least 50 people lost their lives and more than 150 were taken hostage in 197 major acts of international terrorism.[5]

In some parts, political violence has developed into large scale civil or guerrilla war, presenting major world security problems.

---

[4] *Washington Post*, January 14, 1976, p. 3.
[5] *U.S. News and World Report*, January 19, 1976, p. 27.

Mr. Harold Wilson claimed in 1976, for example, that 1,400 political killings had been committed in Ireland since 1969. All told, however, it is apparent that political crime and terrorism account for a mere fraction of all domestic and international crimes of violence. In 10 days of the October War in 1973, Israel lost more lives than during 30 years of Palestinian terrorism. In the United States alone, more people are murdered annually through intrafamily strife or are killed in automobile accidents than meet their deaths through politically inspired violence worldwide.[6]

What then explains the preoccupation of governments, people and the media with terrorism and other forms of political crime? Commentators have observed that the political offender—as opposed to the common criminal—is distinguished both by his claims of altruism and by his denial of the legitimacy of the State or political system which he challenges. Emphasis, too, has been placed upon the terrorist's refusal to limit himself to means proportionate to perceived evils or specified goals resorting, instead, to " violence for effect," viewing a grip of panic as his ultimate goal. Some additional observations need to be made regarding the functions of political violence in modern western societies. In the first place, some political offences—frequently reflected in highly colourful deeds and offenders—must be recognised as antidotes to public apathy and political boredom. Especially in times of relative peace, the exploits of political activists appeal to the news consumer's prurient interest in the unexpected, the unpredictable and the adventurous.

At times, motiveless, psychopathic mass-killers have made the major claim on public attention. At others the media spotlight is turned on organised crime and its " godfatherly " management system. There is increasing indication that white collar and business criminality—ranging from corporate disregard for safety and ethics to the transnational bribery and corrupt dealings of the multi-national corporations—might gain more attention in the future.

Currently, however, the central stage is held by two major classes of political crime, posed like the obverse faces of the Roman god, Janus. On one side are the abuses of those holding the reins of political power. Their official or quasi-official offences may consist of such relatively " mild " abuses of power as political censorship, un-authorised wiretapping and surveillance, electoral harassment and election law frauds (what Kirchheiner[7] terms " political justice "). The offences of those in power might escalate, however, to atrocities such as the " reigns of terror " employed in post-revolutionary France, the Soviet Union and Nazi Germany. On the other side are

---

[6] *Washington Post*, January 31, 1976, A. 17, col. 1.
[7] O. Kirchheimer, *Political Justice* (1961).

crimes committed by those out of power: those who see themselves deprived politically or economically, or as otherwise subjected to racial or ethnic discrimination. Their offences likewise range from mild displays of protest and civil disobedience (at times described as " political offences ") to a full array of such tactics of violence against authority and established institutions that they are properly labelled " siege of terror."

Often, the offences of those out of power are directed against those in positions of eminence (heads of State, politicians, diplomatic personnel, captains of industry), and, in a psychological sense, the victim's status endows the offender with identity. The importance of the victim momentarily elevates the offender to prominence; the mantle of the leader falls for a brief moment upon his assassin. Since the loss of leaders is likely to dramatically affect political, social or economic conditions, nationally and worldwide, the offender temporarily, at least, experiences the pulse of power. To a society suffering from alienation and individual feelings of impotence, in the face of distant government and the anonymity of big business, the political offence comes to epitomise the little man or woman's remaining power to be noticed. He or she can, at least, disrupt, if not stem and re-channel, the flow of distant and unaccountable government powers. Political offenders thus carry the message of many others who feel aggrieved and without opportunities to make themselves effectively heard. Equally important, when government or other established institutions are increasingly perceived to be in the wrong—when they become the dispensers of injustice—the political offender becomes a symbol of popular discontent and opposition, like Robin Hood, anti-slavery leader John Brown, or the heroes of so many modern revolutions.

In the councils of international affairs and law, political crime and terrorism have been equally receiving growing attention because of their challenge to the fundamental institutions and doctrines of international law. First, in a most practical way, terrorism has adversely affected international travel and communications. By seeking out weak links in the international air traffic system, political terrorists have shown themselves able to render not only air carriers, but also governments, virtually helpless in the face of blackmail demands. Not since the heyday of classical piracy has international traffic been so seriously affected. To a lesser degree letter-bombs, for a period, similarly jeopardised the flow of international mail, traditionally immune to such interferences. Secondly, the historical inviolability and special protection of diplomats both in peace and in war, has been totally rejected, if not in theory then at least in practice, by terrorist organisations. Frequently, these agents of international communication are specifically singled out as targets for terroristic activities. Thirdly, previous international efforts to protect the innocent and non-combatants from the ravages of uncontrolled violence, through codifications of the law of war such as the Hague and Geneva conventions, have again been negated both by the practices and doctrines of modern terrorism. Fourthly, modern terrorism's denial of the very concept of innocence and non-combatancy and the overflow of terroristic activities beyond the countries of direct involvement have made the whole globe a battlefield. The traditional efforts to contain war and to protect neutrality have thus been thoroughly challenged by present day terrorism.

It is not surprising, therefore, that despite evidence of relatively limited victimisation, transnational political crime and terrorism have become grave concerns to the international community. For, regardless of national doctrinal shadings, the security of international commerce and travel, diplomatic protection, the safeguarding of non-combatant civilian populations, and preservation of neutrality, are long-standing and indeed classical pillars of the structure of the international system. It is the threat to these international institutions and doctrines that distinguishes modern, international terrorism. Any narrower or lesser definition,[8] while reflecting other possibilities for classification, addresses only part of the international concern.

To all this should be added the terrifying hazards posed by modern technological progress. A shrinking world, due to the revolution in transportation, has redefined the theatres of violence so that no place is safe from terrorism.[9] Weapons of mass destruction, and their ready availability, further afford terrorists an almost boundless expansion of destructive capabilities.

## II—THE POLITICAL OFFENDER'S PRIVILEGED STATUS

Two major obstacles confront those who seek consensus in the response of the community of nations to terrorism. The first is the claim that terrorists are a species of political offenders to whom international law, for over a century, has accorded special privileges. The second is the argument that those engaged in the " siege of terror " should not be singled out for international condemnation while reigns of terror are allowed to continue unaffected.

---

[8] According to W. H. Smith " terrorism is international when the terrorist is of one nationality and at least some of his victims are of another." Smith sees the international significance of terrorism in two ways: (1) When terror is used to exploit the responsibility which governments bear for certain classes of people other than their own citizens, notably diplomats and foreign travellers; and (2) When terror is directed against part or all of the population of another country. See W. H. Smith, " International Terrorism, a Political Analysis," in this *Year Book*, Vol. 31 (1977), pp. 139–140.

[9] It may well be questioned, since Entebbe, whether—given effective international co-operation—any place in the world need remain safe for terrorists.

No productive analysis of new potentials for international agreement can be undertaken without due attention to past political and legal traditions concerning political offenders and offences. It is this heritage which in part accounts for the present impasse. Yet these very traditions might help suggest fruitful future directions. Because most nations have not differentiated political crime from other criminality in their domestic law, the phenomenon has not been subjected to close scrutiny by national legislatures or scholars. The significance of the political nature of an offence has been recognised primarily in the law and practice of extradition. In this limited sphere, the framework for a conceptual analysis of political crime has been developed. Moreover, attempts to define political crime and terrorism have already been made in the context of international agreements to control transnational violence.

The terms " political crime " and " terrorism " cannot be readily defined through a review of the standard literature of the social and behavioural sciences. Similarly, traditional legal materials provide limited assistance.[10] In the Anglo-American tradition, crimes are usually classified according to the objects of the offences—crimes against the person (such as murder and rape), against the habitation (such as burglary and arson), against property (such as larceny), against public order (such as disturbing the peace), and against the State (such as espionage and counterfeiting). Another classification system relies primarily on the severity of the offences and their requisite penalties, thus drawing a line between felonies, which called for capital punishment, misdemeanours, which merited lighter dispositions, and petty offences, which were borderline instances of criminality. While commentators also distinguish ordinary offences from treason, possibly the most despised of all crimes and one which required, at common law, the corruption of blood in addition to drawing and quartering, no general classification for political offences ever came into being in Anglo-American jurisprudence.

Significantly, the United States Constitution, which delegates law-making power to Congress, specifies only one crime, treason—the levying of war against the United States, or the aiding of comforting of its enemies. Despite this constitutional identification of the political crime *par excellence*, American law retains the distinction (which it shares with its English predecessor) of failing to list, identify or recognise political crimes as a distinguishable class in its domestic process.[11] As a matter of both law and policy an

---

[10] For a review of the status of political crime in the United States, see " Comment, Criminal Responsibility and the Political Offender," 24 *American University Law Review* (1975), p. 797.

[11] American law parallels that of the United Kingdom. Thus Brendan Behan commented on " the usual hypocrisy of the English not giving anyone political treatment

offender's political motive, as such, is never to be afforded a forum or hearing.

Other legal systems have specifically defined political crimes in their domestic codes. In so addressing themselves openly and directly to the problems of political crimes, the laws might also decree a differential treatment for political offenders. To draw a distinction between political offenders and common prisoners, points out Alexander Solzhenitsyn, " is the equivalent of showing them respect as equal opponents, of recognising that people may have views of their own." [12] Describing Czarist practices, Solzhenitsyn reports: " Criminals were teamed up and driven along the streets to the station so as to expose them to public disgrace. And politicals could go there in carriages . . . Politicals were not fed from the common pot but were given a food allowance instead and had their meals brought from public eating places." [13] Reflecting this attitude, the German penal system, throughout the Weimar Republic, offered imprisonment in a fortress (*Festungshaft*) as a symbolic confinement when the offender's motives were considered " honourable." It was the benefit of this differentiation which permitted Adolf Hitler, after the failure of his 1923 Munich Putsch, the leisure and facilities for the writing of *Mein Kampf.*

While a great number of countries treated their political offenders leniently, others have responded more harshly. After the Czar came the revolution and the pursued of the past became the new pursuers. The lenient Czarist practice gave way to a totally different and much harsher Soviet response to political crime in the name of socialist justice. Equally, the Nazi and Fascist régimes, as well as other totalitarian governments in the post-Second World War era, have singled out their domestic political offenders for particularly oppressive controls and punishment.

The major recognition and discriminative treatment of political offenders, as noted earlier, occurred not in domestic law but in international practice. In antiquity and throughout the Middle Ages, the offender who committed a crime against the sovereign was more harshly condemned than other criminals: for he had challenged the most sacred of all institutions—setting his hand against divinely-ordained government.[14] In the Middle Ages political offenders,

---

and then being able to say that alone among the Empires she had no political prisoners." B. Behan, *Borstal Boy* (1958), p. 271.

[12] *The Gulag Archipelago* (1973), p. 500.

[13] *Ibid.* pp. 499–500.

[14] See the biblical account of King David's execution of the messenger reporting to him that he slew David's arch-enemy, King Saul. " Thy blood be upon thy head; for thy mouth hath testified against thee, saying I have slain the Lord's anointed." 2 Samuel 1 : 16.

persons guilty of crimes of *lèse-majesté*, became particular targets of extradition from countries to which they escaped, in order to facilitate the meting out of punishments. The first known European treaty dealing with the surrender of political offenders was concluded in 1174 between England and Scotland, followed by a 1303 treaty between France and Savoy. But the Age of Enlightenment and the subsequent ages of revolution revealed government to be less than godly. The sovereign could do wrong. How, therefore, could *all* rebels against authority be labelled evil? More importantly, how could they be returned without differentiation for assured punishment?

One writer has noted that " the French Revolution of 1789 and its aftermath started the transformation of what was the extraditable *offense par excellence* to what has since become the nonextraditable *offense par excellence*." [15] Recognising the nobler public motives of political offenders and the growing diversity of political régimes, Belgium in 1833 became the first country to enact a law withholding the extradition of political offenders. By the middle of the century the doctrine was widely established throughout the continent. Virtually every European treaty gave political offenders, seeking refuge, protection against extradition to the country in which their offence had been committed. While a domestic political offender was often accorded no differential treatment, the offender who committed his crime in his native country and sought refuge abroad was afforded a safe haven.

Who was this privileged offender? The term political offence is still seldom defined in either treaties or domestic legislation. The determination of what constitutes a political offence is reached according to the laws of the haven country and the decision is usually made by the courts of that State. In the practice of extradition the executive branch often retains the final decision. Seeking to establish the proper boundaries for political crime, most courts have drawn a distinction between " pure " political offences and " complex " or " connected " offences. Treason, espionage, sedition, rebellion and incitement to civil war are all viewed as offences exclusively against sovereign authority and are considered pure political offences. Other offences that directly endanger the life or property of individuals, but are carried out in furtherance of, or in connection with, a crime against the State, might be classified as either complex or connected political offences. Viewed alone, the latter offences are common crimes. But when a criminal act (such as the assassination of a head of State) is primarily the " means, method or cloak " [16] for carrying out a

---

[15] M. C. Bassiouni, *International Extradition and World Public Order* (1974), p. 371.
[16] *Re Fabijan* (Supreme Court of Germany, 1933), 6 *Digest of International Law*, Whiteman (ed.) (1968), p. 802.

political objective, the act will be viewed as a complex political crime. When an act affects, primarily, individual life or property, yet is closely connected with other acts against the security of the State (*e.g.* a " fund-raising " bank robbery by revolutionaries), it would be described as a connected political offence.

The political-offence exception was not designed to accommodate the individual conscience of each malcontent or rebel. In the Anglo-American approach, represented by the classic case of *Re Castioni*,[17] the requirement was established that recognised political offences must be " incidental to and formed part of a political disturbance." In the absence of a general political revolt or disturbance, the individual offender, regardless of his political or ideological motivation, was to be viewed as a common criminal. Moreover, the European, and primarily Swiss practice, further sought to curtail excessive violence by conditioning the political-offence exception upon objective standards of proportionality. Accordingly, the ideological beliefs and goals of the offender had to be correlated with the effect of his acts and offences. In the *Ktir* case, a member of the Algerian Liberation movement (FLN) was charged in France with the murder of another FLN member suspected of treason. Ktir fled to Switzerland and contested the French request for extradition. In granting the request the Swiss court held that " the damage had to be proportionate to the aim sought; in the case of murder, this had to be shown to be the sole means of attaining the political aim." [18]

While domestic laws have found it difficult if not impossible to admit the political offender's justification, which challenges the existing legal order, the international legal system has thus found a way to accommodate the conflicting interest of public order and extralegal dissent. The political-offender exception to extradition was certainly an innovative answer. In his own country the political offender often remained a common criminal, but the civilised world community was willing to listen to the defence of conscience. This accommodation for the " right " of political rebellion was reached in the last century. In recent years the old conflict between individual conscience and public order has returned to haunt the international arena. Once again the right violently to resist perceived injustice is being heatedly debated in world councils.

Since the political-offence exception was first created, newer international grounds for its support have gained world acceptance. The First World War ended with a commitment to international self-

---

[17] 1 Q.B. 149 (1891), p. 152. Although this case represents a clarification of the " political offence " concept it is not free from the competing considerations and uncertainties which characterise early English case law on the subject.

[18] 34 I.L.R. 143 (1961), pp. 143–144.

determination; the movement which started with President Wilson's Fourteen Points reached its peak in the post-Second World War era. Only some of this commitment has been reflected in positive international law,[19] but the climate of the world community has certainly supported following the most expeditious routes to self-determination. The conclusion of the Second World War also witnessed a renewed international commitment to the world-wide protection and promotion of individual human rights. In 1948 the General Assembly of the United Nations adopted the Universal Declaration of Human Rights. In the following quarter of a century a host of other declarations, conventions, convenants, and proclamations have been advanced by the United Nations on such topics as economic, social and cultural rights, civil and political rights, racial discrimination, slavery, collective bargaining, rights of children and the right of asylum.[20] While these have been neither uniformly accepted, nor have shared equal legal status, they have nevertheless left an indelible mark on world opinion. Even stronger undertakings for the advancement of human rights have come into being on a regional basis. The European Convention on Human Rights and its enforcement process is a notable example.[21]

These new assertions of the individual's right to political self-realisation have served further to validate the privileged position of the political offender. After all, it is argued, he merely asserts what has already been recognised to be his as a matter of right.

## III—TERRORISM—AND THE RIGHT TO SELF-DEFENCE?

While the terminology of political crime, in international circles, has thus had nearly a century and a half to reach some degree of maturity, terrorism is a relatively unstable newcomer. Most scholars find the origins of modern terrorism in the " reign of terror " which occurred after the French Revolution and in the anarchist movement of the last century. Neither domestic legislation nor international treaties, however, clearly agree upon its elements. Like the political offender, the terrorist often claims to act out of an altruistic rather than an

---

[19] For one of the few examples of an attempt to implement the international commitment of self-determination, see Declaration on the Granting of Independence to Colonial Countries and Peoples (General Assembly Resolution 1514 (xv) of December 14, 1960). See Dec. 2625, in note 3 above.

[20] *UN, Human Rights, A compilation of International Instruments of the United Nations* (1973), No. E. 73. XIV. 2.

[21] See, generally, Robertson, " The United Nations Covenant on Civil and Political Rights, and the European Convention on Human Rights," XLIII *British Yearbook of International Law* (1968–69), p. 21; O'Hanlon, " The Brussels Colloquy on the European Convention on Human Rights," 5 *Irish Jurist* (1970), p. 252; Comte, " The Application of the European Convention on Human Rights in Municipal Law," 4 *Journal of International Community of Jurists* (1962–63), p. 94.

egoistic motive. Unlike the common offender, he proclaims the goal of serving humanity, through violence, rather than his own baser interests. Obvious difficulties arise, though, from regarding the terrorist as just a sub-category of the political offender.

What possibly distinguishes the terrorist from political offenders generally is his lack of sensitivity to proportionality, to traditional notions of innocence, and to the concept of restricted warfare. These differences are implicit in the terrorist's goals, the nature and quality of his deeds and his strategy. The political offender is not necessarily committed to violence. Breaking censorship laws or publishing official secrets is as much a political offence as the assassination of a head of State. The political offender usually seeks to assert rights that he believes the State has improperly denied him: for example, freedom of speech and assembly, or the right to travel. At times a reactionary political offender might even seek a restriction of the civil rights of others. The political offender need not be militant; he may well prefer simply to depart from his own for more compatible societies. The political offender's deed, whatever it might be, is usually directed against those he views as specifically responsible for the conceived ills. The terrorist sees a much fuzzier line between the guilty and the innocent; all too often he views most of society as his proper target. Frequently, the terrorist has a morbid commitment to the violent process as an end in itself, " as a catharsis, not therapy." Thus, while the political offence might be " a passing deed, an event, terrorism is a process, a way to life, a dedication." [22] For the deprived, says Frantz Fanon in *The Wretched of the Earth*, violence is a purifying force.

While the political offender seeks more modestly to remove the specific causes of his discontent, the terrorist believes the social or political order to be so corrupt as to require its total destruction. For the Baader-Meinhof group, the goal was not German reform but rebirth from the ashes. For the Palestinian terrorist, the goal is not a more benevolent Israeli policy but the elimination of Israel. For the violent Irish militant, the aim is not political accommodation with, but the end of, Northern Ireland as a separate political entity.

The true terrorist consciously employs overwhelming fear, hoping to spread panic by maximising uncertainty. To the terrorist his objective can be best attained through bold actions which demonstrate his complete, unconditional and irrevocable opposition to the existing order. Uncertainty exposes the weakness and vulnerability of the existing régime. The final erosion of popular support for the system is to be attained through indiscriminate terrorism which produces equally brutal counter measures. Frequently the strategy is

---

[22] D. C. Rapoport, *Assassination and Terrorism* (1971), p. 37.

to attack the masses, " the very people he wants to liberate, but to attack them in such a way that it is government which appears to be their enemy." [23] A leading nineteenth-century Russian revolutionary proclaimed that " the object is perpetually the same: the quickest and surest way of destroying this whole filthy order." [24]

Judged by motives and deed, the modern terrorist does not fit well in the traditional mould of the political offender. Yet despite the existence of considerable historical, political and legal insights into the nature of modern terrorism, there has been little success in reaching an internationally acceptable definition. The use of the term has been both promiscuous and imprecise. To most western writers the term connotes an undiscriminating commitment to violence differentiating, consequently, the terrorist from other political offenders. In the view of Third-World countries the terrorist label has all too frequently and improperly been attached to " legitimate " national-liberation and revolutionary movements. This confusion and misapplication of labels is demonstrated in many camps. The matter is a judgmental one. Even non-violent conduct has been tagged " terroristic " in indiscriminate usage. An East Berlin court, for example, recently sentenced a West Berliner to 15 years in prison for having helped 96 East Germans to flee to the West. The East Berlin City Court found him guilty of " organised human trafficking, sabotage, espionage and terrorism: " [25] Similarly, South African law provides that a person who has written letters to Africans likely " to encourage feelings of hostility between the white and other inhabitants " will be presumed to have done so with " intent to endanger the maintenance of law and order." [26] Defined by law as a terrorist, such letter writer is subject to the death penalty.

Further complicating the international definition of terrorism is the conflict between diverse camps and ideologies in the world community. The current international disagreement on whether political violence should be universally condemned is not unlike the long-standing domestic debate on whether political offenders should be accorded differential treatment.

One who disobeys the law, does so at his peril. It is a fundamental premise of most legal systems that obedience to the law is an absolute obligation of all citizens, irrespective of the morality of the legal command.[27] While " render unto Caesar " remains the imperative, is it proper to enquire about individuals or groups bound by the

---

[23] *Ibid.* p. 47.

[24] Nachaeveff, *Revolutionary Catechism*, in D. C. Rapoport, *op. cit.* in note 22 above.

[25] *New York Times*, January 27, 1976, p. 2.

[26] Terrorism Act: Nr. 83 of 1967, s. 2, quoted in L. Rubin, *Apartheid in Practice*, UN Publication OPI/553 (1976), p. 40.

[27] A. Fortas, *Concerning Dissent and Civil Disobedience* (1968), pp. 59–64.

conviction that the law is cruel, unjust, immoral or plainly outdated? What about those whose conviction, ideology, conscience or political motivation drive them to disobey or to break the law? In 1849 Henry David Thoreau passionately asked: " Must the citizen even for a moment, or in the least degree, resign his conscience to the legislator? Why has every man a conscience, then? " [28] Despite the compelling resurgence of this question, few legal systems have found satisfactory solutions to the conflict between individual conscience and the dictates of public order. Once the law has been made, it is said, individual conscience may not override it. Indeed, no organised society could survive if the subjective values and judgments of individual citizens were allowed to contradict community rules.

The growing development of internationally recognised rights and duties accruing to individuals and groups has, however, created a jurisprudential as well as a practical dilemma in the community of nations. How are international law and practice to respond to those whose assertion that universal rights are paramount places them in conflict with domestic law?

In the light of the modern international commitment to self-determination, human rights and ethnic and racial survival, it is necessary to search for acceptable tools to secure and enforce those rights. How is the international community to judge those who claim merely to assert these recognised rights? May people press for recognition of these rights through force of arms? May they so protect themselves against abuse? To the " haves," to many others committed to gradual and peaceful means for remedying the claims of the aggrieved—to all those fearing international chaos and anarchy—the tools of violent opposition and rebellion remain unacceptable.

On the other hand, in the eyes of the " have nots "—and many others who believe the international machinery for bringing about political, social and economic justice to be inadequate—the self-help approach is not only pragmatically necessary but totally justifiable. Typically, most efforts in the United Nations and elsewhere designed to condemn and to impose sanctions upon terrorist " sieges of terror " have resulted in Third-World and other countries calling for a parallel curbing of official " reigns of terror." [29] Viewed from these diverse perspectives, those who are terrorists, are to some, evident freedom fighters and, to others, legitimate revolutionaries.

While these ideological and definitional incompatibilities continue no honest and effective co-operation with regard to the control of terrorism can be expected in the international community. Sophisti-

---

[28] *On the Duty of Civil Disobedience* (1968), pp. 413–414.
[29] See, *e.g.* Bennett, " U.S. Initiatives in the United Nations to Combat International Terrorism," 7 *International Lawyer* (1973), pp. 753, 759.

cated technological measures of prevention and surveillance can be developed nationally. Each country might then develop and install its own domestic machinery for the prevention and suppression of terrorist violence. Such countries might further seek assistance and co-operation from other nations with a common mind. As long, however, as a significant number of safe-haven countries remain for terrorists—to supply the weapons for destruction, the training grounds and finally the escape routes—more effective prevention, control and punishment will be difficult. It is in light of this reality and in the aftermath of the Entebbe rescue that much commentary has been heard about the need for " unilateral " action against terrorism.[30] Entebbe is claimed to have demonstrated also the benefits of discreet co-operation between sympathetic governments in lieu of the search for formal international agreements.

### IV—THE SHRINKING POLITICAL OFFENCE AND THE GROWTH OF INTERNATIONAL CRIME

Despite the current unwillingness of many countries to condemn acts committed under claims of self-determination and human rights, there has been an evident trend in international law to narrow the traditional exception granted to political offenders. As early as 1856, Belgium, the first country to embody the political offence protection in its law, amended its requirements by excluding assassinations of chiefs of State from this safeguard. This limitation, called a *clause d'attentat*, was widely copied in both bilateral and regional treaties among European, South American and African States. In several recent treaties all assassinations are excluded from the political offence protection.[31]

Another narrowing of the scope of political offences came at the end of the last century in the face of the growing threat of anarchistic terrorism. The earlier tolerance towards those seeking violently to overthrow a régime turned into a suspicion of those viewed as a danger to all governments. The case of *In re Meunier* [32] held in 1894 that confessed anarchists are not political offenders exempt from extradition. To constitute a political offence, the English court held, there must be two or more parties each seeking to impose the government of its own choice, but " the party with which the accused is identified . . . is the enemy of all governments. Their efforts are directed primarily against the general body of citizens." [33]

---

[30] See, *e.g.*, L. C. Green, " Humanitarian Intervention—1976 Version," 24 *Chitty's Law Journal*, Nr. 7 (1976), pp. 217–225.

[31] Bassiouni, *op. cit.* in note 15 above, p. 410.

[32] 2 Q.B. (1894), p. 415.

[33] *Ibid.* at p. 419.

In subsequent years, domestic laws, international conventions and judicial decisions further restricted the political offence exception. The French Extradition Law of 1927 provided that the exception was not to apply to " acts of odious barbarism and vandalism prohibited by the laws of war." [34] The extradition agreement approved by the League of Arab States in 1952 likewise exempted from the exception premeditated murder or acts of terrorism.[35] Similarly, the Supreme Court of Argentina declared in 1968: " Extradition will not be denied where we are dealing with cruel or immoral acts which clearly shock the conscience of civilized peoples." [36]

In the post-Second World War era an even more drastic restriction was placed on the benefits of the political-offence claim. World revulsion against Nazi and Fascist excesses resulted in the Nuremberg designation of both crimes against humanity and war crimes as international crimes not entitled to the benefit of the political-offence exception. The Nuremberg trial and the subsequent formulation of its principles by the United Nations General Assembly [37] established crimes against humanity which are to be universally condemned. In the recent past, the General Assembly of the United Nations after a discussion of the South African practice of apartheid, labelled it " a crime against humanity." [38] This is more than mere political rhetoric. War crimes, as defined by the 1907 Hague Convention and 1949 Geneva Conventions, also constitute international crimes to which the political-offence exception does not apply. Similarly, the Genocide Convention of 1948 [39] sought to protect national, ethnic, racial and religious groups by defining as an international crime the killing of members of a group, causing them serious bodily or mental harm, or deliberately inflicting conditions of life calculated to bring physical destruction. As an international crime, genocide does not afford its perpetrators the political-offence exception.

The origins of international criminal law date back to the crime of piracy, long considered an offence against all civilised nations.[40] Other early international efforts concentrated on white slavery and

[34] French Extradition Law of 1927, Act of March 10, 1927, Art 5 (2) quoted in I. Shearer, *Extradition in International Law* (1971), p. 185.
[35] Extradition Agreement Approved by the Council of the League of Arab States, September 14, 1952, 159 *British and Foreign State Papers* (HMSO), quoted in Shearer, *op. cit.* in note 34 above, p. 52.
[36] *Re Bohme* (Supreme Court of Argentina), 62 *American Journal of International Law*, (1968), pp. 784–785, quoted in Shearer, *op. cit.* in note 34 above, p. 186.
[37] G. A. Res. 177 (II) (1947).
[38] G.A. Res. 2923, 27 UN GAOR Supp. 30, at 25, UN Doc. A/8730 (1972).
[39] UN, Human Rights, p. 41.
[40] For the most recent statement on piracy, see The 1958 Geneva Convention on the High Seas, 4 Whitman, Digest 647 (1963).

traffic in narcotics. But in more recent years there has been a growing international commitment to limit, through a process of international criminalisation, conduct which could be viewed as political yet which threatened basic institutions of the world community. The definition of counterfeiting as an international crime after the First World War was such a step.[41] Even more demonstrative of the world community's willingness to condemn universally disruptive political violence have been the recent treaties making aircraft hijacking [42] and the kidnapping of diplomats (internationally protected persons) international crimes.[43] So condemned by international law, these crimes can no longer be viewed as political offences affording their perpetrators protection from extradition. Instead, it has become the positive duty of all civilised nations to apprehend the offenders and subject them to either prosecution or extradition (a responsibility summarised in the principle *aut dedere aut punire*).

## V—BETWEEN RIGHTS AND CRIMES:
### AREAS OF DISAGREEMENT

The post-Second World War developments which recognised new international rights, on one hand, and which formulated new international crimes, on the other, have had a profound impact in the classification and status of political offenders. Contradictions, as well as concurrences between international and domestic legal standards are becoming much more critical to international co-operation. In the face of domestic denials of human rights to which the community of nations has given recognition, political offenders may be acting in conformity with recognised international rights even though in violation of domestic laws. At the same time, what were once recognised " political offences " might be turning into international crimes.

The political offender's crime, as previously seen, may range from such relatively " pure " offences as violations of censorship or apartheid laws, to a veritable " siege of terror," involving random and indiscriminate terroristic violence. What traditionally have been defined in extradition law and practice as " pure " political offences —acts which challenge the State but affect no private rights of

---

[41] Convention for the Suppression of Counterfeiting Currency, April 20, 1920; 4 Hudson, International Legislation 692–705 (1931).

[42] See, 1971 Montreal Convention, U.S.T.I.A.S. 7570 (sabotage of aircraft) 1970 Hague Convention, U.S.T.I.A.S. 7192 (hijacking), 1963 Tokyo Convention, U.S.T.I.A.S 6768 (offences committed on board aircraft).

[43] Convention to Prevent and Punish Acts of Terrorism Taking the Form of Crimes Against Persons and Related Extortions that are of international Significance—OAS/ Off. Rec./Ser. p./Doc. 68, January 13, 1971; and Convention on the Prevention and Punishment of Crimes Against Internationally Protected Persons Including Diplomatic Agents, G.A. Res. A/3166 (XXVIIII), February 5, 1974.

innocents—continue to benefit from a privileged status in extradition law. One who commits treason, sedition or espionage continues to be entitled to the political offender exception to extradition. Beneficiaries will also be those who violate State laws limiting freedom of speech or assembly, those who disregard censorship and other secrecy laws, and those who break laws restricting religion or other exercises of human rights. For many of those in the " pure " offender category mere continued benefits of international asylum do not really reflect the full measure of their entitlement. Pressure is mounting, as evidenced by United Nations action on South Africa and Rhodesia, to lift the label of criminality from domestic offences which are a response to, or assertion of, internationally recognised human rights. Part of what was once a political offence is thus on the way to becoming an enforceable domestic right.

On the other extreme of the political-offence spectrum there is a growing list of activities which have lost their political exemption and have become prohibited as outright international crimes. Included here are crimes against humanity, genocide, aircraft hijacking and the kidnapping of diplomats. Most conduct which has been so condemned internationally might be either classed as " complex " or " connected " political offences. Crimes against humanity, genocide and offences against diplomats might be categorised as complex offences. Aircraft hijacking and other offences against innocent victims would fall within the category of connected offences. While it is clear that none of the political offences which have come to be designated as international crimes constitute " pure " political offences, these new crimes do not readily respond to any further classification. They do reflect, by and large, a universal reaffirmation of the classical international law commitment to the protection of transportation and communication routes, and diplomatic personnel. They also represent to a lesser degree an effort to narrow the classes of potential victims and, thus, to protect the innocent.

There now remains an area in the centre of the political-offence spectrum which continues as yet unaffected by the growing recognition of human rights on the one hand, and the increasing expansion of international crimes on the other. Typical of this range of conduct are what might generally be regarded as both complex political offences and connected political offences. Some of these offences might be committed domestically, some transnationally. Complex political offences such as the assassination of a government official in the course of a political uprising, the bombing of military or police headquarters, and violent resistance to an arresting officer come within this class. Also included in this category of behaviour are such connected political offences as bank robberies for the replenishing of an illicit political treasury, the kidnapping of a business executive for extortion, and taking hostages to exchange for political offenders. It is with regard to this wide range of conduct in the middle spectrum, between international rights and international crimes, that uncertainty and ambivalence currently prevail in the international community. Specially troublesome in this still uncharted terrain are those aspects of contemporary terrorism which differentiate it from the traditional political offences. Consider, for instance, the indiscriminate use of violence domestically against victims only marginally associated with an opposing political régime or party, or the assault against such victims in neutral countries remote from the battlefield. Consider a machine-gun assault against a bus carrying school children in Northern Ireland, or the massacre of Christian Puerto Rican pilgrims on their arrival at Israel's Lod airport by Japanese collaborators of the Palestinian terrorists. How should these types of conduct be treated by the international community? Existing international law is silent in these instances. Yet concern with these problems goes back at least 40 years. How effective would the agreements previously offered in response to terrorism have been in dealing with such conduct?

The most comprehensive treaty for the prevention and punishment of terrorism was proposed by the League of Nations in 1937. Following the assassination of King Alexander I of Yugoslavia at Marseilles on October 9, 1934, the French Government urged the Council of the League of Nations to prepare an international agreement for the suppression of terrorism. A committee of experts prepared a draft convention which was later opened for signature at a conference held at Geneva in November 1937. An international criminal court was also proposed, to help in the enforcement of terrorist violations. On January 1, 1941, India became the only country ever to ratify the convention.

Viewing the League of Nations convention today, from the vantage point of some 40 years of historical development, the shortcomings of that effort are readily apparent. The document required all signatories to make acts of terrorism committed on their territories criminal offences. Similarly, signatories were required to either extradite or punish persons who had committed these offences abroad. Acts of terrorism were defined by Article 2 to include: (1) causing death, grievous bodily harm or loss of liberty to heads of State, their spouses and others holding public office, (2) wilful destruction of public property, and (3) acts endangering the lives of members of the public. Article 3 specified further that conspiracy to commit the above acts, as well as incitement and assistance in performing such acts, were likewise criminal offences.

The attempted assassination of Hitler and the successful execution of Mussolini could have readily qualified as internationally condemned terroristic acts under the proposed League convention. Many of the post-Second World War liberation movements would certainly have been defined as terroristic under it. Broadcasting to an oppressed people to encourage them to rise against an exploiting régime would have been condemned as an incitement to commit international crime. It is little wonder that the 1937 document received so little acceptance.

The League convention was clearly predicated on maintenance of the pre-Second World War *status quo* and displayed a willingness to label any future revolutionary or national liberation movement as terrorist. Yet what could have been done about the terrorist excesses of recent years? Why could international consensus not be reached with regard to the suppression of these?

A more reasonable effort to suppress international terrorism was contained in the Draft Convention introduced at the United Nations on September 25, 1972, by the United States. The major, and limited, intent of the proposed Draft was to require countries to either prosecute or extradite those engaging in the *export* of terrorism. To come within the scope of the convention an offender must intend to damage the interests of, or to obtain concessions from, a State or international organisation. The prohibited acts include killing, causing serious bodily harm or kidnapping. Acts are defined as international offences if they are committed outside the offender's own country, and (1) also outside the country against which they are intended, or, (2) within the country against which they are intended but against persons who are not nationals of that State.

The narrower scope of the United States draft convention makes it much less subject to criticism for being oppressive to unorthodox political change. Indeed, the convention has been criticised for having defined its goals so narrowly as to be far-fetched and irrelevant. A German terrorist acting against his own régime would not come under the draft convention. An Irish offender bombing a London café inhabited only by Englishmen would also be exempt. Only when a Greek terrorist, for example, commits an act of violence against a Turkish national living in Switzerland, or against a non-Turkish national in Turkey, would he fall within the confines of the treaty. The basic principle of the United States convention is simple: " Fight your enemies in your country or theirs. Do not export your grievances to distant places where innocent persons are likely to be affected." Yet even these limited goals, which attempt to steer away from ideological conflicts, have not assured the draft convention widespread support. In part, the United States authorship had doomed it from the start. Today any revival of this effort seems unlikely.

### VI—THE NEEDS AND MEANS FOR CONSENSUS

Given the present freeze in the movement towards an international agreement for the control of terrorism, how should civilised nations respond to the problems posed by transnational and domestic political violence? A clear delineation is required, in the first place, between responses to terrorism which are primarily domestic in nature and those which require multi-national co-operation.

Most if not all States already prohibit, by their domestic laws, the major types of violence which are of concern both locally and internationally. Assaults against diplomats, the hijacking of aircraft, the taking of hostages, the mailing of letter-bombs—all these are outside the bounds of legality throughout the world. Existing domestic laws can be readily utilised to proscribe and punish the " unthinkable "—terrorist threats and efforts to poison water supplies of whole cities or to explode atomic and other mass destruction weapons. Clearly police and intelligence agencies of the various countries have undertaken through their surveillance functions to discover potential offenders. Few countries are willing to tolerate terrorist violence on their own territory—regardless of whether the victims are nationals or aliens—without bringing the offenders to justice. The most radical of nations are no more ready to allow non-governmental and unauthorised violence within their boundaries than are the most conservative régimes.

What then can international agreements and co-operation attain beyond the actions of the individual States? In the first place, international conventions may reiterate the duty of States to enforce their domestic laws against certain acts of illegality, committed locally, but which concern the world community. An international agreement could possibly be used to spur State criminal sanctions where local motivations might be lacking. Terrorist attacks on unpopular diplomats or businessmen would be a case in point; domestic political considerations would otherwise make action unlikely.

International agreement might also go one step further towards formalising the international exchange of information regarding the movements of suspected persons, weapons or supplies. Much exchange of this type already is taking place, but on a selective basis. It is evident that those countries most concerned with political violence are not too likely now to make their data available to those suspected of being safe havens to offenders. The existing, narrowly drawn functions of INTERPOL would therefore appear to be marginal at best, in light of the accessibility of this data to all member

nations, regardless of their position concerning terrorism. A crystalli-
sation of international consensus as to which offenders merit universal condemnation might open the way for more meaningful exchange
of information similar to that which now exists in less politically
charged areas as slavery and drug traffic.

More critically needed is added impetus for State action to
prosecute or extradite offenders who commit terroristic actions
abroad and seek local refuge. These instances have raised the greatest
amount of difficulty and controversy in the past. Since no offence to
local law has taken place, neither domestic legality nor local pride
require action. Political considerations predominate over legal ones
where local sympathies are with offenders who escape from hostile or
disagreeable foreign régimes; the traditional political-offender
exception to extradition readily becomes the major block for action
in these instances. Recent Greek difficulties revolving around the
extradition of Baader-Meinhof leader, Rolf Pohle, to Germany well
illustrate this dilemma. The international approach that could most
effectively serve law enforcement interests in the case of escaped
offenders would be a further narrowing of the political-offence
exception to extradition.

The most comprehensive approach, combining the specific goals of
domestic prosecution, exchange of information and extradition,
would continue the search for an international convention that would
define and outlaw all forms of terrorism and related types of political
violence. The enforcement of such prohibitions would be handled
either by all States through universal jurisdiction, as in the case of
piracy, or through a newly created international criminal tribunal, an
echo of the earlier aspirations of the League of Nations. Not disput-
ing the value of such goals, the likelihood of their adoption in the
foreseeable future must be seriously questioned. Not only does the
general content of terrorism continue to escape normative definition,
but a renewal of the past debate, regarding " reigns of terror "
*vis-à-vis* " sieges of terror," is likely to negate the prospects for a
meaningful exercise in international agreement.

A less ambitious approach is the one reflected in the step by step
developments of recent years. Moving from one threatening phenomenon to another, international prescriptions have been developed
first with regard to the hijacking of aircraft, then concerning attacks
on diplomats. The next proposal, which was recently placed on the
United Nations agenda by West Germany, would deal with the
taking of hostages. However result-producing this approach has
proven to be, its major shortcoming is its *ex post facto* character and
the failure to project into future problems areas.

Other efforts designed for the control and containment of terrorist practices through international agreement could come from an altogether different direction. The approaches previously described call primarily for more effective criminal sanctions. They all place heavy reliance on what behaviourists would describe as " negative reinforcement." Yet creative approaches to the curtailment of excessive violence—which is the essence of terrorism—require also the exploration of what might be described as " positive reinforcement."

One such novel approach might be to encourage self-policing and greater conformity by guerrilleros and those designated as terrorists with the traditional rules of war, in exchange for granting them recognition as belligerents rather than criminals. There has been considerable writing recently concerning the status of guerrilleros and other irregular belligerents in international law.[44] Especially with the decline of formal wars, the movement for the regulation of military conflicts short of war has gained momentum. Attention has centred particularly on the question whether guerrilleros and other irregulars in transnational conflicts should benefit from the privileges traditionally extended to belligerents under international law, in particular the prisoner of war status. By and large, the third Geneva Convention of 1949 on Prisoners of War would condition the grant of those protections on guerrillero willingness to comply with specified standards of lawful belligerency, including the wearing of insignias, the open bearing of arms and conformity with the laws and customs of war.

Adherence by guerrilleros and other irregulars to these standards would certainly help reduce the outrages of civil war and especially the abuse of innocent parties. But apart from the reluctance of governments to treat domestic terrorists as belligerents, there is little hope of guerrillero conformity since the effectiveness of guerrilla activities depends in great part on departure from the traditional rules of war. An extension of the belligerency status to terrorists will therefore offer little help to the world community in the combating of excessive violence.

Another effort to infuse civilised standards into civil wars might call for greater enforcement of the requirements contained in Article 3 of all four Geneva Conventions of 1949. This article deals with domestic armed conflicts, seeks to protect persons taking no active part in the hostilities and applies to all parties to the conflict, governments and rebels alike. The article specifically prohibits: (1) violence

[44] See, *e.g.* J. Bond, *The Rules of Riot: Internal Conflict and the Law of War* (1974); G. Schwarzenberger, " Terrorists, Guerrilleros, and Mercenaries," *Toledo Law Review*, (1971), p. 71; Comment, Civilian Protection in Modern Warfare: A Critical Analysis of the Geneva Civilian Convention of 1941, 14 *Vancouver Journal of International Law* (1973), p. 123.

to life and person, in particular murder, mutilation, cruel treatment and torture; (2) taking of hostages; (3) outrages on personal dignity, in particular humiliating and degrading treatment. The fact that these prohibitions do not require reciprocal observance by all parties, as well as other shortcomings, have resulted in widespread disregard of these rules for domestic armed conflicts. It is further questionable whether these requirements are as applicable or enforceable with regard to political offenders and terrorists in situations short of an " armed conflict."

There is no single or simple solution offered for the international regulation of the excessive violence posed by political crime and terrorism. Recent efforts to control these increasingly transnational threats suggest a variety of possible approaches. Several principles should therefore be advanced for further discussion and development.

## VII—RECONCILING PROTECTION OF HUMAN RIGHTS WITH WORLD ORDER

Recognising the expanding boundaries of international crime and the concurrent narrowing of the political-offence protections, a viewer might well conclude that the liberalism exhibited in the nineteenth century's tolerance for extra-legal dissent is coming to an end. Aircraft hijacking and diplomatic abduction are now designated as international crimes. Recently the Federal Republic of Germany's delegate to the United Nations urged that hostage-taking should be similarly proscribed.[45] Other tactics of violence are likely to be outlawed on a case by case basis. Now that the end of colonialism is in sight, governments might be discovering that tolerance, or recognition, of non-governmental violence, even for sympathetic causes, is too risky an enterprise. Established régimes might be closing ranks in self-protection. One committed to the further pursuit of political self-realisation might, therefore, soon confront the central question: within the confines of international legality, what may groups or persons deprived of self-determination or recognised rights do in the defence of their claims?

Another spectator might be reading a different script and developing an altogether different concern. Observing the continuing resurgence of indiscriminate violence, and the existence, as well as emergence, of new safe-haven countries—unwilling to participate effectively or sincerely in international controls—it might be concluded that no more than lip-service is being paid to co-operation. Taking notice of rising new angry minorities (ethnic, religious, linguistic and cultural), and considering evidence of re-tribalisation in

---

[45] Higgins, " International Law and Civil Conflict," in E. Luard (ed.), *The International Regulation of Civil Wars* (1972), p. 183.

the modern nation-State, dire predictions might be advanced of yet new waves of violence. The observer of these trends would articulate his concern differently: given past failures to define and proscribe terrorism, what are the future prospects for the regulation and meaningful control of terrorist excesses?

Essentially, the crux of the problem of domestic as well as transnational political violence is the fact that, while the permissible spectrum of extra-legal political activism is being narrowed, the growing international commitment to self-determination and human rights tends further to legitimise certain political offences. Recent international agreements have already proscribed some of the more extreme measures of political violence. At this point, if there is a need for further codification and regulation, it exists primarily with regard to the middle spectrum of political conduct, consisting mainly of complex and connected political offences. Since the perpetrators of these offences have been, until now, subject only to the *ad hoc* sovereign dispositions of the various countries in extradition cases, and the substance of their offences is frequently complex and controversial, this field remains resistant to international agreement. Last but not least, while a desire to protect innocent and remote victims exists, the fear continues that international legislation will be unduly protective of the rights of existing régimes and overlook the needs of exploited people.

It would be premature, therefore, at this time to call for a new anti-terrorism convention or for the creation of an international criminal tribunal. There is a need, instead, for a more tentative, deliberate, and pragmatic, " step by step " approach. Possibly, what might be required first, before more formal international developments can take place, is a clearer and more open balancing of the conflicting interests. Especially, there is a need to explore potentials for greater consensus regarding the prosecution or extradition of all political offenders, including terrorists. The continued availability of safe havens for terrorists poses a particularly difficult obstacle for effective enforcement and deterrence policies. In the five years between 1970 and 1975, of a total 267 apprehended, transnational terrorists only 50 served prison sentences, while 39 were freed without punishment and another 58 avoided punishment by getting safe conduct to other countries.[46]

Concentration on the reform of the extradition standards for political offenders promises reasonably broad and important results.

---

[46] Since 1970, a total of 267 transnational terrorists were apprehended. Of these 50 were released after serving prison terms and 104 were still confined in mid-September 1975. Another 39 were freed without punishment, 58 avoided punishment by getting safe conduct to other countries and 16 were released from confinement on the demand of fellow terrorists. See *US News and World Report*, September 29, 1975, p. 79.

In the first place, this approach avoids the argument against a comprehensive anti-terrorism convention as an establishment tool. Any proposed convention against terrorism which disregards the claims and needs of the politically abused cannot hope for broad-range support. The exception of political offenders from extradition, on the other hand, has its clear origins in the protection of unorthodox dissent. Already built into the exception is a somewhat sympathetic viewpoint of the political rebel.

Moreover, a restructuring of this exception does not require a total and absolute bar against extra-legal methods of dissent. Instead it would allow for the development of more flexible standards for judgment and response. From its early foundations the political-offender exception has utilised a balancing test. The motivation of the actor, the proportionality of the violence utilised to the claimed wrong, and the effects on innocent persons have been important factors historically. Implicit in this test are principles already known to all countries in their domestic responses to claims of self-defence.

The political-offender exception also affords an opportunity for a broader assault on the unresolved issues of terrorism than would the recent step by step and *ex post facto* approach. The recent approach has been to single out particular types of objectionable and recurring behaviour for treatment as criminal offences. The movement has been from the prohibition of hijacking to the protection of diplomatic persons to the proposed prescription of hostage-taking. Yet too many other weapons and methods of violence, thinkable and unthinkable, remain in the terrorist's arsenal for such progressive control to be satisfactory. The political-offence route offers possibilities for a more comprehensive answer to the trends and threats of the future. It could deal with all manifestations of excessive violence and not merely with a few defined and designated areas.

The reformulation of the exception regarding the political offender would be much simpler, procedurally, than the effort to formulate and agree on the terms of either a comprehensive, or even a narrow, anti-terrorism convention. The need here is not for an international treaty, but for a document of somewhat lower status. While a universal or widely endorsed resolution would be highly desirable, even a lesser formulation by representative international organisations (including, possibly, Amnesty International, the International Association of Penal Law, and the International Committee of the Red Cross) would be an important accomplishment in the search for greater consensus.

Finally, until the ambivalence of the international community in the matter of political and human rights versus increased world order is resolved significantly, resort to the political-exception remedy remains preferable. This traditional route leaves a proper degree of discretion within the national sovereignty, instead of seeking to impose a more demanding international standard such as would be inherent in a terrorism convention. Granted that a reformulated, political-exception resolution will not carry the same weight of authority as an anti-terrorism convention, such lesser but honest step towards world consensus would nevertheless be important in shaping world opinion.

The attempt to deal with the problem of terrorism by means of the extradition exception has already been adopted by the Council of Europe. In a 1974 resolution,[47] the Committee of Ministers pointed out its conviction that extradition is a particularly effective means for the control of terrorism. The Council urged member-States in their response to extradition requests to consider the particular seriousness of terrorist acts which: (1) create a collective danger to life, liberty or safety; (2) affect innocent persons alien to the motives behind the struggle; or (3) employ cruel and vicious means. If extradition is refused in such serious instances, prosecution by competent domestic authorities is required.

Following the regional model of the Council of Europe, it is likely that what could be realistically attained, on a more global scale, is not as an international convention but a less formal declaration, similar to the Council's Resolution on International Terrorism. Such a resolution could be pursued through the United Nations, but a less politicised forum might be more appropriate. Several non-governmental organisations in the field of human rights and international justice could appropriately support such a development.

The narrowing of the political-offence exception deals with only one side of the problem, namely the excesses of political activism. The European Resolution falls short in not addressing itself more directly to the status of those engaged in what might be recognised as legitimate assertions of self-determination and human rights. To maintain a proper balance between human rights and world order, any proposed resolution must deny the proposition that all forms of violence are justified if supported by political claims, but avoid the trap of supporting the other extreme proposition that violent opposition to an established régime is never permissible by any international standards. The principles of self-defence and the requirements of proportionality need to be re-examined, refined and injected more vigorously into this area.

In domestic law, the only justifiable resort to violence is founded on a carefully defined concept of self-defence. Similarly, in the

---

47 Resolution (74) 3, January 27, 1974.

international law of the post-Second World War period, the resort to arms is only justified in the case of self-defence. A modification of this principle would seem useful also in the international response to the problems of terrorism and political crime. Resort to arms by individuals, as a response to denial of recognised human rights, might be viewed, in certain circumstances, as a class of self-defence.[48]

Those claiming the status of political offenders would be required to circumscribe and limit their violent conduct. Acts of self-defence would have to be addressed, as directly as possible, against those exercising the overall, or the most applicable, State power and must avoid all deliberate, or careless, harm to innocent parties. The force used in such acts of self-defence should be appropriate and proportionate to the harm suffered through the right deprived by the authorities, as well as the amount of force utilised by the authorities in the deprivation of the right. To some international scholars and reformers such an endorsement of individual or group self-help might still appear questionable, but " acts of resistance," even though utilising extra-legal means, may be indispensable as long as the international community lacks the means for the effective, world-wide enforcement of fundamental human rights.

A resolution constructed substantially on these principles, with emphasis on the reformation of extradition principles and practices, is unlikely to encounter the same obstacles as other new international legislation might. In this approach there would be continued reliance on a long tradition of exempting from extradition all political offenders with the exception of those who use excessive or indiscriminate violence. This approach offers the possibility of giving weight to considerations of both human rights and world order. While permitting States the ultimate decision in extradition cases, based on the facts in each individual case, it seeks to develop further international consensus in drawing a finer line of demarcation between international rights, international crimes, and non-extradictable political offences.

These might seem meagre goals. In an arena which is rife with world dissension, talking softly while carrying a small stick might, however, be the more desirable course. While it is imperative that States be given a suitable opportunity to condemn and prosecute those forms of conduct destructive of a civilised world community, it is important, at the same time, that they be required more effectively to commit themselves to the support of those universal human rights which they proclaimed nearly three decades ago.

---

[48] For discussion of such an approach see Bassiouni, " Ideologically Motivated Offence and the Political Offence Exception in Extradition—A Proposed Juridical Standard for the Unruly Problem," 19 *DePaul Law Review*, Nr. 217 (1969), pp. 254–257.

VIII—EPILOGUE

Perhaps the experts have been overly pessimistic in their assessment of terrorists as unalterably committed to indiscriminate violence and hopelessly opposed to notions of innocence, proportionality and the concept of restricted warfare. The history of modern terrorism is short, and fails to establish conclusively that terrorists are committed to indiscriminate violence as a way of life rather than a means to an end.

An examination of international terrorist movements indicates a common striving towards legitimacy. However abhorrent the methods, the goals are clearly those of a much more conservative nature: namely, the attainment of a redistribution of political power and recognition by the family of nations. If we can persuade such groups (and their supporters in the community of nations) that protection from extradition and prosecution, as well as possible legitimacy and recognition, have their price in terms of moderation and restraint, the sparing of innocents may be at hand.

# TRANSNATIONAL POLITICS
## *VERSUS*
## INTERNATIONAL POLITICS

By

RONALD J. YALEM

THE purpose of this paper is to undertake an examination of two competing paradigms that are emerging in the study of international politics. By paradigm I mean a conceptual framework for analysing and describing international relations. Particular reference to the challenges of the transnational politics paradigm will be made because of the growing number of scholars who favour its employment.

Paradigm may also be used in the sense of a methodological approach to international studies based on the more traditional procedures of historical analysis and intuition or the more scientific procedures of behavioural scholars who stress rigorous theory, empiricism, and the use of quantitative analysis. The focus of this essay will be on substantive rather than methodological paradigms because the latter has already been widely debated whereas the former has not received the attention it deserves in my judgment. This may be explained by the recent development of the new and competing transnational politics paradigm.

I intend to approach the problem impartially which is usually not the case in the literature. Writers tend to champion the older paradigm of State-centric politics or the newer transnational politics paradigm. A more ambitious purpose of future research would be a reconciliation of their opposing assumptions and philosophies. Whether this may be accomplished by a new synthesis, however, remains doubtful at this time.

### I—THE INTERNATIONAL POLITICS PARADIGM

Until quite recently the international politics paradigm enjoyed unquestioned acceptance as the prevailing framework in the field of international relations, focusing on the interaction of nation-States in the form of various patterns of war, conflict, alliances, and especially the balance of power.[1] The so-called " billiard-ball " approach

---

[1] See, *e.g.* J. H. Leurdijk who defines international politics as the relations between States because " in international relations it is the only legitimate yielder of physical power." " From International to transnational politics: a change of paradigms? " XXVI *International Social Science Journal*, Nr. 1 (1974), p. 53.

first described by Arnold Wolfers depicted the arena of world politics as dominated by nation-States.[2] As Wolfers put it, " every State represents a closed, impermeable, and sovereign unit, completely separated from all other States." [3] In fairness to Wolfers, it should be pointed out that he considered this model to be an inaccurate representation of the real world of international politics because of the existence of corporate non-State actors. In fact, Wolfers was probably the first scholar to recognise the existence of such non-State actors although his work stressed the primacy of the State-as-actor approach. As we shall see later, this approach has come under increasing attack by a minority of writers primarily because of its inadequacy as a descriptive and explanatory tool in an increasingly complex international environment. For the moment, however, the international politics paradigm shall be the object of our concern.

In addition to the billiard-ball conception of international politics, the traditional paradigm associated the system of sovereign States with international anarchy: " the sovereign States, recognising no higher authority, are in an international state of nature; the resulting security dilemma forces them to live in a condition of mutual competition and conflict." [4] The possibility for international co-operation under this conception was limited primarily to the formation of alliances to safeguard national and international security and to the limited capacities of general international organisations to alter the prevailing patterns of power politics.

The traditional paradigm also stressed the concept of national power as the fundamental basis for security in a system lacking supranational government. International politics became power politics of necessity. The power politics paradigm was " the most important and influential of the traditional theories and the one that has attracted the greatest number of thinkers in the field of international relations." [5] As a result, it clearly fits Thomas Kuhn's " conception of a paradigm as a model that provides the basis for a coherent tradition in research." [6]

The traditional paradigm also sharply differentiated between international politics and domestic politics. This was clearly implied in the billiard-ball conception which separated international politics from domestic politics and from the writing of numerous scholars who viewed the power politics approach as differing qualitatively with rules and methods at variance with those that operated in the

---

[2] A. Wolfers, *Discord and Collaboration* (1962), p. 19.
[3] *Ibid.*
[4] A. Lijphart, " The Structure of the Theoretical Revolution in International Relations," *International Studies Quarterly*, March 1974, p. 43.
[5] *Ibid.* p. 46.
[6] *Ibid.* p. 55.

domestic field. The implication of such a separation was that international reality and domestic reality are not only analytically separate but are also empirically distinct. It is this conception that has been so strenuously criticised by the transnationalists who tend to blur the distinction between international and domestic politics.

J. Henk Leurdijk has usefully summarised a number of conclusions incorporated in various theories of international politics [7]: (1) the actions of States may be explained by certain power drives or State capabilities rather than upon international processes with the exception of the balance of power; (2) States are defined in terms of territoriality; (3) international politics consists of the study " of the relations among States that constitute the international system . . ."

Balance of power theory has been the chief explanatory device of the traditional paradigm in which the actions of States were considered to be predetermined by the shifting dynamics of various international combinations rather than by individual choice. Central to the theory is the notion of a relatively constant national interest to guide the behaviour of States whose components include the problems of survival and the nature of the international environment. [8]

Additionally, the theory assumed that all States " will react similarly to stimuli from the movement of forces in the international system." [9] As a result, despite existing differences in the character of States their responses to the forces of the international system tend to be uniform rather than diverse. [10]

Oran Young has further clarified the traditional paradigm of international politics in a perceptive essay. [11] He utilises the term State-centric as an alternative; however, it is clear that his analysis is substantially concerned with the international politics paradigm. Young concentrates on sovereignty and territoriality as the chief attributes of Statehood and proceeds to explain why the traditional paradigm has remained unchallenged until recently [12]: (1) ". . . the very notion of international politics . . . subsumes the postulates of the nation-State as the fundamental unit of world politics." (Simply because the term international refers to relations among nation-States); (2) the State has served as the highest point of human loyalties from a historical perspective; (3) the State-centric view is also buttressed by the fact that international law defines States as the fundamental units of world affairs in their roles as the prevailing

---

[7] Leurdijk, *op. cit.* in note 1 above, pp. 54–55.
[8] *Ibid.* p. 55.
[9] *Ibid.*
[10] *Ibid.*
[11] O. Young, " The Actors in World Politics," in J. N. Rosenau, V. Davis, and M. A. East (eds.), *The Analysis of International Politics* (1972), pp. 125–144.
[12] *Ibid.* pp. 126–127.

subjects of the international legal system and because of the attribute of sovereignty; (4) membership in international organisations is limited to States; (5) the State form has acquired additional legitimacy because it has now spread to Africa and Asia.

Despite the variety of attacks that have been made recently by the opponents of the traditional paradigm on the transnationalists, and Young himself is one of their number, he is unique perhaps in acknowledging that recent changes in world politics have not undermined the State as the fundamental unit of world politics.[13] Most scholars still treat such developments as the rise of non-State actors, the interpenetration of domestic and international politics, and the rise of new patterns of transnational activity involving non-governmental organisations as exceptions which do not necessitate any substantial abandonment of the State-centric view.[14]

## II—The Transnational Politics Paradigm

It is natural that any attempt to displace a paradigm that has guided the study of international relations for so long will be extensive and detailed in its criticism. Consequently, we will now examine a number of critiques in order to explicate their main assumptions and assess the legitimacy of their arguments. The arguments will be drawn from many sources in an effort to discover any uniformities and diversities in their approaches. It will become apparent that despite the persuasiveness for a new paradigm, the most ardent supporters acknowledge the difficulty of breaking with the traditional paradigm.

Oran Young has discussed some of the attacks on the older paradigm with admirable clarity and has suggested a more complex mixed-actor model that resembles but does not constitute a new paradigm.[15] According to Young, the critics fall into the following categories:

(1) *Global integrationists*: This group questions the adequacy of the nation-State as a viable institution for the achievement of social welfare and national security.[16] Because of rising interdependencies of States in these two areas, integrationists believe that " the only alternative to the spread of disorder and chaos in world politics is the development of an effective worldwide political community to replace or supplement . . . national political communities." [17] The group would presumably include all supporters of world government and possibly a new group of scholars interested in global reform of the

---

13 *Ibid.* p. 130.
14 *Ibid.*
15 *Ibid.* pp. 128–134.
16 *Ibid.* p. 128.
17 *Ibid.*

international system such as those who participated in and contributed to the World Order Models Project.[18]

(2) *Transnationalists*: Members of this group attack the traditional paradigm not because they believe in the possibility of world political community but because they allege that State boundaries no longer coincide with the new realities of international relations. Transnational activities have been carried on by individuals and nongovernmental groups and organisations in which the State element is either non-existent or marginal at best. Such activities are said to be increasing and to be global in geographic scope. Young distinguishes transnational economic groups, transnational professional associations, transnational revolutionary groups, and various peace research groups.[19] The most articulate and effective challenge to the international politics paradigm has come from the spokesmen of the transnational economic groups.

Young associates transnationalism with the growth of interdependencies among States brought about by improvements in communication, transportation, and military technology. Interdependence is defined as the " extent to which events occurring in any given component unit of a world system affect . . . events taking place in each of the other parts or component units of the system." [20] In particular, he cites John Herz and his familiar doctrine of the " decline of the territorial State " caused by the advent of nuclear weapons. Young concludes that " the realities of world politics now seem closer to a complex pattern of interpenetration among various types of actors within the world system than to the simple and clearcut dichotomy between international politics and domestic politics." [21]

But in another article Young attacks the notion that the growth of interdependencies means that the State system is obsolete because interdependencies create opportunities for conflict as well as for cooperation.[22] This was well illustrated after the imposition of the Arab oil embargo in November 1973 that created conflict between the oilproducing and the oil-consuming nations. Even under conditions of rising interdependence, increased regulation will be required to maintain system stability without any assurances that this will be possible in specific cases.[23]

---

[18] For a report of the contributions to the project, see S. Mendlovitz (ed.), *On The Creation of a Just World Order* (1975).

[19] Young, *op. cit.* p. 129.

[20] O. Young, " Interdependencies in World Politics," XXIV *International Journal*, Nr. 4, Autumn 1969, p. 726.

[21] Young, *op. cit.* in note 11 above, pp. 129–130.

[22] Young, *op. cit.* in note 20 above, p. 728.

[23] *Ibid.* p. 729.

Nevertheless, Young finds additional discrepancies in the State-centric view. Horizontal patterns of State interaction are being supplemented by a third dimension of vertical relations reflected in the rise of new non-State actors that transcend state boundaries.[24]

Young is less satisfactory in his discussion of new patterns of human loyalty beyond the nation-State since he presents no evidence and even admits that the situation is confusing. He nevertheless insists on a kind of tension between States on the one hand and various non-State actors on the other.[25] As yet, however, the development of multiple loyalties ". . . have not undermined the empirical applicability of the state-centric world view in any decisive sense." [26] If this is true, then it is difficult to explain why human loyalties are being shifted to other entities.

Young's main thesis seems to be that we are moving into a world system of mixed actors comprising nation-States and various non-State actors. Unlike Nye and Keohane, however, he does not envisage a continued diminution in the influence and power of States at the expense of new transnational organisations.[27] Rather, he foresees the possibility of a stable system of mixed actors.

On the other hand, his mixed-actor system is similar to Nye and Keohane's world politics paradigm in a number of respects. Interactions among non-State actors would not be based on fixed patterns of dominance-submission characteristic of State interaction.[28] But Young is vague about what kinds of patterns would be operative. Like Nye and Keohane he perceives that the relationships of non-State actors would be non-territorial and that the inclusion of such actors as multinational corporations would add new and broadening dimensions to the scope of world politics hitherto dominated by the activities of States.

Young concludes his essay by asserting that States are assuming new roles as " important but not dominant actors in world politics." [29] But this conclusion is difficult to reconcile with his earlier statements

---

[24] According to Edward Morse, new non-State units, especially multinational corporations with impressive economic capacity, have a kind of direct or indirect interaction with governments. Yet he admits that while such non-State actors may challenge the traditional State-centric view of reality, the effect of such units on foreign policy " . . . is one about which we know very little." They are so complex that " the co-ordination and control of their activities by formal sovereign entities has become difficult." See " The Transformation of Foreign Policies," *World Politics*, April 1970, pp. 390–391.

[25] See also W. Levi who asserts that the growth of functional groups threatens the exclusive loyalty of the individual to his own State. *International Politics* (1974), p. 232.

[26] Young, " The Actors in World Politics," *op. cit.* p. 134.

[27] See also Levi, who envisages the decline of the power of States at the expense of the new transnational and subnational groups. See *op. cit.* in note 25 above, p. 234.

[28] Young, *op. cit.* in note 11 above, p. 136.

[29] *Ibid.* p. 137.

regarding the continuing power and importance of States all over the world.[30] Though importance and dominance may not be the same thing, Young has not persuasively demonstrated that States have lost their dominant position in the international system.

His discussion of the rise of new non-State actors and the consequent emergence of a mixed-actor system is more plausible. The implications he draws from this development, however, regarding the change in the role of States is not supported by empirical evidence. He has not stated a persuasive case for the abandonment of the international politics paradigm but only a case for widening it. This becomes apparent in the conclusions of his essay [31]: (1) the system of world politics is changing from one formerly dominated by one type of actor to one of interactions among different types of actors; (2) mixed-actor systems have been explained as exceptions to the State-centric view of world politics; and (3) mixed-actor systems have reached the stage in which new developments are difficult to explain on the basis of traditional assumptions of international politics. It seems to me that Young has not proven the validity of his third conclusion. Rather, by his own admission he has explained the rise of new non-State actors as subsidiary actors in a world still dominated by nation-States, as in the second conclusion. Young lends credence to this view by conceding that shifting from the State-centric view to a mixed-actor system, in which States are important but not dominant actors, is strongly resisted because of the strength of the traditional paradigm. Such a shift would also " run counter to the goal of conceptual simplicity." [32] He is in fact acknowledging that serious problems of complexity are inherent in any paradigm shift. For example, the relative influence of various types of actors in various types of situations.

A more explicit case for a change in paradigms has been made by J. Henk Leurdijk because the traditional paradigm runs counter to reality and is thus inadequate.[33] Relying heavily on the assumption of increasing interdependence in the form of transnational society, and on non-governmental actors, he argues that " interactions are initiated not by governments but by non-governmental actors. . . ." [34] He also differentiates the two paradigms on the basis of method: the international politics paradigm emphasises force and the threat of force whereas the transnational paradigm concentrates on economic

---

[30] See for example his discussion of the potency of nationalism and the failure of European political integration. *Ibid.* p. 135.

[31] *Ibid.* p. 139.

[32] *Ibid.*

[33] Leurdijk, *op. cit.* in note 1 above, pp. 57–67.

[34] *Ibid.* p. 58.

growth and peaceful co-operation.[35] This is an important distinction
that deserves consideration despite the fact that it oversimplifies
reality. The traditional model of power politics has always permitted
the possibility of international co-operation while the transnational
society paradigm may be fraught with economic conflict as well as
with economic co-operation among non-State actors.

Leurdijk also attacks the traditional paradigm because it presumes
that all States are preoccupied with the pursuit of power and national
security in a period in which the relevance of these assumptions to the
less-developed States is suspect.[36] Such States are more concerned
with the achievement of national prosperity and overcoming income
gaps between themselves and the rich States. The overwhelming
number of States today are less developed and are centrally concerned
with problems of growth and development rather than power expansion. Whether this justifies the abandonment of the traditional
paradigm is another matter because power and security issues are still
vitally important to many if not all States.

In this connection, Leurdijk suggests that the horizontal relationships among States based on the balance of power have declined as
vertical economic relationships based on patterns of economic
supremacy and dependency have increased.[37] While relationships
between rich and poor States may reflect such patterns, it does not
follow that balance of power and security considerations along
horizontal lines have generally diminished in importance either
regionally or globally. Further, while most analysts make a distinction between power and economics, there is an obvious artificial
dichotomy created by such distinctions because of the fact that
economic power and military power are so closely linked. If this
contention is valid, the division of the international system into
horizontal and vertical sectors may be unjustifiable.

Even if such a division of the system is accepted, it is still open to
objections. The notion of a vertically arranged system of supremacy
and dependency implies a kind of centralisation of political and
economic power that may have been valid for the nineteenth century
but not for the twentieth century. The Great Powers do not dictate
policy to the weaker States especially in the nuclear age. During
1973–74 the imposition of the Arab oil embargo by weak States
contradicted the notion of supremacy/dependency. The powerful
became dependent on the weak contrary to the dependence feature of
unequal States in a vertically organised hierarchical system. Among
many students of international politics, there is a tendency to empha-

35 *Ibid.*
36 *Ibid.* pp. 59–60.
37 *Ibid.* pp. 61–62.

sise the limitations of great military power in so far as the achievement of political objectives is concerned.

According to the transnational politics paradigm outlined by Leurdijk, international politics is considered to be more than the behaviour of States but includes all processes that transcend national boundaries with particular stress on the behaviour of non-territorial actors.[38] Intellectual analysis is thereby widened beyond the traditional concerns of conflict, war, and force to embrace the new transnational economic co-operative relationships among non-territorial entities.[39] Still it may be argued that the traditional paradigm with some modifications can accommodate these new international co-operative aspects.

While it may be true that patterns of trade, natural resource distribution, and environmental problems deserve greater attention than they have received from international politics scholars in a new paradigm, it cannot be denied that presently power and security factors are more authoritative in determining the structure of the world system than economic and social issues. A rejoinder to this argument has been developed by Nye and Keohane, but not convincingly in my judgment and will be examined shortly.

Finally, as previously mentioned, the transnational paradigm distinguishes between horizontal and vertical patterns of influence in the world system. This distinction not only implies the growing importance of vertical (non-State) relations as opposed to horizontal (State) relations but also carries implications for the study of international politics [40]: ". . . in the traditional paradigm the object of study (the inter-State system) was distinguished from the study of foreign policy . . . according to the new concept the object of study defined as the world political system is divided into vertical sphere of issue areas, foreign policy implying the study of the horizontal co-ordination of State behaviour in different issue areas." Under this conception there can no longer be any important distinction between the study of foreign policy and the study of international politics.[41] If the world system was exclusively composed of non-territorial actors, then such a distinction need not obtain. But since territoriality is still the basis of Statehood and non-State actors have not displaced State actors, the distinction still holds. Even in issue areas that are not geographically confined by transnational standards such as dis-

---

[38] *Ibid.* pp. 64–65. This view is shared by most transnationalists.

[39] *Ibid.* p. 65.

[40] *Ibid.* p. 66.

[41] According to Leurdijk, international politics would cease to exist as an autonomous discipline because spatial relations between States would be superseded by issue area relations in which territorial boundaries would lose their relevance. Most scholars would have difficulty in accepting such a contention.

armament, human rights, and economic development, the State remains a vital actor and the international system the environment in which it functions and interacts.

## III—THE NYE AND KEOHANE PERSPECTIVE

Perhaps the most comprehensive attempt to establish a new transnational politics paradigm was the effort instigated by Professors Nye and Keohane in their joint editorship of the volume " Transnational Relations and World Politics," published in 1971 as Volume XXV of *International Organization*. For our purposes the introduction and the conclusion of the volume are the most pertinent components.

In common with other transnationalists, the editors recognise the predominance of the international politics paradigm but question its relevance because of the rise of contacts in trade and communications that takes place outside of the control of governments.[42] They discern a neglect of the whole subject at both theoretical and policy levels.

They define transnational relations as " contacts, coalitions, and interactions across State boundaries that are not controlled by the central foreign policy organs of government." [43] Nye and Keohane are interested in exploring the relationships between such interactions and the international system. They recognise that proponents of the traditional paradigm have excluded transnational relations on the assumption " that their direct political importance is small." [44] They even acknowledge the fact that States are the most important actors in world affairs, but prefer a new paradigm which could account for the increasing importance of such relations and non-governmental actors.[45]

In a careful review of the introduction to the Nye and Keohane volume, R. Harrison Wagner maintains that the editors do not discuss carefully the effects of their new paradigm [46]: " They lump together under the generic term ' transnational relations ' all types of relations in which non-governmental actors participate. The immediate effect . . . is to dissolve the traditional actors in international politics into shifting and poorly defined components and to embed them in a series of poorly differentiated transnational relationships."

Wagner believes that these ambiguities with regard to what he refers to as the disaggregation process of the State raise doubts about

---

[42] Joseph Nye and Robert Keohane, " Transnational Relations and World Politics: An Introduction," XXV *International Organization*, Summer 1971, p. 330.

[43] *Ibid.* p. 331.

[44] *Ibid.* pp. 343–344.

[45] *Ibid.* p. 344.

[46] R. H. Wagner, " Dissolving the State: Three Recent Perspectives on International Relations," XXVIII *International Organization* (1974).

the case for a new paradigm.[47] Supposedly new explanations of government decisions are to result but ". . . their argument can also be construed as implying no more than a shift in our attention to new areas of international politics (economic issues), where transnational relations have always been studied but which have not been at the centre of attention of political scientists." [48]

Wagner concludes that the effect of the abandonment of the State-centric paradigm " would be to direct our attention to the political conflict associated with these (economic) issues and to the relation between them and other issues. . . . But the Keohane-Nye paradigm does not really say anything about the analytical problems involved in such an enterprise." [49]

He is especially concerned with the problems of integrating international economic theory into the paradigm. Even if such difficulties could be overcome, Wagner is sceptical that " this would necessarily require any really novel emphasis on non-governmental actors nor is it clear that it requires a new paradigm of analysis." [50]

Nye and Keohane, however, save their strongest arguments for a new paradigm in the conclusion of the volume on transnational relations. They attribute the need for a new paradigm to two primary factors: an increasing sensitivity of national societies to international developments and to the growth of transnational economic and social organisations that are exercising increasing influence.[51] Societies have become more sensitive to one another because politics and economics are not separated as in the nineteenth century but are intertwined. And while international political organisations such as the United Nations have declined economic and social organisations have increased in importance.

Despite all of these developments, Nye and Keohane are sensitive to the followers of Stanley Hoffmann who argue that transnational relations are a kind of " low politics " of economic and welfare issues that do not affect the " high politics " of security and power in international relations. In my judgment, however, they do not make an effective case to refute Hoffmann's hypothesis first elaborated in an important article in 1966.[52] They cite only the international monetary crisis of 1971 as an example of the fusion of " high politics " and " low politics." [53] While it may be true, as they also assert, that butter may

---

[47] *Ibid.* p. 441.
[48] *Ibid.*
[49] *Ibid.* p. 445.
[50] *Ibid.*
[51] Nye and Keohane, *op. cit.* in note 42 above, pp. 725–726.
[52] Stanley Hoffmann, " Obstinate or Obsolete? The Fate of the Nation-State and the Case of Western Europe," *Daedalus*, Summer, 1966.
[53] Nye and Keohane, *op. cit.* in note 42 above, p. 729.

come before guns in New Zealand diplomacy, for many States the distinction is still relevant and recognised even if we acknowledge that an increasing number of non-governmental activities have political implications. The point to be made here is that transnationalists have failed to demonstrate except in rare instances that the effect of international economic interactions spills over into the political and security fields of the international system. They have demonstrated that such interactions are increasing and have been de-emphasised too much by followers of the traditional international politics paradigm. Spill-over has been conspicuously absent not only on the regional but also on the global level.

### IV—The World Politics Paradigm

In the Nye and Keohane paradigm bargaining supersedes power and influence as the main phenomenon in a system of different types of actors.[54] Their purpose is to break down " the ' level-of-analysis ' problem by broadening the conception of actors and by conceptually breaking down the ' hard shell ' of the nation-State." [55] Figure 1 illustrates their position [56]:

### Figure 1: Actors in World Politics

|  | Governmental | Inter-governmental | Non-governmental |
|---|---|---|---|
| Maximal central control | A<br>States as units | C<br>International organisations as units | E<br>Transnational organisations as units |
| Minimal central control | Governmental subunits | Subunits of international organisations | Subunits of trans-national organisations; also certain individuals |

A + C=Actors in the State-Centric Paradigm
B + D=Actors in Transgovernmental Interactions
E + F=Actors in Transnational Relations

As can be seen from this figure, States are involved in only two out of six cells. The result of this complex paradigm is that " transnational relations include both transnational and transgovernmental inter-

---

[54] *Ibid.* p. 730.
[55] *Ibid.*
[56] *Ibid.* p. 730. See also S. Brown, who predicts that changing forces in international relations " appear to be leading towards a global society in which conflicts would have to be resolved primarily on the basis of ad hoc bargaining." He adds that States, subnational groups and transnational groups would compete for the support and loyalty of individuals. See *New Forces in World Politics* (1974), p. 186.

action—all of world politics that is not taken into account by the State-centric paradigm." [57]

Nye and Keohane conclude their volume by humbly admitting that they have raised more questions than answers and that their intent is not to argue that States are obsolete or that transnational relations will produce peace.[58] Only that transnational relations are increasing in importance and constitute an integral dimension of world politics. They believe that the traditional paradigm diverts attention from such transnational relations which can be accommodated in their new paradigm encompassing three distinct types of interactions. This may be true but in the process of broadening the scope of world politics they have of necessity de-emphasised the role of States as actors and over-emphasised perhaps the role of non-State actors. They have produced a multifaceted matrix of relationships that may be an accurate representation of the increasing complexity of world politics, but they have failed to provide us with any systematic knowledge that would interrelate the relative influence of various types of actors within their complex matrix. Nevertheless, Nye and Keohane have alerted us to a broader range of relationships that are possible within the traditional paradigm. It is obvious, however, that their work is only a beginning and will need to be further clarified in the future.

## V—CONCLUSIONS

Werner Levi reflects the dilemma caused by the inadequacies of the traditional framework of international politics and the newer forces generated by transnational politics. He notes changes in the international system that most advocates of a new paradigm would support such as the growth of international co-operation and interactions; the breakdown of the isolation of States because of improvements in communication; economic growth and development concerns as rivals to the traditional tools of power politics; and the consequent activities of individuals and corporations that have undermined the monopoly position of the State.[58] Yet Levi believes that despite such changes their impact on world politics will be modest [59]: " no strong pressures for fundamental changes to improve the prevailing situations have come from any government. Apparently the satisfactions to be derived from the existing nation-State system and the anxieties to be derived from unforeseeable consequences of radical change sustain a general attachment to the traditional system."

John Weltman also reflects similar views. He believes that the new

---

[57] *Op. cit.* in note 42, above, p. 748.
[58] Levi, *op. cit.* in note 25 above, pp. 226–227.
[59] *Ibid.* p. 228.

issues of international relations such as monetary, trade, and development relations are distinct from traditional power politics and require a kind of co-ordination in which co-operation is stressed over conflict.[60]

But he admits that " even if we accept the view that interdependence between States has greatly increased, this by itself still does little to ensure that the behaviour necessary to reap the benefits of interdependence will follow "; as long as the State system exists, security problems flourish, and the threat of war has not been eliminated, the concepts of strategy and power remain relevant.[61] The interactions between domestic and foreign policy produced by the salience of economic issues and the declining utility of war still lead Weltman to conclude that " some wars may well remain useful and effective means for accomplishing the ends of State action even within a clear context of the declining utility of war." [62] Weltman in effect presents in his essay the contradictory views of " low politics " and " high politics " within the context of the phenomenon of war without any attempt at reconciliation. It is just as unlikely that the international politics paradigm and the transnational politics paradigm can be reconciled given their differing assumptions and orientations.[63]

Until more fundamental changes occur in the relative influence of State as opposed to non-State actors in which the latter become perceptibly more influential than the former, it would be premature to abandon the traditional paradigm in favour of the transnational politics paradigm. This does not deny the validity of many of the arguments of the critics of the traditional paradigm regarding its lack of explanatory capacity for the many new phenomena thrown up by the growth of transnational activities. The more pragmatic course would be to expand the traditional paradigm to include new non-State actors, issue areas, and transnational economic activities in an effort to improve the deficiencies of the traditional framework noted by the transnationalists. Such an effort is beyond the scope of the present essay but seems to be an important task for future development of the study of international politics.[64]

---

[60] J. Weltman, " On the Obsolescence of War: An Essay in Policy and Theory," *International Studies Quarterly*, December 1974, p. 400.

[61] *Ibid.* p. 405.

[62] *Ibid.* p. 415.

[63] For example, A. J. R. M. Groom mentions that while transnational systems may undermine the billiard-ball model of international politics, we forget that " the State apparatus is impinging more and more into our daily lives. . . . We have, then, something of a paradox. Escape from the billiard-ball model, yet reinforcement of it in other functional dimensions." *The Study of World Society: A London Perspective*, Occasional Paper Nr. 1, International Studies Association, 1974, p. 46.

[64] The author wishes to express his appreciation for the financial support of this study provided by the Research Grants Committee of the University of Alabama.

# THE PLACE OF INTERCULTURAL RELATIONS IN THE STUDY OF INTERNATIONAL RELATIONS

## By

## ROY PREISWERK

IN scientific knowledge, concepts play a central role in helping to structure reality.[1] " Science *creates* its objects," says Gaston Bachelard in connection with conceptualisation.[2] The extent of possible knowledge is determined, among other things, by the choice of concepts. According to a widespread view, each concept ought to be exclusive to a single field of knowledge, since only specialisation at the highest level leads to expansion and improvement of scientific knowledge. However, this tendency is offset by a new development, in as much as a concept can have central meaning in the most diverse disciplines. This is, for instance, the case of the concept of structure which is used not only in mathematics and logic, but also in physics, biology, psychology, sociology and linguistics.[3]

Up to now, the concept of culture was assigned a modest place in the study of international relations. However, cultural diversity is one of the most obvious phenomena in human development. What understanding would we have if this problem were linked to that of inter-State relations?

## I—THE OBJECT OF INTERCULTURAL RELATIONS

In everyday language, the term "culture" conveys an idea of artistic and intellectual creation in a given society. But as far back as 1843, G. F. Klemm gave it a much wider meaning when introducing religion, family, customs, general knowledge and aptitudes, utensils, habitats, dress, etc., as objects of a science of culture. Thus, he endowed anthropology, in particular, with an essential analytical tool. Expanding further on this meaning, we can today define culture as a totality of values, institutions and forms of behaviour transmitted within a society, as well as the material goods produced by man. It must be noticed that this wide concept of culture covers *Weltanschauung*, ideologies and cognitive behaviour.[4]

---

[1] For critical comments on the first draft, the author is indebted to Michael Flack, Daniel Frei, Urs Luterbacher, Peter Meier, Fabrizio Sabelli and Noa Zanolli.

[2] G. Bachelard, *Epistémologie* (1971), p. 135.   [3] J. Piaget, *Le structuralisme* (1970).

[4] On some problematic aspects of the global and syncretic culture concept, see R. Preiswerk and Dominique Perrot, *Ethnocentrisme et histoire: l'Afrique, l'Amérique indienne et l'Asie dans les manuels occidentaux* (1975).

In ethnology or anthropology, this broad culture concept has been mainly applied to relatively small human groups, such as tribes or ethnic minorities. Melville Herskovits, among others, went even further when he attempted to define culture areas.[5] While science does not provide us with precise conceptual delimitations, however, different dimensions, or levels of culture, have found their way into everyday language. Thus, one frequently speaks of western or African culture, of Occident versus Orient, of Arabic or Slav culture, and so on. Conceptually, we can differentiate between at least four levels of culture: (1) *micro-culture* can be used to describe the particularity of smaller units such as tribes, minorities, village communities, social classes and sub-cultures; (2) one speaks of *national culture*, a very frequently used expression (*e.g.* " French culture "), mostly in the narrow sense of artistic and intellectual creation. But, in so far as the nationals of a country, despite differentiated micro-cultures, have certain common values, institutions and forms of behaviour, one can here also speak of culture in the broad sense; (3) the cultural particularity of a nation is limited to specific cultural characteristics; in other respects it is part of a wider cultural area in so far as it shares other characteristics with neighbouring nations within a *regional culture*; (4) beyond this level one can speak, in the broadest sense, of *macro-cultures* to describe characteristics which are common to a number of cultures despite local, national and regional differences.

The individual human being lives culture as a totality. As far as socially transmitted values and forms of behaviour are concerned, he does not always distinguish, or perhaps never distinguishes which aspects are to be attributed to a micro-culture (*e.g.* Scotland, Ewondo), the national culture (Great Britain, Cameroon), the regional culture (Anglo-Saxon, Bantu), or the macro-culture (western world, Africa). Nevertheless, the differentiation is justified for analytical reasons. As will be shown later, it corresponds to a human and political reality which is significant in international relations.

The differentiation of culture dimensions or culture levels revives old problems in the never-ending debate about the culture concept. Surely one objection must be taken seriously. Recently, in a new attempt to re-examine the culture concept, Paul Bohannan points out the difficulty of delimiting cultures. For him the delimitation is impossible and this leads him to the conclusion that one may speak of culture, but not of cultures. The latter would mean reification of a " reality " merely designated by an analytical concept.[6] Bohannan is certainly right when he underlines the problem of delimitation: even

---

[5] M. Herskovits, *The Human Factor in Changing Africa* (1967), p. 57.

[6] P. Bohannan, " Rethinking Culture: A Project for Current Anthropologists," 14 *Current Anthropology*, October 1973.

on the level of micro-cultures, it is often impossible to determine precisely where one culture ends and the other begins. All the more, one must admit that a delimitation between a national culture, a regional culture and a macro-culture can, in most cases, be only inaccurate. The identity of the observer who determines a culture and the choice of criteria which supposedly characterise the particularity of a culture raise enormous epistemological problems.

Nevertheless, some conceptualisation is necessary. The culture concept facilitates the distinction between different groups and societies, the reality of which should not be denied even if the differences cannot be defined and described in a clear-cut and precise way. Inasmuch as culture merely serves to describe the behaviour of individuals and groups, it is not reified, since individuals and groups are a social reality.

Parallel to a broad definition of international relations, intercultural relations may be defined as relations between members of different groups and societies identified by culture (as opposed to nationality). Occasionally, the same meaning is given to the term " cultural encounters." Theoretically, three kinds of intercultural relations can be distinguished. " Cultural export " means the transfer of characteristics attributed to one culture to another cultural unit which, from our point of view, can be demarcated as different. " Cultural import," on the other hand, is the integration or acceptance of foreign cultural characteristics. " Cultural exchange " can be regarded as a reciprocal process. Marked differences in military and economic power largely determine the direction of cultural influence. A *colloquium* on " Cultural Relations for the Future " in this respect states: " The growing instability of the international order affects cultural relations, among other things, by the differential in access to the international communication system. The problem is, therefore, not simply a matter of a gap in wealth, nor a gap in knowledge, it is also a gap in access to opportunity. It is, in short, a gap in power." [7]

Intercultural relations, according to content and, in so far as they correspond to conscious motivations, according to their aim, may take various forms. Under certain circumstances, individuals and international actors seek a human fulfilment through contacts with other cultures. Inversely, members of a given society feel the need to express their cultural identity and make it understandable to others. The study of other cultures is indispensable or even the main objective of disciplines such as anthropology and social psychology. As a new aspect, intercultural problems are also increasingly dealt with by

---

[7] P. Braisted, Soedjatmoko, K. Thompson (eds.), *Reconstituting the Human Community* (1972), p. 10.

communication science. One may define intercultural communication as the " process of transmission of thought and meaning between human beings belonging to different cultures." [8]

But intercultural relations, above all, cover the desire of powerful States to expand their political and territorial sphere of interests through projection of their ideologies, modes of behaviour and value systems. What is sometimes called " cultural imperialism " is in this case an instrument for political domination and economic exploitation. A quotation from a French Foreign Ministry document is significant in this respect, particularly in relation to Africa: " Cultural expansion (language, the radiance of its culture and its ideas, literature, science, art, significance of its teaching methods) contributes directly to the international power position of our country." [9] Hostile or expansive forms of cultural encounters can also be found in depreciation of foreign cultural characteristics, discrimination against the cultural alien, the segregation or even persecution of persons who seem culturally different. The assimilation of individuals or the acculturation of entire groups to a dominant culture can also be deemed, in certain circumstances, as a destruction of culture. Ethnocide occurs, in the extreme case, when the identity of a group is completely annihilated.

Cultural encounters are not always the result of intentional behaviour. Cultural change, where it occurs, often is not intended. Thus, for instance, the introduction of industrial products such as automobiles or transistor radios into rural areas leads to socio-cultural consequences which were neither intended nor predictable. In this connection, three essential media of cultural influence should be mentioned: (1) language and writing, in personal communication or through mass media, are generally considered an important means of culture transfer; (2) behaviour, as an expression of a cultural model, today is probably equally important in view of the massive exchange of cultural agents (*e.g.* development experts, scholarship students); (3) objects and consumer goods, such as the above-mentioned means of transport and communication, also play an increasing role in the transfer of ways of life and values or in stirring up needs.

## II—The Juxtaposition of " Intercultural " and " International " as an Epistemological Problem

The attempt to circumscribe the subject-matter of a new field of knowledge as compared to existing disciplines raises epistemological

[8] G. Maletzke, " Interkulturelle und internationale Kommunikation," in *Interkulturelle Kommunikation zwischen Industrieländern und Entwicklungsländern* (1967).
[9] Suzanne Balous, *L'action culturelle de la France dans le monde* (1970), p. 13.

questions. On the one hand, there is the problem, dealt with in the theory of science, of the specificity of the field and its delimitation or, more generally, of its precise place in a classification of sciences.[10] On the other hand, it is necessary to determine what kind of knowledge is being sought, with the aid of which cognitive processes and methods that knowledge can be attained and on what basis the validity and veracity of findings are based.[11]

Intercultural relations were defined above as a multi-disciplinary field of study, the aim of which is to examine relations between members of different groups and societies defined by their culture. The basic disciplines on which they draw for both substance and method are anthropology, social psychology, psychology, communication science, comparative studies in the most diverse fields (*e.g.* comparative legal studies, comparative government), as well as area studies, also a multi-disciplinary field. This list is indicative of the attempts made in practically every field of the sciences of man to scrutinise knowledge emanating from a given cultural context as to its possible correspondence with identical or similar situations in other cultures.

The aim of this discussion is not to point out the possible development, in the field of " intercultural relations," leading towards more interdisciplinarity and homogeneity, but to clarify its relationship to the equally heterogeneous field of " international relations." In theory, three possibilities can be envisaged: (1) " Intercultural relations " can be seen as part of the study of international relations. This is already the case when the word culture is used in the narrow sense of everyday language. Indeed, for a few years now, the pursuit of " cultural relations " has been considered as a new dimension of foreign policy. In this sense, intercultural relations are promoted through art exhibitions, concert tours, student exchanges, scientific congresses, distribution of teaching materials, and so on.[12] But the question becomes more interesting when one examines the implications of the wider culture concept. If the previously mentioned four dimensions of culture were to be introduced into the analytical

---

[10] J. Piaget, *Epistémologie des sciences de l'homme* (1970), p. 16.

[11] The distinction between the French term " épistémologie " (meaning: theory of science, in German " *Wissenschaftslehre* ") and the English term " epistemology " (meaning: theory of knowledge, in German " Erkenntnislehre ") is rather outdated. The term " epistemology " can now be used to cover both aspects. The distinction can be retained for the construction of models of non-scientific cognition (mystical, ethical, " magical ") and for a possible critical evaluation of scientific knowledge from such a point of view.

[12] See such authors as Barghoorn, Blum and Coombs. M. Flack regrets that intercultural relations in this narrow sense are also neglected in international relations textbooks. " Cultural Diplomacy: Blindspot in International Affairs Textbooks," *International Educational and Cultural Exchange*, Winter 1972–73.

framework of international relations, one would be confronted with what has repeatedly been called the level-of-analysis problem.[13] Variables pertaining to macro- and regional cultures would have to be considered in the determination of international sub-systems. Aspects of national culture are significant in the study of decision-making processes. Micro-cultures appear as domestic factors in the foreign relations of States. A universal or world culture, still to be defined, would have to be considered on the level of the international system. (2) " Intercultural relations " can be designated as a field of knowledge as distinct from international relations. In this case, the distinction of cultural dimensions is not a level-of-analysis problem for international relations, but a unit-of-analysis problem in intercultural relations. (3) " International relations " can be considered as part of the study of intercultural relations. Indeed, the opinion is justified that even questions examined in the classical study of international relations concern relations between different types of societies which can be distinguished on the basis of cultural characteristics.

Fundamentally, it appears that different " specialists " are looking at the same object of study from different angles and using different methods. From the point of view of intercultural relations, multi-national corporations, for instance, are not of interest *per se* as producers of material goods, carriers of technology or distributors of merchandise. Their activity modifies forms of production, consumer habits, even value systems, social structures and cognitive styles. Inter-State negotiations are not only the expression of a political power constellation or the exercise of diplomatic skill, they are also the confrontation of different images of the world, different processes of thought, possibly threatening cultural identity.

If, so far, a strict delimitation of the two fields cannot be based on compelling arguments, nevertheless a distinction is necessary for reasons pertaining to the theory of knowledge. The need for the study of intercultural relations partly arose from an epistemological crisis of " international relations " in the era of decolonisation. With the massive entry of a majority of new States of non-western tradition into an international system created largely under western influence, " internationalists " sooner or later had to become aware of the fact that their analytical tools were no longer adequate for the understanding of their object of study. This means, in fact, a coming awareness of ethnocentrism in cognition. Maybe this insight was easier for " internationalists " well versed in the social sciences (mainly sociology and social psychology) or in philosophy, than for those of predominantly historical-legal-institutionalist tradition. In

---

[13] D. Singer, " The Level-of-Analysis Problem in International Relations," in J. Rosenau (ed.), *International Politics and Foreign Policy* (1969).

this respect, although it is dangerous to be too schematic, one can argue that an epistemological break with this tradition is at present taking place in the perspective which we have called intercultural. It is felt that the break is necessary because a cognitive style, predominant in western countries, such as " purpose-rational " (*zweckrational*) thought or a form of behaviour such as instrumental action, are not necessarily conducive to the understanding of other people.[14] The break is also required because the study of international relations in industrial countries (both in the private- and State-capitalistic societies) is based on evolutionist interpretations of history which place their own culture at the top of a list of honours and expect the development of non-western peoples to be oriented towards that model.[15]

In the study of intercultural relations, the cognitive process will have to be based largely on dialectics and hermeneutics. Dialectics is concerned in so far as the relationship between a subject (in this case an actor or observer belonging to culture X) and an object (culture Y as object of action or study) is of primary importance. In this relationship, subject and object do not appear as clearly separate entities but as elements of a praxis or of a cognitive process which modify each other reciprocally through interaction. This element must be taken into account particularly when intercultural aspects are examined empirically in direct contact with the foreign culture. Of equal importance for the understanding of intercultural relations is the interpretation of assertions made within a given cultural area about other cultures. Sources of all kinds (literary, philosophical and scientific works, teaching materials, children's books, proverbs, etc.) must be hermeneutically examined beyond their manifest ethnocentric content for underlying thought structures and images of the world.[16]

Despite this serious reservation, a strict delimitation of the two fields is not indispensable from the point of view of the theory of knowledge. On the contrary, this would result in a further compartmentalisation of fields of knowledge (as is common between sciences and even within individual disciplines), with deplorable consequences

[14] The re-examination of some of Max Weber's concepts by J. Habermas is of particular value here, although (as appears on p. 65) the intercultural perspective is not emphasised *Technik und Wissenschaft als Ideologie* (1968).

[15] These and other aspects of cognitive ethnocentrism are dealt with in *Ethnocentrisme et histoire, op. cit.* in note 4 above.

[16] See H. P. Fagagnini, " Wissenschaftstheorie und Politische Wissenschaft," 13 *Schweizerisches Jahrbuch für Politische Wissenschaft*, (1973), pp. 32–34. Methodologically, we must consider here qualitative and critical content analysis as it has been developed, among others, by G. Lukacs and L. Goldmann. J. Piaget also underlines the sociological and epistemological significance of such a method. *Etudes sociologiques* (1965), pp. 78–81. See also J. Ritsert, *Inhaltsanalyse und Ideologiekritik: Ein Versuch über kritische Sozialforschung* (1972).

for the study of human relations. This becomes particularly manifest, when one examines the potential of the two fields not only to describe such relations but also to explain them. Comprehension and explanation are no doubt two different degrees of scientific cognition. Nevertheless, the description of certain processes (necessary for their comprehension) can explain other processes.[17] In this sense, inter-cultural studies can help explain international relations. Thus, for instance, the *description* of the image of African cultures held by western people, or that prevailing of industrial society among African élites, can help the *explanation* of the behaviour of inter-State actors in relations between Africa and the West.[18] The classical study of international relations is predominantly of a descriptive and norma-tive nature; its explanatory potential is minimal. It increases when new developments in the social sciences are considered. In the era of a pluricultural international system, this includes the disciplines which are particularly meaningful in the study of intercultural relations.

### III—CONCRETE POSSIBILITIES OF LINKING THE TWO FIELDS

In order to give concrete meaning to what so far has only been indicated in a general way, different possible links will now be illustrated with the aid of a typology. The starting point is the assumption that the relations between States I and II can be examined in the light of the previously defined four cultural dimensions. In both cases, two micro-cultures (A and B) are considered within the national contexts. Furthermore, one has to ascertain in the case of State II whether it belongs to the same regional culture as State I (D) or to another one (G). Also the question must be asked whether it is part of the same macro-culture (E) or of another one (H).

From the Table it appears that theoretically 35 combinations are possible. However, the numbering shows that only 13 categories were considered relevant to the study of international relations. Identical numbers mean either, for formal-logical reasons, identity of cases or, on empirical grounds, analogy of situations.

All categories cover international relations in the sense of relations between nationals of different States. Only in 10 categories do we also find intercultural relations, whereas the three remaining ones (1, 9 and 12) concern intracultural relations (between persons of the same cultural area).

---

[17] L. Goldmann, *La création culturelle dans la société moderne* (1971), p. 21; and " Epistémologie de la sociologie," in J. Piaget (ed.), *Logique et connaissance scientifique* (1967), p. 1008.

[18] R. Preiswerk, " Neokolonialismus oder Selbstkolonisierung? Die Kulturbegeg-nung in den europäischafrikanischen Beziehungen," 24 *Europa-Archiv*, (1973), p. 845 *et seq.*

*Table*: CONCRETE POSSIBILITIES OF LINKING
INTERCULTURAL AND INTERNATIONAL RELATIONS

| | Micro-culture A within II | Micro-culture B within II | National culture F of II | II as part of regional culture D | II as part of regional culture G | II as part of macro-culture E | II as part of macro-culture H |
|---|---|---|---|---|---|---|---|
| Micro-culture A within I | 1. intra-cultural A | 2. A-B | 3. A-F | 4. A-D | 4. A-G | 5. A-E | 5. A-H |
| Micro-culture B within I | 2. A-B | 1. intra-cultural B | 4. B-F | 4. B-D | 4. B-G | 5. B-E | 5. B-H |
| National culture C of I | 3. A-C | 3. B-C | 6. C-F | 7. C-D | 7. C-G | 8. C-E | 8. C-H |
| I as part of regional culture D | 4. A-D | 4. B-D | 7. D-F | 9. intra-cultural D | 11. D-G | 10. D-E | 10. D-H |
| I as part of macro-culture E | 5. A-E | 5. B-E | 8. E-F | 10. E-D | 10. E-G | 12. intra-cultural E | 13. E-H |

State II

State I

The following examples can be used as illustrations of each category in the Table:

(1) Contacts between language minorities of different countries (French-speaking minorities in Canada, Belgium and Switzerland); efforts of minorities within several States to create their own national State (Kurds in Iraq, Iran, Turkey, Syria).

(2) Reciprocal support in efforts to preserve or promote cultural identity given by culturally not identical minorities in different countries; participation in efforts to strengthen international protection of minorities.

(3) Relations between a State and language minorities in another State (France-Quebec); irredentist movements.

(4) Situation of micro-cultures within individual States with respect to movements towards unity or identity reaching beyond existing frontiers (Italian Tyrol and pan-germanism, Peruvian Indians and " indigenismo "). Similar to 1.

(5) This category is difficult to differentiate from 4, since the conceptual distinction between regional culture and macro-culture may in some cases appear far-fetched. It is also of relatively little interest from the point of view of international relations. In terms of intercultural relations, this category takes two forms: micro-culture in relation to a wider embracing macro-culture (A-E and B-E) or to a different macro-culture (A-H and B-H).

(6) Inter-State relations are examined here for their cultural characteristics in so far as it is possible to isolate the national culture of a State within the wider macro-culture. The aim is to broaden knowledge about the decision-making and negotiating style of the representatives of a country in order to meet heavy demands or threats of force in the defence of one's own interest. American authors have undertaken " bilateral " studies of this kind. Historians have also sought retroactively, to reveal the cultural background of decisions, the significance of which became apparent only later.[19]

(7) This category is close to 6 and 8 when one bears in mind again that national cultures are part of regional and macro-cultures. Possible cases are relations between the United States and countries of luso-hispanic tradition in the western hemisphere (illustrating the consequences of strong cultural differences) or between France and

---

[19] *e.g.* for the relation between Japan and Germany or the United States and Greece: H. Triandis, *The Analysis of Subjective Culture* (1972). For Japan–United States, see also M. Armacost, " U.S.–Japan Relations: Problems and Modalities of Communication," *Department of State Bulletin*, January 15, 1973. Of particular interest in a historical perspective is A. Bozeman, *Politics and Culture in International History* (1960). An attempt of a condensed presentation of American culture for use in the study of international communication is made by E. Stewart, " The Simulation of Cross-Cultural Communication," in *op. cit.* in note 8 above.

francophone Africa (showing conditions of political dependence partly created through cultural indoctrination).

(8) Here again there are two situations: a State as part of a wider context defined by macro-culture (C–E) or in relation to another macro-culture (C–H). Regarding the first situation, above all one should note the position of the United States and the Soviet Union within the western macro-culture, the two super-Powers being politically in a conflict situation although they share a considerable number of cultural characteristics. The present *rapprochement* may have something to do with this, particularly when one bears in mind that highly industrialised societies are dependent on each other for markets, technology and capital. To illustrate the second situation, intercultural studies on the relations between Japan and the West could be mentioned.[20]

(9) In this case, we are dealing exclusively with international relations among States of a relatively narrow cultural area (Scandinavian, Central American or Arab countries) and the relations that States of such a region have with the outside world.

(10) This is a less relevant category. In its variation E–D, it could mean: Germany as part of the western macro-culture in relation to Sweden as part of a Scandinavian regional culture which belongs to the same macro-culture as Germany. Correspondingly, the variation D–H would be: Sweden as part of Scandinavia in relation to Senegal as part of the African macro-culture (inversely E–G).

(11) Relations between States of different regional cultures (North and South America, Slavic and Germanic States).

(12) Similar to category 9, but on the wider level of macro-culture.

(13) This is perhaps the most important category of intercultural aspects for the future of international relations: the relations between States of different macro-cultures. This view is based mainly on the fact that China and Japan begin to exercise their role of Great Powers while most of the other peoples of Asia and Africa have attained their independence at least in a formal-legal sense. Two particularly important aspects of the most recent past need to be stressed. On the one hand, cultural encounters play a central role in international co-operation for development which has been launched in the late 1940s. More precisely the problem is that of a massive western cultural export being part of a relationship which, in formal-legal terms, brings together equal partners. This question has been dealt with elsewhere, but we shall return to it briefly further on.[21]

---

[20] *e.g.* D. Krusche, *Japan-Konkrete Fremde: Eine Kritik der Modalitäten europäischer Erfahrung von Fremde* (1973); T. Leuenberger, *Kriege um den Frieden in Ostasien* (1973), ch. 3.

[21] R. Preiswerk, *Entwicklungshilfe als Kulturbegegnung* (1972).

On the other hand, cultural encounters cannot go unnoticed in the creation of an international legal order. Older natural law theories were distinctively ethnocentric, because they postulated a God-given (given by a Christian God) or universally valid human reason as the basis of a legal order. The present foundations are essentially different, but in many respects no less ethnocentric. Thus the famous Article 38 of the Statute of the International Court of Justice, which mentions, as a source of international law, the general principles of law recognised by " civilised nations." [22] In the 1960s, it was the merit of the Hague Academy of International Law to promote works on Buddhist, Hindu and Islamic conceptions of law. Approximately in the same period, one can situate the point from which the codification of international law was undertaken with the participation of State communities representative of cultural differences.

In this connection, it may be in order to mention that certain legal norms and rules of diplomatic intercourse considerably hamper intercultural relations. State authorities frequently adopt the point of view that communication with other peoples may only take place through official channels. A case in point is the debate on the recently proposed law on co-operation between Switzerland and the developing countries. The demand, raised in various circles, that the law should express the principle of co-operation with the poorest segments of the population in the countries concerned, was already rejected at the drafting stage. The reason for this was the fear of interference in domestic affairs of partner States. The justification for such an argument can be based only on diplomatic, not even on legal, considerations. What should be stressed, however, is that in this way, the views of governments in the developing countries are in most cases accepted as solely authoritative. This means that one takes sides in the domestic cultural encounters between the élite and the mass (the " westernised " against the " traditional ") as well as in the political power relationship between the governing and the governed. Very often, existing structures are legitimised and consolidated through foreign contributions. Not only international law, but even simple rules of diplomatic relations on the level of protocollary behaviour, fulfil functions of ideological legitimisation.

The student of international relations may object that some topics deemed worthy of enquiry from the point of view of intercultural relations, have been dealt with already. In many instances, this is indeed the case. But one should not forget that the emphasis is different and that new insight can be gained with the help of methods that hitherto have been neglected in the study of international

---

[22] D. Frei, *Zur Regelung der Gewaltanwendung* (1972), p. 29.

relations. Even if the object of study is the same, the viewpoint and methodologies are different.

In two respects, the 13 construed linkages do not completely cover the issue raised. On the one hand, the international consequences of intercultural relations within a State are of particular interest. South Africa, whose apartheid policy is an important factor in the determination of its international position, is a striking example. Many other internal crises, such as the Biafra conflict or the situations in Pakistan (separation of Bangladesh), Cyprus or Northern Ireland, also illustrate this point. On the other hand, there is the question of the cultural foundations of internationalist endeavours. Is there an international public opinion and an " international conscience," or are these mere projections of the West on opinion-forming classes in other countries? If one pays so much attention to cultural differences, does a basis for the codification of human rights exist at all? Such vital questions can only be raised here, because the study of a possible universal culture has hardly commenced.

## IV—CENTRAL CONCEPTS
### IN THE STUDY OF INTERCULTURAL RELATIONS

Similarly to individual scientific disciplines, a multi-disciplinary field must have at its disposal central concepts as instruments for describing insufficiently apprehended factual material. Although such a conceptual framework does not yet exist in a coherent form for use in intercultural relations, we can nevertheless indicate four groups of relatively closely linked concepts:

(1) With *cognitive ethnocentrism* we designate the attitude of placing the culture of one's own group in the upper part of a hierarchy and of viewing other cultures through one's own frame of reference. It is based on *mental images* which the observer has acquired largely under the influence of his in-group and which inadequately represent other groups in so far as they consist of insufficient factual material, subjective valuations, stereotypes and prejudice. With this concept, the distortion of the object of study " foreign culture " can be examined at all levels of cognition: not only in everyday sensory perception (which, in an intercultural context, becomes an extraordinarily complex matter), but in conceptualisation, theory formation and scientifically founded empirical investigation.

(2) Intercultural understanding, or *empathy*, depends on group ideology as well as on the cognitive style and affective constellation of the individual. This is related to the problem of *cultural distance*, not to be understood in the evolutionist sense—*i.e.* that certain cultures are " ahead " of others in the progression towards an ideal model—but simply as the extent of differences with respect to all

imaginable spheres of culture. Gerhard Maletzke expresses this when he makes intercultural understanding, misunderstanding or non-understanding dependent " upon the extent of common traits and differences in frames of reference, value systems, world views of the cultures involved, upon their cognitive and affective distance. . . ." [23] *Culture shock* may consequently be defined as the sudden awareness of a strongly felt cultural distance. Among the categories of inter-cultural problems linked to international relations, some show a weak cultural distance (A-B, A-E, E-D, C-D, etc.), whereas others are marked by large differences, or can be marked so depending on the partner States (C-F, C-G, D-H, E-H).

(3) With the issue of culture, the question of *group identity* arises. [24] Each individual takes part in a variety of groups (according to sex, age, class, profession, etc.). In addition, the question of cultural identity arises at each of the four levels from micro-culture to macro-culture. Furthermore, each culture is continuously changing and the individual at least partially adapts to new cultural models through *internalisation*. When he becomes aware that a considerable cultural distance exists between various internalised cultural elements, the possibility of an *identity crisis* arises. In this case, he no longer knows to which cultural area he wants to belong. An identity crisis has hit many of the post-colonial élites in new States. Minorities in western States raise similar questions (Indians and Blacks in the United States, Basques in Spain, Jews in the Soviet Union, etc.).

(4) A particularly difficult and, as already pointed out, a relatively unexplored question is that of a world or *universal culture*. In the most diverse cultures, and certainly not only in the West, people imagine the whole world to be only just what the world image pro-duced by their own culture allows to permeate. This is ethnocentrism resulting from a lack of differentiation. In more recent times, another idea of world culture has emerged. It is based on the opinion, current in the West and among westernized élites in the so-called developing countries, according to which there is a progressive elimination of cultural differences.

Although one should be wary of phenomena said to be universal and concepts propounded as universally valid, the increasing significance of *intercultures* should not be denied. Besides the vertical culture delimitations stressed so far, new horizontal stratifi-cations appear according to interest groups, professional specialisa-tion and social status or role. Intercultural communication geared to

---

[23] Quoted in *op. cit.* in note 8 above, p. 23.

[24] Marisa Zavalloni, " L'identité psycho-sociale, un concept à la recherche d'une science," in S. Moscovici (ed.), *Introduction à la psychologie sociale* (1973); E. Erikson, *Identity: Youth and Crisis* (1968).

specific interests is in many cases more intensive than relations measured with intra-cultural or national criteria. Intercultures are sometimes called international role cultures.[25] It is also interesting to note that some international organisations have made it their aim to create intercultures through congresses, associations and publications of all kinds.[26] From an international standpoint it is particularly interesting that an interculture of development technocrats who, despite many national and cultural differences, share similar views about the development process, has emerged. It is of course, questionable whether such intercultures can resist possible open conflicts of universal significance.

### V—PROSPECTS FOR FUTURE INTERCULTURAL RELATIONS

A world without cultural diversity seems unthinkable today. But on this point also opinions are divided. To conclude, one should indicate at least two clarifying speculative theories.

We designate as " levelling theories " all those attempts which establish, predict or postulate as desirable the birth of a " world society " and the " disappearance of clear group identities." [27] They are predominant in the most diverse western social sciences dealing with non-western societies. In sociology and political science, they often appear with the concept of modernisation. Economists, planners or investors base their practical action on explicit or implicit conceptions which one may call diffusionism or extension theories. According to this view, economic development begins with certain " modern " poles and then spreads gradually to the entire " hinterland." In a new variety, Claude Lévi-Strauss has based a levelling theory on the concept of entropy, borrowed from physics.[28] Generally (but not in the case of Lévi-Strauss),[29] levelling theories have an underlying cultural-evolutionist interpretation of human history, still anchored in nineteenth-century thought. In this view, cultural differences are regarded only as backwardness which is eliminated when societies progress through the same stages the West has known in its own development.

The advocates of levelling theories can advance some overwhelming factual material. It cannot be denied that, today more than ever, a

---

[25] M. Flack, *The Role of Culture in International Operations* (1967).

[26] M. Flack, " Cultural Politics in Discourse: Political Aspects of Communication between Industrialised and Developing Societies," in *Interkulturelle Kommunikation, op. cit.* in note 8 above, p. 117.

[27] J. Habermas, *Kultur und Kritik* (1973), pp. 390, 392.

[28] See J. Grinevald, " L'entropolitique ou la théorie du nivellement politique: Eléments d'épistémologie," 13 *Schweizerisches Jahrbuch für politische Wissenschaft* (1973).

[29] C. Lévi-Strauss, " Race and History," in *The Race Question and Modern Science* (1969).

massive export of culture from the West to the rest of the world takes place. This is very often considered as desirable by the élites of the receiving countries. New developments in science and technology will contribute to an intensification of these exports. Let us think of communication satellites which, according to an expert, will make it possible before the end of the century to receive, in every village of Africa, Asia and Latin America, " television and radio programmes emanating from New York, Hollywood, London, Paris, Moscow, Tokyo, and other localities." [30] The list is significant: the author does not foresee the possibility that any non-industrialised country could produce and diffuse programmes.

In spite of this, it is not frivolous to continue to defend theories of cultural pluralism. These interpretations do not ignore the levelling process, but take into account the considerable resistence of non-Western cultures. In radical opposition to evolutionist thinking, the view is that non-Western peoples can internalise Western culture in the most diverse ways and still retain a certain identity. The orientation towards a single possible model springs from Western cultural arrogance and a naïve-realistic view of processes which all-too-soon are accepted as " evident " and " irreversible."

Some peoples have refused to accept Western culture for centuries. Among Amerindians this resistance went as far as collective suicide. Everywhere, cultural identity movements are manifest. " Negritude," " Black Power," meetings of Afro-Asian writers, attempts of a Julius Nyerere, or a Kenneth Kaunda, to find new development models and a new humanism, the American Indian Movement, separatist movements of all kinds (also in Western countries) are signs of resistance against the predominant societal model in the West. The cultural revolution in China may also be seen as an attempt to retain specificity in the use made of a European-born ideology. Even if Westernised élites in most developing countries have adopted our development models, it is not foreseeable how entire populations will force themselves to collectively negate cultural identity in the name of a new " rationality," welfare and " progress." If culture could be determined ideologically and imposed through social manipulation, one could concur with such a development. But above all culture is the behaviour of a society in a given ecological context (which science and technology can transform only to a limited degree) and the specific historical experience of that society, which is always deeply instilled. Finally, one should remember that the western development model is itself beginning to stagger (environment problems, inflation, psychological problems of individualisation, exhaustion of raw

---

[30] Carroll Newsom, " Communication Satellites: A New Hazard for World Cultures," in 5 *U.N. and Outer Space* (1973), p. 30.

materials and energy resources, etc.) and faces problems of immense dimensions. While most developing countries are desperately trying to become industrial nations, futurology cannot predict conditions in the West even 20 or 30 years hence.

What is certain, if present demographic trends continue, is that in the year 2000, close to 85 per cent. of the world's population will live in countries which one calls today "Third World." Should we truly believe that all these human beings will be oriented towards the same behavioural model, thus making the study of intercultural relations superfluous?

# EQUALITY AND DISCRIMINATION IN INTERNATIONAL ECONOMIC LAW (VIII):

## THE UNITED NATIONS REGIONAL ECONOMIC COMMISSIONS

By

## B. G. RAMCHARAN

This is the eighth contribution to the series on *Equality and Discrimination in International Economic Law*, initiated by Professor Schwarzenberger's paper under this title in the 1971 Volume of this Annual, and continued in the 1972 Volume by G. G. Kaplan on *The UNCTAD Scheme for Generalised Preferences* and B. G. Ramcharan on *The Commonwealth Preferential System*, in the 1974 and 1975 Volumes by P. Goldsmith and F. Sonderkötter on *The European Communities* and *The European Communities and the Wider World*, and in the 1977 Volume by A. Sutton on *Trends in the Regulation of International Trade in Textiles* and C. Stoiber on *The Multinational Enterprise—Managing Editor*, Y.B.W.A.

ACCORDING to Article 12 of the Charter of Economic Rights and Duties of States, " States have the right, in agreement with the parties concerned, to participate in sub-regional, regional and inter-regional co-operation in the pursuit of their economic and social development." [1] The regional economic commissions of the United Nations are the managerial, economic and social development centres within the United Nations system entrusted, within their respective regions, with the formulation, co-ordination and implementation of programmes for the promotion of intra-regional and inter-regional co-operation. In recent years increasing importance has been attached to the role which they should play in implementing United Nations policies and programmes for the establishment of a New International Economic Order and for the promotion of development and international economic co-operation. By its resolution 2043 (LXI) entitled " Strengthening of the regional commissions for regional

---

[1] All views expressed in this paper are those of the author in his personal capacity.

and inter-regional co-operation," adopted on August 5, 1976, the United Nations Economic and Social Council affirmed that the regional economic commissions should exercise team leadership and responsibility for inter-sectoral co-ordination and co-operation at the regional level. The Council requested other relevant organisations in the United Nations system to intensify their co-operation with the secretariats of the regional economic commissions, with a view to making them centres for the formulation, co-ordination and implementation of programmes for the promotion of co-operation among States which are members of the respective commissions.

One of the main concerns of the United Nations in the economic field has been to promote genuine equality in trade and economic relations by removing discriminatory barriers and, where appropriate, by granting preferential treatment to developing countries. This has made the issue of equality and discrimination a central question of international economic law. In this paper we shall look at some of the issues of equality and discrimination which have arisen in the work of the regional economic commissions of the United Nations.[2]

---

[2] See generally: *Documents* E/5607 and Corr. 1 and Add. 1–2: Report of the Joint Inspection Unit on the Decentralisation of the United Nations Economic, Social and Related Activities and the Strengthening of the Regional Economic Commissions: Note by the Secretary-General; E/5727 and Add. 1–2: Reports of the Joint Inspection Unit; Report on the Regional Structures of the United Nations System; E/5801: Regional Co-operation: Regional Structures of the United Nations System: Report of the Secretary-General; E/5835 and Corr.1, and Add.1; E/Res.1756 (LIV): Study on Regional Structures; E/Res/2043 (LXI): Strengthening of the regional commissions for regional and interregional co-operation.
*Annual Reports*: (1970–1976) *ECE*: E/4822; E/5001; E/5136; E/5276; E/5470; E/5651; E/5781.
*ECLA*: E/4806; E/4883; E/5027 and Add.1; E/5135; E/5275; E/5495; E/5608; E/5784.
*ECA*: E/5824; E/4997; E/5117; E/5253; E/5471; E/5687; E/5783.
*ESCAP*: E/4823; E/5020; E/5134; E/5277; E/5469; E/5656.
*ECWA*: E/5539 (1974); E/5658; E/5785.
*The Work of the United Nations Economic Commission for Europe, 1947–1972*, United Nations Publications, Sales Nr. 72.II.E.3.
*United Nations Economic Commission for Latin America*, United Nations Office of Public Information, OPI/227 (1966).
*ECAFE in Brief* (1972).
E/ECE/574, *Compendium of ECE Resolutions*.
E/ECE/642, *Studies and other publications issued under the auspices of the ECE, 1947–1967*.
*Multilateral Economic Co-operation in Latin America*, United Nations Publication, Sales Nr. 62.II.G.3.
*The United Nations Economic Commission for Africa*, United Nations Office of Public Information, OPI/330 (1969).
*Books and Articles*
J. S. Magee, " ECA and the Paradox of African Co-operation," *International Conciliation*, Nr. 561, January 1967.
J. Siotis, " ECE in the Emerging European System," *International Conciliation*, Nr. 561, January 1967.
D. Wightman, " Toward Economic Co-operation in Asia," *The United Nations ECAFE* (1963).

I—NATURE AND FUNCTIONS
OF THE REGIONAL ECONOMIC COMMISSIONS

The regional economic commissions of the United Nations consist of the Economic Commission for Africa (ECA), the Economic and Social Commission for Asia and the Pacific (ESCAP),[3] the Economic Commission for Europe (ECE), the Economic Commission for Latin America (ECLA) and the Economic Commission for Western Asia (ECWA).

The Economic Commission for Europe was the first to be created, in 1947, with the primary task of dealing with problems of post-war reconstruction in Europe. Following the period of reconstruction, the Commission became increasingly a major instrument for regional economic co-operation, especially between countries with different economic and social systems. ECLA was created in 1948, ESCAP (ECAFE) in 1947, ECA in 1958 and ECWA in 1973.

The terms of reference of the five regional commissions, as laid down by the Economic and Social Council are basically similar but they do provide for regional differences. The principal functions of the regional commissions are identical inasmuch as they are called upon, in their respective regions, to initiate and participate in measures facilitating concerted action for economic development and for raising the levels of economic activity. They are required to initiate and participate in measures for maintaining and strengthening the economic relations of the countries in their respective regions, both among themselves and with other countries of the world. The five commissions also have similar terms of reference with respect to: (1) making or sponsoring investigations and studies of economic and technological problems and developments within their respective regions; (2) undertaking or sponsoring the collection, evaluation and dissemination of such economic, technological and statistical information as the commissions deem appropriate. The terms of reference give the four regional commissions that serve the developing areas broad functions relating to technical co-operation and other forms of operational activities. Practical action for the promotion of development is one of the basic tenets in the commissions' activities.[4]

When ECA and ECWA were established, in 1958 and 1973 respectively, the Economic and Social Council provided in their terms of reference that in carrying out their functions these commissions should " deal as appropriate with the social aspects of

---

[3] Prior to 1974, this Commission was known as the " Economic Commission for Asia and the Far East " (ECAFE). In 1974, the Economic and Social Council adopted resolution 1895 (LVII) changing the name of the Commission to the Economic and Social Commission for Asia and the Pacific.

[4] E/5081, paras. 9–10.

economic development and the interrelationship of the economic and social factors." The Council added that provision to the terms of reference of ECAFE and ECLA in resolution 723 (XXVIII), after it had referred the matter to those commissions and to ECE for their consideration and advice. In the absence of any recommendation on the question from ECE, no change was made in that commission's terms of reference.

Since their establishment, the regional commissions have been adapting their activities to the changing economic and social conditions in their respective regions and adjusting their work to the realities, needs and aspirations of the regions they serve.

## II—EQUALITY AND DISCRIMINATION

### (a) *Implementation of global economic policies and programmes*

In the Programme of Action on the Establishment of a New International Economic Order which was adopted on May 1, 1974, the General Assembly of the United Nations pledged to make full use of the United Nations system in the implementation of the programme and in working for the establishment of a New International Economic Order.[5] It entrusted all organisations, institutions, subsidiary bodies and conferences of the United Nations system with the implementation of the Programme of Action.[6] The Economic and Social Council was charged with the task of defining the policy framework and co-ordinating the activities of all such organisations. For this purpose, those organisations, institutions and subsidiary bodies concerned were requested to submit progress reports to the Economic and Social Council on the implementation of the programme at least once a year.[7]

As institutions within the United Nations system, the regional economic commissions are under a duty to implement the programmes and policies of the United Nations for the establishment of a New International Economic Order, particularly as contained in the Declaration on the Establishment of a New International Economic Order (General Assembly resolution 3201 (S-VI); the Programme of Action on the Establishment of a New International Economic Order (General Assembly resolution 3202 (S-VI) ); the Charter of Economic Rights and Duties of States (General Assembly resolution 3281 (XXIX) ); and measures for Development and International Economic Co-operation (General Assembly resolution 3362 (S-VII) ). These resolutions contain a series of provisions providing for various forms of equality and discrimination. Inasmuch as the regional

---

[5] General Assembly resolution 3202 (S-VI), part IX, article 1.
[6] *Ibid.* article 4.
[7] *Ibid.* article 3 (a) and (b).

economic commissions are required to implement these policies they are the general framework for a discussion of equality and discrimination in relation to the work of the regional economic commissions.

The foregoing resolutions of the General Assembly contain more or less the same scheme of equality and discrimination, providing, *inter alia*, for: (1) The general principle of equal treatment in international economic relations except where otherwise provided for; (2) A general prohibition of discrimination except where expressly allowed; (3) Preferential treatment for developing countries; (4) A higher degree of preferential treatment for certain developing countries usually referred to as " the least-developed, land-locked and island developing countries "; (5) Preferences among developing countries *inter se*, particularly within the framework of sub-regional, regional and inter-regional co-operation.

The regional economic commissions, particularly ECLA, ESCAP, ECA and ECWA, have played an important role in the establishment and subsequent development of the Generalised Scheme of Preferences (GSP). As an example of the kind of role which they continue to play, we may note the following passages from the report of ECLA for 1975 on the question of the export of manufactures *vis-à-vis* the operation of the Generalised Scheme of Preferences [8]:

" 76. Efforts to export manufactures to the developed countries should be continued and intensified. Since these are fairly new activities in the developing countries, they should receive compensation for the fact that they are entering the world markets at an initial disadvantage . . . (t)he countries which are not yet in a position to compete on an equal footing with the developed countries should receive compensation for the disadvantage at which they find themselves. This compensation should take the form of preferential treatment of the developing countries to grant incentives to their export industries. In turn, the developing countries should grant adequate subsidies within reasonable limits."

" 77. One of the important elements of the special treatment afforded to exports of manufactures from the developing to the industralised countries is the Generalised System of Preferences . . ."

" 78. The experience of recent years, during which the Generalised System of Preferences has been in effect, has brought to light some of its major shortcomings and the modifications that would have to be introduced for the System to become a really effective instrument for expanding the exports of manufactures from the developing countries. Essential improvements that should be considered include the need for the preference schemes to cover numerous products that are

---

[8] E/5608/Rev.1, paras. 76–79.

subject to customs duties (especially processed agricultural goods), the elimination of quota systems, the adoption of principles and norms for resorting to escape clauses, the harmonisation of the preference schemes of various countries, the adoption of more flexible criteria regarding rules of origin, the simplification of administrative formalities for taking advantage of the preferences, the extension of preferential treatment without reciprocity to non-tariff barriers, the establishment of a prior consultation system when for reasons of *force majeure* it becomes necessary to restrict the application of the System, and the adoption of other supplementary measures aimed not only at making better use of the various schemes, but also at institutionalising the Generalised System of Preferences on a firm and clearly defined multilateral basis." [9]

The regional economic commissions have also set about the implementation of the other United Nations policies, programmes and measures referred to earlier. Resolution 3362 (S-VII) of the General Assembly, for example, indicated the overall policy framework for action by the competent bodies and organisations of the United Nations system in the following seven fields: international trade; transfer of resources and international monetary reforms; science and technology; industrialisation; food and agriculture; co-operation among developing countries; and restructuring of the economic and social sectors of the United Nations system. The regional commissions have work programmes and activities with an integrated approach covering the first five fields.

In 1976, the Economic and Social Council (ECOSOC) " noted that the regional economic commissions have been adapting their work programmes and activities to conform to the decisions adopted by the General Assembly." [10]

### (b) *Promotion of Regional Interests*

The regional economic commissions strive to promote the development of their respective regions and to get the most advantageous trade and economic terms for their members. In consequence, some of the commissions have supported, either openly or tacitly the formation of customs unions and free trade areas in their respective regions. ECLA participated actively in the creation of the Latin American Free Trade Association, the Central American Common Market and SELA. It has also co-operated in the implementation of the aims and objectives of the Andean Group and the Caribbean Common Market.[11] ECA rendered technical support for the establishment of

---

[9] See, similarly, the report of ECAFE for 1974, E/5469, para. 34.
[10] ECOSOC resolution 2043 (LXI) of August 5, 1976.
[11] United Nations ECLA, OPI/227, pp. 3–5.

the Economic Community of West African States.[12] Such economic associations have the effect, generally, of granting preferential treatment to their respective members and discriminating against outside countries.

The incidence of such discrimination has arisen frequently within the ECE. Ever since the creation of the European Economic Community and the European Free Trade Area, an issue which has frequently arisen in the ECE has been the allegedly discriminatory effects of these sub-regional régimes on the trade and commercial relations of countries within the ECE not belonging to EEC or EFTA.[13] At its tenth session in 1957, the ECE Committee on the Development of Trade recommended that Governments participating sub-regional economic groups, and those which are non-participants in those groups, should meet as frequently as necessary to solve, according to procedures agreeable to both sides, trade problems arising between them.

The regional economic commissions have recently been requested by ECOSOC " to work out a program of work and priorities for their respective regions in the field of co-operation among developing countries." [14] This has to be done within the framework of relevant policy guidelines laid down by superior organs. In this regard, article 21 of the Charter of Economic Rights and Duties of States provides that " developing countries should endeavour to promote the expansion of their mutual trade and to this end may, in accordance with the existing and evolving provisions and procedures of international agreements where applicable, grant trade preferences to other developing countries, without being obliged to extend such preferences to developing countries, provided these arrangements do not constitute an impediment to general trade liberalisation and expansion." The Declaration on the Establishment of a New International Economic Order states that the New International Economic Order should be founded on full respect for, *inter alia*, the principle of " strengthening through individual and collective actions, of mutual economic trade, financial and technical co-operation among the developing countries, mainly on a preferential basis." In the Programme of Action on the Establishment of a New International Economic Order, the General Assembly invited developing countries to take further steps, *inter alia*, to ensure that no developing country accords to imports from developed countries more favourable treat-

---

[12] A/31/304, para. 31.

[13] See, more recently, ECE report 1974, E/5470, para. 199; P. Goldsmith and F. Sonderkötter, " Equality and Discrimination in International Economic Law " (IV): The European Communities; and (V): " The European Communities and the Wider World," in this *Year Book*, Vol. 28 (1974), p. 262 *et seq.* and Vol. 29 (1975), p. 265 *et seq.*

[14] ECOSOC resolution 2043 (LXI) of August 5, 1976, para. 6.

ment than that accorded to imports from developing countries. Taking into account the existing international agreements, current limitations and possibilities, and also their future evolution, preferential treatment should be given to procurement of import requirements from other developing countries. Wherever possible, preferential treatment should be given to imports from developing countries and the exports of those countries. The General Assembly also invited developing countries to promote close co-operation in the fields of finance, credit relations and monetary issues, including the development of credit relations on a preferential basis and on favourable terms.

The regional commissions are currently engaged in working out their programmes. It can be expected that the foregoing principles concerning preferences among developing countries will feature prominently among them.

### (c) *Intra-regional Perspectives*

In a statement to the 57th session of the ECOSOC in 1974, Mr. E. V. Iglesias, Executive-Secretary of ECLA stated: " Intra-regional co-operation must now cover new areas as well as pressing forward in its present fields. Above all, however, it will be necessary to distinguish clearly between the relative situation of the different countries in order to perfect in consensus the ideal of non-equal treatment for non-equal countries. The perfecting of the concept of preference among the countries [of the region] is absolutely imperative." [15] In a statement to the 61st session of the ECOSOC in 1976, Mr. M. S. Al Attar, Executive-Secretary of ECWA " cited imbalances in economic structures and the persistence of the large income disparities between and within the countries [of ECWA] as being among the serious and long-standing problems facing the region. Kuwait, for example, with a *per capita* income of more than $11,000 was in sharp contrast with Democratic Yemen and the Yemen Arab Republic with *per capita* income levels still below $15." [16] Disparities in the levels of development and available resources are to be found in the membership of all of the regional commissions. In each case arrangements have been made to grant varying degrees of preferential treatment to the less privileged members. The following are some of the techniques which have been utilised for this purpose.

The ECE's Committee on the Development of Trade has studied the trade problems of the least-developed countries of ECE [17] and has made suggestions for dealing with specific problems.[18] The

---

[15] XIX *Economic Bulletin for Latin America* (1974), p. 7.

[16] United Nations Press Release, ECOSOC/810, p. 2.

[17] ECE report, 1968—E/4491, para. 235.

[18] See on this, E/5470, para. 194.

Commission also assists less developed countries outside the ECE region, *inter alia*, by making its accumulated technical and other information and experience more readily available to them.[19]

By resolution 169 (XXXII) of April 2, 1976, entitled " Special measures in favour of the least-developed, land-locked and island countries " the ESCAP, *inter alia*, called on member countries, to the extent possible: (1) to adopt favourable treatment for the least-developed, land-locked and island developing countries to assist in bringing about harmonious and balanced development; (2) to give special attention to the trade requirements of the least-developed, land-locked and island countries; (3) to assist the least-developed, land-locked and island countries of the region in the structural transformation of their economies. It also called on member countries to provide the necessary assistance to land-locked countries of the region through the adoption of practical measures to facilitate their free access to and from the sea, and to alleviate the transit difficulties of the land-locked countries of the region.

### (d) *Inter-regional Perspectives*

We have seen earlier in this paper that developing countries have been seeking from the developed countries better terms of trade and preferential treatment for their products. Nearly all of the developed countries are members of the ECE, the developing countries being members of the remaining commissions. This demarcation is significant because the ECE can, and has, played a significant role as a forum for working out concessions from developed to developing countries. The members of the ECE can work out constructive proposals among themselves.

This spirit was evident at the 31st session of the Commission in 1976. In a message to the session, the Secretary-General, Mr. K. Waldheim, observing that the Commission had made a positive contribution to the work of the United Nations in assisting to establish the guidelines for the implementation of the New International Economic Order,[20] enjoined it as follows: " While the problems facing the Governments of the region are your main priority, it is essential that these should be approached in the context of the wider need to meet the massive economic and social issues which confront the whole international community. In this regard, I am convinced that the Commission can make a major contribution towards reaching this goal." [21] The ECE Secretary, J. Stanovnik, called on the Commission to make the maximum effort possible within its

---

[19] E/5651, para. 173. E/5781, para. 51.
[20] UN press release ECE/GEN/7, March 30, 1976.
[21] *Ibid.*

mandate to contribute to the efforts by the United Nations in implementation of resolution 3362 (S-VII) on development and international economic co-operation.[22] He indicated that the Commission could be of assistance to the less privileged countries outside the ECE region by making accumulated technical and other information and experience more readily available to them, and by more intensive and direct contacts among the secretariats of the regional commissions.[23]

The relationship between ECE and the United Nations Conference on Trade and Development (UNCTAD) may also be mentioned.[24] The ECE has co-operated closely with UNCTAD, both in the preparations for the four general conferences of UNCTAD held up to now, and in the implementation of the programmes of UNCTAD. By resolution 3 (XXIX) of April 30, 1964, for example, the ECE requested its Executive Secretary to award high priority to those activities of the Commission which, within the framework of the Commission's programme of work, might contribute towards the implementation of the recommendations of UNCTAD. The ECE has also instructed its secretariat to respond expeditiously to requests it may receive for assistance on projects or studies of UNCTAD and co-operate in this connection to the fullest extent practicable within its competence and resources. ECE and UNCTAD maintain a joint reference centre in Geneva.

(e) *Countries with Different Economic Systems*

Within the Economic Commission for Europe the most central and crucial issue which has faced it since its establishment has been the relationship between countries with differing economic systems. Much of the history of ECE's activities has been a continuing search for solutions to problems of common concern to these groups of countries, for appropriate forms of contact between them, for methods of exchanging experiences and for techniques and procedures with the help of which specific agreements adjusted to the various interests as well as to the institutional differences involved could be negotiated.[25] The ECE has concentrated on: promoting facilities for trade between centrally-planned and market-economy countries, particularly through the standardisation and unification of trade practices and the development of legal and technical norms applicable to trade relations among them; " clearing house " functions performed by ECE

---

[22] UN press release ECE/GEN/9, March 30, 1976, p. 4.

[23] *Ibid.*

[24] See generally, G. G. Kaplan, " Equality and Discrimination in International Economic Law (II): The UNCTAD Scheme for Generalised Preferences," in this *Year Book*, Vol. 26 (1972), pp. 267–285.

[25] Fifteen years of activity of the ECE. UN publication, Sales Nr. 64.II.E.6, p. 3.

Committees; and efforts designed to eliminate obstacles to trade among countries with different socio-economic systems.[26]

In the early years of the Commission a major source of difficulty between market-economy and centrally-planned countries was the complaint by the East European countries that discriminatory trade and export licensing policies were practised against them. In 1949, a Committee on the Development of Trade was established. It held two sessions in February and May, 1949, but owing to the political climate then prevailing, it did not meet again until 1954. With the " thaw " in East–West relations, it met again in 1954 and has since met regularly. In 1963 the ECE established an *ad hoc* Working Group of Experts to study certain policy problems of East–West trade, including: (1) examination of the role of customs tariffs in the trade of member countries with different economic systems and the bearing of pricing and taxation policies on external trade; (2) the most-favoured-nation principle and non-discriminatory treatment as applied under different economic systems and problems concerning the effective reciprocating of obligations under the different systems; and (3) the possibility of further multilateralisation of trade and payments.[27]

On the first point, the experts agreed that, in negotiations between countries with different economic systems aimed at trade expansion, it was necessary to take into account not only tariffs and the discrimination which might exist in this regard, but also other forms of State policy determining access to markets, and to seek to attain equality of treatment as a basis of undertakings which would have mutual advantages and equivalent trade effects in both types of economy.[28] There was general consensus among the experts that " export-price policies, while permitting fair competition, should not cause injury to the interests of other countries." [29]

In regard to the most-favoured-nation clause, the discussion

[26] J. Siotis, *op. cit.* in note 2 above, p. 23. Rodolphe Nötel, " The Role of the United Nations in the Sphere of East–West Trade," XVIII *Economica Internazionale* (1965).

[27] ECE resolution 4 (XVIII). See also the work of the United Nations Economic Commission for Europe, UN publication Sales Nr. 65.I.10, p. 17. See generally ECE Analytical Report on the State of Intra-European Trade 170; ECE. The work of the Economic Commission for Europe 1947 to 1972 (1972), p. 49. ECE, Analytical Report on industrial co-operation among ECE countries (1973); Economic Bulletin for Europe: Vol. 16, Nr. 2 (1964), pp. 31–87: " Trade problems between countries having different economic and social systems "; Vol. 20, Nr. 1 (1968), pp. 43–54; " Note on institutional developments in the foreign trade of the Soviet Union and East-European Countries "; Vol. 24, Nr. 1 (1972), pp. 36–49: " Recent changes in the organization of foreign trade in the centrally-planned economies "; Vol. 25, (1974), pp. 49–74: " Review of East–West Commercial Policy Developments, 1968–1973."

[28] ECE Doc. TRADE/AD HOC GROUP/1/2, p. 5.

[29] *Ibid.*, p. 6. See Report of the International Law Commission on the Work of its 28th Session (1976), A/31/10, Chap. II: The most-favoured-nation clause.

brought out two problems: (1) the general problem of the significance of the most-favoured-nation provision in the relations between countries with different economic systems; and (2) the special problem of the application of this provision by certain West European countries in connection with their entry into the EEC and EFTA.

Regarding the general question of the meaning of the most-favoured-nation clause as it affects international trade between countries with different economic systems, experts from countries with market economies pointed out that because of the differences in systems it is difficult to define in practical terms and to verify the meaningful application in planned economies of most-favoured-nation undertakings. They also stated that certain provisions of bilateral trade and payments agreements may lead to practices difficult to reconcile with the most-favoured-nation principle.

The experts from countries with planned economies stated that there was no difficulty in applying the most-favoured-nation principle in countries with planned economies, or in verifying that real benefits were granted under this principle to exporters from countries with market economies: foreign trade organisations were autonomous bodies obliged by law and regulations to operate according to commercial considerations, and the planning of import policy did not discriminate between foreign suppliers or fail to take into account the availability and prices of goods which could be imported. They pointed out that quotas and quantitative indications in bilateral trade and payments agreements did not mean that foreign trade transactions would take place under other than competitive conditions; these provisions of bilateral agreements were not in any sense discriminatory and had never been regarded as involving practices incompatible with the most-favoured-nation principle. They also pointed out that the application to their countries of discriminatory quantitative restrictions and tariffs in certain market economies was incompatible with the principle of most-favoured-nation treatment and that such practices took place in spite of provisions in bilateral agreements or, in the case of Czechoslovakia, also of the GATT.

The experts from countries with planned economies stated further that a number of countries in Western Europe which, under bilateral agreements, had undertaken to apply to countries with planned economies most-favoured-nation treatment in the matter of tariffs, were unjustifiably violating these undertakings in connection with their entry into the EEC and EFTA, thus hindering the normal development of East–West trade.

The experts from the countries with market economies argued that there were certain recognised exceptions to the most-favoured-nation obligation, such as customs unions and free trade areas, purchases by government agencies for their own use, some traditional preferences as in regard to the Commonwealth, and the franc zone.

The experts from countries with planned economies replied that unconditional most-favoured-nation treatment was a basic element in international trade relations. It comprised non-discriminatory treatment in regard not only to tariffs but to other trade facilities as provided normally in existing trade agreements. In some agreements exceptions to the rule are recognised to be justified for customs unions, frontier trade and trade between neighbouring countries, etc., but these exceptions must be specifically agreed as such. If questions arise concerning the detailed application of the most-favoured-nation principle or exceptions to the principle, they should be settled by negotiation between the States concerned. The argument that, as a customs union, the EEC fell outside the régime of the most-favoured-nation clause was untenable, they said, since the EEC could not be regarded as a customs union either in substance or in form. As to the common trade policy of the countries members of the EEC towards third countries, they pointed out that some points of this policy provided for discriminatory treatment towards them. The proposals made in connection with the above considerations by a number of planned-economy countries to certain West European countries regarding the carrying out of bilateral negotiations on customs tariff questions were designed to promote the development of trade with those countries on a basis of mutual advantage and non-discrimination.

The experts from countries with market economies replied that customs unions and free trade areas constituted rightful exceptions to the clause, on the basis either of customary international law and/or of multilateral conventional law (in particular the GATT) and bilateral agreements (many treaties as for example the commercial agreement between France and the Soviet Union provide for an exception in favour of customs unions). This exception clearly applied to the measures necessary for the purpose of the establishment of these unions or areas, for otherwise their formation would in practice be prevented since such formation virtually necessitated a period of transition. Consequently, the member-States of the European Economic Community and of the European Free Trade Association were not legally bound to extend to the third countries to which they granted most-favoured-nation treatment, the special régime applied between the signatory States of the Treaties of Rome and of Stockholm. They observed that judgments on the legitimacy of exceptions to the most-favoured-nation clause benefiting customs unions or free trade areas and applied in a manner which discriminated according to the particular countries comprising these groups, would constitute specific violations of most-favoured-nation treatment. They noted with interest the proposal that these divergencies of views should be settled by negotiation between States.

Following the discussion there was a general consensus that detailed talks on the theoretical concept of the most-favoured-nation clause and its application in trade between countries with different economic systems would be less profitable than a realistic and practical approach to the subject. It was agreed that the general objective should be to achieve an equitable and mutually advantageous balance and increased trade on the basis of the principle of the most-favoured-nation concept. To this end it would be useful to work out a *quid pro quo* technique for negotiating multilaterally meaningful and balanced concessions on the basis of effective reciprocity under different economic systems. The experts agreed that at a future date a review should take place jointly of practical problems involved in the application of the most-favoured-nation principle; such a review should concentrate on the main obstacles to trade expansion, and on establishing a basis for negotiations to remove trade obstacles to the maximum extent possible under prevailing conditions.

The *ad hoc* Group also examined the problem of effective reciprocity in trade and trade obligations of countries with different systems. Although the experts understood and interpreted this concept somewhat differently—in the opinion of the experts of countries with planned economies, it signified trade conducted on the basis of mutual advantage and equality, while, in the opinion of the experts of countries with market economies, it also signified the practical equivalence of advantages and obligations received and granted— they agreed on the following: (1) The aim should be to achieve effective reciprocity/mutual advantage by means of a realistic and practical approach to this problem both in intergovernmental negotiations and in joint discussions within the framework of the ECE and/or other appropriate bodies; (2) Effective reciprocity/ mutual advantage should be measured in terms of concrete and comparable results, *i.e.* the increase in the volume and composition of trade between countries with different systems which would satisfy the trading partners and would serve as a basis for its further development on a long-term and balanced basis; (3) The acceptance of mutual obligations with respect to the application of the most-favoured-nation treatment, non-discrimination in customs tariffs, quantitative restrictions, licensing etc., will not, however important in themselves, necessarily lead to the desired development of trade. In this connection, it appeared useful that these obligations, whenever possible and appropriate, be accompanied by concrete mutual

commitments of the trading partners intended to result in the maximum increase of the volume and in the widening of the composition
of imports (combined with a corresponding increase in exports). In
endeavouring to achieve trade expansion it is necessary to give due
consideration to the need for a fair degree of continuity and stability
in the pattern and composition of trade.

In the opinion of experts from countries with planned economies,
the most appropriate way of reaching the above-mentioned aims
would be the mutual application of most-favoured-nation treatment,
the removal of discriminatory obstacles to trade, the conclusion of
long-term trade agreements and a more flexible payments system.

The experts agreed that a more continuous and detailed exchange
of information, with due regard to security and commercial-interest
considerations, about the criteria and methods used for national and
regional planning affecting foreign trade, and about foreign trade and
market policies and practices, could substantially influence the
development of commercial relations between countries with different
economic systems.

At its next meeting from November 30 to December 11, 1964, the
*ad hoc* Group proposed certain measures for attaining a further
expansion of trade between ECE countries having different economic
systems by adopting practical measures in view of the application of
the most-favoured-nation clause. In their comments on the report,
certain countries felt that the *ad hoc* Group had gone too far in
elaborating its suggestions, especially those on the application of the
most-favoured-nation clause and on multilateralisation of trade and
payments.[30] The largest group of countries agreed with the substance
of the experts' conclusions and was prepared to go a step further.
They declared that, on the basis of the *ad hoc* Group's work, " specific
recommendations should now be drawn up for the removal of economic, administrative, and trade policy obstacles . . ." [31] A third group
of countries expressed the point of view that the Committee on the
Development of Trade " should begin to draft concrete recommendations aimed at removing trade barriers on the basis of the UNCTAD
recommendations." [32]

In resolution 8 (XX) [33] of May 8, 1965, the Commission requested
the Committee on the Development of Trade to indicate to the *ad hoc*
Group areas where it should concentrate its work and decided that
the Group should continue in being for a further period. At the
Committee's 14th session it could not reach agreement on recommen-

[30] E/ECE/553/Add. 3.
[31] E/ECE/581, p. 48.
[32] E/ECE/581, p. 48.
[33] E/4031, para. 219.

dations or on problems for future study and consequently the *ad hoc* Group was not reconvened.[34] At the 15th session of the Committee, a contact group was appointed to seek an accord on recommendations, but was also unable to reach agreement or produce an agreed text.[35]

In 1967, the ECE adopted a Declaration to celebrate the 20th anniversary of the Commission, paragraph three of which stated that " the member countries of the ECE shall . . . continue their common efforts towards the expansion of trade and to this end shall seek to remove the economic, administrative and trade policy obstacles to the development of trade." [36] At the same session the ECE adopted resolution 2 (XXII) in which, wishing to assist member countries in their efforts to give effect to the provision just stated, it decided to convene, prior to the 16th session of the Committee on the Development of Trade, a meeting of governmental experts from any ECE member country interested in participating, with the mandate of drawing up, for the consideration of the Committee on the Development of Trade at its 16th session, practical proposals, including possible draft recommendations, for the removal of the economic, administrative and trade-policy obstacles to the development of trade.

The meeting, which was held in September 1967, produced no useful results, however.[37] On May 2, 1968, the Commission adopted resolution 1 (XXIII) in which it: " invited countries members of the Commission to take all possible measures to permit a broad expansion of intra-European trade, which could bring them considerable economic advantages and would be likely to contribute to the strengthening of peaceful and friendly relations. It requested the Committee on the Development of Trade to continue its efforts with a view to the preparation of mutually acceptable recommendations on the removal of economic, administrative and trade policy obstacles to the development of trade between countries with different economic and social systems, and drew the attention of the Committee to the desirability of preparing practical measures which would contribute to the further development of trade, and in particular to the importance which a study of the following problems might have: the use of long-term agreements and contracts in economic and trade relations between countries with different economic and social systems; long-term export and import forecasts for certain categories of goods; the practices followed for trade in machinery, equipment, patents and licences, having regard to the growing importance of industrial and commercial co-operation; measures likely to facilitate the development of contacts between businessmen."

---

[34] E/4177, paras. 208–209, E/ECE/TRADE/80.
[35] ECE Report 1967, E/4329, para. 190.
[36] E/4329, para. 260.          [37] E/4491, para. 226.

Issues of equality and discrimination continue to be of importance in the work of the ECE. Some of the most important questions of international political and economic relations are considered within the ECE. Relations between the United States and the Soviet Union, for example, have been seen to depend, partly, in recent years upon the question of most-favoured-nation treatment for the Soviet Union. One of the negotiating forums where this issue has been discussed has been the ECE. In 1974, for example, a number of East-European delegations emphasised that the removal of discriminatory practices and the full application of most-favoured-nation treatment were indispensable for the normalisation of trade relations between countries having different economic and social systems and for the sustained expansion and diversification of trade. Other West-European delegations could not, however, agree with the implication that the remaining quantitative import restrictions which their governments still maintained on certain goods, constituted an unjustified obstacle to the development of trade with East-European countries, those restrictions being the consequence, they asserted, of the different nature of the economic systems involved.[38]

In 1976, some delegations in the ECE emphasised the great importance they attached to action being undertaken with a view to the reduction or progressive elimination of all kinds of obstacles to the development of trade and recalled in this connection the relevant provisions of the Helsinki Final Act. A number of delegations stated that in their view progress towards the elimination of discriminatory restrictions during the past year had been slow and that certain countries had introduced new obstacles adversely affecting traditional trade flows. These delegations maintained that international contractual obligations and, in particular, those concerning the accordance of the most-favoured-nation treatment should be faithfully observed. The delegation of the Soviet Union emphasised the necessity of eliminating discrimination and all artificial barriers in international trade, and all manifestations of inequality.[39] The issues are still very current.

The relationship of the concept of reciprocity to that of equality is also still very current. The view was recently advanced that the harmonious development of East–West trade must be inspired by the concept of improving access to markets under conditions of effective reciprocity.[40] In the ECE in 1976, the delegate of Hungary called attention to the fact that in the Helsinki Final Act the notion of reciprocity was strictly linked with the principle of equality and with

---

38 E/5470, para. 189.
39 E/5781, para. 225.
40 E/5470, para. 190.

that of the respect for bilateral and multilateral agreements. He stressed that a genuine reciprocity could prevail only in conditions of non-discrimination and of faithful observance of international contractual obligations.[41] It has also been suggested, however, that a search for a precise and legalistic balancing of rights and obligations is likely to be less rewarding, if only because of difficulties in translating concepts into practically comparable practices in the two types of economy, than attempts to assure by other means an effective reciprocity over the whole field.

### III—CONCLUSIONS

The issues of equality and discrimination which have arisen in the work of the regional economic commissions of the United Nations are a mirror of the main issues in international economic relations generally.

The regional economic commissions operate within the frame-work of policies decided upon by the superior organs of the United Nations, such as the General Assembly and the Economic and Social Council. In so far as they touch on equality and discrimination, these policies mesh, on the whole, with the interests of the regional economic commissions and their respective member-States. With the partial exception of the ECE, the members of the regional economic commissions are mostly developing countries striving to be able to co-exist in the economic world and seeking to accelerate their development. The ECE also shares a desire to help these countries.

In terms of their impact on the formation and implementation of policies involving equality and discrimination, the regional economic commissions are mostly concerned to obtain preferential treatment for their developing members in order to enable them to co-exist on a basis of meaningful equality and in order to accelerate their economic development. They also strive for a requisite amount of equity in international economic relations in seeking to obtain special treatment for the least developed or particularly disadvantaged countries.

The ECE has done important work in seeking to arrange for the conduct of trade and economic relations between centrally-planned and market-economy countries on an equal and non-discriminatory basis. It will be of interest to observe the continuing effort within the ECE to promote East-West trade on mutually favourable terms and to eliminate restrictive and discriminatory practices. Another area of interest will be to observe how the regional commissions proceed to lend permanence to preferential treatment for their respective developing countries in the context of co-operation among developing countries.

---

[41] E/5781, para. 228.

# ARE DEVELOPING STATES MORE EQUAL THAN OTHERS?

By

## WERNER LEVI

THE developing States have become aware of the realities of their situation and are demanding justice and equal treatment as a matter of right, announced Salvador Allende of Chile to the 27th opening session of the United Nations General Assembly. An Algerian Minister of Justice, Mohammed Bedjaoui, defined as the basic goal of new States the purification of traditional relationships between States of " unequal content." [1] The new States have opted, as one of their spokesman expressed it, to reconcile the irreconcilable by complementing the commonly accepted legal equality of States with their factual equality. [2] In taking this stance, the new States are embracing and furthering equality, at least among States, as an objective of civilised ambition, together with liberty—already partially achieved—and fraternity—yet to be adopted. At the same time they are also exploiting the demand for equality as " the most powerful moral imperative of our time." [3] They seem undaunted by failures of men in the past to rationalise the postulation of equality among men and nations in the face of their unequal endowments. And they are certainly unwilling to accept that the facts of international life in the past must be the conditions of the future; when the major Powers, with the acquiescence of the minor States, directed the affairs of the world. The developing States have made equality as a right of States the leitmotif of their appeals, agitation, and argumentation in all international councils.

---

[1] M. Bedjaoui, " Problèmes récents de succession d'états dans les états nouveaux," Académie de Droit International, *Recueil des Cours*, 130 (1970 II) p. 469.

See also the series on *Equality and Discrimination in International Economic Law*, initiated by Professor Schwarzenberger's paper under this title in the 1971 Volume of this Annual, and continued in the 1972 Volume by G. G. Kaplan on *The UNCTAD Scheme for Generalised Preferences* and B. G. Ramcharan on *The Commonwealth Preferential System*, in the 1974 and 1975 Volumes by P. Goldsmith and F. Sonderkötter on *The European Communities* and *The European Communities and The Wider World*, in the 1977 Volume by A. Sutton on *Trends in the Regulation of International Trade in Textiles* and C. Stoiber on *The Multinational Enterprise*, and in this Volume by B. G. Ramcharan on *The United Nations Regional Economic Commissions*. See also J. Stone, *Of Law and Nations* (1974), pp. 365–369.

[2] B. Boutros-Ghali, " Le principe d'égalité des états et les organisations internationales," Académie de Droit International, *Recueil des Cours*, 100 (1960 II) p. 30.

[3] Z. Brzezinski, " U.S. Foreign Policy: The Search for Focus," 51 *Foreign Affairs* (1973), p. 726.

## I—LAW AS A POLITICAL TOOL

The principle of equality must have a place in the legal formulation of the reciprocal rights and obligations of States, affirmed the Yugoslav delegate at an international law conference, and he submitted a clause for international agreement that every State is entitled to the assistance of the international community in making equality effective. Czechoslovakia, with the strong support of the developing States asserted at the same conference that international co-operation towards such an end was not merely a moral or political concept but a part of international law.[4] The " Group of 77 " developing countries, comprising few paragons of democracy, announced at the United Nations Conference on Trade and Development (UNCTAD) that " developing countries attach cardinal importance to democratic procedures which afford no position of privilege in the economic and financial, no less than in the political sphere." [5] In a great many variations, this theme recurs over and over again.

There are precedents for the practice of these States to use international law for the achievement of political goals. One of its last dramatic illustrations was the opposition of the smaller States at the San Francisco Conference on the United Nations to the preferential treatment of the major nations. The developing States are now hoping, by committing States legally to some basic changes in the international legal system, to legitimise favourable unequal and special treatment of them with the aim of overcoming underdevelopment.

In contrast to past demands, the new States have in mind legal commitments much broader than the traditional " sovereign equality." They include equality in the economic and social sphere, or more broadly still a general obligation to " narrow the gap " between developing and developed States.[6] " Le principe égalitaire devra de plus en plus se charger d'un sens concret pour devenir une égalité de conditions au lieu et en place d'une égalité de droits," wrote Boutros-Ghali.[7]

The attempt of the developing States to begin solving their problem of material inequality by legal means is a reversal of the historical process. In the past, developed States established their superiority *de facto* and thereafter reinforced it by foisting discriminatory,

---

[4] United Nations, 1966 A/AC. 125/SR. 34, p. 5; 1964 A/5746 p. 149. Communist states generally support the positions of the Third World States. Because the Chinese make " mutual benefit " an integral part of the concept " equality " they should have difficulty supporting the unilaterally favourable demands of the Third World. *Cf.* J. A. Cohen and H. Chiu, *Peoples China and International Law* (1974), pp. 131–132; G. Kaminski, *Chinesische Positionen zum Völkerrecht* (1973), pp. 168, 199–217.

[5] UNCTAD, March 23–June 16, 1964. Final Act. Report, vol. I, E/Conf. 46/141, p. 67.

[6] United Nations, 1964, A/AC. 119/SR. 35, p. 10.

[7] Boutros-Ghali, " Le principe d'égalité," p. 12.

unfavourable and unequal treaties on the dominated States. The law was used to confirm and legalise an existing situation. The developing States want to bring about a desired situation with the help of law. But their conception of material equality in a very broad sense could hardly be more than a political slogan. Without further definition it could not be operated as a legal obligation. As long as this equality remained little more than an exhortation (that is until quite recently), the developing States could exclaim it in unison while the developed States could sign resolutions containing it without much risk. An undefined equality imposed no specific legal obligation to implement any promise. Yet the developing States were untroubled for a long time by the difficulty of specifying either the kind or the substance of the equality they were demanding. Perhaps they were satisfied with creating a moral atmosphere in which then to make very concrete demands. They seemed reluctant to define their ultimate goals, except for their insistence on the " narrowing of the gap " in the name of justice. Gradually, and presumably in the face of no favourable response to the general demand for equality, the developing States provided particulars.

## II—THE DEMAND FOR POLITICAL EQUALITY

The developing States are freely and voluminously elaborating on the means by which they propose to bring about equality. They are much more generous in outlining with considerable detail the behaviour they expect from the developed States than in itemising what their own contributions could be. They have drawn up a long catalogue of actions to which the developed States are to be committed. This catalogue is publicised on every possible occasion, so that it can be found in many international documents, though rarely anywhere else. Among these more important documents are the 1967 Charter of Algiers of the " Group of 77 "; the 1971 International Development Strategy for the Second United Nations Development Decade; the 1971 Declaration and Principles of the Action Program of Lima; and the " Manila Declaration " of the " Group of 77 " of February 1976. Parts of the catalogue can also be found in resolutions of regional organisations in Asia, Africa and Latin America; in declarations of meetings of Third-World States; or in the records of international agencies and committees, especially those dealing with trade, development, and the codification of international law.

In the sphere of politics, the developing States are exploiting the idea of " sovereign equality " to the utmost, providing always that doing so furthers their aspirations. They are jealously guarding their " personality " and are highly sensitive to any reference touching their internal affairs. They would, for instance, on this ground, strongly reject proposals for the pursuit of internal or external economic policies which they do not hesitate to prescribe for the developed States. Interference with sovereign equality is liberally defined, to the point of almost suspending the very existence of politics (if politics is defined as involving, minimally, an attempt by one party to influence another).

The extreme sensitivity of these States was very evident during a discussion of the legal regulation of force. Like all States they confessed opposition to the use of force in international relations. But unlike other States, they included all forms of political or economic pressure in the definition of force. Such an extensive interpretation was alleged to be in line with today's " dynamism." Under modern conditions, they argued, the result of economic pressure is equivalent to the use of physical violence in the past. It must, therefore, be prohibited as the illegal use of force. Some of these States consequently supported a legal norm prohibiting " all forms of economic and political pressure." Others were willing to qualify the prohibition by adding: " which have the effect of threatening the territorial integrity or political independence of any State." [8] Such a norm could make international politics illegal, since any attempt at influence could be interpreted as pressure. That these States have no intention of consistently adhering to such a norm was demonstrated, *e.g.* by their demand for forceful British intervention in Rhodesia, their applauding the Arab oil boycott during 1973–74, or generally their militant, even bellicose stance towards South Africa and Portugal (before the liberation of Angola).

Another political right demanded in the name of equality is participation of the developing, or, for that matter, of all States in multilateral treaties or international conferences likely to generate important, or generally valid, legal rules. A sovereign right of States to choose their treaty or conference partners is denied. The United Arab Republic insisted that " participation in the formulation of general norms of international law was an inherent right of the independent statehood of sovereign members of the community of nations." With much support from the developing States, Yugoslavia proposed a legal norm to the effect that sovereign equality included " the right to legal equality and to full and equal participation in the life of the community of nations and in the creation and modification of rules of international law." [9]

A rationale for this position is the reluctance of States to be bound by rules in whose creation they had no part. In supporting this

---

[8] United Nations, 1968 A/Conf. 39/7 p. 11; 1966 A/AC. 125/Sr. 25 p. 12, /L23 p. 2, /L21 p. 1, /L16 p. 2.
 [9] United Nations, 1968 A/Conf. 39/11 p. 3.

position, the Soviet Union asserted " all States, as equal members of the international community, had the same right to participate in the settlement of common interest." [10] The claim of developing States is that treaties create situations affecting them as much as if they had been parties. Moreover, they want to use the right to take part in multilateral treaties as a " strategy of participation " (Richard Falk), and as a means of undermining the dominance of the big Powers. These States hope to gain through their legal role access to a political role which their low political status denies them. Their demand implies that equality before the law must imply equality in making it.

A third area within the political sphere in which the strictest equality is demanded is non-interference in domestic affairs. Traumas suffered in the past under colonialism could easily explain strict adherence to the principle. But expediency for political advantage is noticeable here too. Depending on the interests at stake, matters are measured with different rods.

The treatment of racism is most illuminating. The persistent attempts of developing States to intervene against alleged racism in other States or to make political capital of it require no elaboration. Less noted is their almost exclusive concern with white racism against blacks, or its appearance in conjunction with alleged colonialism practised by white, non-communist peoples.[11]

Other forms of racism, such as white against white, black against black, brown against brown, yellow against yellow, or any combination of them have either been ignored or explained away as something else (*e.g.* " aesthetics " in the case of the preference for light Indians in northern India). Typically, the Rapporteur of the Third Committee in a report to the General Assembly (21st session, 1,452nd meeting), stated that there had been general condemnation of the violation of human rights, " but especially and primarily of the policy of racial segregation and discrimination in Southern Rhodesia, in the territories under Portuguese administration and other dependent territories, and of the South African Government's policy of *apartheid*." Immediate complaints of " neo-colonialism," " intervention," " imperialism " about any suggestions of economic measures recipients of foreign aid might take, are daily occurrences.

### III—THE DEMAND FOR ECONOMIC EQUALITY

Economics is, *par excellence*, the sphere in which the developing States are making their demands for unilateral commitments. In the

---

[10] United Nations, 1968 A/Conf. 39/11 p. 2.

[11] G. Ladreit de Lacharrière, " L'influence de l'inégalité de développement des états sur le droit international," Académie de Droit International, *Recueil des Cours*, 139 (1973 II), pp. 250–251.

name of creating substantive equality the " special " treatment expected is fully elaborated and very specifically described. The favours developing States are asking of the developed States are comprehensive. They cover commodity policies, trade in general and particularly in manufactured and semi-manufactured goods, financing, shipping and insurance. The developed countries are to open their markets freely; throttle competition of their own economies with those of developing States; gear their national economies to the needs of the developing economies; grant most-favoured-nation treatment unilaterally; provide guarantees against deteriorating terms of trade; make nominal conditions for financing development projects, with at least 90 per cent. of public development aid to be free gifts or interest-free loans; cancel public debts of the poorest countries; impose a development tax in the developed countries; and obtain prior approval for the application of any escape clauses designed to save the developed economies from danger. The developing countries are to be free to manipulate their internal and external economies unilaterally to their advantage. They may decree prices; use quota systems; interfere in the free market mechanisms; tax imports and exports; increase or decrease production; and make single or collective arrangements to maintain or increase prices on their products.

No immediate or direct returns are offered by the developing countries for all these concessions. They have, however, agreed that " the primary responsibility for their development rests on them " and that they " are determined to contribute to one another's development." The frequency of this assertion is matched by the rarity of its implementation. Few details have ever been outlined on the discharge of this responsibility or on the contributions to mutual aid. Of the 17 objectives enumerated in the " Manila Declaration " of 1976, only one refers—vaguely—to greater economic co-operation among the developing countries. At the Colombo Conference of the Non-aligned Nations (1976), foreign minister Malik of Indonesia called it an " illusion " to think that effective economic co-operation among developing countries was within easy or immediate grasp. When failure to co-operate is mentioned at all, it is always done with some reminder that " a fuller mobilisation and more effective utilisation of domestic resources of developing countries is possible only with concomitant and effective international action " (Charter of Algiers, International Development Strategy), or a warning that the developed countries must abstain " from adopting any kind of measure or action which could adversely affect the decisions of the developing countries in favour of the strengthening of their economic co-operation . . ." (UNCTAD at Nairobi, May 1976). In this manner the blame for inadequate mutual co-operation among developing countries is, at least in part, again placed upon the developed countries.

### IV—ASSUMPTIONS AND PRINCIPLES
### BEHIND THE DEMANDS

Underlying the catalogue of demands for equality are several assumptions; and a few basic principles are consistently applied to bring forth their fulfilment.

The most fundamental assumption is that equality as part of justice is a goal of the international society, and must therefore be a resultant of international law. All States would agree to this assumption, though their behaviour often belies their conviction. This is true of the developing States as well. The extensive one-sidedness of their demands does not quite fit the conceptions of either justice or equality, at least not as these States themselves understand and advocate them. Nor is it altogether justified or relevant on their own grounds. What justification other than political expediency could there be for a double standard on racism, or in condemning economic boycott as aggression only when undertaken by developed States? When the Algerian delegate to the planning conference for a major international energy conference in 1975 remarked, " We have one card to play and that is the energy card. We have to take advantage of it because it won't be good for long," [12] he was advocating economic pressure and possibly boycott otherwise condemned as destructive of equality. More positively, equality is a condition to be achieved by common effort. States must act to produce it and refrain from actions undermining it. Development as a step towards equality requires basic internal effort and reforms in the developing countries no less than the contributions of the developed countries. If it is admissible to remind the developed States of their obligations in this regard, it is no less admissible to do the same towards the developing countries. The developing States consider their demands on the developed States as a rectification of discriminatory and disadvantageous structures and practices—past and still present—in international society. They may well be, but as put forward the catalogue is incomplete, especially in regard to the commitments of the developing States.

Other assumptions (to be discussed later) are that some kind of material, but undefined, equality is possible; and that the developing States are unjustly disfavoured by the prevailing inequalities and the international law which permits their existence.

The foremost principle—to be induced rather than openly expressed—is that developed States must act for the benefit of the

---

[12] *Los Angeles Times* Service, April 12, 1975.

developing States, with little regard for the consequences for the actors. The justification is that the required behaviour may not immediately, but will eventually, benefit all States. The Charter of Algiers avers: " In a world of increasing interdependence, peace, progress and freedom are indivisible. Consequently the development of developing countries will benefit the developed countries as well."

The second principle follows. Reciprocity as a basic condition of international law, if not all international politics, is no longer operative. Indeed, one-sided benefits resulting from one-sided obligations are specifically stipulated in the proposals of the developing countries. The Charter of Algiers, for instance, demands that in discussions on the liberalisation of trade, the principle of reciprocity " should in no way be introduced."

A third principle is that, where (traditionally postulated) absolute " sovereign " equality benefits the developing countries, it is to be scrupulously maintained and interpreted in the most orthodox manner. However, it is laid down in innumerable international resolutions that benefits from equal rights should, as the standard phrase has it, accrue " in particular " to the developing countries— making these in fact more equal than others! This formulation is particularly ironic in regard to ocean resources. For, although these have been declared the " common property of mankind," and are to be explored and exploited for the benefit of mankind, this is to be done " taking into account the special interests of the developing countries, whether land-locked or coastal." [13]

Benefit to the developing countries becomes the major criterion by which international behaviour is to be oriented. It eliminates the dilemma of having to choose between the kinds of equality desired, whether there is to be absolute, commutative equality (an eye for an eye), or distributive equality or compensating inequality (taxes according to ability to pay; support according to need). The developing States expect any kind of equality as long as it assists in their development and advances substantive equality. They apply Jean Jaurès' formula—" la véritable égalité, c'est la proportionnalité "— in the sense that they should be entitled to special privileges where necessary to reach the goal, but should also receive the same privileges when this should be more favourable. This alternative or cumulative equality is needed, they argue, if they are ever to achieve substantive equality.

## V—THE NEW (?) INTERNATIONAL LAW

Granting the demands of the developing States would lead to the disappearance of sovereign equality and reciprocity as hitherto

[13] United Nations resolutions in 1968, 1969, 1970 and on several occasions thereafter.

understood in international relations. The developing States claim that these concepts have been largely formal and meaningless anyway. States, they point out, have always used their power to obtain unilaterally favourable treatment. International courts and arbitrators have recognised the discrepancy between equality in law and in fact.[14] Whether the proposals of the developing States would improve equality and justice in the international system—as they claim—is dubious. More likely, their proposals would perpetuate the present system, albeit with a reversal of its beneficiaries. Inequalities would favour the weaker rather than the stronger States.

The developing States are ahead of the older States—willy-nilly— in basing their demands on a " new " international law of co-operation rather than trying to enforce them by means of arms. This approach may give them high standing in the eyes of moralists, whose influence in world politics is, however, extremely limited. They have achieved very little. " Co-operation for the benefit of mankind," the slogan of the " new " international law, began to become effective only very recently (as will be seen later on) when the developing States finally realised that the international world is not a charitable institution and that reciprocity remains the essential basis for a good deal.

Justification of this complex of demands and counter-demands through equality and justice makes the issue part of the eternal debate over the reconciliation of equality in the name of justice with inequality in fact. The exploitation of law for the solution of this problem is tempting because in the minds of men, equality is related to justice and law is the realisation of justice. Legal philosophers have argued this position and statesmen have occasionally accepted it, not for philosophical but for the practical political reason that it helped them in gaining support for their policies. There can in any case be no doubt that justice can be made operative if it is embedded in legal rules which are obeyed. But it is also true that interests can be satisfied when they are supported—regardless of their justice—by a law that can be enforced. For the one or the other reason (as well as some additional ones), States find it useful to have international law. The developing States accept international law. They do so, like all States, as a political instrument. They naturally wish to make it useful for their purposes. Their efforts in international councils are directed, therefore, towards abolishing unacceptable rules, giving new meaning to old rules, or creating new rules. By shaping law they

---

[14] *Lake Lanoux Arbitration*, 24 *International Law Reports* (1957), p. 126. See also on the problem dealt with here Ladreit de Lacharrière, " L'influence de l'inégalité "; R. A. Klein, *Sovereign Equality among States: The History of an Idea* (1974) pp. 143–168; D. Schröder, *Die Dritte Welt und das Völkerrecht* (1970) pp. 49–63.

hope to shape politics. The quibbling over legal formulations in the General Assembly, the International Law Commision, the United Nations Conference on Trade and Development (UNCTAD), and similar bodies is usually in fact a struggle over substantive political issues. What has the appearance of a conflict over noble moral principles in international relations is frequently a battle over national interests.

The approach of developing States to international law is self-serving. They explicate their interests and the norms needed to serve them. But, like older States, they hesitate to admit selfishness and instead take refuge in the standard diplomatic formula that their interests happen to coincide with those of the international society. Occasionally, clothing the pursuit of selfish interests into high moral principles leads to contradictions—as when special treatment has to be explained in terms of equality. Such difficulties dissolve themselves, however, when the reasoning of these countries is accepted that their goal is to overcome with an expedient change of international law the inequalities inherited from colonial times. To these countries, international law is the means for achieving a balance between the " have " and the " have-not " States. This attempt involves a significant alteration in the international order and, as a prerequisite, a revolutionary change in the motivations which move nations. The welfare of every State ceases to be its own sole responsibility under sovereign independence. It also becomes the responsibility of the community of States in the name of international co-operation. The benefit to the developing States of such an arrangement is obvious as long as the general welfare is to be achieved by a redistribution of the world's existing goods rather than by a common effort to augment the supply of these goods.

There is nothing unusual or disreputable in States trying to formulate or interpret legal norms to suit their interests. Law is not an end in itself. It is always a means for reaching goals. Every law is the end-product of a political process in which usually conflicting interests are defined, evaluated, adjusted and finally firmed in norms. Developing countries accept this process because it enables them to use law occasionally as one of the tools available to them in defence of their interests. It is, however, inevitable that these norms, resulting from political processes, reflect both differing interests as well as differing power potentials between the parties. To the extent that the power available to States is unequal and supports conflicting interests, legal norms will fail to establish substantive, material equality. This condition of international politics makes the developing States, like many smaller or weaker States before them, restive. An amelioration is not likely to come from simple pressure for a reinterpretation of the concept of legal equality, or from demanding legal inequality if it favours the developing States. It has come in the past from balancing power, but was inadequate even then as long as conflicting interests were not balanced by common interests.

Hitherto, laws confirming unequal treaties or the institution of distributive " justice " (*e.g.* weighted voting and veto rights) usually favoured powerful States—reflecting exactly the interest and power relationships of the parties in the traditional manner. The open demand of the developing States for favourable unequal treatment— even if in the name of equality—amounts to a metamorphosis of the formal international legal system. But whether, in an otherwise unchanged nation-State system, the legalisation of inequalities in the name of equality is a desirable way—even if it were feasible—of satisfying " just " claims and promoting general respect for inter- national law, is questionable. The reluctance of most developed States to comply with the broad, general demands of the developing States beyond rhetoric indicates that they too do not cherish being the unfavoured party to unequal treaties. The creation of an un- defined and perhaps undefinable general equality is not a goal to which States are willing to commit themselves legally. In fact, it would be very difficult to discover any legal specific obligation States have entered into for the sake of a high principle like justice. Yet that principle is fundamentally the major justification for the equality demand of the developing States.

## VI—JUSTICE, EQUALITY AND LAW

Appealing to justice for satisfying national interests raises the prob- lem of the individual versus the group. Though for obvious reasons States try to skirt this problem, they occasionally have to face it. Moral principles, in particular, become readily corrupted when they are transferred from application to individuals to such abstract entities as States. The United Nations resolution on International Development Strategy solved the problem by blithely ignoring it. The resolution asserts: " equality of opportunity should be as much a prerogative of nations as of individuals within nations." Such a personification of States—a near-inevitable practice of law for dealing with corporate persons—facilitates the task of statesmen in making demands on behalf of their peoples. But it does not assist, it may even aggravate, resolving many difficulties of determining when equality in justice has been achieved for its beneficiaries who ulti- mately are human beings.

Developing States explain, at any rate, their demand for favoured unequal treatment in part as a retribution for the evils of colonialism and as nullification of neo-colonialism. The underlying belief must be that justice is done when a generation in the developed countries pays for the colonial sins of their fathers or, more likely, great-grandfathers; or, when the problem of moral principles in relation to collectivities is considered, that an entire people is responsible for the sins of the colonialists and neo-colonialists among them. Such collective responsibility has traditionally been posited in international relations and law. But the practice does not very well fit the moral posture many developing States assume, and there are hints (*e.g.* war criminals) that it may be changing. It seems hardly more just to make people in developed countries work for the benefit of developing States than it was to make colonial people work for their foreign masters. This argument appears especially relevant in the absence of guarantees that, first, the conscience money will benefit those suffering most from the legacy of colonialism, and that, secondly, those within developing countries enabling outsiders to be neo-colonialists will have to cease their activities—in other words that justice will indeed be done on all sides. Even then the difficult proof remains to be supplied, if retribution is in deference to justice, that the ills blamed on old and new colonialism are indeed such.[15]

Assuming that it is meaningful to speak of justice among social collectivities, there is the question of what justice is in such a situation. If justice for all is to be served, as States say it must be, equality and inequality can be measured only by some universal standard equally applicable to all States. No such standard exists, nor is one likely to be agreed on in the light of the great differences between States. Measurements along some arbitrarily chosen dimensions are not likely to satisfy the sense of justice of all concerned. There can be agreement, on humanitarian grounds, on the need to raise intolerable standards of living for vast sections of mankind. There is a possibility of agreement also on some minimum standards for reasonably measurable matters of universal interest (*e.g.* nutrition, health, working conditions). But the demands of the developing States are comprehensive and vague, going beyond the limited scope of such standards. On the basis of their proposals, there can be only unending striving among States for " equality " on some undefined and indefinable level. Such a situation is already in an incipient stage among some developing countries, vying for special advantages and preventing regional organisation and co-operation. For example, mutual accusations of breaking pricing agreements have been exchanged among oil producing countries.

---

[15] German payments to Jews, Israel and some countries conquered by them during the Second World War were unusual and part of a special situation. These payments were ordered by occupation authorities, but aso made voluntarily to relieve the conscience of many Germans and to restore Germany's reputation and standing.

Far from resulting in equality, a striving for equality produces jealousies, frustrations and hostilities. The inadequacy of this approach was well illustrated when an extra-special form of special treatment was advocated for the least developed countries, landlocked and island countries and those most seriously affected by the world economic crisis (*e.g.* Manila Declaration), and when sub-categories within existing categories of developing countries (especially in Latin America) formed themselves with some covert and some overt friction resulting. In praising the faithfully observed equality among States in the Organisation of African Unity, Boutros-Ghali speculated with disarming frankness that this might be due to the facts that no African State has yet the power to dominate others or—being preoccupied with internal developments—has not yet the will to do so.[16]

With no definition of the measure by which equality is to be judged, it would be extremely difficult to create a universally acceptable rule of law to make the types of equality demanded by the developing States an obligatory end. With no such end, legal commitments to means for reaching it would lose their *raison d'être.*

There is no way of determining " justly " when an initial inequality has disappeared. Demands for favourable unequal treatment by some States in the name of creating material equality could go on for ever. Because no two States are alike, every State could ask for special treatment to catch up with the conditions, or a particular condition, of the next " higher " State. There will always be a majority of " unequal " States when they choose to compare themselves to the " highest " State on the basis of some selective criterion. The practice of obtaining favourable unequal treatment can then be institutionalised *ad infinitum* in the name of the " new " international law of equality, co-operation and justice. The institution would become a powerful disincentive for States to provide for their own welfare by their own efforts, whether they are developed or developing. The complaint can already be heard within, and even more without, the developing States that they do indeed rely too much on outside assistance and fail to live up to their own recognition that " the primary responsibility for the development of developing countries rests upon themselves."

The German chief delegate to the UNCTAD conference at Nairobi created much discomfort when he explained that the German *Wirtschaftswunder* after the Second World War was achieved by acquiring know-how, working hard, and using foreign aid rationally and sensibly, and implied that developing countries might follow this recipe.

---

[16] B. Boutros-Ghali, *L'organisation de l'Unité Africaine* (1969), p. 41.

## VII—THE RESULT

The chances are that the developing countries will continue to find poor response to their comprehensive demands. The reasons are many. States are notoriously opposed to committing themselves to broad, complex schemes with unforeseeable consequences. States also most rarely engage in activities without some noticeable benefits to their own interests. And impulses towards charity quickly weaken when there are no signs that those in distress strain to overcome their misery.

The strong emphasis of the developing States on legal methods may also be a handicap. By nature and function law is a confirmation of political processes, not their substitute. In trying to bring about a situation with the help of law which has not previously been acceptable politically, they are placing too great a burden on law. Their method is understandable. None of the developing countries is sufficiently powerful to exert significant influence on developed States. Their unity is based on shared resentments and like hopes, not a strong basis for joint political action. Attempts to strengthen it in the image of the Organisation of Petroleum Exporting Countries (OPEC)—itself turning out not to be as solidary as it first appeared—have so far failed. The flurry of new or renewed cartel formations during 1975 (copper, bananas, tungsten, mercury, sugar, silver, rubber, tin) has not produced noticeable results. Algerian President Boumedienne's hope [17] that they would become the pillars of a new global economic order is likely to remain unfulfilled in the face of very strong opposition at the Nairobi UNCTAD conference—by some major developed countries—to cartels or buffer stocks, designed to keep raw material prices at artificially high levels and interfere with a free global market economy. The aid OPEC is giving, at least to non-Muslim countries, is meagre. Votes in the United Nations do not indicate groupings according to the North–South division. And in the Law of the Sea conferences positions were taken according to individual national needs. Yet in spite of the inadequacy of the developing countries' broad-gauged approach and the weakness of their unity, they have made headway in some respects. And there are good reasons for it.

Developed States are not impervious to the idea that they could benefit in the long run from the development of the developing countries. Individual corporations are reaping benefits in developing countries which they reward by using their political influence at home in favour of the developing countries (as *e.g.* the Congressional hearings in the United States on multinational corporations indicated). Some " humanitarian " pressures (one would like to think) have induced States to agree to certain minimum standards and to

[17] *Die Zeit*, June 6, 1975.

give their support everywhere in such organisations as International Labour Organisation, World Health Organisation, and Food and Agriculture Organisation.

Some limited concessions were made in the General Agreement on Tariffs and Trade (GATT), especially the Kennedy Round. The GATT report affirmed that the developing countries had made some gains, in particular through the play of the most-favoured-nation clause " without their having to grant equivalent concessions in return." The United States negotiator reported that no " reciprocal contributions " were expected from the developing countries for the assistance given to them.[18] The Lomé Convention of February 1975, between the European Community and 46 developing States of Africa, the Caribbean and the Pacific (replacing the Yaoundé Convention) is—in the words of the Senegalese finance minister, Babacar Ba—a " revolutionary " agreement, presumably because it makes a number of concessions to the demands of the developing countries.[19] There are numerous international conferences on specialised subjects in which developed and developing States are edging towards what they hope will be some limited agreements on specific economic items.

In September 1975—preceded and followed by much talk about a new world economic order—the Seventh Special Session of the United Nations General Assembly provided evidence for some meeting of minds between the developed and developing countries. The Assembly went more than half-way towards meeting the developing countries, thanks to some conciliatory proposals made by the United States during the opening session, and included an appeal for selectivity and specificity.[20] The optimism generated by the Session was expressed by the United States delegate, Daniel Moynihan, when he summed it up by saying " we have all learned a lot," and by an Asian delegate affirming that the Third-World States wanted to talk business and did not want " an ideological showdown or political victories but practical short-term solutions to their real problems." [21]

In this spirit, the year-long Conference on International Economic Co-operation began in Paris in December 1975. By distributing its work among four substantive committees—energy, raw materials, development and finance—it was hoped that forums would be

[18] GATT, *The Activities of GATT 1967–68* (1969–72), p. 6; U.S. Department of State, *Bulletin* (June 12, 1967), p. 880.
[19] *The Times*, February 3, 1975; *Le Monde*, February 27, 1975; *European Community*, Background Information, Background Note Nr. 6/1975 Revised, February 13, 1975; *Die Zeit*, February 14, 1975; *Europa Archiv*, March 25, 1975, pp. 177–188, D164–D170.
[20] U.S. Department of State, Bureau of Public Affairs, Office of Media Services, The Secretary of State, Speech, September 1, 1975.
[21] *New York Times*, September 22, 1975.

created, to use Henry Kissinger's words, " in which participants can be expected to act responsibly," and in which there would be a change in the substance of discussions " from ideology to consideration of practical actions." At the half-way point, the Conference had at least drawn up working papers detailing the situation regarding its four major topics. But it was still far removed from working out action programs. Observers noted that, so far, confrontations had been avoided and all 27 participating nations were struggling to reach substantive agreements.

A similar spirit prevailed at the fourth UNCTAD meeting at Nairobi. While no solutions to major problems were reached, there was at least sufficient agreement to continue " the dialogue." At the fifth conference of the Non-aligned Nations at Colombo in August 1976, the attitudes towards the developed States seemed less aggressive than formerly, and more devoted to achieving concrete and specific economic results. But at the meeting of the International Bank and Monetary Fund in October 1976 at Manila, confrontation was again prominent.

### VIII—THE LESSON

This very limited progress of the developing States towards their goals, and the slightly more co-operative spirit at the various international conferences during 1976, can serve as signposts of a path the developing countries might tread more successfully than hitherto. Suggestions dealing with limited, detailed and specific items might replace complex, sweeping demands for special treatment or comprehensive plans for the entire economy. Some of the developed countries, for instance, showed a willingness at Nairobi to discuss mutually satisfactory arrangements for a given raw material, while absolutely rejecting broad schemes for the control and regulation of the world market for raw materials in general.

Two advantages developing countries perceive in their strategy are outweighed by a number of disadvantages. The first advantage is that a broad, general approach facilitates a united front. Against that possibility a number of observations can be made: that States rarely make legal commitments to broad generalities; that those developing States having something to offer in return for concessions lose the opportunity of so doing by being associated with all developing States (including those of the Fourth World), and thus have their bargaining power minimised; and that all too many of the developing States cannot in any case resist the occasional temptation of striking individual bargains with developed States, thus breaking the unity.[22]

---

[22] *Cf.* R. D. Hansen, " The Political Economy of North-South Relations: How much Change?" 29 *International Organization* (1975), pp. 937–940.

The second advantage is in the returns the developing States have received so far. But these are mostly rhetorical. In UNCTAD, the main forum for action by the developing States, they have achieved few successes, these stemming mainly from more specialised agencies, such as GATT, the International Monetary Fund, the European Community and the International Bank.[23]

Quite apart from the empirical evidence which shows that carefully circumscribed agenda items are likely to lead more reliably to legal commitments, there is the additional evidence that the approach hitherto used by the developing States has outworn its usefulness, if it ever had any. There is little satisfaction in being part of a majority passing flourishing, but non-binding resolutions. They are boring, as the French delegate of the 29th General Assembly complained, " each longer than the last, one a repetition of the other—virtually unreadable and sometimes not read, even by their sponsors." The unity among the developing States is becoming increasingly frail as these States develop and evolve special interests.[24] The increasing homogeneity of developing countries with greatly varying capabilities and bargaining potentials, as well as of the developed countries, provokes a north–south confrontation. Both sides meet on the basis of the lowest common denominator: the developing States on the basis of the least all of them combined have to offer; the developed States on the basis of the least all of them combined have to concede.

The present case demonstrates the tenacity of certain principles of international politics. States are little moved by high moral principles, but love impressive sounding rhetoric. States will not readily enter into broad, sweeping legal commitments. Legal norms are results, not generators of political agreements. Co-operative action for dubious benefits is readily sacrificed for individual action resulting in concrete gain. Reciprocity and mutual benefit are virtually the only foundations for international agreement. The application of these principles to the situation in which the developing countries find themselves would suggest a return to traditional processes of bargaining. They will not immediately produce the much vaunted equality. Some States may in any case never reach that stage (however defined). Equality is, after all, a condition that cannot be created directly. It is a resultant of many components. It would be Utopian to expect that all these components could be adjusted at once to create equality as their combined end-product.

---

[23] *Cf.* R. S. Walters, " International Organizations and Political Communications: The Use of UNCTAD by Less Developed Nations," 25 *International Organization* (1971), pp. 823–825.

[24] A. P. Sereni, " Les nouveaux états et le droit international," 72 *Revue Générale de Droit International Public* (1968), p. 321.

# THE HISTORY OF INTERNATIONAL LAW:
## *A COMPARATIVE APPROACH*

### By

### A. M. CONNELLY

### I—APPROACHES TO THE HISTORY OF INTERNATIONAL LAW

MANY international lawyers have regarded and many would still regard international law as peculiar to relatively modern times. For them, a history of international law comprises tracing the genesis of the present or contemporary system of international law and studying its development. The present system of international law has been thought to have originated at various points in time: in the post-1945 period, at the end of the First World War or earlier, with the Congress of Vienna of 1815, the Peace of Westphalia of 1648, or even the Middle Ages.[1] In so far as such histories have concentrated on the practice of States and the authors have thereby sought to elucidate the evolution of contemporary rules and principles of international law, these studies make a valuable contribution to the better understanding of this law.

It is appropriate at this point to issue a *caveat*, not because a note of caution has not been sounded before [2] but because, despite its reiteration, the trap still claims some victims. The trap or danger is that of failing to distinguish between doctrine and State practice. Jurists' musings on the law, their opinions and suggestions should be clearly separated from what the rules and principles of international law are or were at any particular point in time. *Lex ferenda* must not be so intertwined with *lex lata* that the two become indistinguishable. Histories of international law which have failed to distinguish, either adequately or at all, between doctrine and State practice are thereby

---

[1] See *e.g.* J. H. W. Verzijl, *International Law in Historical Perspective*, (1968–75); and L. Oppenheim, *International Law*, Vol. 1 (8th ed. by H. Lauterpacht, 1955), p. 6: " International law in the meaning of the term as used in modern times did not exist during antiquity or the first part of the Middle Ages. It is in its origin essentially a product of Christian civilisation, and began gradually to grow from the second half of the Middle Ages. But it owes its existence as a systematised body of rules largely to the Dutch jurist Hugo Grotius, whose work, *De Jure Belli ac Pacis, libri iii*, appeared in 1625, and became the foundation of all later development." For a division of the history of international law during the last 500 years into six phases see G. Schwarzenberger, *The Dynamics of International Law* (1976), pp. 32–33, or 25 *Current Legal Problems* (1972), p. 219 *et seq.*

[2] By, *e.g.* Sir J. Macdonell in C. Phillipson, *The International Law and Custom of Ancient Greece and Rome* (1911), p. xxiii; and G. Schwarzenberger, *The Frontiers of International Law* (1962), p. 43.

limited as an aid to the understanding of actual rules of international law.

The so-called " fathers " of international law have been ill-named. No Grotius or Victoria spawned a system of international law. They thought and wrote about the legal aspect of State relations in their day. Some of what they wrote provides a record of the actual rules observed by States in their dealings with one another; some of it is speculation; some of it gives the attitude of the writer on a particular matter—an attitude which was not necessarily widely held at the time; and some of it is merely reflection on the desirable legal position. The various strands of thought constitute historical evidence of a different nature. Grotius' argument that the seas are free and open to all nations and their peoples was in fact polemical.[3] He was hired to state the case of the Dutch East India Company: that it had the right to sail its ships by way of commerce to and from the East Indies without let or hindrance; and to refute the contemporary claims of Spain and Portugal to ownership of vast chunks of the oceans. In fact, an English jurist, John Seldon, proceeded to write and publish a tract in reply to Grotius, showing how the oceans are capable of being owned by one or more States to the exclusion of their use by others.[4] Grotius' statement of the case in favour of the freedom of the seas is certainly of relevance to an understanding of the evolution and content of a principle of international law which subsequently came to be generally recognised by States, but it should not be taken as an authoritative exposition of the actual position in law with regard to the use of the sea in the early seventeenth century. The history of doctrine and the history of State practice should not be confused.

The practice of focusing on the immediate past as a key to the understanding of the present has been common and is not to be denigrated. Coming events cast their shadows before and perception of these shadows not only can aid in an appreciation of current events but also provide a guide to the future. But not all historians of international law have dealt exclusively with the practice of States, especially European States, in the last few centuries or, more particularly, with the evolution of the modern rules and principles of international law. Some writers have shown an awareness of rules of international practice in earlier times.

Many of these writers, in particular, those who profess to have written a general history of international law, have cast only a cursory glance at pre-mediaeval State practice.[5] One historian who

---

[3] *Mare Liberum*, translated into English with a revision of the Latin text of 1633 by Magoffin, 1916.

[4] *Mare clausum* (1635).

[5] See, *e.g.* A. Nussbaum, *A Concise History of the Law of Nations* (1962); T. A.

was early to recognise that a general history of international law might embrace the whole of human history, nevertheless limited his own study to the post-Middle Ages as being the period in which modern civilisation arose.[6] Even among those who have paid more attention to the juridical aspect of the relations of States in earlier times there has been a marked hesitancy to regard the legal rules and concepts deserved as pertaining to international law.[7] There have occasionally been voices raised to the contrary but, until recently, they were by and large few and far between. However, in the last few decades, these voices have multiplied.

With regard to the more remote past, several studies have recently been made of the law governing the relations between States in ancient China.[8] These studies have been confined to a reasonably well-defined period of time, 722–481 B.C., known to historians of China as the Ch'un-ch'iu or Spring and Autumn Period. Less well-defined is the time span covered by studies of the law recognised by the States of ancient India in their relations with one another.[9] These studies have treated the relations of States at any time between the Aryan invasion of India in the twelfth century B.C. and the ascendancy of Islam in the early eighth century A.D., but in general they have tended to focus on various writings on polity known as *Arthasastras* and *Dharmasastras*, especially on the *Arthasastra* of Kautilya written in the last quarter of the fourth century B.C.

As regards the less distant past, some attention has been paid to the relations of the Italian States from the middle of the twelfth to the middle of the sixteenth century A.D.[10] Also, at least one writer has studied the system of international law which was in operation in the sixteenth, seventeenth and eighteenth centuries A.D. in what he has

Walker, *A History of the Law of Nations* (1899); and A. Wheaton, *History of the Law of Nations* (1845).

[6] E. Nys, *Les origines du droit international* (1894).

[7] See, *e.g.* W. S. Armour, " Customs of Warfare in Ancient India," 8 *Transactions of the Grotius Society* (1923), p. 71, at pp. 83–84; A. Nussbaum, *op. cit.* p. 9; L. Oppenheim, *op. cit.* p. 6; and T. A. Walker, *op. cit.* p. 38.

[8] See R. S. Britton, " Chinese Inter-State Intercourse Before 700 B.C.," 29 A.J.I.L. (1935), p. 616; S-T. Chen, " The Equality of States in Ancient China," 35 A.J.I.L. (1941), p. 641; and R. L. Walker, *The Multi-State System of Ancient China* (1953).

[9] See W. S. Armour, *op. cit.*; C. J. Chacko, " International Law in India; Ancient India," 1 *Indian Journal of International Law* (1960–61), p. 184; " International Law in India; Ancient India (Part II)," *ibid.* p. 589; " International Law in India; Ancient India (Part III)," 2 *Indian Journal of International Law* (1962), p. 48; H. Chatterjee, *International Law and Inter-State Relations in Ancient India* (1958); N. N. Law, *Inter-State Relations in Ancient India* (1920); T. M. P. Mahadevan, " Kautilya on the Sanctity of Pacts," 5 *Indian Year Book of International Affairs* (1956), p. 342; M. K. Nawaz, " The Law of Nations in Ancient India," *ibid.* Vol. 6 (1957), p. 172; and K. A. N. Sastri, " International Law and Relations in Ancient India," *ibid.* Vol. 1 (1952), p. 97. Some caution is required in using these studies to separate doctrine from the actual practice of States.

[10] By A. P. Sereni, *The Italian Conception of International Law* (1943), Chaps. 1–6.

termed the " East Indies," that is, India, Ceylon, Burma, Thailand, the Indonesian islands and, to a limited extent, Persia.[11]

These studies are illustrative of a fresh attitude to the history of international law. They range over a wide period of time limited only by the historical evidence and emanate from a global perspective. The historian has displayed a certain ability to detach himself from the present. International law is no longer viewed as the creation of European States or the preserve of States in the last few centuries, but as a feature or phenomenon of human society. This view " liberates us from the impediments, the limitations that are imposed on our experience of man when we situate him in a certain society at a certain moment of his evolution,[12] and " brings about a veritable catharsis, a liberation of our sociological subconscious somewhat analogous to that which psychoanalysis seeks to establish on the psychological level." [13]

In the above two approaches to the history of international law, the focus of research is either on the present or on a past period of history. These are not the only methods of conducting historical research. Another is possible. Events, ideas and institutions may be taken from their chronological slot in history and compared with other events, ideas and institutions of a comparable nature belonging to another point in time. The purpose of such comparison is that, by it, light may be thrown, for example, by one event on another occuring at a different historical period. Such an approach is based on the premise that similarities afford a key to the understanding of human phenomena. Also it is assumed that there is a certain amount of repetition in human affairs that " what happened in the past will, in accordance with man's nature, happen again in the same or much the same way in the future." [14]

One of the first of modern scholars to adopt such an approach to the study of history was Arnold Toynbee.[15] Toynbee regarded history as primarily a study of various civilisations which " are intrinsically comparable with one another." [16] He spoke of " the philosophical contemporaneity of all civilizations " [17]; and embarking ambitiously on a review of the whole of the history of mankind, discerned some 21 civilisations.

It has taken many years for this comparative approach to filter through into the particular field of the history of international law.

---

[11] C. H. Alexandrowicz, *An Introduction to the History of the Law of Nations in the East Indies* (1967).
[12] H. Marrou, *The Meaning of History* (1966), p. 282.
[13] *Ibid.* p. 283.
[14] Thucydides, *The Peloponnesian War* 1.22.
[15] See *A Study of History* (1934–1963).
[16] *Ibid.* Vol. 1 (2nd ed. 1935).     [17] *Civilisation on Trial* (1948), pp. 8 and 36–37.

In the 1950s Chatterjee treated the law governing the relations of the States of ancient India with, where appropriate, brief comment by way of comparison with modern rules of international law.[18] Fourteen years later, Schwarzenberger has put the case for a comparative history of international law.[19] But, by and large, the comparative approach to the history of international law is still in its infancy.

For a comparative study to be fruitful, comparative material is essential. A study of incomparables is not likely to be rewarding. Before embarking on such a study, it is necessary to discern the comparables. An apple may be compared with an orange. Both are varieties of fruit and both are roundish in form, but there is little other similarity between the two. The dissimilarities predominate. They are different in taste, texture and colour, to mention but a few of the differences, and neither these differences nor the few similarities may be thought to add much to our knowledge of these fruits. Likely to be similarly unrewarding would be the comparison of an apple with a banana. However, the comparison of one type of apple, say a Golden Delicious, with another, say a Worcester, may be more instructive. The similarities are greater. Both are varieties of the same fruit. There are similarities of taste, texture, composition. Comparison may show, for example, that difference in colour is linked with variation in sweetness, and this knowledge may be of use in experiments to create a new strain of apple.[20]

Similarity, then, is important in determining the basis of a comparative study. At least two comparables are needed for such a study, the comparables being determined by a number of intrinsic similarities. For Toynbee, the comparables were civilisations; for Schwarzenberger, they are models of international law; for the present writer, they are systems of international law.

In the remainder of this article the latter two approaches to the history of international law will be further explained and examined, the models approach briefly, the systems approach, being that of the present writer, in greater detail. In reality they are not two different approaches, but variants of the same approach. The comparables are different, but the methodology is the same: a comparative approach.

## II—THE SYSTEMS APPROACH

As stated above, the comparables in this approach to the history of international law are systems of international law. But how are such

---

[18] *Op. cit.*

[19] 25 *Current Legal Problems* (1972), p. 219 *et seq.*; or *The Dynamics of International Law* (1976), Chap. 3. See also A. Connelly, *International Law Across the Ages*, unpublished doctoral thesis, McGill University, 1975.

[20] These are purely hypothetical examples of the possible results of comparison and of the use to which such results may be put.

systems to be recognised? What are the intrinsic similarities by which they may be identified?

It is believed that there are five conditions which are essential to any system of international law or, alternatively phrased, that there are five prerequisities for the existence of international law. First, there must exist several distinct political units. Secondly, these units must enter into relations with one another. There can be no international relations if these bodies do not enter into contact with one another but either are geographically isolated or purposely adopt a policy of isolation. Thirdly, these relations must be based on the concept of political equality. The units need not necessarily enjoy the same political power or influence, but must acknowledge that they all possess the same character or personality, that is, they must recognise one another as political equals. Fourthly, they must not be subject to superior authority but each must be sovereign in its own right. Where entities possess the same political status but are subordinate to a higher authority, their relations do not, strictly speaking, fall within the province of international law. The fifth prerequisite for a system of international law is that these entities must regard their relations as subject to law, that is, there must exist an *opinio juris*. They must recognise that certain conduct on the part of one towards another is legally permissible and certain conduct impermissible.

Some writers would add the condition that there must exist a substantial number of shared moral values. It is not denied that there must exist some common values.[21] For example, the belief that agreements should be honoured, commonly expressed by the Latin maxim, *pacta sunt servanda*, is essentially a moral attitude. However, it is denied that the shared values need be substantial. Today States of many different, even radically divergent, political ideologies enter into legal relations with one another; that is, even though they uphold separate social values, they nevertheless regard their relations with one another as governed by law. Moral values undoubtedly affect the content of the law as do other factors, such as political power or considerations of expediency, but the only moral value which is absolutely essential to the existence of international law is

---

[21] See *e.g.* V. Martin, *La vie internationale dans la Grèce des cités* (1940), pp. 7–8; C. W. Jenks, *A New World of Law?* (1969), pp. 292–299, where the author discusses the moral basis of the world community and formulates it in eight basic propositions; and on the relationship between international law and social values in general, W. G. Friedmann, *The Changing Structure of International Law* (1964), Chap. 7, where the author discusses " the perennial dilemma of natural law philosophy, the postulation of permanent and absolute values in a world deeply divided by conflicts of national interests and social values " (p. 75); and M. S. McDougal, " International Law, Power and Policy," 82 *Hague Receuil* (1953), p. 137, where at p. 141, he describes as one of the tasks of a policy-oriented approach to the study of law the clarification of the goal values of the society within which the law operates.

that which is at the very basis of respect for the law and which might be expressed in some such way as that " the law should be respected."

Other writers stress the sanctional aspect of law.[22] For them there can be no law without sanctions, and hence no international law without sanctions. From a practical viewpoint, it is agreed that sanctions play an important role in the functioning of law, but from a theoretical point of view, it is not agreed that they are essential to the existence of law. If all those subject to the law were law-abiding, there would be no need for sanctions, but man being what he is and a political unit being a collectivity of men, as long as men and political societies break the law, there will be a need for sanctions. This, however, is not quite the same thing as saying that sanctions are essential to the existence of law. Law is conceivable without sanctions.

There is, then, some disagreement as to the actual number of conditions which must be met for the existence of a system of international law; but, whatever the precise number of conditions, whether it be five, seven, or 70, fulfilment of these conditions signifies the existence of a system of international law.

Accepting for the present that there are only five conditions which are essential to a system of international law, does the available historical evidence suggest that there has, in fact, been a number of such systems? It does. A few examples may be given.

From approximately the seventh to the fourth century B.C., there existed in the Mediterranean basin a number of Greek city-States or *poleis*. Many of these communities were politically independent, recognising no superior political authority. Many fought fiercely to retain this independence. These city-States entered into relations not only with one another but also with various non-Greek communities. These non-Greek peoples were on the whole those which were geographically contiguous with the Greek States, the various tribes of Europe, for example, in the Thracian region, communities in north Africa, especially the Egyptians, and Asiatic peoples, notably the Persians. It is, furthermore, clear that to a certain extent these communities regarded their relations with one another as governed by law.[23] There was, then, a system of international law in operation between various communities in the Mediterranean region in the seventh to fourth centuries B.C. This period is termed by historians the Greek classical age.

---

[22] See *e.g.* L. Oppenheim, *op. cit.* pp. 13–14; H. Kelsen, *The Legal Process and International Order* (1935), *General Theory of Law and State* (1945), pp. 328–341, and *Principles of International Law* (2nd ed. rev. by R. W. Tucker, 1966), p. 16 *et seq.*

[23] See A. Connelly, *op. cit.*; V. Martin, *op. cit.*; C. Phillipson, *op. cit.*; and G. Tènékidès, *La notion juridique d'indépendance et la tradition hellénique* (1954), and " Droit international et communautés fédérales dans la Grèce des cités," 90 *Hague Recueil* (1956), p. 469.

In the latter part of the fourth century B.C., due largely to the activities of Alexander, King of Macedon, many of the Greek city-States lost their independence and became incorporated, along with many non-Greek communities, into the Macedonian Empire. After Alexander's death in 323 B.C., this vast Empire split up into a number of separate kingdoms. Many of the Greek city-States of this period still entered into relations with one another on a basis of political equality, but they virtually all acknowledged a duty of allegiance to one of the great Hellenistic kingdoms; and, though the relations of such States may greatly resemble those of independent, sovereign bodies, on account of their political subjection to a higher authority, they lack one of the conditions essential to the existence of international law. This does not, however, mean that there was no system of international law during this period. Though the Greek and other non-Greek communities were in a subject status at the time, the various Hellenistic kingdoms frequently went to war and concluded agreements with one another. In other words, these kingdoms allowed that their relations with one another were to some degree regulated by law. A system of international law did exist, but the subjects of the law had changed. The political units of the system were no longer the comparatively small Greek city-States and the non-Greek communities with which these States had entered into relations, but much larger bodies, the products of an imperial age.[24]

The five conditions have been present at yet other historical periods. They were present in the Italian peninsula from the fifth century B.C. or earlier until the end of the third.[25] They were also probably present from the late eighth to early fifth century B.C. in ancient China.[26] They may possibly be found at some time between the twelfth century B.C. and the early eighth century A.D. in ancient India,[27] and again in the Italian peninsula from the middle of the twelfth to the middle of the sixteenth century A.D.[28] They are, of course, existent at the present time.

---

[24] This period is known as the Hellenistic age.
[25] See C. Phillipson, *op. cit.*
[26] See above, n. 8.                                    [27] See above, n. 9.
[28] See above, n. 10. These Italian States were for long, strictly speaking, subordinate to the Holy Roman Emperor, but it has been ably argued by Sereni that this allegiance was little more than nominal and that their relations both with one another and with other States may be regarded as possessing an international character: in other words, that these Italian States entered into relations *de facto* on a basis of political equality, while *de jure* subject to the Holy Roman Emperor. This distinction between the *de jure* and *de facto* position is also relevant with respect to the relations of States in ancient China and India. The studies of these States make it clear that at each period there was a complex system of vassalage, but that there was also a number of States whose relations can be regarded as having been conducted on a basis of equality. However, it is not always possible, on the available historical evidence, to tell where the ultimate sovereignty in law resided.

There has, then, been a number of systems of international law, and these systems provide comparables for a comparative study of international law. It is hoped, by comparing them, to gain a better understanding of each system.

Though a comparative study is based on the identification of certain similarities, this does not mean that differences are always or necessarily unimportant. Similarities will determine the framework of the study, but within the study differences will be noted and some examined. For example, if similar problems have existed in different societies and different solutions have been devised in the different societies to what is essentially the same problem, it may be instructive to study and compare these different solutions. However, if the problems have been entirely different, it is unlikely that comparing them will be a rewarding pursuit unless, perhaps, they are observed to have had the same or a similar solution.

In the systems approach to international law, each system is studied in the light of the juridical rules and concepts observed in the other system or systems with which it is being compared. Where the rules and concepts in each system have differed, they are not subjected to minute examination unless they appear to be a response to a similar problem. Where they overlap or are markedly similar, the rule or concept in one system is studied with particular reference to the comparable rule or concept in another.

For the purpose of illustrating the application of this method to the history of international law, two particular systems of international law will be chosen, one the present system, the other that found in the Mediterranean region in the seventh to fourth centuries B.C. and centred on the relations of the Greek city-States.[29]

Examination of the attitude of States in each system to the use of the sea and the regulation of activities at sea reveals that the problems were largely different. Much of the modern law of the sea deals with problems which have arisen as a result of the great technological strides taken in modern times. Nuclear-powered vessels and massive oil-tankers have left in their wake such problems as that of pollution and damage to coastal States. The exploitation of the mineral and other natural resources on and under the seabed has in recent years become an actuality thanks to the invention and perfection of the equipment necessary for mining at great depths. Such mining has raised problems of international concern. Who owns the ocean floor? Will freedom of navigation suffer as a result of mining operations? These problems are peculiar to the modern period and to the modern system of international law. The question of the regulation by law of

---

[29] A comparison of these two systems of international law was undertaken in *International Law Across the Ages*. See above, n. 19.

many activities at sea did not arise in the classical age of the Greek city-States and, though the number of these questions is today, by contrast, appreciable, since there existed no practice in this respect in the earlier system which would provide the material for a fruitful comparison, mention would be made of these differences, but the modern law with regard to such activities would not be examined in any detail.

However, while the differences between the two systems regarding the use of the sea are great, the problems have not been entirely disparate. Piracy was a menace to shipping throughout antiquity. In the heroic age it was even a respectable profession, but by the classical age an embryonic *opinio juris* can be discerned that it was not to be tolerated. Piracy is no longer a pressing problem, but it has not altogether been suppressed. In contrast to antiquity, the juridical position with regard to this practice is now clear. A pirate is universally regarded as a *hostis humani generis*. Hence the concept of piracy would have to be studied to see whether or not it has signified essentially the same pursuit in both periods.

Though there is some material of value for a comparative study of the legal rules and principles pertaining to the use of the sea, regulation of activities at sea is one of the fields in which the differences between the two systems predominate. A field in which the material for a comparative study is more promising is the regulation of the use of force.

States have in both periods used force against one another for various reasons, but in neither has the use of force been considered legitimate in all circumstances. States have sought to regulate resort to force by one State against another on a legal basis and have claimed legal justification for their action when they employed it. Today, with the realisation that war can have disastrous consequences even for the victor, States have bound themselves to pursue a common policy of peaceful co-existence and have formally proscribed the use of force in international relations except in certain limited circumstances, most notably, in self-defence. The attitude of the Greek States towards the use of armed force was somewhat different. The heroic tradition, most aptly exemplified by Sparta in the classical age, taught men that it was glorious and noble to fight and to die for one's country. War was an accepted aspect of life. Nevertheless, even when a State's primary motive for going to war was economic or political, it usually claimed some legal ground for its action, and one of the grounds most commonly invoked by Greek States was that of self-defence. Hence it is found that though the attitude of States towards the use of force has been markedly different in each system, self-defence has been recognised in both as legally justifying resort to arms. But what today is understood by self-defence in international law? And what did the concept signify in the relations between the States of the classical age? It would be necessary in such a comparative study to examine the scope and content of the concept in each system in order to determine whether one of the recognised grounds for the use of force has in fact been the same in both. On the other hand, where, owing to the different attitudes to the use of force, practice and its regulation have been different in the two periods, the differences would be noted but not subjected to further analysis.

The material is even more promising when the regulation of disputes in general is considered. Resort to force has not been the only method adopted by States either in the modern era or in the classical age to settle a dispute. States have also had recourse to various peaceful means of settling their disputes. Negotiation, mediation, conciliation and arbitration are forms common to both periods, but whereas these categories by and large cover the range of procedures used in the classical period to deal with the pacific settlement of disputes, an additional form has today attained some importance, that of judicial settlement. The States of the classical age do not appear to have attempted an experiment in international adjudication by establishing a permanent judicial organ to deal with international disputes. However, the Greek arbitral tribunals show several affinities with modern judicial organs in composition and procedure and must to some extent have fulfilled the same purpose. What was understood by each of the various forms of pacific settlement in the classical age, in what way, if at all, they were interrelated, and to what extent they resemble the modern forms are questions which fall within the scope of such a comparative study.

### III—THE MODELS APPROACH

For a full exposition of this approach, the reader is referred to a chapter of *The Dynamics of International Law* (1976) [30] in which the author, G. Schwarzenberger, makes a " plea for a radical re-appraisal of the treatment of the history of international law as a subject of teaching and research." [31] The treatment he advocates is the application of a comparative technique based on the identification of historical models of international law. Here mention will be made only of some of the salient features of this technique and a few comments ventured on it.

This approach also stems from an " awareness of the rise, plurality

---

[30] Chap. 3. entitled " Historical Models of International Law " or *loc. cit.* above, note 19, (1972) p. 225 *et seq.* Concerning models of international law in general see, further, *International Law and Order* (1971), Chap. 14 by the same author.

[31] At p. 32.

and passing of individual civilisations since the dawn of recorded history " [32] and of former " defunct or arrested systems of international law." [33] The models which are the object of comparison are either systems or rules of international law; and these systems or rules are of interest in so far as they " represent models which correspond to present-day needs or show failings which are more clearly discernible at a distance than in a contemporary setting." [34] In other words, the focus is essentially on the international law of today. These models provide yardsticks for the evaluation of present rules of international law and enable a more informed choice of alternatives for the future. The past is studied as a guide to the present and to the future.

In explaining this approach, Schwarzenberger emphasises the dichotomy between international law and order. [35] An international order or quasi-order may break down, yet the rules of international law at the time may not undergo any radical change. They may even continue essentially unaltered by the " destruction of their correlated political and legal frameworks." [36] Examples given are the Westphalian Peace Treaties of 1648, the Vienna Peace Treaties of 1815 and the Paris Peace Treaties of 1919. The reason afforded for such continuity in the rules of international law as distinct from the international order or quasi-order is that such rules fulfil the stereotyped needs of international societies. A war may destroy an international order, but provided it does not destroy international society altogether, it will not necessarily entail a change in the rules of international law, in particular those of customary international law, as the needs of the international society in the post-war period are likely to be similar to the needs of the international society in the pre-war period. This is because, in Schwarzenberger's view, such societies " are motivated by the quest for power rather than law and based on the co-existence of entities which consider themselves as ends rather than means." [37]

With regard to international law itself, he delineates five historical models. These he has termed the model of omnipotence, the *jus strictum* model, the *jus aequum* model, the oceanic model, and the unionist model. The models are distinguished one from another in that each comprises a distinct system of inter-locking rules of international law. [38]

The first, the model of omnipotence, is illustrated by a State [39]

---

[32] At p. 33.
[33] At p. 55.
[34] At p. 36.
[35] See pp. 34–36 and 53–54.
[36] At p. 35.
[37] At p. 54.
[38] See pp. 36 and 55.
[39] There may be one or a number of such States at a given time.

which claims supremacy over a particular piece of territory, maintains a reasonable degree of actual control over this territory and refuses to concede equality of status to any other entity within this area.[40] The Roman Empire and imperial China provide such models.

For the second, the *jus strictum* model, there must exist at least two separate entities neither of which is subordinate to the other.[41] These bodies may recognise one another as sovereign and equal in status, or they may not, in which case any relations which may exist between them will be of a *de facto* peaceful or warlike character. An example of this model is the Declaration of Arbroath of 1320 and the subsequent recognition of Robert Bruce as King of Scotland by the Pope and by Edward III of England.

In describing the third, the *jus aequum* model, Schwarzenberger concentrates on a treaty of the early thirteenth century B.C. between King Ramesses II of Egypt and King Hattusitis of Hatti.[42] The treaty provided for eternal peace and brotherhood between the two kingdoms, respect for one another's territorial integrity, a defensive alliance, assistance to be afforded by one if the government of the other was threatened by internal strife, in particular, if the normal succession to the throne was challenged, and the extradition of fugitives; and is described in some detail to show that the relations between the parties were conducted on a basis of good faith in the positive meaning of this term. Whereas in the *jus strictum* model, rights and obligations are treated as absolute and are strictly interpreted, in the *jus aequum*, they are regarded as relative to be interpreted in the light of what would be considered just, fair and reasonable in the circumstances.

The fourth, the oceanic model relates to the situation where the subjects of international law have regulated their relations at sea.[43] The rules of international law observed by European States in the Middle Ages and the present system of international law are examples of this model.

The fifth model, the unionist, denotes various forms of union.[44] There are four major sub-models: (i) the hegemonial; (ii) the confederate; (iii) the federal; and (iv) the unitary.

In the hegemonial sub-model, the relations between the units are hierarchical in nature. Examples are the vassal treaties of Hittite and Assyrian rulers. In the confederate form of union, all or some of the constituent units retain their own sovereignty. The Germanic Confederation of 1815 is an illustration of this sub-model. The

[40] See pp. 36–38.
[41] See pp. 38–39.
[42] See pp. 39–49.
[43] See pp. 49–51.
[44] See pp. 51–53.

federal sub-model may itself take one of two forms, political or functional federation. The example afforded of the political form is the establishment of the German Reich 1870–71, of the functional, the present European Communities. The unitary sub-model denotes a political union whereby two or more independent states merge to create a new sovereign body. The union in 1707 of England and Wales with Scotland exemplifies this sub-model.

As stated above,[45] these models are differentiated by the fact that each comprises a number of rules of international law peculiar to itself. In the second, third and fourth models, the *jus strictum*, *jus aequum* and oceanic, these rules are reasonably clear and distinguishable. Basic to the *jus strictum* model are rules on sovereignty and recognition. Included or implied are some rules with respect to international responsibility, the use of force and some formal agreements. Furthermore, good faith in the sense of the absence of bad faith or treachery in the relations between States is a feature of this model. The *jus aequum* model also comprises rules on sovereignty, recognition, international responsibility, the use of force and the conclusion of agreements, but these rules are infused with an equitable spirit. In this model good faith signifies more than merely the absence of bad faith. For example, with regard to international responsibility, there is a recognised rule that if a party breaks the terms of a treaty, it is thereby under a duty to make reparation to the offended party or parties for this breach. In the oceanic model, besides rules on sovereignty, recognition, international responsibility, the conclusion of agreements and good faith, there is provision for the regulation of the use of the sea and more limited justification for resort to force.

It is the distinguishing features of the first, the model of omnipotence, and the fifth, the unitary model, which are open to question. What rules of *international* law are peculiar to these models? Certainly the omnipotence model is founded on a concept of sovereignty, sovereignty in the sense of overall or absolute supremacy whether in internal or external affairs. But what rule of *international* law does it illustrate? Similarly, it may be asked whether the unionist model, at least in its federal and unitary state forms, necessarily represents any rules of international law. Are these two models, in fact models of international law?[46]

At times Schwarzenberger himself seems to recognise that not all the models pertain, properly speaking, to the realm of international

---

[45] p. 314, above.

[46] These questions may also be asked of the form of the *jus strictum* model in which relations are conducted purely on a *de facto* basis without mutual recognition by States of their sovereign and equal status.

law. For example, in dealing with the hegemonial sub-model of the unionist model, he explicitly states that the relations between the units which characterise this sub-model may be of an international, national or quasi-international character and consequently governed by either international law, national law or law of a hybrid variety.[47] That the omnipotence model and the federal and unitary State variants of the unionist model do not belong to the field of international law is in fact made clear by a diagram showing the relationship between each model, its order, and what Schwarzenberger has termed the fundamental principles of international customary law.[48] No rule of international law features in these models. They connote, in Schwarzenberger's words, a "state of pre-international or internal law."

If it is allowed that not all these historical models in fact pertain to the field of international law, is there not some inconsistency in distinguishing the various types of model by applying the test that each should "call its own a distinct system of rules of international law?"[49]

To state that certain models, for example, the political form of the federal model, are not truly models of international law is not to assert that the study of such models will necessarily contribute nothing to the understanding of actual rules and systems of international law. There is undoubtedly some affinity between the law of a federal system and the law of an international society, and the study of one may help in an appreciation of the other; but the basic difference between the two should not be obscured. International law governs essentially the relations between political units which recognise one another as equal and sovereign. They acknowledge no higher political authority, but allow that their relations with one another are subject to law. In a federation, the units may be equal in status, but they will not be sovereign in all matters affecting their interests. The units of a federal State all cede a certain amount of their sovereignty to a central or federal authority.[50] In other words, sovereignty is divided or shared. In certain matters the federal units retain sovereignty, in others they are subordinate to the federal authority.

IV—THE SYSTEMS AND THE MODELS APPROACHES COMPARED

Both the systems and the models approach to the history of international law have much in common. They both favour a selective use

---

[47] See p. 52.
[48] See p. 43. On these fundamental principles see "The Fundamental Principles of International Law," 87 *Hague Recueil* (1955), p. 195.
[49] At p. 55.
[50] Sovereignty is usually ceded in respect of, *e.g.* defence and foreign affairs.

of historical material and distinguish clearly between the history of doctrine and of State practice. In both the present system of international law is studied with a considerable degree of detachment fed by an awareness of the existence of previous systems of international law, a consciousness that international law is not exclusive to the modern era, but is a recurrent historical phenomenon. Most importantly, both are founded on a belief in the value of comparative research.

There are, however, differences. In the models approach, the basis for comparison is a number of rules of international law. In the systems approach, the comparables are particularly systems of international law, that is, systems which meet the five or more conditions for the existence of international law.[51]

Both approaches stress similarities in rules and systems, but the models approach to a greater extent than the systems. Models, especially analytical models,[52] are by their nature standard. They are composed of salient features. Details are regarded as of minor importance, if not altogether ignored. Implicit in this approach is the view that variations in rules or systems may be accommodated within one type of model, and such accommodation could on occasion lead to an oversimplification of the actual situation. The systems approach is also principally concerned with the drawing of analogies, but more attention is likely to be paid than in the models approach to differences in the systems and rules. It will be asked whether the differences merit further study because either they are different legal responses to an analogous social problem or are different problems which have been regulated by law in a similar manner.

Both types of study have posed a further question relating either to the basic structure of international law or of international society.

The models approach reveals that certain rules of international law have occurred in more than one historical context. They have been repeated at various points in time throughout the history of man. The question raised is why these models or rules should feature in different historical periods. The answer given by Schwarzenberger is that they all pertain to international societies with essentially the same political infra-structures, those of power politics or power politics in disguise.[53]

The question posed by the systems approach has yet to be answered. A comparison of various systems of international law shows that certain rules, legal concepts and institutions are found in all or most

---

[51] *op. cit.* pp. 5–6.

[52] On the analytical type of model see G. Schwarzenberger, *International Law and Order* (1971), pp. 257–258 and 259–261.

[53] For the meaning of these terms see G. Schwarzenberger, *The Frontiers of International Law* (1962), Chap. 2, in particular the definitions at p. 24.

of these systems. For example, the rule that an envoy should be inviolable while on an official mission between units of international society has apparently been recognised in all the systems referred to earlier. Is there a number of such rules which are fundamental [54] to international law in the sense that they are found in every known system or are characteristic of international law in that they are found in most systems? Definition of such rules would aid in an understanding of the basic structure of international law. It would thereby be possible to separate out those rules of an intrinsic nature from those of more peripheral significance. The comparative studies which have to date been carried out would suggest that there are indeed certain legal rules, concepts and institutions which are basic to or characteristic of international law as a legal system, but a definitive answer to this question can only be given after much further research into the various known systems of international law.

---

[54] It is desirable to distinguish between fundamental in the sense of essential and in the sense of basic but not necessarily essential. In the systems approach, at least five conditions are regarded as prerequisite to the existence of a system of international law. There must exist several distinct political units; these units must not be subordinate to any superior political authority; they must enter into relations with one another; these relations must be conducted on a basis of equality; and they must be regarded as subject to law. Since these conditions are essential to a system of international law, such principles as that of equality or sovereignty are fundamental to international law in the sense that they are essential to it. They are principles of a somewhat different nature to those which are basic to or characteristic of a system of international law, but which are not essential to its existence.

# COMPARATIVE LAW
# IN THE COURT OF JUSTICE
# OF THE EUROPEAN COMMUNITIES

By

## ANNA BREDIMA

### I—CONDITIONS OF USE OF THE COMPARATIVE LAW METHOD

THE European Community Treaties are framework treaties (*traités-cadre*).[1] They have established a *sui generis* legal order and do not pretend to govern in an absolute manner all eventualities, foreseeable or not. They hide a number of *lacunae*. As it was characteristically said: " A creation of such a novel character could not emerge from the Treaties as perfect as Goddess Athena from the head of Zeus." [2] Therefore, very early it was realised that the provisions of the Treaties and of secondary Community Acts were not sufficiently comprehensive to resolve all disputes.

To this effect, the European Court of Justice entrusted with the

---

[1] For detailed bibliography see: Sinclair, " The Principles of Treaty Interpretation and their application by the English Courts," I.C.L.Q., 1963, p. 517; Toth, " The Individual and European Law," I.C.L.Q., 1975, p. 659; Lorenz, " General Principles of Law," A.J.C.L., 1964, pp. 1–29; Donner, " National Law and the Case Law of the C.J.E.C." C.M.L. Rev., 1963, 8, 11; Reuter, " *Le Recours de à la C.J.E.C.* a *des principes généraux de droit,*" *Melanges Rolin,* Paris, Pédone, 1964, pp. 263–283; Pescatore, " International Law and Community Law," C.M.L. Rev., 1970, p. 167; Jeantet-Kovar, *Jurisclasseur de Droit International,* 1960, vol. II, Fasc. 161c; Usher, " *The influence of national concepts on decisions of the European Court of Justice,*" *European Law Review,* 1976; Brinkhorst, " *European Integration,*" Penguin, 1972, pp. 304–322; Colin, " *Le Gouvernement des Juges,*" p. 107; Lipstein, " *The Law of the European Economic Community,*" p. 16; Schlesinger, " *Le fonds commun des systemes juridiques,*" R.I.D.C., 1963, p. 508; Guggenheim, " *Traité de Droit International Public,*" 1967, pp. 304–306; Boulouis-Chevallier, " *Grands Arrêts de la C.J.C.E.,*" Paris, Dalloz, 1974, t. 1, pp. 78–89; Kapteyn-Verloren, " *Introduction to the Law of EEC,*" p. 25; Cheng, " *General Principles of the Law,*" London, Stevens, 1953, pp. 390–392; Migliazza, " *La C.J.C.E.,*" Milan, Giuffré, 1961, p. 355, 367; Batailler, " *Le juge interne et le droit communautaire,*" A.F.D.I., 1965, p. 741; Teitgen " *Droit Institutionnel Communautaire,*" pp. 202–204; Migliazza, *Osterreichische Zeitschrift für Offentliches Recht,* 1962, p. 332; Rosenne, " *The Law and Practice of the International Court,*" Leyden, Sijfthoff, 1965, vol. 2, p. 610; Schwarzenberger, " *The Inductive Approach,*" pp. 36–37; Cartou, " *La C.J.C.E.,*" *Melanges Waline,* p. 171; Pescatore, " *Law of Integration,*" p. 75; Bebr, " *Judicial Control in E.E.C.,*" p. 29; McMahon, " The C.J.E.C."; B.Y.I.L., 1961, p. 326; Aubert, " *La C.J.C.E.,*" R.T.D.E., 1971, p. 78; Constantinesco, " *Dix Ans de Jurisprudence,*" p. 206; Wolf, *ibid.* pp. 193–200; Scheuner, " Fundamental Rights in E.E.C. Law and in National Constitutional Law," C.M.L. Rev., p. 171, 185.

[2] Constantinesco, " *Contribution au problème des rapports entre l'orde de la Communauté et l'ordre juridique interne des Etats Membres.*" (1957), pp. 213–214.

interpretation and application of the Treaties,[3] in the exercise of its discretionary powers and of its creative law-making activity, has frequently had recourse to national concepts and general principles of the law which were derived and elaborated by means of the comparative law method of interpretation. In this way, unwritten law has afforded a solution to numerous problems to which Community Law provided no written answer.[4] Such development is by no means unique to the European Court, but it has acquired an unprecedented predominance in its case law. Indeed, it is a universal phenomenon of legal civilisation [5]: suffice it to remember article 38 (1) (*c*) of the Statute of the World Court establishing " the general principles of law recognised by civilised nations " as one of the sources of law applied by it. However, in spite of this instigation both World Courts have shown little enthusiasm for this source.[6] On the contrary, the comparative law method has been used by the European Court even when there is no express provision for reference to the " general principles " in the Treaties and Regulations.[7] This source has acquired such an importance in the framework of the Communities that refusal to have recourse to it may amount to a denial of justice.[8]

The nature of such principles is a highly controversial issue. According to the prevailing view,[9] a distinction must be drawn between " Rules " and " Principles." The former are binding legal norms that can be inductively verified as the products of law-creating processes. The latter are abstractions from the former and provide the common denominator for a number of related rules; they are mere rubrics and indications of the legal rules. In fact, the European Court, and the literature appertaining thereto, do not draw a clear line of distinction

---

[3] Arts. 31 ECSC, 164 EEC and 136 EURATOM.

[4] In *Merlini* v. *HA*, 108/63 Rec. XI 1, the Court expressly stated: " The fact that such a rule [estoppel] is not mentioned in the written law is not sufficient proof that it does not exist."

[5] Pescatore, " *Law of Integration,*" p. 75.

[6] In many instances, the ICJ refused the application of general principles of the law because " particular practice must prevail over general rules "; see Rosenne, *op. cit.,* p. 610. This source was invented to minimise the possibilities of *non liquet* by the World Court: Schwarzenberger, *Current Legal Problems* (1955), p. 212, remarks that its existence " forestalls any argument that there are gaps in International Law which prevent an International jurisdiction from rendering a judgment on the substance of any dispute."

[7] Occasionally, the Court refers to " general principles applicable even in the absence of a text referring to them," *Erzbergbau* v. *HA*, 3–18/58, 26–26/58 Rec. VI 367 or says: " we must include the general principles of law in the rules relevant to the application of the Treaty " *F. Walzwerke* v. *HA*, 21/58, Rec. V 215, but usually it explicitly states to what general principle it is referring.

[8] Migliazza, *op. cit.* in note 1 above, p. 362.

[9] Schwarzenberger, " *Manual,*" pp. 42–45. According to another view, general principles of the law are " not so much generalisations reached by the application of comparative law as particularisations of a common underlying sense of what is just in the circumstances "; Rosenne, *op. cit.,* in note 1 above.

between general principles and rules.[10] Both categories are used
indiscriminately and interchangeably; in fact, each category as it will
be demonstrated, corresponds to a different stage in the interpretative
process of the Court.

In what way does the Court extract, refine and apply the legal
principles common to the laws of the member-States? [11] In what
manner does it conduct the analysis and synthesis of the municipal
laws in order to arrive at a meaningful interpretation of the Community Law? Schematically, it proceeds at two levels; first, it carries
out a comparative analysis of the laws of member-States in order to
establish the existence of a general principle. Secondly, if a principle is
established, it elaborates on the synthesis to derive a detailed rule
from it. Thereafter, the application to the facts of the case follows.

It must be borne in mind that the Court has not, so far, furnished
expressly any explanations on the conditions of its recourse to the
general principles, but limited itself in declaring that a certain principle existed or not. The comparative studies that supply information
relevant to the cases before the Court, are carried out by its staff; one
finds, however, reference to them not in the judgments but in the
conclusions of the Advocates-General.

National concepts furnish a point of reference, a " store room " of
indications and orientations, but not ready-made solutions. The
Court usually proceeds on the " common core " (*fonds commun*)
found to exist in the various national laws, upon their congruence on
fundamental points. To this common core, it applies the modern
method of critical comparison according to which the general
principle is not necessarily the solution accepted in the highest
number of States. The technique adopted is not to have a " quasi-
mechanical superimposition of municipal laws " in order to retain the

---

10 Teitgen, *op. cit.* in note 1 above, pp. 201–208.

11 The Court may also refer to general principles of International law but only in so
far as they correspond to the needs of European integration; *e.g.* the European Convention on Human Rights (1950) was referred to in *Rutili* v. *Minister for the Interior*, 36/75
[1976] E.C.R. 1219 and in *Nold* (Nr. 2) 4/73 [1974] E.C.R. 507. In *Interfood*, 92/71 Rec.
1972, 243 for reference to GATT principles for interpretation of the classification rules
in the Community customs tariff; *Commission* v. *Italy*, 8/70, Rec. XIII 931; *Commission*
v. *Italy* 10/61 [1962] C.M.L.R. 201; *Société Anonyme Cimenteries* v. *Commission*, 8–11/68
Rec. XIII 931. On the whole, however, concepts of International Law are unsuited to
the solution of problems arising in a system of integration. Community law publicists
agree that they are rather more a disruptive than a constructive element of interpretation
(Zweigert, " *Droit des Communautés Européennes*," *Les Novelles*, p. 422; Pescatore,
C.M.L. Rev., 1970, 177. The Court has *expressis verbis* rejected reference to such princi-
ples: *Commission* v. *Luxembourg, Belgium* 90/91/63 [1965] C.M.L.R. 58; *Commission* v.
*Italy* 7/61 [1962] C.M.L.R. 39; *Commission* v. *Luxembourg, Belgium* 2, 3/62 [1963]
C.M.L.R. 129; *Germany* v. *Commission* 52, 55/65 [1967] C.M.L.R. 22 to the effect that
Member States cannot do justice to themselves, nor invoke the exception " *tu quoque* " or
" *non adimpleti contractus*," nor the state of necessity, nor reciprocity, neither the fault
of Community organs.

elements that overlap.[12] The Court avoids a " servile imitation " [13] and does not stick to details, but follows the general trend, not what Pascal called: "*plaisante justice qu'une rivière borne, la vérité en deçà des Pyrénées erreur au delà.*" [14] The use of the comparative law method is not an *a priori* intent to find the highest common factor (*dénominateur commun*), *i.e.* to recognise a principle only where the law of each member-State provides for it—nor the theory of lowest common denominator, but an intent to trace elements from which legal rules can be built for the Communities. The judges consider less the common nature of a principle than its ability to enter in the Community legal order and the ability of this order to absorb it. They choose the solutions which appear to be the most progressive,[15] *viz.* those in accord with the economic and political climate of the Communities and their objectives, not the mean quantity between solutions prevailing in the national legal systems. Sometimes, the law of one member-State may suffice if it serves best the Community purposes.[16] If the national laws reveal some identity, the Court may use them as a starting point; if they are contradictory, it evaluates the differences, reconciles them and shapes them according to the Community purpose. Hence, finality becomes the decisive element in these cases.

The elements thus adopted undergo " naturalisation," are acclimatised as European and are applied by the Court as such. This process of incorporation is qualified by Boulouis[17] as " selective integration "

---

[12] Reuter, *op. cit.* in note 1 above, p. 263. Similarly, it has been stated that the way in which International law borrows from this source is not by means of imposing Private Law institutions " lock, stock and barrel " ready-made and fully equipped with a set of rules.

[13] *Steel Industries in Luxembourg* v. *HA* 7, 9/54 Rec, II 87 *per* A. G. Roemer.

[14] " Pleasant justice surrounded by a river. Truth on this side of the Pyrenees, falsity on the other " in *Pensées* fragment 294, Ed. Brunschweig, quoted by Cheng, *op. cit.* in note 1 above, p. 390.

[15] A.G. Lagrange in *Hoogovens* v. *HA* 14/61 [1963] C.M.L.R. 72 was explicit: " The object is not merely to reach a solution by means of some kind of mathematical average between the various national solutions but to choose from the legal systems of the member-States those solutions that seem the best ones in view of the aims of the Treaty."

[16] *Assider* v. *HA*, 5/55 Rec. I 263 per A.G. Lagrange on " *detournement de pouvoir.*" Art. 215 para. 2 EEC requires " common principles." If one interprets it literally one has to find the common denominator of rules of national laws. This would eventually result into rules of such a high generality that their legal efficacy would be very much curtailed. In favour of the view that a principle derived from the law of one member-State may suffice is the fact that several provisions of the Treaties themselves were solely based on the law of one member-State, for instance, art. 40 E.C.S.C. modelled upon French Administrative Law. The opposite view tends to curtail the discretionary power of the Court in the search for principles; in favour of the common denominator see, McMahon, J.C.M.S., 1962, p. 1 *et seq.*: " the Court examines the jurisprudence of the member-States relating to this concept and extrapolates the principles common to most of the States "; Toth, *op. cit.* in note 1 above, p. 659 concurs that the Court cannot rely upon the law of one member-State.

[17] *Mélanges Waline*, p. 154.

of external sources. Notions having an archaic flavour, inadequate to meet the Community needs [18] are rejected; still, if the case is presented, the Court may refer to the historical origins of certain rules of national laws.[19] Thus, the choice is freely made for the purpose of creating a homogeneous law.

The theory of mathematical average or common denominator has its origins in the misunderstanding as to the difference between principles and rules. Constantinesco [20] rightly distinguishes between " *éléments déterminants,*" *i.e.* fundamental, which are identical in all member-States, and " *éléments fongibles,*" *i.e.* the technical differences in municipal laws. As far as the latter are concerned, the Court may either adopt a rule as existing in one or several member-States or elaborate a new rule. As for the former, the Court seeks to establish if a general principle exists in the majority of member-States but nothing like a mathematical average is adopted. No particular national law may claim any preference over the others, unless it can offer a superior solution to a problem.[21] As Zweigert [22] remarked, it is not desirable to have " *a brouillard* " consisting of diverse national legal systems, but rather an adequate solution germane to the legal order of the Communities. It is not a quantitative solution [23] that prevails but a qualitative one, in the last analysis, determined by functional considerations. Thus, comparative law study [24] has a positive, practical and concrete purpose; it is no longer a struggling new academic discipline but becomes a directly creative method of the embryonic European Community Law. It has, however, been stressed since the early judgments that this study should not be confused with the problem of direct application of the rules of municipal laws. The Court bases its refusal on the distinctiveness of its

[18] *E.g. Glucoseries Réunies* v. *Commission*, 1/64 [1964] C.M.L.R. 596.

[19] For reference to the Roman law origins of a common tradition in the laws of member-States, see: *Klomp* v. *Inspektie*, 23/68 Rec. XV 43.

[20] *Op. cit.* in note 2 above, pp. 205–206.

[21] See: *Algera* v. *Common Assembly*, 7/56, 3–7/57, Rec. III 81 where the Court withheld the solution of Italian Administrative law that withdrawal of an administrative act is possible within a reasonable time. In *Hoogovens* v. *HA*, 14/61 [1963] C.M.L.R. 73, it adopted the solution of German Administrative law.

[22] " *Die Rechtsvergleichung im Dienste der Europaischen Rechtsverzeinheitlichung,*" *Rabels Zeitschrift* (1951), p. 388; Lorenz, *op. cit.* in note 1 above, p. 11.

[23] The test adopted by international judges seems to be that the principle must be recognised in substance by all the main systems of law and it must not do violence to the fundamental concepts of any of those systems. Hence, it is not necessary for it to be applied by all States *in foro domestico* but by the most representative systems of national law.

[24] Elaboration of the case law would have been rendered very difficult without this method. Yet, certain publicists refuse to recognise the value of the comparative method. Assuming that the Court is an International Court and based on the voluntarist theory of Jellinek—that the origin of International law is limited to the will of States—they stressed the difference between sources of International law and principles of national law.

mandate, limited to the application of Community law: " This is not a case of application of Italian Law, nor French Law, nor of the law of any other member-State of the Community but of the law of the Treaty, and it is solely in order to achieve the elaboration of this law of the Treaty that the Court must undertake the study of the national legal solutions, whenever it appears necessary for that purpose." [25]

## II—APPLICATION OF THE COMPARATIVE LAW METHOD BY THE EUROPEAN COURT OF JUSTICE

If the Court of Justice may use the comparative law method in order to fill in the outlines of Community legislation due to the affinities of the latter in its tenor and legal technique with the municipal systems, it is not open to the Courts of member-States to fill in the *lacunae* in Community law [26] by reference to their own national law.[27]

From what *reservoir* is the comparative law method going to draw? Civil law or Administrative law? Administrative laws of the member-States provide most of the material but this does not preclude rules derived from private law from playing a role. It is remarkable that the Advocates-General refer not only to national law but also to precedents [28] drawn from national courts and to textbook writers [29] of the member-States.

Explicit reference to the general principles is made in a number of articles of the Treaties,[30] the most important to be found in articles 215, paragraph 2 of the European Economic Community (EEC) [31] and 188, paragraph 2 of the European Atomic Energy Agency (EURATOM) which read as follows: " In the case of non-contractual liability, the Community shall in accordance with the general principles common to the laws of the member-States, make good any damage caused by its institutions or by its servants in the performance of their duties."

Some of the general principles adopted by the Court are so fundamental and broad that they cannot be ascribed only to the laws of

---

[25] *Assider* v. *HA*, 3/54 Rec. I 148; *Molkerei Zentrale* 28/67 [1968] C.M.L.R. 167.

[26] Since the majority of writers on Community law and the practice of the European Court do not make a strict separation between principles and rules, the exposition of this part will not distinguish between them.

[27] *Hannoverische Zucker* v. *Hauptzollamt Hannover*, 159/73 [1974] E.C.R. 121, 129.

[28] In *Limburg Coalmines* v. *Ha*, 17/57 Rec. V 36, the Court referred to the *Merveilleux* case 26/5/1944 Rec. p. 155 and *Cercat* case 24/4/1953 Rec. p. 195 of the French Conseil d'Etat.

[29] Reuter is frequently cited by the Court: *Stork* v. *HA*, 1/58 Rec. V. 83.

[30] Arts. 40 ECSC, 92 ECSC, 70 (2) ECSC, 96 ECSC, 99 ECSC, 58 para. 2 EEC, 211 EEC, 192 EEC, 164 EURATOM, 185 EURATOM.

[31] Non-contractual liability in art. 215, para. 2 EEC means administrative liability. It refers to the same concept as governmental liability (*Amtshaftung*) in the member-States; see *Kampffmeyer* v. *Commission*, 5–7/66, 13–24/66 Rec. XIII 318, for the notions of " *faute de service*," " *damnum emergens* " and " *lucrum cessans*."

member-States but are inherent in every legal system. The following can be considered as the most important findings of the comparative law method: The principle of legality (*principe de la légalité, Gesetzmässigkeit der Verwaltung*) *i.e.* that a norm of a lower rank must respect the rules established by a higher norm. In an early case, however, the Court ruled that: " in the exercise of its functions, the High Authority must conciliate the principle of legality with legal certainty." [32]

The principle of legal certainty (*respect de la sécurité juridique, Wahrung der Rechtssicherheit*) has been recently used for interpretation of Community Acts so as to ensure their validity rather than as a criterion for determining their validity. In the two *Deuka* cases,[33] it was stated in almost identical terms: " it is right to apply in the interests of legal certainty, for the computation of the amount of the denaturing premium, the provisions in force at the time the application was lodged, even if the technical mixing is not done until a subsequent date." Interpreted in such a way, the relevant Regulations (reducing and abolishing a denaturing premium) were held to be valid. The same principle has been used in the field of competition, concerning articles 85 (1) and 86 EEC, to the effect that they produce direct effects and cannot be modified or limited by Regulation 17/62.[34] In the absence of provision in the EEC Treaty and Regulation 17 as to the prescription of actions for breaches of competition, it was held that the time limit had to be fixed in advance to fulfil the necessity of legal certainty.[35] Recently,[36] in a case of conflict between legal certainty and the principle of equality of remuneration between male and female workers for identical work, it has been held that the former prevailed at least for past periods.

In France, an aspect of legal certainty comes under the label of " respect of acquired rights " (*respect des droits acquis, wohlerworbene Rechte*). The Court consecrated it in one of the leading staff cases which concerned the *ex nunc* revocability of an illegal act conferring

---

[32] *Breedband* v. *Société des Aciériés du Temple*, Ha, 42, 49/59 Rec. VII 101, 103.

[33] *Deuka* v. *Einfuhr*, 78/74, 5/75 [1975] E.C.R. 421, 759. Concerning the organisation of agricultural markets, the principle of legal certainty compelled reference to the law in force when the text was applied: *Henck* v. *Hauptzollamt Emmerich*, 14/71 Rec. XVII 774, 787.

[34] Reg. 17/62, OJ, 1962, 204 (13/3/62); see also *BRT* v. *Sabam*, 127/73 [1974] E.C.R. 51; *Brasserie de Haecht* v. *Wilkin*, 48/72 [1973] E.C.R. 77.

[35] *Chimiefarma* v. *Commission*, 41/69 Rec. XVI 64; *Buchler* v. *Commission*, 44/59 Rec. XVI 733; *Boehringer* v. *Commission*, 45/69 Rec. XVI 769. In *De Geus* v. *Bosch*, 13/61 [1962] C.M.L.R. 1, it was held to be contrary to the legal certainty to strike with nullity certain agreements before knowing to what kind of agreements art. 85 EEC applies. In *Imperial Chemical Industries* v. *Commission*, 48, 49, 51, 52, 54, 55, 57/69 [1972] C.M.L.R. 557 the Court created a kind of praetorian prescription to satisfy the needs of legal certainty.

[36] *Defrenne* v. *Sabena*, 43/75 [1976] C.M.L.R. 98.

individual rights. Certain European Coal and Steel Community (ECSC) employees had their employment regulated by the ECSC Statute of Service and the problem was whether admission to it could subsequently be withdrawn. It was held: " As for the possibility of revocation of such acts . . . a study of comparative law makes it clear that if an administrative act is illegal, the law of all member-States accepts the possibility of withdrawal." Yet, the Court admitted that if this principle is generally recognised, the conditions of its exercise vary. Further on: " If the act in question were legal and individual rights had been acquired under it, then it could not be revoked, because of the need to protect the expectations thus created." [37]

The principle of the protection of legitimate expectation [38] (*protection de la confiance légitime, Vertrauensschutz*) has been recently used in connection with non-contractual liability, *i.e.* that a Community institution can be liable for harm caused by an act infringing this principle even where the legality of the act itself is not in question.

The English doctrine of estoppel or " he who comes to equity must come with clean hands " under the latin label " *non venire contra factum proprium* ": in a case [39] concerning Tunisian exports of fat products to France, it was held that the inaction of the Commission—in failing to make propositions to the Council as to levies on imports from third States—allowed the Court not to find that France was in default. The reason was that the inaction of the Commission created the French default.

Equity or its expression in the principle of Penal law " *non bis in idem*," *i.e.* that a person may not be punished twice for the same offence, was mainly used for staff disciplinary matters.[40] In *Walt Wilhelm* v. *Bundeskartellamt* [41] it was held that " equity necessitates to take into consideration a previously imposed sanction when determining a new one."

The principle of " good faith " (*bona fides*) which requires obedience to a standard of honesty, loyalty, fair dealing and morality and

---

[37] *Algera* v. *Common Assembly.* 3–7/57, 7/56 Rec. III 115; *Simon* v. *CJEC*, 15/60, Rec. VIII 242; *Breedband* v. *HA*, 42 49/59 Rec. VII 159; *Snupat* v. *HA*, 32, 33/58 Rec. V 299; it has also been held that the principle of non-discrimination overrides the respect of acquired rights: *Mannesmann* v. *HA*, 37/64 Rec. XI 916; *Lemmerzwerke* v. *HA*, 111/63 [1968] C.M.L.R. 280; *Societe des Aciéries du Temple* v. *HA*, 39/64 Rec. XI 957.

[38] *CNTA* v. *Commission*, 74/74 [1975] E.C.R. 533; *Commission* v. *Council*, 81/72 [1973] E.C.R. 575, 584.

[39] *Commission* v. *France*, 26/69 Rec. XVI 565; *Sorema* v. *HA*, 67/63 [1964] C.M.L.R. 358; *Alfiera* v. *European Parliament*, 3/66 [1967] C.M.L.R. 110; *Klocknen* v. *HA*, 17, 20/61 [1962] E.C.R. 325, 342; *Europemballage, Continental Can* v. *Commission*, 6/72 [1973] E.C.R. 215, 241.

[40] *Gutmann* v. *Commission*, 18, 35/65 [1966] E.C.R. 103, 119.

[41] 14/68, Rec. 1969, 16 p. *per* A.G. Roemer.

advocates the non-abuse of rights has also been used. In an early case [42] it was held that the acts of administrative authorities concerning contracts are subject to respecting good faith. Recently, [43] A.G. Trabucchi formulated an analysis of Italian, French, German and English law in order to determine the extent to which the State is liable for failure to carry out undertakings given in the exercise of a discretionary power, and concluded that whilst the extent differed from State to State, the principle as such was recognised.

The principle of " *audi alterem partem* " or " *audiatur ed altera pars* " (*droit de la défense*): case in which a person who may be aggrieved by an administrative procedure, is entitled to a hearing on the questions in point before the decision is taken. In *Snupat* v. *HA*, [44] it was expressly stated that " it would amount to a violation of an elementary principle of law to base a decision on facts of which the parties were unable to take cognisance and on which they were unable to take any position."

The principle of equality before the public charges: under the ECSC Treaty, reference was made in several cases to the French concept of " *égalité devant les charges publiques*," *i.e.* comparableness of situations. [45] Now, however, this principle has been subsumed in the wider principle of equality of treatment or non-discrimination. [46]

The principle of proportionality (*Verhaltnismässigkeitsgrundsatz*) means that there must be a proportional gravity between a wrongful act of an individual and the response of the High Authority or Commission to it [47]; *viz.* that the punishment must fit the crime. It is, perhaps the best known principle and has its origins in German theory. It requires that Community legislation should not have the effect of imposing on traders unnecessary burdens to effect the object

---

[42] *Lachmüller* v. *Commission*, 43, 45, 48/59 Rec. VI 933, 956; *Fiddelaar* v. *Commission*, 44/59 Rec. VI 1077, 1099.

[43] *Compagnie Continentale France* v. *Council*, 196/73 [1975] C.M.L.R. 578, 585; in *West Zucker* v. *Einfuhr Fur Zucker*, 1/73 [1973] E.C.R. 723.

[44] 42, 49/59 Rec. VII 146; *Alvis* v. *Council*, 32/62 [1963] C.M.L.R. 403; *Leroy* v. *HA*, 35/62 [1964] C.M.L.R. 562; *Huber, Willane* v. *Commission*, 11/64, 110/63, 19/63, 65/63, [1966] C.M.L.R. 231, 261; *Kergall* v. *Common Assembly*, 1/55 Rec. II 9. Recently, in *Transocean Marine Paint Association* v. *Commission*, 17/74 [1974] C.M.L.R. 459, 477, the Court annulled part of a Commission Decision extending an exemption of art. 85 (3) EEC, the part annulled being an onerous condition of which the plaintiffs had not had foreknowledge and on which they were unable to present contrary argument, *cf.* also Submissions invoking the English concept of " natural justice," at p. 468, 471.

[45] *Meroni* v. *HA*, 14, 16, 17, 20, 24, 26, 27/60, 1/61 Rec. VII 319, 338; *E. Longdoz, Hainaut-Sambre* v. *HA*, 3–4/65 [1966] C.M.L.R. 146; *Kergall* v. *Common Assembly*, 1/55 Rec. II 9, 44; *Hauts Fourneaux Belges* v. *Ha*, 8/57 Rec. IV 230.

[46] *Louwage* v. *Commission*, 148/73 [1974] E.C.R. 81, 89.

[47] *Fedechar* v. *HA*, 8/55 Rec. II 304; *Alma* v. *HA*, 8/56 Rec. III 179, 192; *Boehringer* v. *Commission*, 7/72 [1973] C.M.L.R. 864. In *Reich* v. *Hauptzollamt Landau*, 64/75 [1975] C.M.L.R. 396 a particular application of this principle consisted in the requirement that in certain cases, traders should be relieved of the consequences of effects amounting to *force majeure*.

that the legislation has in view. A.G. de Lamothe defined it as follows: " citizens may only have imposed on them, for the purposes of the public interest, obligations which are strictly necessary for those purposes to be attained." [48] It has recently been used as a criterion to test Community measures designed to combat the problems arising from fluctuating exchange rates. In a preliminary reference [49] on agricultural matters, the question was raised whether Council Regulation 974/71,[50] introducing the system of monetary compensatory amounts conflicted with the principle of proportionality. The Court declared that it was not satisfied that the Council had " imposed burdens on traders which were manifestly out of proportion to the object in view," but it did state that " the Institutions must ensure that the amounts which commercial operators are charged, are no greater than is required to achieve the aim which the authorities are to accomplish."

The principle of requirement of good administration of justice was referred to in a case [51] involving the power *ad litem* (power of attorney). The Court adopted a liberal view that a Counsel representing a party before it is only required to establish his professional status as an advocate and not to produce a specific power of attorney. A.G. Roemer draws argument from the Rules of Procedure, adding that similar results were reached by examining the national administrative procedures. In particular in French and German law such a power can be produced subsequently to regularise breaches to the rules of procedure.

The principle of undue enrichment: it has been held [52] that recovery of undue payments should depend on the absence of *justa causa*, in accordance with this principle of the Civil law of accession of the member-States.

The rule that a written declaration (*inter absentes*) becomes effective as soon as it reaches the internal sphere of the addressee [53] was elaborated after an examination of the posting rules in operation in the member-States.

Recently, A.G. Warner [54] considered an English rule not obliging an administrative authority when entrusted with discretion to be

---

[48] *Internationale Handelsgesellschaft* v. *Einfuhr*, 11/70 [1972] C.M.L.R. 255.

[49] *Balkan-Import-Export* v. *Hauptzollamt Berlin-Packhof*, 5/73, [1973] E.C.R. 1091, 1112.

[50] Reg. 974/71, O.J., 1971, L 106/1.

[51] *Barge* v. *HA*, 14/64 [1965] C.M.L.R. 215, 218; *Vloeberghs* v. *HA*, 9, 12/60, Rec. VII 395, 448.

[52] *Mannesmann* v. *HA*, 4/59, 13/59 Rec. VI 24; *Megancy* v. *Commission*. 36/72, [1973] E.C.R. 527, 534.

[53] *Alma* v. *Ha*, 8/56 Rec. III 189; *Chambre Syndicale* v. *HA*, 9/57 Rec. IV, 367.

[54] *Commission* v. *Council* (*Re Civil Service Salaries*), 81/72 [1973] C.M.L.R. 632 annotation of Dubois, *RTDE*, 1973, p. 761; A.G. Warner also considered two English

bound in advance as to how they will exercise it, whereas the Court adopted the opposite Continental view embodied in the maxim *legem patere quam fecisti*.

In another recent case,[55] the Court withheld the principle of no payment for days in which work was stopped as follows: " According to a principle recognised in the labour law of the member-States, wages and other benefits pertaining to days on strike are not due to persons who have taken part in that strike. This principle is applicable in the relations between the institutions of the Communities and their officials." [56]

In the process of investigations undertaken by the comparative law method, a particular place was allotted to the respect of fundamental rights. Neither the Treaty of Paris nor the Treaties of Rome contain a provision concerning the safeguarding of these rights, because it was thought that the economic objects of the Treaties did not necessitate the existence of such rights. In practice, though, economic and social objectives are interrelated. The mission of the Court as custodian of the Treaties is extensive and, consequently, it must draw its inspiration not only from the Treaties but from the " common core " [57] of constitutional traditions of the member-States with regard to fundamental rights. The evolution of its attitude is remarkable. Whilst in 1959 and 1960 [58] it refused to consider the violation of fundamental rights as ground for annulment under article 31 ECSC, in 1969 and 1970 [59] it accepted that they formed part of the Community legal order and that, in safeguarding them it drew its inspiration from the common constitutional tradition of the member-States. Since 1974 [60] it has been orientated towards an optimal standard of these rights by not admitting measures incompatible with the fundamental rights recognised and guaranteed by the Constitutions of the member-States. Obviously, their elaboration in

---

cases: *Cory* v. *London Corporation* [1951] 2 K.B. 476 and *Ellen Street Estates* v. *Ministry of Health* [1934] 1 K.B. 590 and the exceptions to them. Similarly, in *Commission* v. *Council* (Nr. 2) 70/74 [1975] C.M.L.R. 287 it was held that the Council will be bound by the criteria fixed in advance for the exercise of its discretion.

[55] *Acton* v. *Commission*, 44, 46, 49/74 [1975] E.C.R. 383, 395.

[56] It is arguable whether we are dealing with a general principle or a particular rule. Comparative studies concerning particular aspects of the freedom of trade union activity of Labour law were also carried out in: *Union Syndicale* v. *Council*, 175/73 [1974] E.C.R. 917, 925; *Syndicat General* v. *Commission*, 18/74 [1974] E.C.R. 933, 944. For the principle of continuity of legal structures through changes in the legislation see: *Klomp* v. *Inpektie der Belastingen*, 23/68 Rec. XV 43 per A.G. Gand.

[57] According to Scheuner, *op. cit.* in note 1 above, p. 171, 185, the Court has adopted a negative criterion that rights which are not respected in the legal orders of all member-States cannot be protected at Community level.

[58] *Stork* v. *HA*, 1/58 Rec. V 43, 63; *Nold* v. *HA*, 40/59 Rec. VI 827, 859.

[59] *Stauder* v. *Ulm*, 29/69 [1970] C.M.L.R. 112; *Internationale Handelsgesellschaft* v. *Einfuhr*, 11/70 [1972] C.M.L.R. 255.

[60] *Nold* v. *Commission*, 4/73 [1974] C.M.L.R. 338.

the practice of the Court is going to be a slow and long-lasting process. The following rights have hitherto been adopted at Community level: the right of human dignity and general liberty [61]; the freedom of trade and industry [62]; the right of property and free exercise of work [63]; and the right of equality of remuneration between male and female workers for identical work.[64]

The comparative law method has also been used in order to elucidate the meaning of certain undefined notions contained in the Treaties. Since these notions were borrowed from the national laws, it was natural that the Court would turn to national laws for their interpretation. The Treaties contain terms such as: misuse of power (art. 33 ECSC, 173 EEC), legal person (art. 173 EEC), undertakings (art. 85 (1) EEC), members of Government (art. 146 EEC), " wrongful act or omission in the performance of duties " (art. 40 ECSC),[65] competition (art. 85 EEC), workers (art. 48 (1) EEC), " companies or firms constituted under civil or commercial law " (art. 58 para. 2 EEC), *force majeure* (art. 39 of the Protocol on Statute of the Court).

Perhaps the most noteworthy example of a notion interpreted in the light of national laws concerns the misuse of power of articles 33 ECSC, 173 EEC and 146 EURATOM. This concept was subjected to an extensive analysis by A.G. Lagrange,[66] who prefaced his incursion into national laws, saying: " It seems to us that a recourse to the national laws is imperative. The concept of *détournement de pouvoir* has not been invented by the authors of the Treaty and in order to formulate an opinion on what the *détournement de pouvoir* should be in the application of the Treaty . . . we must, first, know what is the meaning in the respective laws of our Member States. . . ." and he finally concluded that it was similar to the French and Belgian law and the law of Luxembourg, and quite different from the Italian *sviamento di potere*, the German *Ermessensmissbrauch* and the Dutch *misbruik van bevoegdheid*.

In the *Nold* v. *HA* (Nr. 1) case,[67] the Advocate-General referred to German law in order to determine the legal capacity of a German company in liquidation: " It is a question of legal capacity and in the absence of particular provisions in Community Law, we must appreciate it according to the rules of national law, therefore, of German law, since a German company is in question."

The precise meaning of *force majeure* has to be decided by reference

---

[61] *Stauder* v. *Ulm*, 29/69 [1970] C.M.L.R. 112.
[62] *Internationale Handelsgesellschaft* v. *Einfuhr*, 11/70 [1972] C.M.L.R. 255.
[63] *Nold* (Nr. 2), 4/73 [1974] E.C.R. 491.
[64] *Defrenne* v. *Sabena*, 43/75 [1976] C.M.L.R. 98.
[65] *Feram* v. *HA*, 23/59 Rec. V 517; *Fives Lille Cail* v. *HA*, 19, 21/60, 2, 3/61 [1962] C.M.L.R. 281.
[66] *Assider* v. *HA*, 3/54 Rec. I 123 (author's translation).    [67] 18/57 Rec. V 110, 160.

to the legal context in which it is intended to operate but which cannot be confined to absolute impossibility.[68] The Court has extended it to include " abnormal circumstances outside the control of the importer, arisen in spite of the fact that the titular holder of the licence had taken all the precautions which could reasonably be expected by a prudent and diligent trader." [69] Nevertheless, in a recent case [70] it recognised that there was an implied *force majeure* clause in a Regulation which did not specifically provide for one, on the basis that such clauses were contained in parallel Regulations.

Finally, it must be said that in the course of its comparative studies, the Court and mainly its Advocates-General take cognisance of concepts embedded in the laws of non-member-States. Such a reference demonstrates the flexibility of its approach and the experimental character of Community law, a strange phenomenon for a law based on Civil law origins. The most frequent reference has been to the anti-trust law of USA [71] on which articles 85, 86 EEC and 60 ECSC have been modelled, as well as the relevant parts of English and German law.[72]

### III—CONCLUSIONS

In spite of certain isolated voices of scepticism as to the interpretation of European Community law in the light of concepts and principles of municipal law, based on the premise that complex economic ideas of the Treaties can scarcely be clarified by recourse to traditionally and generally recognised legal principles, the overwhelming tendency in theory and practice is in favour of their use. This is so because the comparative law method as used by the European Court has been a valuable instrument in peeling off the differing appearances to reach a more or less common substratum. This was expressly stated by A.G. de Lamothe: " The general principles of national legal systems contribute to forming that philosophical, political and legal substratum common to the member-States from which through the case-law an unwritten Community law emerges." [73]

---

[68] *Norddeutsches Vieh und Fleischkontor* v. *Einfuhr* 186/73 [1974] E.C.R. 533, 550; *Kampffmeyer* v. *Einfuhr*, 158/73 [1974] E.C.R. 101, 110.
[69] *Einfuhr* v. *Pfutzenreuter*, 3/74 [1974] E.C.R. 589.
[70] *Reich* v. *Hauptzollamt Landau*, 64/74 [1975] C.M.L.R. 396; *Unger* v. *Bestuur*, 73/63 [1964] C.M.L.R. 330.
[71] For reference to the Sherman Act and the Robinson-Patman Act (1936) see: *Acciaierie Ferriere di Modena* v. *HA*, 16/61 [1962] C.M.L.R. 221; *Imperial Chemical Industries* v. *Commission*, 48, 49, 51, 52, 53, 54, 55, 56, 57/69 [1972] C.M.L.R. 557; A.G. Roemer cited approvingly American anti-trust cases in *Italy* v. *Council, Commission* 32/65 [1969] C.M.L.R. 39; *Geitling* v. *HA*, 13/60 [1962] C.M.L.R. 113; *Erzbergbau* v. *HA*, 3–18/58, 26/58 Rec. VI 386.
[72] The Court has also referred to the Swiss Federal Statute on Cartels (1962) and to the United Kingdom Restrictive Trade Practices Act (1956).
[73] *Internationale Handelsgesellschaft* v. *Einfuhr*, 11/70 [1972] C.M.L.R. 255.

Although it is thought that the rules of the Treaties are often modelled on French Administrative law, this is not the case concerning the elaboration of Community rules by recourse to the comparative law method. Indeed, it is difficult to establish a definite influence of a certain member-State in this process. At most, it can be maintained that certain of these rules have a formulation closely resembling that current in Germany. Recently English concepts are beginning to make their presence felt [74]; nevertheless, the enlargement of the Communities to Nine requires a more refined comparative method in order to determine the common core of continental and Anglo-Saxon laws. However, the comparative process possible for the Community of Six is still feasible in the Community of Nine.

The general principles thus derived are established in the case law so as to become principles of Community law, but they are still distinguished from the general principles of the law of the Community Treaties: *i.e.* in social affairs the notion of equality of treatment; in business law the requirement that competition should not be eliminated; in external trade, the notion of Community preference; and between member-States the notion of solidarity. In cases of conflict between these two sets of general principles, the latter always prevail over the former.

It is to be expected that, day by day, new general principles will emerge and, by means of the comparative law method, will be integrated in Community law. This is an ingenious way of indirectly achieving harmonisation of national laws. In fact, as A.G. Lagrange [75] characteristically remarked, two or three Advisory Opinions of the Court concerning basic legal principles are more conducive to harmonisation of national laws than years of learned scholarly discussion between those attending even the most outstanding congresses of Comparative law. The comparative analysis undertakes a tremendous work in that it has to establish principles and rules best suited to express a common tradition and compatible with the Community structure. The overriding consideration of this interpretation is that the principle and rule must be consistent with the basic aims and objectives of the Community and best serving European integration. Thus, comparison of the law serves not only in getting a better comprehension of our own law through the study of comparable foreign systems, but is conditional for the creation of a twentieth-century European *ius commune*. [76]

---

[74] *Transocean Marine Paint Association* v. *Commission*, 17/74 [1974] C.M.L.R. 459.

[75] A.J.C.L. 1966, p. 709, 724.

[76] Brinkhorst, *op. cit.* in note 1 above, p. 320.

# METHODOLOGICAL INNOVATIONS
# IN SOVIET INTERNATIONAL
# LEGAL DOCTRINE

By

## W. E. BUTLER

THE newer methodological approaches to international law and
relations developed during the past three decades are finding their
adherents among Soviet international lawyers. Many factors are
doubtless responsible. Soviet international legal writing is taking
fuller account of a broader range of publications abroad and in doing
so is engaging in a more sophisticated and differentiated critique of
contrary views rather than simply dismissing them.[1] Of greater
significance perhaps is the influence of Sociology and International
Relations, still relatively young as separate disciplines in the Soviet
Union, in encouraging experimentation with empirical and comparative investigations of phenomena.[2] Not only has their emergence had
no deprecatory effect on international law, as some Soviet jurists
once feared, but they have infused a new vitality and possibly a new
style into doctrinal writings.

Until the late 1960s the overwhelming inclination, based on
decades of tradition in doctrinal exegesis, was to approach international law methodologically through the materialistic dialectic
while emphasising normative analysis: the general concepts and
principles of international law, emanating from the concordance of
the wills of States and comprising part of the superstructure of the
economic base of society in every State, were to be considered in
conjunction with the economic base which delimited the will of the
State and also with other superstructure elements, such as politics,
municipal law, morals, and legal consciousness, that influence a
State's will and thus, indirectly, influence international law. These

[1] See G. I. Tunkin, " Zadachi nauki mezhdunarodnogo prava v svete reshenii
XXIV s'ezda KPSS," *Sovetskoe gosudarstvo i pravo,* Nr. 7 (1972), pp. 30–36.

[2] W. Zimmerman, *Soviet Perspectives on International Relations* (1969). On the
development of Soviet sociology, see E. A. Weinberg, *The Development of Sociology in
the Soviet Union* (1974). International lawyers also take part in the Soviet Association of
Political (State) Science, founded about 1961. The Association commenced publication of a Yearbook in 1976 under the title, *Mezhdunarodnye otnosheniia, politika i
lichnost'. Ezhegodnik. 1975.* The inaugural issue published information on research in
progress at various academic centres and reproduces the text of the Charter of the
Soviet Association of Political Science. One contribution is by an international lawyer,
V. A. Kartashkin, " Mezhdunarodnoe pravo i lichnost' ," pp. 115–122.

concepts and principles were then examined in historical context, with due regard for the socio-political objective of States and the socio-political consequences of applying rules of international law to particular situations.[3]

That other " special methods " of research used in various branches of the social sciences (bearing in mind that in the Soviet Union and in the rest of Europe law is regarded as one of the social sciences) could fruitfully be utilised in International Law was forcefully argued by Iu. Ia. Baskin and D. I. Fel'dman at the twelfth annual general meeting of the Soviet Association of International Law in 1969. Their prospectus for international legal research was later expanded into a monograph.[4] Within the framework of the materialist dialectic and its basic laws, Baskin and Fel'dman dwelt at length on such scientific and special methods of research in International Law as systems analysis, modelling, cybernetics, game theory, and empirical sociological enquiries. They also explored the limitations and merits of " quasi-scientific methods," including the application of formal logic, the historical method, and the comparative method.

Among the first Soviet international lawyers to pursue these new methodologies is I. I. Lukashuk, Professor of International Law at the Kiev State University in the Ukraine. He is intrigued by the interaction between international law and the international order. In his recent monograph, the first of its kind in the Soviet Union, he has applied systems analysis to international law as a means of explaining and comprehending that interrelationship.[5] His technique will be of interest to those elsewhere of a similar inclination, but his broader observations and conclusions convey a refreshing perception of the international community and the role that law plays, or ought to

---

[3] See D. B. Levin, "Metodologiia sovetskoi nauki mezhdunarodnogo prava," *Sovetskoe gosudarstvo i pravo*, Nr. 9 (1969), pp. 62–63.

[4] Iu. Ia. Baskin and D. I. Fel'dman, *Mezhdunarodnoe pravo; problemy metodologii* (1971).

[5] I. I. Lukashuk, *Mezhdunarodno-pravovoe regulirovanie mezhdunarodnykh otnosheni* (1975). Professor Lukashuk was born at Kharkov in 1926 and graduated from the Kharkov Juridical Institute in 1947. He received the degree kandidat iuridicheskikh nauk in 1951 and doktor iuridicheskikh nauk in 1961. From 1950–63 he taught at the Saratov Juridical Institute before assuming the Chair of International Law at Kiev State University. He is a member of the Permanent Court of Arbitration at the Hague and also of the Executive Committee of the Soviet International Law Association. He has represented the Ukraine at the Vienna Conference on the Law of Treaties, the United Nations Human Rights Commission, and the Sixth Committee of the United Nations General Assembly. His recent publications in English include " Parties to Treaties—The Right of Participation," CXXXV *Recueil des cours* (1972), pp. 231–328 and a basic student manual, *International Law* (Kiev, 1968). He is the co-author of the standard Ukrainian textbook on international law, *Mizhnarodne pravo* (1971), reviewed in the LXVI *American Journal of International Law* (1972), pp. 666–668. In 1974 he collaborated with G. I. Tunkin, R. L. Bobrov, and A. N. Talalaev in editing another text, *Mezhdunarodnoe pravo* (1974).

assume, in a conceptual language far more comprehensible and even palatable to the western psyche. And this is perhaps not inappropriate in a volume devoted to demonstrating how international law can assist in furthering détente.

Lukashuk begins by defining and developing the systemic notion of " international legal regulation " (hereinafter ILR—to translate the Russian acronym which the author employs). ILR in his view is the ". . . purposeful authoritative influence in international relations jointly exercised by States with the aid of international law for the purpose of satisfying their own national and international interests " (p. 8). This is in effect a form of social management or administration [*sotsial'noe upravlenie*] by States, that is, an application or use of State authority to influence international relations, working on the premise of the sovereign authority of each State.

Administration of affairs is an " objectively necessary " function of any social system, he notes, and an international system of sovereign States cannot function normally without ILR. International law establishes or records the general standards for normal behaviour in the international community as a requisite of maintaining international peace and security, indeed, of international life itself. Those standards embodied in general principles of international law are of special importance because their breach is an infringement of the proper functioning of the entire international system. Or, putting it another way, the author says that generally recognised norms of international law are an expectation of behaviour laid down in a special way. Conduct contrary to these expectations is anomalous or deviant conduct. Revolution, meanwhile, poses an enormous strain on ILR. Periods in which great social revolutions occur, Lukashuk argues, are those in which profound contradictions exist between the constantly developing international system and obsolete international legal standards. To this extent, he suggests, the dysfunctional conduct of revolutionary States is itself normal and necessary. But, he adds, the modern system of ILR has itself improved " mechanisms " for the progressive development of international law, and these presumably reduce the objective necessity of abnormal behaviour by new States.

ILR as a system is said to consist of two subsystems: the system which is the *object* of ILR, that is, relations between States, and the system which is the *subject* of ILR, the system of means of exerting international legal influence. A profound understanding of the object of ILR is essential, and not surprisingly Lukashuk believes it is to be found in Marxist-Leninist theory, most especially the Marxist sociological understanding of international affairs. He cautions strongly in this connection that one cannot mechanically carry over the experience of municipal legal regulation into the international order. ILR itself is also said to have two basic phases: the creating of law and the applying of law, as well as an adjunctive correctional phase based on the experience of the initial two phases.

As the international community becomes more interdependent, the highest possible degree of unity is essential in the generally obligatory conduct of sovereign States. This would be impossible to achieve, Lukashuk observes, without ILR, and hence the latter's role must inevitably grow. But the discipline of International Law, or as he prefers, the science of International Law, with few exceptions rarely invokes this systemic approach. Some Soviet jurists (he mentions P. I. Stuchka and V. M. Shurshalov) have urged that legal concepts must include not only the norms themselves but their application in social relations, as also have western jurists (he names Julius Stone). Most western international lawyers in his view, however, associate themselves with Kelsenian positivism and by implication presumably most Soviet international lawyers are content to retain their traditional methods. Lukashuk believes with Professor L. Henkin that there is little understanding of the role of international law in international relations.

A legal norm, he argues, is in one sense a model of proper conduct for the subjects of the international system. The creation of an optimal model does not automatically transform the reality of international relations. Implementation is more complex than adopting or creating the norm. The advantage of ILR is that it allows one to consider the dynamics of international law, instead of dwelling, as international legal science now does, on the static elements of the system. As ILR develops, systemic concepts such as " international legal order " and " international legality " become more significant, for " international legal order " results from putting international relations in good order with the aid of international law. International legality, Lukashuk suggests, is a historically conditional level of the realisation of the principles and norms of international law (p. 18). This entails the universality of international legality, the universal binding nature of international law, and the equally binding nature of generally recognised norms on all subjects of international law.

Lukashuk then turns to consider the place of ILR in the administrative system of international relations. As co-operation among States increases, the administrative dimension of the international system becomes more important. He defines " administration " as a complex " system of means, forms, and methods with whose aid States purposefully influence international life " (p. 19). The international system is one of the self-administering types of social system, *e.g.* the States or subjects of the system administer it through co-operation. ILR is one method of administration, a basic form of normative legal regulation. Indirectly, municipal law also regulates the conduct of States on the international level and influences international relations.

Foreign policy is characterised as the strategy of a State's entire activity in the administration of international relations, and the author cites former Senator William Fulbright on the importance of style for an effective foreign policy. States, Lukashuk acknowledges, use all appropriate means at their disposal in their international relations: political, economic, ideological, legal, scientific, technical, and others. When considering the co-relation of political and legal regulation, the author recognises that the basic problems of States touching vital interests are political issues and not juridical ones and consequently should be decided politically with the assistance of political methods and means (p. 24). However, he adds, political regulation of these issues rarely exceeds the legal bounds. On the other hand, he argues that, because most international disputes are political, institutions such as the International Court of Justice cannot be used to great advantage. Purely legal disputes, he believes, are not very significant ones for the international community, but this in no way reduces the absolutely essential role of international law in the proper functioning of the international system, the more so since the use of force is now prohibited in the settlement of political disputes. Moreover, international law offers something that political means cannot: a standardised approach. ILR necessarily embraces common interests and generally recognised principles of international law. While international law cannot avert all cataclysms, neither can politics without law regulate everything.

Having defined the role and concept of ILR. Lukashuk turns to the " systems approach." This he defines as " the aggregate of methods and means with whose aid the laws of the structure and functioning of a system as a uniform whole are studied " (pp. 35–36). Particular attention is given to the structural interlinkages of systemic element which, he believes, can best be appreciated if the systems approach is based on dialectical and historical materialism. The approach is especially useful in assessing the prospects for and results of international legal regulation of urgent international issues. To a systems analyst, Lukashuk suggests, neo-colonialism for example is not an isolated phenomenon but an " interstate system born of imperialism and adapting to new conditions " (p. 45). The decline of colonialism is not the consequence of a changed relationship between the metropolitan and colony, but rather of alterations in the entire world system.

The author considers at some length the possible importance of the systems approach for international legal science. He draws on more than 100 foreign works, and almost as many Soviet contributions. The western sources, as one might expect, fall almost equally between international law and international relations. Soviet writings show the receptiveness to systems analysis among philosophers, sociologists, legal theorists, mathematicians, and specialists in international relations. But it is ungenerous for Lukashuk to minimise the contributions of western international lawyers in this connection (p. 74), although he criticises another Soviet jurist who suggests that "bourgeois science has not even raised the problem of legal regulation" (p. 73).

Next Lukashuk returns to a question raised at the very outset of his enquiry: international relations as the object of ILR. He is careful to point out that he is employing the term differently from its ordinary usage in international law as the object of law as a whole or of specific norms of law and legal relations or of international treaties. The objects of ILR must be capable of being realised and be objectively necessary from the viewpoint of the normal functioning of the national and international systems. Thus, he observes, not anything can be the object of an international treaty, for a valid treaty must treat with issues that fall within the sovereign authority of the parties. The domestic affairs of a State could not be the object of ILR.

This leads to a discussion of how the systems approach can be useful in delimiting differences between the municipal and international legal systems. While acknowledging that many western theorists have used systems theory to prove the opposite, Lukashuk contends that distinctions in principle are neither blurred nor is a merger of different social systems implied by the undoubted deepening interrelationship between domestic and foreign affairs. Rather, he suggests, we see a more active interaction while qualitative differences are preserved. He nonetheless is concerned that one delineate as precisely as possible the notion of "internal affairs." Concepts of world law, transnational law, and global law all ignore, in his view, the significance of the object being regulated and presuppose that rules from different legal systems belong to a whole. Since relations between States are basically different from those between physical and juridical persons, any attempt to create world law would undermine international law. Areas in which the author sees interaction between the municipal and international legal systems expanding include national economic planning and the regulation of natural resources. He also notes how international notions of racism have altered the concept of internal affairs.

Lukashuk anticipates that ILR will continue to expand, although he cautions that one must not confuse ILR with mere negotiations. The expansion of ILR will take the form of greater universality, embracing all States, of extending to areas of political and economic international relations which in the past were precluded from the purview, and of being applied to new forms of State relationship— cultural, scientific, and technical.

Next the author considers the system of ILR itself as a special kind of social system comprised of various interlinked but more limited systems. Of the possible criteria for subdividing ILR into analytical units, Lukashuk prefers that of socio-class distinctions: socialist, capitalist, and developing countries. Other possible criteria include the scale of the system; *e.g.* universal, world, regional, group, and bilateral relationships. Yet a third possibility is the types of social activity served by a particular system. More traditional criteria would be the status of the subjects of ILR (States, international organisations) or the methods of ILR (treaty, customary law, auxiliary sources).

He then dwells at some length on the scale of system approach, considering the possible insights and working in turn from the larger to the smaller. A strong case is made for the universality of ILR as an absolutely essential condition for the adequate and effective regulation of modern international relations. There is criticism of both cold-war and Peking-revisionist policies, but more interestingly also of those international lawyers who have queried the universality of international law by either suggesting there exist " multinational laws " (McDougal) or particular regional or continental international laws (Moreno Quintana). Bloc ideologies and regional international laws which undermine universal international law are thus soundly rejected.

There are nonetheless, he believes, regional and socio-political sub-systems of ILR which lead to the strengthening and unification of ILR. The Organisation of African Unity and the socialist system of ILR are singled out as constructive examples, whereas the Organisation of American States is treated as an unconstructive one. On the level of bilateral ILR, Lukashuk notes the importance of the Vienna Convention on the Law of Treaties in constraining the freedom of contracting parties to conclude agreements which are contrary to ILR. He also places emphasis on the preambular language of bilateral treaties of friendship and co-operation among socialist countries in this connection. Even the ILR activities of a single State are significant for insight into how one entity co-ordinates its relationship with others. The author regards Peter Rohn's *World Treaty Project* as an admirable contribution to systems analysis at this level.

Future prospects for the development of ILR are discussed

together with what the author calls the Soviet programme for peace. The existence of a new international law, he says, is now acknowledged by international lawyers of widely divergent ideological predispositions. And since the international order is bound to become even more interdependent as a consequence of dialectical changes therein, the importance of ILR must grow. This places responsibilities on States to co-ordinate both their short-term and long-term interests with regard to the systemic implication of ILR, and it also means that violations of international law are necessarily a general concern of all States. The monograph closes with a resounding endorsement of détente.

While the merits of the author's concept and application of systems analysis must be left to his fellow systems analysts it will be apparent to even the non-initiate that Lukashuk's basic description of the international system and the possible and actual roles of international law within it sound far more congenial and familiar than those couched in rule-oriented Marxist normativism. As the emphasis is on interdependence and co-operation in the world community, the exposition is less conflict-oriented and combative than we have been accustomed to, which adds to its persuasiveness. But there is more to this monograph than a new style and image. The traditional points of exacerbation between western and Soviet approaches to international law are more muted in substance as well. A significant barometer is the treatment of the regional sub-systems of international law. Priority is given clearly to universality, and socialist international legal regulation is seen as one among several sub-system supports in that direction. The author postulates not the convergence of two opposed social systems, but an increasingly universal system of international regulation forged out of the growing interdependence of the international community. This is not pure functionalism, although manifestly one may expect areas of functional co-operation to be among those most rapidly promoting universal ILR. Nor is the message entirely a new one, for the tensions in Soviet international legal doctrine have existed for decades between theories of international law which stress the exclusivity and qualitative distinctiveness of socialist international legal relations and those which emphasise either the necessary or desirable interlinkage of the socialist States and the outside world. It has been a continuum between inward and outward looking theories in a sense, as well as a continuum between a conflict or a conciliation emphasis. Professor Lukashuk's exposition must be numbered among the most outward-looking in the entire history of Soviet international legal doctrine.

# INDEX

343